COMMUNICATING ACROSS CULTURES

THE GUILFORD COMMUNICATION SERIES

Editors

Theodore L. Glasser, Stanford University
Marshall S. Poole, Texas A & M University

Advisory Board

Charles Berger   Peter Monge   Michael Schudson
James W. Carey   Barbara O'Keefe   Linda Steiner

Recent Volumes

COMMUNICATING ACROSS CULTURES
Stella Ting-Toomey

COMMUNICATIONS POLICY AND THE PUBLIC INTEREST:
THE TELECOMMUNICATIONS ACT OF 1996
Patricia Aufderheide

THE BUSINESS OF CHILDREN'S ENTERTAINMENT
Norma Odom Pecora

CASE STUDIES IN ORGANIZATIONAL COMMUNICATION 2:
PERSPECTIVES ON CONTEMPORARY WORK LIFE
Beverly Davenport Sypher, Editor

REGULATING MEDIA: THE LICENSING
AND SUPERVISION OF BROADCASTING IN SIX COUNTRIES
Wolfgang Hoffman-Riem

COMMUNICATION THEORY: EPISTEMOLOGICAL FOUNDATIONS
James A. Anderson

TELEVISION AND THE REMOTE CONTROL:
GRAZING ON A VAST WASTELAND
Robert V. Bellamy, Jr. and James R. Walker

RELATING: DIALOGUES AND DIALECTICS
Leslie A. Baxter and Barbara M. Montgomery

DOING PUBLIC JOURNALISM
Arthur Charity

SOCIAL APPROACHES TO COMMUNICATION
Wendy Leeds-Hurwitz, Editor

PUBLIC OPINION AND THE COMMUNICATION OF CONSENT
Theodore L. Glasser and Charles T. Salmon, Editors

COMMUNICATION RESEARCH MEASURES: A SOURCEBOOK
Rebecca B. Rubin, Philip Palmgreen, and Howard E. Sypher, Editors

PERSUASIVE COMMUNICATION
James B. Stiff

Communicating Across Cultures

STELLA TING-TOOMEY

THE GUILFORD PRESS
New York   London

© 1999 The Guilford Press
A Division of Guilford Publications, Inc.
72 Spring Street, New York, NY 10012
http://www.guilford.com

Printed in the United States of America

This book is printed on acid-free paper.

Last digit is print number: 9 8 7 6 5 4

Library of Congress Cataloging-in-Publication Data

Ting-Toomey, Stella.
   Communicating across cultures / Stella Ting-Toomey.
      p.   cm.
   Includes bibliographical references and index.
   ISBN 1-57230-445-6 (pbk.)
   1. Intercultural communication. 2. Communication and culture. 3. Oral communication. 4. Nonverbal communication. 5. Culture conflict. 6. Conflict management. I. Title.
GN345.6.T56   1998
302.2—dc21   98-49353
                                                         CIP

About the Author

Stella Ting-Toomey, PhD, is Professor of Speech Communication at California State University, Fullerton. She is the author and editor of 11 books. Three recent titles are *Communicating Effectively with the Chinese* (coauthor); *The Challenge of Facework: Cross-Cultural and Interpersonal Issues*; and *Communication in Personal Relationships Across Cultures* (coeditor). She has published extensively on cross-cultural facework, intercultural conflict, Asian communication patterns, and the effective identity negotiation model. She has held major leadership roles in international communication associations and has served on numerous editorial boards. An experienced trainer in the area of transcultural communication competence, she has lectured widely throughout the United States, Asia, and Europe on the topic of intercultural facework management.

Preface

I have written this book for use as an intermediate text for undergraduate courses in intercultural communication. This book is for students, teachers, and practitioners who would like to integrate knowledge and skills in practicing mindful intercultural communication. Mindfulness means being particularly aware of our own assumptions, viewpoints, and ethnocentric tendencies in entering any unfamiliar situation. *Simultaneously*, mindfulness means paying attention to the perspectives and interpretive lenses of *dissimilar others* in viewing an intercultural episode.

The book presents a new framework, namely, the identity negotiation perspective, to explain why we experience emotional vulnerability in communicating with dissimilar others. Our group-based identity (e.g., cultural identity) and person-based identity (e.g., personality traits) influence our particular ways of perceiving, thinking, and behaving in our everyday cultural milieu. However, when we encounter *dissimilar others*, our habitual ways of seeing and thinking are often thrown into disequilibrium.

As cultural beings, we are like fish in an aquarium—who can live comfortably inside their aquatic milieu without realizing the importance of the water or the tank that surrounds them. In encountering people who are culturally different from us, their dissimilar ways of thinking and behaving challenge our fundamental ways of experiencing. In encountering people who are culturally dissimilar, or when we are staying in an unfamiliar culture, our identities undergo turmoil and transformation. Emotional vulnerability is part of an inevitable identity change process.

The key, however, is to prepare ourselves with competent knowledge and skills so that we can enjoy this eye-opening intercultural learning journey. This book offers you the foundational concepts and skills so you can travel effectively across a diverse range of intercultural situations. Through the theme of mindfulness and the framework of identity negotiation, we put a compass and a map in your backpack to guide you through your different intercultural excursions.

This is a culture-general book that uses examples from many different cultures to support or clarify the various concepts. Since many of you will be engaged in different types of intercultural encounters, a culture-general book will prepare you to cross diverse cultural boundaries flexibly and adaptively. The ideas presented here are drawn from my years of intercultural research and the work of renowned scholars in the intercultural discipline. They are also reflective of some of my informal "ethnographic" observations of people and behaviors in many intercultural encounter scenes.

My own research and the research of other distinguished theorists led me to this one observation: In order to communicate effectively across cultures, we have to be mindful of our own identity issues and the identity issues that arise in others. We have to learn to understand and respect identity-based issues in any communication process. Identity-based issues (e.g., cultural or gender issues) constitute the substance of "who we are" and act as the focal points that guide our verbal and nonverbal actions. Identity-based issues are influenced by our cultural beliefs, values, norms, scripts, and meanings—all of which we use to interpret our own and others' behaviors.

The book is organized in four parts. Part I presents the conceptual foundations of the study of intercultural communication. Chapter 1 gives the reasons why we should pay close attention to intercultural communication and examines the urgent need in these times of studying the subject in depth. It also addresses the questions What is culture? and What is intercultural communication? Chapter 2 maps out the identity negotiation perspective. This approach or theory emphasizes the importance of understanding the various identity domains in mindful intercultural encounters. The chapter concludes by presenting a model of mindful intercultural communication in which the various knowledge blocks, motivational factors, and skills for competent communication are identified.

Part II consists of three chapters and covers the core concepts of the intercultural communication *process*. Chapter 3 highlights the importance of understanding cultural values as a starting point in practicing mindful intercultural communication. Cultural values such as individualism–collectivism and power distance shape our various identities, and these identities, in turn, sculpt the way we communicate. Chapter 4 underscores the importance of knowing the features and functions (e.g., group identity, perceptual filter) of language. It presents ample intercultural examples to compare and contrast low-context (i.e., direct and to-the-point) and high-context (i.e., indirect and spiral) verbal style differences. It also draws out implications for how different cross-cultural verbal styles can create frictions and clashes. Chapter 5 addresses the complex system of nonverbal communication. While language is the *key* to the heart of a culture, nonverbal communication is *the heartbeat* of a culture. The chapter highlights the different functions (e.g., reflecting identities, expressing emotions) of cross-cultural nonverbal communication. It also uses a diverse range of intercultural examples to illustrate each interesting nonverbal function. All three chapters end with specific recommendations for practicing mindful intercultural skills (e.g., mindful listening, verbal empathy) in managing value-based and communication-based differences.

Part III focuses on boundary regulation and intergroup–interpersonal dynamics in intercultural contacts. The motif is developed in three chapters. In Chapter 6, which focuses on the intergroup encounter, identity-based concepts such as ethnocentrism, stereotypes, and prejudice are discussed. In order to manage in-group/out-group boundaries mindfully, the skills of ethnorelativism (e.g., viewing a behavior from the other's cultural perspective) and mindful stereotyping (e.g., using loose categories) are introduced. Chapter 7 identifies the critical themes (e.g., vulnerability and security, autonomy and connection) that affect the formation and maintenance of intercultural personal relationships. Intercultural research studies are used to highlight some of the diverse expectations that can confuse matters between different cultural members in dealing with their relationships. Chapter 8, focusing on constructive conflict management, is a comprehensive analysis of the underlying goals and factors that shape an intercultural conflict episode. The chapter also recommends many practical skills (e.g., facework management and collaborative dialogue) that can be used to manage conflicts productively across many cultures.

Finally, Part IV addresses ideas of identity transformation and transcultural competence. In Chapter 9, a new model that incorporates antecedent, process, and outcome factors of intercultural adaptation is explained. The developmental experiences of sojourners (i.e., individuals who reside overseas for a short- or medium-term stay) and immigrants (i.e., individuals who reside in a new culture permanently) are traced. The costs of our inattention to diversity in our changing society are also identified. In Chapter 10, the transcultural communication competence theme is developed. The mindfulness component, as it relates to knowledge and skills, is revisited in more depth and in practical terms. Last but not least, the important issues of acting as an ethical, transcultural communicator are addressed. A specific set of transcultural competence guidelines serves as a conclusion to the book.

Five features distinguish this book from others. First, this book is guided by a practical theme, namely, mindfulness. Through mindful thinking, experiencing, and behaving, individuals can make a qualitative difference in their own lives and the lives of dissimilar others. Second, as an explanatory framework, the identity negotiation perspective emphasizes the importance of integrating knowledge, identity-based motivations, and skills in practicing competent intercultural communication. Third, at the end of Chapters 3–10, specific recommendations for how to integrate the newly acquired knowledge and skills are presented in easy-to-follow terms. Fourth, many chapters present key ideas and concepts concisely in tables and figures. They will enable readers to link ideas coherently in easy-to-visualize frameworks.

Fifth, the book is multidisciplinary in nature. It draws from diverse research sources such as work in cross-cultural psychology, sociology, language, international management, and communication. While the book is theoretically directed, the accessible writing style should appeal to students, teachers, and practitioners who want to learn more about mindful intercultural communication. The book is aimed at intercultural communication courses but can also be used as a supplemental text to many existing communication offerings.

Writing a book of this nature is a major undertaking. It is an immense commitment of time and energy, and its evolution involves the lives of many others. This book has been several years in the making, and during the course of writing it I have benefited greatly from the wise comments of many individuals. First of all, I want to acknowledge the "voices" of many undergraduate students, graduate students, and participants in my past intercultural courses and workshops. Their "voices" and questions helped me to clarify my own thinking over the many ideas presented here. I want to thank you for your inquiring minds and supportive hearts. I also want to thank the series co-editor, Scott Poole, and an anonymous reviewer for their perceptive comments and encouraging feedback on an earlier version of this manuscript. To Peter Wissoker, my editor at The Guilford Press, I would like to acknowledge his enormous patience and continuous faith in me and the book. Without his gentle nudging, it would not have been completed. I also want to extend my appreciation to Bert Zelman, the copy editor, as well as Anna Nelson and the entire production staff of The Guilford Press for their meticulous and professional help in the production of this book.

I am indebted to four special individuals who reviewed a complete draft of this book at different stages: Bill Gudykunst, Jill Bennett, John Oetzel, and Beth-Ann Cocroft. To Bill Gudykunst, your insightful comments on the "big picture" of the book contributed greatly to its conceptual organization and development. To Jill Bennett, your detailed remarks on an earlier draft contributed immensely to the clarity of ideas. To John Oetzel, your astute suggestions on the "flow" of the manuscript improved enormously the quality of the text. To Beth-Ann Cocroft, your keen eye and proofreading made the book more comprehensible. To all four of you, I am grateful for your insights and support. I also want to offer my special acknowledgment and thanks to Peter Lee, who helped me in preparing the tables and figures. Peter, you always came through as the computer "whiz" in times of computer crises and crashes. Without your help, this book could not have made it to the finish line.

I would like to take this opportunity to acknowledge with gratitude the ceaseless support of my past graduate students, notably Leeva Chung, Ge Gao, Wintilo Garcia, Angela Hoppe, Atsuko Kurogi, Kimberlie Yee-Jung, and many others, whose enthusiasm for this book and whose heartfelt caring for my "well-being," have meant a great deal to me throughout the years. To my own colleagues and staff in the Department of Speech Communication of California State University, Fullerton, I thank you for providing a comfortable and calming environment in which to conduct my scholarly work.

Last but not least, I want to thank my two precious family members—Charles and Adrian—for their endless patience and good humor throughout the years of working on this project. My 12-year-old son Adrian Toomey grew up along with this book.

Adrian, for all your extraordinary warm bugs and specialness—I dedicate this book to you.

Stella Ting-Toomey
Fullerton, CA

Contents

I. CONCEPTUAL FOUNDATIONS

1. Intercultural Communication: An Introduction   3

Why Study Intercultural Communication?   4
    Global Diversity Trends   4
    Domestic Diversity Trends   5
    Interpersonal Learning Opportunities   7
What Is Intercultural Communication?   9
    Conceptualization of Culture   9
    Conceptualization of Intercultural Communication   16
Intercultural Communication: Five Core Assumptions   21

2. Mindful Intercultural Communication: An Identity Negotiation Perspective   25

The Identity Negotiation Perspective   26
    The Theoretical Background   27
    Primary Identity Domains   28
    Situational Identities   36
    Summary   39
The Identity Negotiation Theory   39
    Core Theoretical Assumptions   40
    Assumptions 1–4   41
    Assumptions 5 and 6   42
    Assumption 7   44
    Assumption 8   45
Mindful Intercultural Communication   45
    Threefold Outcomes of Mindful
        Intercultural Communication   46
    Mindful Intercultural Communication:
        Criteria and Components   48

II. THE INTERCULTURAL COMMUNICATION PROCESS: DISSIMILAR ASSUMPTIONS

3. Value Orientations and Intercultural Encounters   57

Classical Value Orientations   58
    Basic Assumptions   59
    People–Nature Value Orientation   60
    Temporal Orientation   61
    Human Nature Orientation   63
    Activity Orientation   64
    Relational Orientation   65
Cross-Cultural Organizational Value Dimensions   66
    Individualism–Collectivism: The Core Dimension   66
    The Power Distance Dimension   69
    The Uncertainty Avoidance Dimension   71
    The Masculinity and Femininity Dimension   72
    The Confucian Dynamism Dimension   74
    Loose and Tight Social Structures   75
Values, Self-Conception Consequences, and Interaction   76
    Independent and Interdependent Self-Construal   76
    Personal and Collective Self-Esteem   80
    Universalistic-Based versus
    Particularistic-Based Interaction   81
Summary   82
Recommendations   82

4. Mindful Intercultural Verbal Communication   84

Human Language: A Coherent System   85
    Arbitrariness   85
    Multilayered Rules   86
    Speech Community   90
Languages across Cultures: Diverse Functions   91
    The Group Identity Function   91
    The Perceptual Filtering Function   94
    The Cognitive Reasoning Function   94
    The Status and Intimacy Function   97
    The Creativity Function   98
Cross-Cultural Verbal Communication Styles   100
    Low-Context and High-Context Communication   100
    Direct and Indirect Verbal Interaction Styles   103
    Person-Oriented and Status-Oriented Verbal Styles   106
    Self-Enhancement and Self-Effacement Verbal Styles   107
    Beliefs Expressed in Talk and Silence   110
Recommendations   111

5. Mindful Intercultural Nonverbal Communication   114

Nonverbal Communication:
    Specific Functions and Patterns   115
    Reflecting and Managing Identities   117
    Expressing Emotions and Attitudes   119
    Conversational Management   123
    Impression Formation and Attraction   126
Space and Time across Cultures   127
    Interpersonal Spatial Boundary Regulation   128
    Environmental Boundary Regulation   131
    Temporal Regulation   134
Interpersonal Synchrony and Nonverbal Cautions   137
    Interpersonal Interactive Synchrony   137
    Nonverbal Cautions   139
Recommendations   140

III. BOUNDARY REGULATION AND INTERGROUP–INTERPERSONAL RELATIONSHIP DEVELOPMENTS   145

6. Identity Contact and Intergroup Encounters

Social Identity Theory and Its Associated Constructs:
A Boundary-Regulation Approach   146
    Social Identity Theory   147
    Social Categorization   149
    Social Comparison   150
Intergroup Attribution: A Sense-Making Process   152
    Attribution Theory   152
    Intergroup Attribution Theory   154
Mindsets: Affective and Cognitive Filters   156
    Intergroup Perception   156
    Ethnocentrism and Communication   157
    Stereotypes and Communication   161
    Prejudice and Communication   164
    Reduction of Prejudice and Discrimination   169
Recommendations   171

7. Intercultural Personal Relationship Development:
Identity- and Relational-Based Themes   174

Personal Relationship Developments:
    Membership and Contextual Conditions   175
    Cultural and Ethnic Membership Values   176
    Gender Expectations and Norms   177
    Individual Personality Attributes   178
    Situational Contact Conditions   179

Four Identity- and Relational-Based Themes 181
The Identity Vulnerability and Security Theme 181
The Identity Autonomy and Connection Theme 184
The Relational Dissimilarity and Similarity Theme 186
The Relational Openness and Closedness Theme 188
Summary 192
Recommendations 192

8. **Constructive Intercultural Conflict Management** 194

Intercultural Conflict: Definitional Characteristics 195
Conflict Goal Issues 195
Conflict-Related Characteristics 198
Contributing Factors Affecting Intercultural Conflict 201
A Cultural Variability Perspective 202
Cultural-Based Conflict: Different Lenses 210
Intercultural Conflict Management Skills 219
Operational Skills Needed for Constructive
Conflict Management 219
Collaborative Dialogue and
Communication Adaptability 224
Recommendations 227

IV. **IDENTITY TRANSFORMATION AND
TRANSCULTURAL COMPETENCIES**

9. **Identity Change and Intercultural Adaptation** 233

Intercultural Adaptation: Antecedent Factors 234
Systems-Level Factors 235
Individual-Level Factors 239
Interpersonal-Level Factors 241
Intercultural Adaptation: The Identity Change Process 245
Managing the Culture Shock Process 245
Sojourners' Adjustment Models 247
Minority and Immigrants' Identity Change Models 254
Intercultural Adaptation: Effective Outcomes 257
Systems-Level and Interpersonal-Level Outcomes 257
Personal Identity Change Outcomes 258
Recommendations 259

10. **Transcultural Communication Competence** 261

Criteria of Transcultural Communication Competence 262
The Appropriateness Criterion 262
The Effectiveness Criterion 263
The Satisfaction Criterion 265

Components of Transcultural Communication Competence 265
  The Knowledge Blocks Component 266
  The Mindfulness Component 267
  The Communication Skills Component 269
From Intercultural to Transcultural Ethics 271
  Ethical Absolutism versus Ethical Relativism 272
  Moral Exclusion versus Moral Inclusion 275
Final Recommendations 276

References 277

Index 301

1

CONCEPTUAL FOUNDATIONS

1

Intercultural Communication: An Introduction

Why Study Intercultural Communication? 4
    Global Diversity Trends 4
    Domestic Diversity Trends 5
    Interpersonal Learning Opportunities 7
What Is Intercultural Communication? 9
    Conceptualization of Culture 9
    Conceptualization of Intercultural Communication 16
Intercultural Communication: Five Core Assumptions 21

As we enter the 21st century, there is a growing sense of urgency that we need to increase our understanding of people from diverse cultural and ethnic backgrounds. From interpersonal misunderstandings to intercultural conflicts, frictions exist within and between cultures. With rapid changes in global economy, technology, transportation, and immigration policies, the world is becoming a small, intersecting community. We find ourselves in increased contact with people who are culturally different, working side by side with us. From workplace to classroom diversity, different cultural beliefs, values, and communication styles are here to stay. In order to achieve effective intercultural communication, we have to learn to manage differences flexibly and mindfully.

The study of intercultural communication is about the study of cultural differences that really "make a difference" in intercultural encounters. It is also about acquiring the conceptual tools and skills to manage such differences creatively. The aims of this chapter are threefold. The first is to outline the reasons why we should pay mindful attention to the study of intercultural communication. The second is to explain what intercultural communication is. The third is a summary of the five core assumptions concerning intercultural communication.

WHY STUDY INTERCULTURAL COMMUNICATION?

There are many practical reasons for studying intercultural communication. We offer three reasons here: global diversity trends, domestic diversity trends, and interpersonal learning opportunities.

Global Diversity Trends

Workplace diversity on the global level represents both opportunities and challenges to individuals and organizations. In order to develop these opportunities, individuals and organizations in the forefront of workplace diversity must rise to the challenge of serving as global leaders. Adler (1995) suggests that global leaders in today's world need to work on five cross-cultural competencies: (1) understanding the worldwide political, cultural, and business environment from a global perspective; (2) developing multiple cultural perspectives and approaches to conducting business; (3) being skillful at working with people from many cultures simultaneously; (4) adapting comfortably to living in different cultures; and (5) learning to interact with international colleagues as equals, rather than from a superior-inferior stance. Global leaders, in sum, must forge a transcultural vision that is not bound by one national definition. They must also have the necessary communication skills to translate this vision into practice in the diverse workplace. In sum, they need to practice transcultural communication competence skills (for a detailed discussion, see Chapter 10).

Successful business today depends on effective globalization. Effective globalization, in part, depends on dealing with a diverse workforce. Factors that contribute to the diversity of the workforce on the international level include, but are not limited to, the development of regional trading blocs (e.g., the European Union; the North American Free Trade Agreement, or NAFTA), communication technology (e.g., fax, E-mail, the Internet), immigrant worker and guest worker policies (e.g., Turkish migrant workers in Germany) on the international level (Banks, 1995). In this era of global economy, it is inevitable that employees and customers from dissimilar cultures are in constant contact with one another. They buy and they sell, all the while negotiating multiple facets of their cultural differences.

According to a recent Workforce 2020 report (Judy & D'Amico, 1997), in the span of 15 years (i.e., 1980–1995), international trade grew by about 120% on the global level. Four out of every five new jobs in the United States are generated as a direct result of international business. Additionally, 33% of U.S. corporate profits are derived via import–export trade. Even if we do not venture out of our national borders, global economy, and hence global contact, becomes a crucial part of our everyday work lives (Brake, Walker, & Walker, 1995).

In order to communicate effectively with dissimilar others, every global citizen needs to learn the fundamental concepts and skills of mindful intercultural communication. The U.S. workplace reality indicates the following (Kealey, 1996, p. 83):

- Although most U.S. international employees are considered technically competent, they lack effective intercultural communication skills to perform satisfactorily in the new culture.
- Overseas business failure rates, as measured by early returns, are about 15–40% for U.S. business personnel, and of those who stay, less than 50% perform adequately.
- It is estimated that U.S. firms alone lose $2 billion per year in direct costs because of premature returns.

U.S. businesses have often overlooked the area of intercultural communication competence in their overseas personnel selection process. While many sojourners are well prepared technically for their overseas assignments, they fall short of possessing the knowledge and skills to function effectively in the new cultural environment.

Beyond global business, increased numbers of individuals are working in overseas assignments such as government service, humanitarian service, peace corps service, and international education. Acquiring the knowledge and skills of mindful intercultural communication is a necessary first step in becoming a global citizen of the 21st century.

Domestic Diversity Trends

The study of intercultural communication in domestic U.S. society is especially critical for several reasons. First, immigrants, minority group members, and females will account for a third of the total *new entrants* into the U.S. workforce in the next decade. Second, while European Americans constitute 78% of the total U.S. labor workforce today, they will drop to 68% in 2020. Thus approximately one-third of the total U.S. workforce will consist of immigrants (many non-English speakers) and minority group members. Third, over the next 20 years, the Asian and Latino/a shares of the U.S. labor force will grow dramatically to 6% and 14%, respectively (mostly in the South and West of the United States), and the share of African Americans in the labor force will remain constant, at 11% (Judy & D'Amico, 1997). Fourth, over the next 20 years, Latino/a Americans will account for 47% of population growth in the United States; African Americans will account for 22%; and Asian Americans and other minority group members will make up 18% of this increase. European Americans will account for only 13% of the population growth. Even if we never step foot outside U.S. borders, it is inevitable that we will encounter people from diverse cultures and ethnicities in our own backyards. Learning to understand such cultural differences will serve as a major step toward building a more harmonious, multicultural community.

Beyond the cultural domestic diversity dimension, there are many other diversity dimensions that are deemed important by different individuals. The term *diversity* refers to a rich spectrum of human variations. Loden and Rosener (1991) state that "diversity is *otherness* or those human qualities that are different from our own and outside the groups to which we belong, yet present in other individuals and groups. *Others*, then, are people who are different from us along one or several dimensions such as age, ethnicity, gender, race, sexual/affectional orientation, and so on" (p. 18; emphasis in original).

There are two sets of dimensions that contribute to the ways groups of people differ from one another within any culture (Loden & Rosener, 1991). One set, the *primary dimensions of diversity*, refers to those "human differences that are inborn and/or that exert an important impact on our early socialization and an ongoing impact throughout our lives" (p. 18), for example, ethnicity, gender, age, social class, physical abilities, and sexual orientation. Comparatively, the other set, the *secondary dimensions of diversity*, refers to conditions that can be changed more easily than the primary dimensions, including "mutable differences that we acquire, discard, and/or modify throughout our lives, [most of which] are less salient than those of the core" (p. 19), for example, educational level, work experience, and income.

The primary dimensions of diversity more than the secondary dimensions, shape and mold our individual self-image and direct our thinking, feelings, and behavior. Additionally, others often interact with us in initial encounters based on those stereotypic, group-based images. Individuals may define primary and secondary dimensions of identity differently, depending on their particular life stage. For example, age identity may not be an important identity for young adults in their 20s, whereas it becomes quite salient for older adults in their 60s. Persons in their 20s may not discuss retirement issues, whereas adults in their later life stage may consider those topics as salient. It is also important to grasp that another person's perception concerning a holder's salient identity dimensions may differ from the holder's preferred self-definition. For example, person X may describe person Y as "a Hispanic-looking clerk who loiters around in the store." However, person Y's self-description is "a second-generation Mexican American student who is working long hours to support his or her family."

Use of ethnic labels such as "Hispanics," "Latino/a," and "Mexican American" is subject to individual preference. While the term *Hispanics* refers to individuals who "reside in the [United States] and who were born in or trace the background of their families to . . . Spanish-speaking Latin America . . . [e.g., Mexico, Panama, Costa Rica; Venezuela, Colombia; Puerto

Rico, Cuba] or Spain," *Latino* implies that a person is "from a Latin American country . . . [and the term] does not signify the conqueror Spain" (Paniagua, 1994, p. 38). *Mexican Americans* implies that individuals who reside in the United States can trace their family background to Mexico. Likewise, for the African American group, terms such as "Blacks," "Black Americans," and "African Americans" have been used. Hecht, Collier, and Ribeau (1993) find that the "Black" respondent group is the most conservative and accepting of racial status quo, the "Black American" group is caught in between two extremes, and that the "African American" respondent group is the least conservative and views verbal assertiveness as a strategy to deal with interethnic communication problems. Thus, the membership labels that individuals use, or prefer to be used, can tell us a lot about them. Furthermore, understanding the strength and content in which they identify with particular membership groups can help us to develop more effective communication with them.

In order to communicate effectively with dissimilar others, we need to be mindful of how others prefer to be "named" and identified. Other people's perceptions and evaluations can strongly influence our self-conceptions, or our views of ourselves. Mindful intercultural communication requires us to be sensitive to how others define themselves on both group membership and personal identity levels. The feelings of being understood, respected, and supported are viewed as critical outcome dimensions of mindful intercultural communication (for a detailed discussion, see Chapter 2).

Interpersonal Learning Opportunities

As we enter the 21st century, direct contacts with dissimilar others in our neighborhoods, schools, and workplace are an inescapable part of life. Each intercultural contact can bring about identity dissonance or stress because of attributes such as an unfamiliar accent, way of speaking, way of doing things, and way of nonverbal expression. In a global workplace, people bring with them different work habits and cultural practices. For example, cultural strangers may appear to approach teamwork and problem-solving tasks differently. They may appear to have a sense of different time, and they may appear to have different spatial needs. They also may look and move differently.

Most of us prefer to spend time with people who are similar to us rather than different from us. Among people with similar habits and outlooks, we experience interaction predictability. Among people with dissimilar habits and communication rules, we experience interaction unpredictability. In a familiar cultural environment, we feel secure and safe. In an unfamiliar cultural environment, we experience emotional vulnerability and threat.

However, the time and energy we invest in learning to deal with our own feelings of discomfort *and* in reducing the discomfort of others may pay off substantially in the long run. It is through the mirror of others that we learn to know ourselves. It is through facing our own discomfort and anxiety that we learn to stretch and grow. Encountering a dissimilar other helps us to question our routine way of thinking and behaving. Getting to *really know a dissimilar stranger helps us to glimpse into another world*—a range of unfamiliar experiences and a set of values unlike our own.

From a human creativity standpoint, we learn more from people who are different from us than from those who are similar to us. At the individual level, creativity involves a process of "taking in new ideas, of being thrown into disequilibrium and trying to reach some accommodation, achieve a new synthesis. . . . The same is true at the societal level. In the most creative periods there has been a tremendous infusion of diversity: new ideas and cross-cultural encounters" (Goleman, Kaufman, & Ray, 1992, p. 173). In absorbing dissimilar ideas, it is important for us to suspend our usual ways of thinking and try to see things in a different light—and from a crooked angle.

In meeting people who are similar to us, we practice similar routines and scripts, and with predictable rhythms and outcomes. In meeting and working with people who are different from us, we may have to open our minds, ears, eyes, and hearts with more alertness and closer attention. Whether we are embarked abroad on a student exchange program or are going overseas for business reasons, we must learn to embrace uncertainty and face our vulnerability. Emotional vulnerability is part of an intercultural learning journey. With mindful vulnerability, we can listen with greater thoughtfulness and see things through fresh lenses.

In sum, our ability to communicate effectively with cultural strangers will help us to uncover our own diversity and "worthiness." As Hall (1983) concludes,

> Human beings are such an incredibly rich and talented species with potentials beyond anything it is possible to contemplate that . . . it would appear that our greatest task, our most important task, and our most strategic task is to learn as much as possible about ourselves [and others]. . . . My point is that as humans learn more about their incredible sensitivity, their boundless talents, and manifold diversity, they should begin to appreciate not only about themselves but also others. (p. 185)

Mindful intercultural communication will enrich our understanding of a diverse range of meanings concerning human work and leisure. Mindful communication takes patience, commitment, and practice. Our willingness to explore and understand such cultural differences and complexities will ultimately enrich the depth of our own life experiences. We now turn to a discussion of the definitional elements of "intercultural communication."

WHAT IS INTERCULTURAL COMMUNICATION?

"Culture" is an elastic, dynamic concept that takes on different shades of meaning—depending on one's perspective. The word "communication" is also fluid and subject to different interpretations. While both culture and communication reciprocally influence one another, it is essential to distinguish the characteristics of the two concepts for the purpose of understanding the complex relationship between them. In this section we venture to answer the following two questions: What is culture? What is intercultural communication?

Conceptualization of Culture

Definition of Culture

Culture is an enigma. It contains both concrete and abstract components. It is also a multifaceted phenomenon. What is culture? This question has fascinated scholars in various academic disciplines for many decades. As long ago as the early 1950s, Kroeber and Kluckhohn (1952) identified more than 160 different definitions of the term "culture." The study of culture has ranged from the study of its external architecture and landscape to the study of a set of implicit principles and values to which a large group of members in a community subscribe.

The term "culture" originates from the Latin word *cultura* or *cultus* as in "*agri cultura*, the cultivation of the soil. Later [the word] culture grabbed a set of related meanings: training, adornment, fostering, worship. . . . From its root meaning of an activity, culture became transformed into a condition, a state of being cultivated" (Freilich, 1989, p. 2). D'Andrade (1984) conceptualizes "culture" as follows:

Learned systems of meaning, communicated by means of natural language and other symbol systems . . . and capable of creating cultural entities and particular senses of reality. Through these systems of meaning, groups of people adapt to their environment and structure interpersonal activities. . . . Cultural meaning systems can be treated as a very large diverse pool of knowledge, or partially shared cluster of norms, or as intersubjectively shared, symbolically created realities. (p. 116)

This integrative definition of culture captures three important points. First, the term culture refers to a diverse pool of knowledge, shared realities, and clustered norms that constitute the learned systems of meanings in a particular society. Second, these learned systems of meanings are shared and transmitted through everyday interactions among members of the cultural group and from one generation to the next. Third, culture facilitates members' capacity to survive and adapt to their external environment.

Drawing from D'Andrade's conceptualization of culture, we define *culture* in this book as a complex frame of reference that consists of patterns of *traditions, beliefs, values, norms, symbols, and meanings that are shared to varying degrees by interacting members of a community* (see Figure 1.1).

Culture is like an iceberg: the deeper layers (e.g., traditions, beliefs, values) are hidden from our view; we only see and hear the uppermost layers of cultural artifacts (e.g., fashion, trends, pop music) and of verbal and nonverbal symbols. However, to understand a culture with any depth, we have to match its underlying values accurately with its respective norms, meanings, and symbols. It is the underlying set of beliefs and values that drives people's thinking, reacting, and behaving. Furthermore, to understand commonalities between individuals and groups, we have to dig deeper into the level of universal human needs (such as safety, security, inclusion, dignity/respect, control, connection, meaning, creativity, and a sense of well-being).

On a communal level, culture refers to a patterned way of living by a group of interacting individuals who share similar sets of traditions, beliefs,

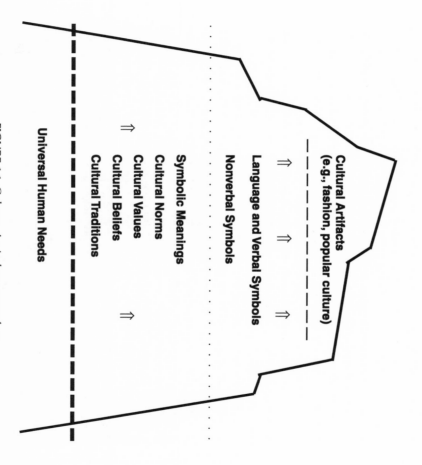

Cultural Artifacts (e.g., fashion, popular culture)

Nonverbal Symbols

Language and Verbal Symbols

Symbolic Meanings

Cultural Norms

Cultural Values

Cultural Beliefs

Cultural Traditions

Universal Human Needs

FIGURE 1.1. Culture: An iceberg metaphor.

values, and norms. This is known as the *normative culture* of a group of individuals. On an individual level, members of a culture can attach different degrees of importance to this complex range and layers of cultural traditions, beliefs, values, and norms. This is known as the *subjective culture* of an individual (Triandis, 1972).

Culturally shared traditions can include myths, legends, ceremonies, and rituals (e.g., celebrating Thanksgiving) that are passed on from one generation to the next via an oral or written medium. *Culturally shared beliefs* refer to a set of fundamental assumptions that people hold dearly without question. These beliefs can revolve around questions as to the origins of human beings; the concept of time, space, and reality; the existence of a supernatural being; and the meaning of life, death, and the afterlife. Proposed answers to many of these questions can be found in the major religions of the world such as Christianity, Islam, Hinduism, and Buddhism. People who subscribe to any of these religious philosophies tend to hang onto their beliefs on faith, often accepting the fundamental precepts without question.

Beyond fundamental cultural or religious beliefs, people also differ in what they value as important in their cultures. *Cultural values* refer to a set of priorities that guide "good" or "bad" behaviors, "desirable" or "undesirable" practices, and "fair" or "unfair" actions (Kluckhohn & Strodtbeck, 1961). Cultural values (e.g., individual competitiveness vs. group harmony) can serve as the motivational bases for action. They can serve as the explanatory logic for behavior. They can also serve as the desired end goals to be achieved. To understand various communication patterns in a culture, we have to understand the deep-rooted cultural values that give meanings to such patterns. An in-depth discussion of the content of cultural values will appear in Chapter 3.

Cultural norms refer to the collective expectations of what constitute proper or improper behavior in a given situation (Olsen, 1978). They guide the scripts (i.e., appropriate sequence of activities) we and others should follow in particular situations (e.g., how to greet a professor, how to introduce yourself to a stranger). While cultural beliefs and values are deep seated and invisible, norms can be readily inferred and observed through behaviors. Cultural traditions, beliefs, and values intersect to influence the development of collective norms in a culture. Oftentimes, our ignorance of a different culture's norms and rules can produce unintentional clashes between us and people of that culture. We may not even notice that we have violated another culture's norms or rules in a particular situation.

A symbol is a sign, artifact, word(s), gesture, or behavior that stands for or reflects something meaningful. The *meanings* or interpretations that we attach to the symbol (e.g., a national flag) can have both objective and subjective levels. People globally can recognize a particular country by its national flag because of its design and colors. However, people can also hold subjective evaluations of what the flag means to them, such as a sense of pride or betrayal. Another such example is the linguistic symbol "home." "Home" on the objective level refers to "a family's place of residence." However, members of different cultures may hold different subjective meanings for this richly textured symbol. For example, for a Tomalithli Native American, "home" means an experiential place where "time and space, as well as collective and individual perceptions blur into impressionistic totality. . . . [That is, the place of] the people who live on the high ground or bluffs. [Home is] the place of our birth vested indelibly in us, an identity, since we have always been and will always be there with the spirits of relatives of past, present, and future" (Grinde, 1996, p. 63).

The linguistic symbol "home," for different individuals, can connote spirituality, kinship, belonging, identity, a sacred space, and a sacred time. While the word "home" sounds simple, it can conjure diverse cultural and personal meanings. To understand a culture, we need to know in depth the values and meanings of its core symbols. Oftentimes, we learn the values and meanings of a cultural community through the acquisition of its core linguistic symbols.

Functions of Culture

What does culture do for human beings? Why do we need culture? As an essential component of the effort of human beings to survive and thrive in their particular environment, culture serves multiple functions. Of all these functions, we identify five here: identity meaning, group inclusion, intergroup boundary regulation, ecological adaptation, and cultural communication.

First, culture serves the *identity meaning function*. Culture provides the frame of reference to answer the most fundamental question of each human being: Who am I? Cultural beliefs, values, and norms provide the anchoring points in which we attribute meanings and significance to our identities. For example, in the larger U.S. culture, middle-class U.S. values emphasize individual initiative and achievement. A person is considered "competent" or "successful" when he or she takes the personal initiative to realize his or her full potential. The translation of this potential means tangible achievements and rewards (e.g., an enviable career, a good salary, a coveted car, or a dream house). A person who can realize his or her dreams despite sometimes difficult circumstances is considered to be a "successful" individual in the context of middle-class U.S. culture.

This valuing of individual initiative may stem, in part, from the milieu of the predominantly Judeo-Christian belief system in the larger U.S. culture. In this belief system, each person is perceived as unique, with free will and responsibility for his or her own growth. Additionally, some immigrants may seize the opportunity for personal mobility and advancement with more ambition than is shown by native-born individuals.

Thus, the concept of being a "successful," "competent," or "worthwhile" person and the meanings attached to such words stem from the fundamental values of a given culture. The identity meanings we acquire within our culture are constructed and sustained through everyday communication. For example, in the Chinese culture, the meaning of being a "worthwhile" person means that the individual respects his or her parents at all times and is sensitive to the needs of his or her family. In the Mexican culture, a "well-educated" person (*una persona bien educada*) means that the person has been well taught by his or her parents the importance of "demonstrating social relationships *con respeto* (with respect) and *dignidad* (dignity). Therefore, if a child is called *mal educado* (without education), the implicit assumption . . . is that this child did not receive education from his or her parents concerning the treatment of others (particularly persons in a position of authority) with *respeto*" (Paniagua, 1994, pp. 39–40).

Second, culture serves the *group inclusion function*, satisfying our need for membership affiliation and belonging. Culture creates a comfort zone in which we experience in-group inclusion and in-group/out-group differences. Within our own group, we experience safety, inclusion, and acceptance. We do not have to constantly justify or explain our actions. With people of dissimilar groups, we have to be on the alert and we have to explain or defend our actions with more effort.

A shared common fate or a sense of solidarity often exists among members of the same group. For example, within our own cultural group, we speak the same language or dialect, we share similar nonverbal rhythms, and we can decode each other's nonverbal mood with more accuracy. The need to be seen as sharing something similar propels us to identify with salient membership groups and involves the general process of group-based inclusion.

However, with people from a dissimilar membership group, we constantly have to perform guessing games. We tend to "stand out," and we experience awkwardness during interaction. The feeling of exclusion or differentiation leads to interaction anxiety and uncertainty (Brewer, 1991; Gudykunst, 1993). The urge toward group inclusion addresses our need to be seen as similar to others and to fit in with them. The group inclusion need also creates boundaries between "us" and "them."

Third, culture's *intergroup boundary regulation function* shapes our in-group and out-group attitudes in dealing with people who are culturally dissimilar. An *attitude* is a learned tendency that influences our behavior. Culture helps us to form evaluative attitudes toward in-group and out-group interactions. Evaluative attitudes also connote positive- or negative-valenced emotions.

According to intergroup research (Triandis, 1994a), we tend to hold favorable attitudes toward in-group interactions and hold unfavorable attitudes toward out-group interactions. We tend to experience strong emotional reactions when our cultural norms are violated or ignored. We tend to experience bewilderment when we unintentionally violate other people's cultural norms. While our own culture builds an invisible boundary around us, it also delimits our thoughts and our visions.

Culture is like a pair of sunglasses. It shields us from external harshness and offers us some measure of safety and comfort. It also blocks us from seeing clearly through our tinted lenses because of that same protectiveness. In brief, culture nurtures our ethnocentric attitudes and behaviors. The term *ethnocentrism* refers to our tendency to consider our own cultural practices as superior and consider other cultural practices as inferior. As cultural beings, we are all ethnocentric to some degree. We often consider our own cultural way of seeing and sensing as much more "civilized" and "correct" than other cultural ways. More often than not, we are unaware of our own ethnocentric biases. We can also be ethnocentric about different aspects (such as language, architecture, history, or cuisine) of our culture or identity group. We acquire the lenses of ethnocentrism as we are enculturated into our own social world.

Fourth, culture serves the *ecological adaptation function*. It facilitates the adaptation processes among the self, the cultural community, and the larger environment (i.e., the ecological milieu or habitat). Culture is not a static system. It is dynamic and changes with the people within the system. Culture evolves with a clear reward and punishment system that reinforces certain adaptive behaviors and sanctions other nonadaptive behaviors over time. When people adapt their needs and their particular ways of living in response to a changing habitat, culture also changes accordingly. Surface-level cultural artifacts such as fashion or popular culture change at a faster pace than deep-level cultural elements such as beliefs, values, and ethics (see Figure 1.1). Triandis (1994a) makes the following observation:

Ecologies [the physical environment, geographic features, climate, and fauna and floral where survival depends on hunting and fishing are different from ecologies where survival depends on successful farming. . . . In agricultural cultures, cooperation is often required. For example, many farmers work together digging irrigation canals or constructing storage facilities. A person who is not dependable or does not conform would not be a good coworker. As a result, socialization in such cultures emphasizes dependability, responsibility, and conforming. The realities of the environment create conditions for the development of particular cultural, socialization, and behavioral patterns. (p. 23)

Culture rewards certain behaviors that are compatible with its ecology and sanctions other behaviors that are mismatched with the ecological niche of the culture.

Fifth and finally, culture serves the *cultural communication function*, which basically means the coordination between culture and communication. Culture affects communication, and communication affects culture. The noted anthropologist Hall (1959) succinctly states that culture *is* communication and communication *is* culture. It is through communication that culture is passed down, created, and modified from one generation to the next. Communication is necessary to define cultural experiences. Cultural communication shapes the implicit theories we have about appropriate human conduct and effective human practices in a given sociocultural context.

Cultural communication provides us with a set of ideals of how social interaction can be accomplished smoothly among people within our community (Cushman & Cahn, 1985). It binds people together via their shared linguistic codes, norms, and scripts. Scripts are interaction sequences or patterns of communication that are shared by a group of people in a speech community (i.e., a group of individuals who share a set of common norms regarding appropriate communication practices; Hymes, 1972).

For example, people in a particular speech community have established a set of norms of what constitutes a polite or impolite way of meeting strangers. In Western Apache culture, remaining silent is the most proper way to behave when strangers meet. As Basso (1990) observes, "The Western Apache do not feel compelled to 'introduce' persons who are unknown to each other. Eventually, it is assumed, strangers will begin to speak. However, this is a decision that is properly left to the individuals involved, and no attempt is made to hasten it. Outside help in the form of introductions or other verbal routines is viewed as presumptuous and unnecessary. Strangers who are quick to launch into conversation are frequently eyed with undisguised suspicion" (p. 308). While norms are implicit expectations concerning what "should" or "should not" occur in an interaction, scripts refer to expected interaction sequences of communication. As already noted, people in the same speech community often subscribe to a shared set of norms and scripts in particular situations.

Cultural communication serves to coordinate the different parts of a complex system. It provides the people in a particular speech community with a shared consensus way of understanding (Cushman & Cahn, 1985). It serves as the superglue that links the macro levels (e.g., family units, education, media, government) and micro levels (e.g., beliefs, values, norms, symbols) of a culture. A change in one part of the cultural system is expressed and echoed in another part of the system via symbolic communication. Thus, communication coordinates and regulates the multiple facets of a culture in a stable yet dynamic direction.

In sum, culture serves as the "safety net" in which individuals seek to satisfy their needs for identity, inclusion, boundary regulation, adaptation, and communication coordination. Culture facilitates and enhances individuals' adaptation processes in their natural cultural habitats. Communication, in essence, serves as the major means of linking these diverse needs together. Drawing from the basic functions of culture as discussed above, we can now turn to explore the characteristics and assumptions of the intercultural communication process.

Conceptualization of Intercultural Communication

The term "cross-cultural" is used in the intercultural literature to refer to the communication process that is *comparative* in nature (e.g., comparing conflict styles in cultures X, Y, and Z), while the term "intercultural" is used to refer to the communication process between members of different cultural communities (e.g., business negotiations between a Dutch importer and an Indonesian exporter). To put it more succinctly, in *intercultural communication*, the degree of difference that exists between individuals is derived primarily from cultural group membership factors such as beliefs, values, norms, and interaction scripts; the term *intergroup communication* implies that a degree of difference exists stemming from general group membership factors (e.g., ethnicity, gender, social class).

Intercultural communication takes place when our cultural group membership factors (e.g., cultural norms and scripts) affect our communication process—on either an awareness or an unawareness level. Individuals may be aware that some cultural differences exist between themselves and the other group members. Nevertheless, they still need to learn the knowledge and skills to manage such differences constructively. On the contrary, individuals may not be aware at all that some cultural difference exists between themselves and dissimilar others. They may attribute the communication missteps to factors (e.g., personality flaws) other than culture-level factors. They may also be totally oblivious that the seeds of intercultural discord have been sown.

However, if intercultural communicators continue to ignore group-based *and* person-based factors that have an impact on their encounters, their misinterpretations may spiral into major escalatory conflicts. Alternatively, individuals may stay in a very superficial relationship without ever moving the relationship to a satisfactory level. To develop a quality intercultural or interpersonal relationship, communicators need to integrate knowledge and skills and practice mindfulness in their communication process.

Mindfulness means being aware of our own and others' behavior in the situation, and paying focused attention to the *process* of communication taking place between us and dissimilar others. Mindlessness, in comparison, implies habitual ways of thinking and behaving without ever moving the awareness of our underlying intentions and/or emotions (Langer, 1989, 1997; Thich, 1991). In mindful communication, we encounter ourselves and others in the "flow" of the interaction moment. In mindless communication, we are consumed by either our habits, reactive/defensive emotions, or biased ethnocentric cognitions. To become an effective communicator in diverse cultural situations, we must first be mindful of the different characteristics that constitute the process itself.

Intercultural communication is defined as the *symbolic exchange process whereby individuals from two (or more) different cultural communities negotiate shared meanings in an interactive situation.* The major characteristics of this definition include the following concepts: symbolic exchange, process, different cultural communities, negotiate shared meanings, and an interactive situation.

Explanations of Intercultural Communication Characteristics

In any intercultural encounter process, people use verbal and nonverbal messages to get their ideas across. The first characteristic, *symbolic exchange,* refers to the use of verbal and nonverbal symbols between a minimum of two individuals to accomplish shared meanings. While verbal symbols represent the digital aspects of our message exchange process, nonverbal symbols or cues (i.e., the smallest identifiable unit of communication) such as smiles represent the analogical aspects of our message exchange process. Digital aspects of communication refer to the content information that we convey to our listener. The relationship between a digital cue (e.g., the word "angry") and its interpretation is arbitrary. The word "angry" is a digital symbol that stands for an intense, antagonistic feeling. The word itself, however, does not carry the feeling; it is people, as symbol users, that infuse the word with intense emotions.

In comparison, analogical aspects of communication refer to the "picturesque" meanings or the affective meanings that we convey through the use of nonverbal cues. Nonverbal cues are analogical because there exists a "resemblance" relationship between the nonverbal cue (e.g., a frown) and its interpretation (e.g., dislike something). Furthermore, while verbal cues are discrete (i.e., with clear beginning and ending sounds), nonverbal cues are continuous (i.e., different nonverbal cues flow simultaneously with no clear-cut beginning and ending) throughout the message exchange process. While verbal messages always include the use of nonverbal cues such as accents and vocal intonations, we can use nonverbal messages such as touch without words. As babies, we acquire or soak up the nonverbal cues from our immediate cultural environments before the actual learning of our native tongues.

The second characteristic, *process,* refers to the interdependent nature of the intercultural encounter. Once two cultural strangers make contact and attempt to communicate, they enter into a mutually interdependent relationship. A Japanese businessperson may be bowing, and an American businessperson may be ready to shake hands. The two may also quickly reverse their nonverbal greeting rituals and adapt to each other's behavior. This quick change of nonverbal postures, however, may cause another awkward moment of confusion. The concept of process refers to two ideas: the transactional nature and the irreversible nature of communication (Barnlund, 1962; Watzlawick, Beavin, & Jackson, 1967).

The transactional nature of intercultural communication refers to the simultaneous encoding (i.e., the sender choosing the right words or nonverbal gestures to express his or her intentions) and decoding (i.e., the receiver translating the words or nonverbal cues into comprehensible meanings) of the exchanged messages. When the decoding process of the receiver matches the encoding process of the sender, the receiver and sender of the message have accomplished shared content meanings effectively. Unfortunately, more often than not, intercultural encounters are filled with misunderstandings and second guesses because of language problems, communication style differences, and value orientation differences.

Furthermore, intercultural communication is an irreversible process because the receiver may form different impressions even in regard to the same repeated message. Once a sender utters something to a receiver, he or she cannot repeat the same message exactly twice. The sender's tone of voice, interaction pace, or his or her facial expression will not stay precisely the same. It is also difficult for any sender to withdraw or cancel a message once the message has been decoded. For example, if a sender utters a remark such as "I have friends who are Japs!" and then quickly attempts to withdraw the message, this attempt cannot succeed because the message has already created a damaging impact on the receiver's decoding field. Thus, intercultural communication process is irreversible (Barnlund, 1962). Throughout this book, we will use examples of intercultural acquaintance relationships, business relationships, friendships, and dating relationships to illustrate various intercultural communication processes. We also encourage you to think of additional examples and questions to clarify your own understanding of important concepts that affect the intercultural communication process. By reading each chapter mindfully *and* practicing the concepts and skills recommended there, you will uncover constructive choices and multiple pathways that lead to effective intercultural communication.

The third characteristic, *different cultural communities*, is defined as a broad concept. A cultural community refers to a group of interacting individuals within a bounded unit who uphold a set of shared traditions and way of life. This unit can refer to a geographic locale with clear-cut boundaries such as a nation. This unit can also refer to a set of shared beliefs and values that are subscribed to by a group of individuals who perceive themselves as united even if they are dispersed physically (e.g., Jews who, although dispersed throughout the world, perceive themselves as a united cultural community via their religious beliefs).

Broadly interpreted, a cultural community can refer to a national cultural group, an ethnic group, or a gender group. It is, simultaneously, a group-level construct (i.e., a patterned way of living) and an individual's subjective sense of membership in or affiliation with a group. The term *culture* here is used as a frame of reference or knowledge system that is shared by a large group of interacting individuals within a perceived bounded unit. The "objective" boundaries of a culture may or may not coincide with its national or political boundaries. The term can also be used on a specific level to refer to a patterned way of living by an ethnocultural group (i.e., an ethnic group within a culture).

The fourth characteristic, *negotiate shared meanings*, refers to the general goal of any intercultural communication encounter. In intercultural business negotiations or intercultural romantic relationships, our first level of concern is that we want our messages to be understood. When the interpretation of the meaning of the message overlaps significantly with the intention of the meaning of the message, we have established a high level of shared meanings in the communication process. The word "negotiate" connotes the creative give-and-take nature of the fluid process of human communication. For example, if both communicators are using the same language to communicate, they may ask each other to define and clarify any part of the exchanged message that is perceived by them as unclear or ambiguous. Every verbal and/or nonverbal message contains multiple layers of meanings. The three layers of meaning that are critical to our understanding of how people express themselves in a communication process are content meaning, identity meaning, and relational meaning.

Content meaning refers to the factual (or digital) information that is being conveyed to the receiver through an oral channel or other communication medium. When the intended content meaning of the sender has been accurately decoded by the receiver, the communicators have established a level of mutually shared content meanings. Content meaning is usually tied to substantive discussion or issues (e.g., business contract details) with verifiable, factual overtones (i.e., "Did you or did you not say that?"). It also involves what is appropriate to say in a particular cultural scene. For example, in many Asian cultures, it is impolite to say "no" directly to a request. Thus, people from Asian backgrounds will tend to use qualifying statements such as "I agree with you in principle, however . . ." and "Maybe if I finish studying and if you still want to borrow my lecture notes . . ." to imply a "no" or "maybe" answer. In most encounters, people more often operate by negotiation of content meaning than by negotiation of identity or relational meaning. They also spend more time and effort debating what has been said or not said (i.e., the content meaning) than reflecting mindfully about the identity meaning and relational meaning that have transpired. Although content meaning is easy to "fix," it is the layers of identity and relational meaning that carry powerful information about our "selves" and about the relationship (see Chapter 2).

Identity meaning refers to the following questions: "Who am I and who are you in this interaction episode?"; "How do I define myself in this interaction scene?"; "How do I define you in this interaction scene?" (Wilmot & Hocker, 1998). Identity meaning involves issues such as the display of respect or rejection and is thus much more subtle than overt, content meaning. Decoders typically infer identity meanings through the speaker's tone of voice, nonverbal nuances, different facial expressions, and selective word choices. The statement "Tomoko, come over here!" can be rephrased as "Ms. Sueda, when you have a minute, I would really like to talk to you" or "Ms. Sueda, don't you understand my English? I need to talk to you right now!" or "Dr. Sueda, please, when you have some time, I would really appreciate hearing your advice on this." These different statements indicate different shades of respect accorded to the addressee.

The verbal and nonverbal cues, the interaction styles, and the salient identities of the communicators are part of the identity meaning negotiation process. Identity is a composite self-conception that encompasses different facets of self such as culture, ethnicity, gender, and personality issues. This important theme is further explored in the discussion of identity negotiation theory in Chapter 2.

Relational meaning offers information concerning the state of the relationship between the two communicators. Relational meanings are inferred via nonverbal intonations, body movements, or gestures that accompany the verbal content level (Watzlawick et al., 1967). It conveys both power distance (i.e., equal–unequal) meanings and relational distance (e.g., personal–impersonal) meanings. For example, the professor says, "I want to talk to you about your grade in this class," which can be inferred as either "You're in serious trouble—better shape up or ship out" or "I'm concerned about your grade in this class—let me know how I can help you."

On the relational level, the above phrase can be decoded with a mildly requesting tone, a strongly demanding tone, or a sincerely caring tone. It can also be decoded with compliance or with resistance. Relational meaning of the message often connotes how the relationship between the communicators should be defined and interpreted. It is closely linked with identity meaning issues. It is also often reflective of the expected power distance dimension of the relationship.

The last characteristic, *an interactive situation,* refers to the interaction scene of the dyadic encounter. An interactive scene includes both the concrete features (such as the furniture or seating arrangements in a room) and psychological features (such as perceived formal–informal dimensions) of a setting. Every communication episode occurs in an interactive situation. Burgoon, Buller, and Woodall (1996, p. 193) conclude that an interactive situation typically includes the following gestalt components:

1. *Elements of behavior.* These are the specific verbal and nonverbal behaviors that occur in a situation.
2. *Goals or motivations of the participants.* For example, is this a business get-acquainted situation or a business negotiation situation? What are the expected goals to be achieved in a particular situation?

3. *Rules of behavior.* The rules for getting acquainted differ from a bargaining/concession-seeking negotiation situation.

4. *Different roles that people must play.* Individuals have different prescribed roles (e.g., buyers vs. sellers' roles) to play in different interactive situations.

5. *The physical setting and equipment.* For example, a classroom environment with chalkboard and straight-row seating is different from an office environment with a desk, file cabinets, and personal objects.

6. *Cognitive concepts.* The psychological features of the situation such as the public–private dimension, formal–informal dimension, task–social dimension, competitive–cooperative dimension.

7. *Relevant social skills.* Appropriate and effective skills are needed to achieve interaction goals in the situation.

The interpretations that we attach to the various components of an interactive situation are strongly influenced by the meanings we attach to these components. We acquire the meanings to these situational components via the primary socialization process within our own culture. For example, whether we define different rooms in our home environment as "public" or "private" spaces (reserved for guests or family members) can vary tremendously from one culture to the next. Furthermore, our expectations of what interaction scripts (i.e., patterns of communication or activities) and how interaction sequences should be carried out (e.g., asking a guest if she or he wants tea, coffee, or an extra bowl of rice) are highly culturally and situationally based. Without situational sensitivity, however, minor intercultural irritations can often turn into major intercultural frustrations and conflicts.

INTERCULTURAL COMMUNICATION: FIVE CORE ASSUMPTIONS

Intercultural communication is viewed as a symbolic exchange process between persons of different cultures. The general goal of effective intercultural communication is to create shared meanings between dissimilar individuals in an interactive situation. However, in Chapter 2, we argue that in addition to creating shared content meanings between two cultural communicators, we need to be mindful of the identity and relational meanings that are being expressed in an intercultural situation. Identity support work is viewed as a crucial perspective in promoting mindful intercultural communication. Mindful intercultural communication requires that we support others' desired self-concepts, including their preferred cultural, ethnic, gender, and personal identities. The following assumptions are presented to increase your understanding of the intercultural communication process.

Assumption 1: Intercultural communication involves varying degrees of cultural group membership differences. When individuals from two cultural groups communicate, there exist both differences and similarities between the two individuals. Intercultural communication takes place when our cultural group membership factors affect our communication process on either a conscious or unconscious level.

The cultural membership differences can include deep-level differences such as cultural traditions, beliefs, and values. Concurrently, they can also include the mismatch of applying different norms, rules, and interaction scripts in particular situations. In practicing mindful intercultural communication, we need to develop an understanding of the valuable differences that exist between identity groups; yet at the same time, we need to continuously recognize the commonalities that exist on a panhuman identity level.

Assumption 2: Intercultural communication involves the simultaneous encoding and decoding of verbal and nonverbal messages in the exchange process. This is the key assumption to understanding the concept of "process" in intercultural communication. From a transactional model viewpoint, both intercultural communicators in the communication process are viewed as playing the sender and receiver roles. Both are responsible for synchronizing their conversational process and outcome. The effective encoding and decoding process leads to shared meanings. Ineffective encoding and decoding process leads to intercultural misunderstanding.

However, beyond the accurate encoding and decoding of messages on the content level, communicators need to cultivate additional awareness and sensitivity along multiple levels (such as identity meaning and relationship meaning) of intercultural understanding. With clarity of understanding, we can mindfully choose words and behaviors that make dissimilar others feel included and affirmed.

Assumption 3: Many intercultural encounters involve well-meaning clashes. Members of different cultural communities have learned different scripts in, for example, conversational opening, maintenance, and termination. They tend to use their own cultural scripts, often on an unconscious level, to evaluate the appropriateness of others' conversational opening or exit. Many intercultural miscommunication episodes start off from well-meaning clashes (Brislin, 1993).

"Well-meaning clashes" basically refer to misunderstanding encounters in which people are "behaving properly and in a socially skilled manner *according to the norms in their own culture*" (Brislin, 1993, p. 10; emphasis in original). Unfortunately, the behaviors that are considered proper or effective in one culture can be considered improper or ineffective in another culture (e.g., using direct eye contact is considered a sign of respect in the U.S. culture, whereas direct eye contact can signify disrespect in the Thai culture). The term "well-meaning" is used because no one in the intercultural encounter intentionally behaves obnoxiously or unpleasantly. Individuals are trying to be well mannered or pleasant in accordance with the politeness norms of their own culture. Individuals behave ethnocentrically—often without conscious realization of their automatic-pilot actions.

Effective intercultural communication starts with the practice of mindful intrapersonal communication. Mindful intrapersonal communication starts with conscious monitoring of our reactive emotions in negatively judging or evaluating communication differences that stem from cultural differences.

Assumption 4: Intercultural communication always takes place in a context. Intercultural communication does not happen in a vacuum. Intercultural interaction is always context bound. Patterns of thinking and behaving are always interpreted within an interactive situation or context.

In order to understand intercultural communication from a contextual viewpoint, we have to consider how different cultural value dimensions influence the symbolic exchange process between communicators in an interactive situation. Additionally, the roles of the players, the interaction goals, the scripts, the timing, and the physical/psychological features of the setting can influence the mood of the interaction. Lastly, cultural knowledge, past cultural visiting experience, and relevant application of effective communication skills form the gestalt components of the context. In order to gain an in-depth understanding of the intercultural communication process, we have to mindfully observe the linkage among communication patterns, context, and culture.

Assumption 5: Intercultural communication always takes place in embedded systems. A system is an interdependent set of ingredients that constitute a whole and simultaneously influence each other. Our enculturation process (i.e., our cultural socialization process from birth) within our own culture is influenced by both macro-level and micro-level ingredients in our environment. On a macro level, we are programmed or enculturated into our culture via our family and educational systems, religious and political systems, and government and socioeconomic systems, as well as the paramount influence of media in our everyday life. On a micro level, we are surrounded by people who subscribe to similar ideologies, values, norms, and expectations. We are the recipients and also the preservers of our culture via the daily messages that we trade. However, culture is not a static web. It is a dynamic, evolutionary process. Human beings are also not static individuals—they are changeable.

In learning about another culture or dissimilar groups, we should commit ourselves to make mindful choices and use different cultural viewfinders so as to see things from their perspective. In viewing things through different lenses, we may ultimately perceive our own routine cultural practices with fresh insights. To become mindful intercultural communicators, we have to develop fresh visions, new ways of listening to others, and a soulful alertness.

2

Mindful Intercultural Communication: An Identity Negotiation Perspective

The Identity Negotiation Perspective 26
    The Theoretical Background 27
    Primary Identity Domains 28
    Situational Identities 36
    Summary 39
The Identity Negotiation Theory 39
    Core Theoretical Assumptions 40
    Assumptions 1–4 41
    Assumptions 5 and 6 42
    Assumption 7 44
    Assumption 8 45
Mindful Intercultural Communication 45
    Threefold Outcomes of Mindful Intercultural
        Communication 46
    Mindful Intercultural Communication:
        Criteria and Components 48

There are numerous approaches to the study of intercultural communication. For example, three approaches are anxiety/uncertainty management (AUM) theory (Gudykunst, 1993, 1995), expectancy violations (EV) theory (Burgoon, 1992, 1995), and systems theory (Y. Y. Kim, 1988, 1995). Each of these approaches emphasizes the different facets of intercultural communication. For example, the AUM approach emphasizes the importance of information seeking in reducing anxiety and uncertainty. The EV approach accentuates the importance of understanding our own and others' expectancies in crossing interpersonal or cultural boundaries. Lastly, the systems approach highlights the interface between factors of the host culture and factors of the newcomers' adaptation to the new culture. Each approach is supported by a body of theoretical and empirical work substantiating its ideas (see also, Wiseman, 1995).

    The perspective that guides the development of this book is labeled the *identity negotiation theory*. The identity negotiation theory focuses on the

25

motif of identity security–vulnerability as the base that affects intercultural encounters. Understanding the motif of identity security–vulnerability in any intercultural encounter is critical for the following reasons:

First, individuals bring their sense of "self-image" or "identity" to any type of communicative encounter. The meaning of "self-image," or our view of ourselves, is profoundly influenced by cultural, personal, situational, and relational factors. In this book, we propose that culture plays the primary shaping role in our view of ourselves. It is through core cultural values and practices that the meanings of identities such as ethnicity, gender, and age are defined and differentially valued.

Second, individuals acquire their identities via interaction with others in their culture. Whether we perform an identity role effectively or ineffectively, appropriately or inappropriately, is defined by the consensual norms and scripts developed by people in the culture. What constitutes competent interaction (e.g., verbal assertiveness) may be viewed as incompetent in another culture. What may be perceived as incompetent interaction (e.g., conflict avoidance) may be perceived as competent in another culture. Thus, understanding how various cultural norms endorse and mold communication ideals in a culture is critical to any effective intercultural communication.

Third, individuals tend to feel secure when communicating with people whom they view as supportive and with a high sense of familiarity. They tend to experience identity vulnerability when interacting with people whom they view as unfamiliar. With similar others, individuals tend to share common set of values, norms, and scripts. With dissimilar others, individuals' habits of norms and routines are constantly being questioned or contested. Thus, the theme of identity security and vulnerability is viewed as a springboard from which other facets of intercultural communication are affected.

This chapter will explore these three reasons that surround the motif of identity security and vulnerability in some depth. The chapter is organized in three main sections. First, the theoretical background and the identity domains of the identity negotiation theory are addressed. Second, the theoretical assumptions of the identity negotiation perspective are explained. Third, mindful intercultural communication from the identity negotiation model is discussed.

THE IDENTITY NEGOTIATION PERSPECTIVE

The identity negotiation perspective emphasizes the linkage between cultural values and self-conception. It explains how one's self-conception profoundly influences one's cognitions, emotions, and interactions. It explains why and how people draw intergroup boundaries. It illustrates the different needs and wants of individuals in desiring inclusion–differentiation and connection–autonomy in their relationships. It also maps out the factors that contribute to identity shock—as when individuals move from a familiar cultural milieu to an unfamiliar one.

The identity negotiation perspective is an integrative theory that draws from the work of social identity theory (e.g., Abrams & Hogg, 1990; Brewer & Miller, 1996), symbolic interactionism (e.g., McCall & Simmons, 1978; Stryker, 1981, 1991), identity negotiation (e.g., Ting-Toomey, 1988, 1989a, 1993), and relational dialectics (Baxter & Montgomery, 1996). Social identity theorists derive their ideas from the social psychological discipline. Symbolic interactionists draw their ideas from the sociological arena. The identity negotiation and dialectical approaches reflect theoretical and research work in the communication discipline.

In sum, the identity negotiation perspective is an integrative theory that draws inspirations from three major scholarly disciplines. Integrating many of the empirical research studies conducted in the three academic spheres, the theoretical ideas of the identity negotiation perspective are formed. This section is organized in three parts: (1) the theoretical background; (2) primary identity domains; and (3) situational identity domains.

The Theoretical Background

The fundamental basis of the identity negotiation theory posits that individuals in all cultures desire to be competent communicators in a diverse range of interactive situations. They learn to be competent communicators within their own cultures through repeated practice. They also learn to deal with others appropriately and effectively through habitual routines. Two sources of identity typically influence an individual's everyday interaction: group-based identity and person-based identity.

Our awareness of our group membership identity and personal identity stems primarily from the internalization of the viewpoints of others around us (Mead, 1934). For example, when significant others consistently regard us in a favorable light, we tend to develop positive conceptions of ourselves. Conversely, when relevant others consistently view us in an unfavorable light, we tend to develop negative conceptions of ourselves.

The core processes of individuals' reflective self-conceptions are formed via symbolic communication with others (McCall & Simmons, 1978). It is through communication that we acquire our generalized views of ourselves and others. It is also through communication with others that we acquire particular ways of thinking about ourselves and others in different situations.

In developing the social identity theory, Tajfel and his associates (Tajfel, 1981, 1982; J. C. Turner, 1985, 1987) propose that *social identities* refer to an individual's conceptualizations of the self that derive from memberships in emotionally significant categories or groups (Brewer & Miller, 1996).

Personal identities, on the other hand, refer to an individual's self-conceptions that "define the individual in relation to (or in comparison to) other individuals" (Brewer & Miller, 1996, p. 24).

Social identities can include cultural or ethnic membership identity, gender identity, sexual orientation identity, social class identity, age identity, disability identity, or professional identity. Personal identities, on the other hand, can include any unique attributes that we associate with our individuated self in comparison to those of others. In collectivistic group-oriented cultures, for example, people may be more concerned with group membership-based issues (Marsella, De Vos, & Hsu, 1985). In individualistic cultures, however, people may be more concerned with individuated-based identity issues.

The social identity theory further assumes that we typically relate to others via two types of perception: intergroup-based versus interpersonal-based perceptions (Tajfel, 1981). In intergroup-based relationships we pay exclusive attention to the group membership attributes of the individuals. In interpersonal-based relationships we pay selective attention to the idiosyncratic attributes of the individuals.

In actual intercultural encounters, however, both types of relatedness are present. Intergroup-based perceptions are salient, for example, when we experience in-group/out-group membership distinctions that arise from the social categorization process (e.g., Black and White racial group memberships). Interpersonal-based perceptions are salient when we get a chance to share or find out more unique information about the person in the encountering process. Both types of perception can contribute to an either effective or ineffective interaction outcome, depending on how we use the group-based or person-based information (see the "Mindful Intercultural Communication" section below).

Finally, both the social identity and the symbolic interaction theories make it clear that the process of defining a personal self is inevitably a social process. No individual person develops a sense of self in a vacuum. Personal identity is developed in conjunction with social identity, and vice versa. Both social identity and personal identity are acquired and developed within the larger webs of our culture (Rosaldo, 1984). Thus, culture is the prime regulator in influencing how we attach meanings, develop labels, and draw boundaries in constructing others' and our own social and personal selves.

Primary Identity Domains

The term *identity* is used in the identity negotiation perspective as the reflective self-conception or self-image that we each derive from our cultural, ethnic, and gender socialization processes. It is acquired via our interaction with others in particular situations. It thus basically refers to our reflective views of ourselves—at both the social identity and the personal identity levels. Regardless of whether we may or may not be conscious of these identities, they influence our everyday behaviors in a generalized and particularized manner.

The identity negotiation perspective emphasizes eight identity domains in influencing our everyday interactions. They are discussed as cultural identity, ethnic identity, gender identity, personal identity, role identity, relational identity, facework identity, and symbolic interaction identity (see Figure 2.1). The first four identity or self-image domains (i.e., cultural, ethnic, gender, and personal identities) are viewed as primary identities that exert an important, ongoing impact throughout our lives. The other four identity domains (i.e., role, relational, facework, and symbolic interaction identities) are situational dependent, that is, changeable from one situation to the next.

Both primary and situational identities mutually influence one another. For example, our gender identities and gender-linked expectations influence our evaluations of how females or males "should" or "should not" behave in a given situation. Our ethnic identities may influence the choice of a particular language or dialect we use in a particular interethnic scene, as well as the nonverbal style that pairs with the language or dialect usage.

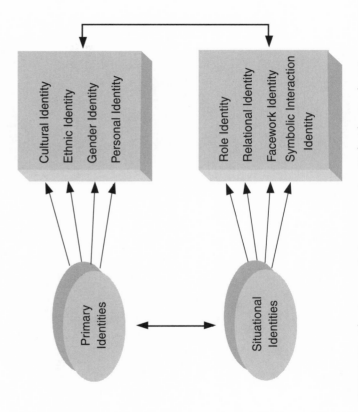

FIGURE 2.1. Identity negotiation perspective: Eight identity domains.

Both language and nonverbal styles represent part of our symbolic identity. The four primary identities definitely influence the other situational identities in an interaction scene. Additionally, situational identities (e.g., through competent or incompetent communication skills) can also influence the way we view ourselves—in a positive or negative direction.

Taken together, these eight identity domains are viewed as a "composite self-conception" of individuals of any culture. In being aware of this composite self-conception, we can begin to mindfully listen to the concerns and issues that surround a person's identity-related stories in a communication episode. We can also learn to reflect back and affirm some of the desired identities of the speaker from another membership group or culture. We begin our discussion with cultural identity.

Cultural Identity

All individuals are socialized within a larger cultural membership group. For example, everyone born and/or raised in the United States has a sense of being an "American" (in this book, to avoid ambiguity, we shall use the term "U.S. American"). Our cultural identities can be so impregnated that unless we encounter major cultural differences, we may not even notice the importance of our cultural membership badges.

Individuals acquire their cultural group memberships via parental guidance and responses during their formative years. Furthermore, physical appearance, racial traits, skin color, language usage, education, mass media, peer groups, institutional policies, and self-appraisal factors all enter into the cultural identity construction equation. The meanings and interpretations that we hold for our culture-based identity groups are learned via contacts with others.

Cultural identity, from the identity negotiation perspective, is defined as the emotional significance that we attach to our sense of belonging or affiliation with the larger culture. To illustrate, we can talk about the larger Brazilian cultural identity, or the larger Canadian cultural identity. To understand cultural identity more specifically, we need to discuss two issues: content and salience.

One way to understand the content of cultural identity is to look at the value dimensions that underlie people's behavior. While there are many value content dimensions in which cultural groups differ, one dimension that has received consistent attention from intercultural researchers around the world is individualism–collectivism (see, e.g., Gudykunst & Ting-Toomey, 1988; Hofstede, 1991; Triandis, 1995). In order to negotiate mindfully with people from diverse cultures, it is critical that we understand the value contents of their cultural identities.

Individualism refers to the broad value tendencies of a group in emphasizing the importance of individual identity over group identity, individual rights over group rights, and individual interests over group interests. Australia, Belgium, Germany, Switzerland, Canada, and the United States have been identified as prototypical individualistic cultures (Triandis, 1995). In comparison, *collectivism* refers to the broad value tendencies of a group in emphasizing the importance of the "we" identity over the "I" identity, in-group obligations over personal rights, and in-group needs over individual desires. China, Japan, South Korea, Vietnam, Ghana, Saudi Arabia, and Mexico have been identified as prototypical collectivistic cultures (Triandis, 1995).

Understanding the individualistic and collectivistic tendencies of various cultures provides one means for examining the value contents of cultural identity. The knowledge can lead us to understand the social behavior of diverse people from a broad range of cultures. The extent to which our culture influences our behavior is dependent in part on how strongly we identify with that culture.

Salience of cultural identity refers to the strength of affiliation we have with our larger culture. Strong associations of membership affiliation reflect high cultural identity salience. Weak associations of membership affiliation reflect low cultural identity salience. The stronger our self-image is influenced by our cultural identity salience, the more we are likely to practice the norms and interaction scripts of our culture. The weaker our self-image is influenced by our cultural identity salience, the more we are likely to practice norms and scripts of our own inventions. Salience of cultural identity can operate on a conscious or an unconscious level. Salience of cultural identity is often a taken-for-granted phenomenon: we live within our own culture as a habitual way of life; we do not need to "justify" or explain its impact unless outsiders inquire about it. We should also clarify here that while the concept of "national identity" refers to one's legal status in relation to a nation, the concept of "cultural identity" refers to the sentiments of belonging or connection to one's larger culture.

To illustrate, as an immigrant society, residents in the United States may mix some of the larger cultural values with that of their ethnic-oriented values and practices. In order to negotiate cultural and ethnic identities mindfully with diverse cultural/ethnic groups, we need to understand in depth the content and salience of cultural *and* ethnic identity issues.

Ethnic Identity

Ethnic identity is "inherently a matter of *ancestry*, of beliefs about the origins of one's forebears" (Alba, 1990, p. 37; emphasis in original). Ethnicity can be based on national origin, race, religion, or language. For many people in the United States, ethnicity is based on the countries from which their ancestors came (e.g., those who can trace their ethnic heritage to an Asian or a Latin American country).

Most Native Americans—descendants of people who settled in the Western Hemisphere long before Columbus, sometime between 25,000 and 40,000 years ago—can trace their ethnic heritage based on distinctive linguistic or religious practices. However, most African Americans may not be able to trace their precise ethnic origins because of the pernicious slavery codes (e.g., a slave could not marry or meet with an ex-slave; it was forbidden for anyone, including Whites, to teach slaves to read or write) and the uprootedness coerced upon them by slaveholders beginning in the 1600s (Schaefer, 1990, p. 207). Lastly, many European Americans may not be able to trace their ethnic origins precisely because of their mixed ancestral heritage. This phenomenon stems from generations of intergroup marriages (say, Irish American and French American marriages, or mixed Irish/French American and Polish American marriages, and the like) starting with the great grandparents or grandparents.

Ethnicity, of course, derives from more than the country of origin. It involves a subjective sense of belonging to or identification with an ethnic group across time. In order to understand the content and the salience of someone's ethnicity, we also need to understand the content and the salience of that person's ethnic identity in particular. For example, with knowledge of the individualism-collectivism value tendencies of the originating countries, we can infer the value contents of specific ethnic groups. Most Asian Americans, Native Americans, and Latino/a Americans, for example, who identify strongly with their traditional ethnic values, would tend to be group oriented. Those European Americans who identify strongly with European values and norms (albeit on an unconscious level) would tend to be oriented toward individualism. African Americans might well subscribe to both collectivistic and individualistic values—in blending both ethnic African values and assimilated U.S. values—for purposes of survival and adaptation.

Beyond ethnic identity content, we should address the issue of ethnic identity salience. The role of ethnic identity salience is linked closely with the intergroup boundary maintenance issue across generations (e.g., third-generation Cuban Americans in the United States). *Ethnic identity salience* is defined as the subjective allegiance to a group—"large or small, socially dominant or subordinate—with which one has ancestral links. There is no necessity for a continuation, over generations, of the same socialization or cultural patterns, but some sense of a group boundary must persist. This can be sustained by shared objective characteristics (language, religion, etc.), or by more subjective contributions to a sense of 'groupness,' or by some combination of both" (Edwards, 1994, p. 128). Thus, ethnic identity has both objective and subjective layers. The objective layers can include racial classifications, shared religion, or shared language. From such a layered outlook, ethnicity is an inheritance and an immutable historical fact.

The subjective layers, on the other hand, imply that an ethnic group consists of people who conceive of themselves as being a distinctive group and are united by common historical, emotional, or symbolic (e.g., language) ties. On the individual identification level, members who identify strongly with an ethnic group believe that they share a common history, heritage, and descent.

Ethnicity is, overall, more a subjective experience rather than an objective classification. While a political boundary (e.g., delimiting Chechnya—formerly the Chechno-Ingush Autonomous Soviet Socialist Republic—from Russia) can change over generations, the continuation of ethnic boundaries (i.e., an identity inclusion/differentiation issue) is an enduring, long-standing phenomenon that lasts in the hearts and minds of its members. Ethnic minority group members, in the context of intergroup relations, tend to be keenly aware and sensitive to the intersecting issues of ethnicity and culture. For ethnic minority members, the perceived imbalanced power dimension and power inaccessibility dimension within a society lead them to draw clear boundaries between the dominant "powerholder" group and the nondominant "fringe" group (Orbe, 1998; Yinger, 1994).

While individuals often use social identity to address in-group/out-group boundary issues (e.g., my turf vs. your turf), they tend to use personal identity to differentiate their unique attributes from the other's unique qualities (e.g., "I'm hardworking, and he is always tardy"). By understanding how others define themselves ethnically and on a personal identity level, we can communicate with them with more sensitivity and understanding. We can learn to lend appropriate self-conception support in terms of ethnic identity issues. Uncovering and supporting others' self-conceptions requires mindful identity negotiation work.

Gender Identity

The meanings of gender terms such as "feminine" and "masculine" are reflective of how the larger culture or ethnic group constructs the images of females and males. While sex is a biological attribute that is determined by genetics and hormones, gender is a learned phenomenon via our primary cultural socialization process (Belenky, Clinchy, Goldberger, & Tarule, 1986; Wood, 1996, 1997). While sex is a static concept, gender is a dynamic construct. We can learn and unlearn gender role expectations.

Gender identity, in short, refers to the meanings and interpretations we hold concerning our self-images and expected other-images of "femaleness" and "maleness." For example, females in many cultures are expected to act in a nurturing manner, to be more affective, and to play the primary caregiver role. Males in many cultures are expected to act in a competitive manner, to be more emotionally reserved, and to play the breadwinner role. The orientations toward femaleness and maleness are grounded and learned via our own cultural and ethnic practices. Gender identity is a culturally constructed phenomenon that consists of the meanings "culture attributes to men and women and the personal and social effects of those meanings on individuals' concrete lives. . . . As we interact with family members, friends, intimates, and work associates, we participate in the cultural creation of gender" (Wood, 1996, p. 14).

To illustrate, in traditional Mexican culture, child-rearing practices differ significantly in socializing girls and boys. At the onset of adolescence, the difference between girls and boys becomes even more markedly apparent. The female is likely to remain much closer to home and to be "protected and guarded in her contact with others beyond the family. . . . The adolescent male, following the model of his father, is given much more freedom to come and go as he chooses and is encouraged to gain much worldly knowledge and experience outside the home" (Locke, 1992, p. 137). Gender identity and cultural/ethnic identity intersect and form part of an individual's composite self-conception.

Although gender difference is pervasive in our everyday lives, it is difficult to pinpoint its effect. As Wood (1996) observes insightfully, "Just as we seldom notice air and fish are unaware of water, for the most part we do not realize the myriad ways in which gender infuses our everyday lives as individuals and our collective life as a culture. This is because the meanings of gender that our [U.S.] society has constructed are normalized, making them a constant taken-for-granted background that can easily escape notice" (pp. 8–9).

Our gender identities are created, in part, via our communication with others. They are also supported and reinforced by the existing cultural structures and practices. The gender identities we learned as children affect our communication with others. They affect how we define ourselves, how we encode and decode messages, and how we develop expectations of what constitute sex role appropriate or inappropriate behavior. We are not, however, prisoners of our gender identities. We can choose to behave differently or to reframe our evaluations in viewing gender-based identity performance. As indicated in the identity negotiation theory, every human being has a diverse range of identities, and she or he can choose to communicate mindfully and flexibly in different cultural situations. To engage in flexible communication behaviors, we need a conceptual compass or working model such as the identity negotiation perspective to guide our diverse actions. A conceptual perspective can add more depth to our understanding of a complex process such as the interface among culture, ethnicity, and gender.

Personal Identity

Beyond group membership identities, individuals develop distinctive personal identities due to unique life histories, experiences, and personality traits. We develop our personal identities—our conceptions of a "unique self"—via our observations of role models around us and our own drives and reinventions.

Personal identity is defined as the sentiments and information an individual has regarding her or his personal self-images. These personal self-images are linked to her or his unique personalities, drives, goals, and values. Personal identity can have two facets: actual personal identity and desired personal identity.

The term *actual personal identity* refers to those unique attributes that an individual exhibits frequently and that are also perceived by others (e.g., traits such as assertiveness, talkativeness, decisiveness). However, the labeling of such attributes may vary markedly between one's own perception and that of others (e.g., the self-perception of being "decisive" can be labeled by others as being "pushy"). The term *desired personal identity*, on the other hand, refers to the preferred attributes that an individual considers to be assets in an interaction (Cahn, 1987). The more others affirm such desired identities in the interaction, the more the person feels that he or she is being understood, respected, and supported. The premise of the identity negotiation approach rests on the importance of supporting others' desired, salient identities more than their actual identities.

Beyond actual and desired personal identity facets, we should also consider specific personality trait factors in the identity negotiation process. To differentiate trait-level analysis versus culture-level analysis, Markus and Kitayama (1991) coined the terms "independent construal of self" and "interdependent construal of self" (see Chapter 3).

"Independent-self" individuals tend to be motivated by personal goal achievements, personal assertion, and personal fairness and rewards. Comparatively, "interdependent-self" members tend to be motivated by group-oriented goal achievements, collective consensus, and in-group harmony and rewards. According to past research, the independent-self pattern tends to predominate in individualistic cultures and the interdependent-self pattern tends to predominate in collectivistic cultures (Triandis, 1995). Thus, on a desired identity level, independent-self individuals tend to strive for personal self-esteem validation such as by someone acknowledging their personal attributes and competence. On the other hand, interdependent-self members strive for collective self-esteem validation such as through their team effort and collective group success.

Overall, individuals may change their conceptions of composite identities at different age brackets, at different life stages, and with different life experiences. When one facet of our self-conception encounters stress (e.g., initial cultural identity shock in an overseas assignment), other facets of our composite identity can also experience the vibrations. A threat to our cultural identity can be perceived as a threat to our personal self-esteem level. For example, when someone says to a nonnative speaker, "I don't understand your heavy accent. How did you ever get this job in the first place?" the hearer's cultural identity can be threatened and simultaneously her or his personal self-esteem level can plummet. Likewise, a perceived threat directed to our personal identity level can also evoke defensive alarms in our other identity domains. For example, when someone says in a belittling tone, "Are you sure you're competent enough to handle this job yourself?" the hearer's personal self-esteem level can suffer and he or she may also wonder whether the speaker is acting out of his or her racist or sexist bias.

We have completed the discussion of the four primary identity domains—cultural, ethnic, gender, and personal identities. We now turn to a discussion of situational identities.

Situational Identities

As already noted, the situational identities refer to role, relationship, facework, and symbolic identities that are adaptive self-images and highly situational dependent. These identities are changeable—dependent on the configuration of the interaction goals, individual wants and needs, roles, statuses, and activities in the situation. Compared to the four primary identities (above), they are less stable and are driven by external situational features and are subsequently internalized by individuals operating in the society.

Role Identity

Role identities are closely linked to the situational parameters of the intercultural encounter (see Chapters 3 and 4). The concept of "role" is a theatrical metaphor that is shaped by expectancy norms within a particular situation in a particular society (Burke, 1945; Goffman, 1959; Stryker, 1987, 1991).

The term *role* refers to a set of expected behaviors and the values associated with them that a culture or ethnic group defines as proper or acceptable. Norms refer to what "should or should not" happen in an interactive situation. They are prescribed expectations of how things should be accomplished (e.g., how to greet someone politely) in a cultural community. The norms of the situation shape what constitutes proper or improper role enactment. Cultural, ethnic, and gender-related values underlie the reinforcement and interpretation of situational norms and roles.

For example, the norms in some individualistic classrooms (e.g., in the United States) encourage students to take initiatives and express personal opinions freely. Ideally, teachers operating in a U.S. classroom should play the friendly, democratic role. They should elicit questions and generate an open atmosphere in the classroom, while students should ask questions and express their opinions freely. In contrast, the norms in collectivistic classrooms (e.g., in Japan) often emphasize team cooperations and classroom obedience. Ideally, teachers in collectivistic classrooms should play the authoritarian expert role. They should disseminate expert opinions and facts, and the students should take notes seriously and respectfully without questions. Cultural values such as individualism–collectivism and power distance (see Chapter 3) undergird the interpretations of appropriate role performance of different actors in a given situation. For role performance to be effective, the actors need to internalize their role scripts for different situations and must accept certain situated behaviors as part of who they are.

Relational Identity

People in every culture are born into a network of family relationships. First and foremost, for example, we acquire the beliefs and values of our culture within a family system. The rules that we acquire in relating to our parents, siblings, extended families, peers, and teachers contribute to the initial blueprint of our relational identities or reflective relational images.

For example, through our family socialization process, we learn to deal with boundary issues such as space and time. We also learn to deal with authority issues such as gender-based decision-making activities (e.g., who did what household chores) and power dynamics (e.g., which parents or siblings held what status power). We also acquire the scripts for emotional expressiveness or restraint, as well as for nonverbal eloquence or gestural nuances, from similar others in our own cultural setting.

Beyond forming relational identities within the family, we also develop voluntary relationships with others such as social relationships or friendships. The self-conception support from intimate friends and significant others can be a powerful form of identity approval (Cupach & Metts, 1994). However, the development of an intimate relationship between persons of two contrastive cultures is a complex phenomenon.

Some relational partners may move quickly from culture-based interaction to person-based interaction. Other partners may spend a lifetime negotiating the meanings of cultural identities, on the one hand, and the meanings of relational/personal identities, on the other (see Chapter 7). One of the basic stressors that people often experience in their relational identities revolves around the theme of facework.

Facework Identity

The term *face* refers to identity respect issues and other consideration issues within and beyond the intercultural encounter process (see Chapters 4 and 8). It is tied to a claimed sense of social esteem or regard that a person wants others to have for him or her. It is therefore a vulnerable identity resource in social interaction because it can be threatened, enhanced, undermined, and bargained over. Face is an identity resource that is manifested and comanaged in communication with others (see Chapter 8 for a detailed discussion).

The term *facework* refers to the specific communication behaviors that we engage in to "save" our own and/or others' face. Individuals, as resourceful communicators, often use creative facework behaviors to protect their vulnerable emotions such as pride and shame, or honor and dishonor. While the concept of face (i.e., identity respect issue) is a universal phenomenon, how we "do" facework differs across cultures (Ting-Toomey, 1985, 1988, 1994a; see also, Brown & Levison, 1987). Face and facework can only be meaningfully interpreted within the communication ideals of the larger cultural system.

In a mindful facework negotiation process, honoring others' face and helping others' to save face may be one way to manage favorable interactive identities across cultures. We should also take into serious consideration intercultural facework competence. For example, in international business negotiations, speaking assertively may be prized in Western cultures and is often viewed as competent facework action. However, from the standpoint of many Asian cultures, speaking tactfully and circumspectly may well be considered a more skillful facework response.

While human beings in all cultures desire identity respect in the communication process, what constitutes the proper way to show respect and consideration for face varies from one culture to the next. Additionally, the emotions (e.g., pride, shame, honor, hurt, anger) that are generated in reaction to different face-saving issues may differ from one person to the next. Different situational contexts and goals call for different rules of facework appropriateness and effectiveness.

Symbolic Interaction Identity

Facework identities are developed and sustained via symbolic interaction. Additionally, all identity domains are implicitly or explicitly expressed via symbolic interaction. Symbolic interaction identity refers to the verbal and nonverbal communication process through which we acquire our reflective self-images and the associated values of our group-based and person-based identities (Blumer, 1969; Blumstein, 1991; Mead, 1934). Through our communication with others and the viewpoints they embody, we develop our composite self-conceptions.

Additionally, in symbolic interaction with others, individuals tend to use certain preferred styles of linguistic and nonverbal codes in relating with others (see Chapters 4 and 5). For example, Francophones in Montréal prefer to use French to converse, whereas Anglophones there prefer to use

English to interact with others. Symbolic interaction consists of the exchange process of verbal and nonverbal messages that constitute the dynamics of communication between people across ethnic groups or cultures.

Verbal and nonverbal symbolic cues serve as the emblems of our composite identities. Individuals in all cultures use culture-based language and nonverbal movements to communicate, to manage impressions, to persuade, to develop relationships, and to elicit and evoke their desired identity badges. These verbal and nonverbal patterns tell others something about ourselves and how we want to be perceived and treated. The language or dialect we engage in reflects our group membership affiliation.

In the first few minutes of interaction with strangers, we form impressions of them, develop attraction or repulsion, and draw in-group/out-group boundaries based on respective symbolic identity assessments. In order to increase the likelihood of positive interaction outcomes with unfamiliar others, we must become mindful of our symbolic interaction process with cultural strangers.

Summary

We have identified eight identity domains that play a critical role in the mindful intercultural communication process. These eight domains are cultural identity, ethnic identity, gender identity, personal identity, role identity, relational identity, facework identity, and symbolic interaction identity.

In order to engage in mindful identity negotiation, we have to increase our knowledge base, our awareness level, and our accuracy in assessing our own group membership and personal identity issues. Concomitantly, we have to understand the content and salience issues of identity domains in direct correspondence with how others view themselves in a variety of situations.

There are many more identities (e.g., social class, sexual orientation, age, disability) that people bring into an interaction. However, for the purposes of this interculturally oriented book, we shall emphasize the above eight identity domains as constituting the nucleus of the identity negotiation framework. The theoretical assumptions we pose in the next section are cast as a set of basic human needs that carry both culture-general and culture-specific meanings.

THE IDENTITY NEGOTIATION THEORY

The identity negotiation theory emphasizes that identity or reflective self-conception is viewed as the explanatory mechanism for the intercultural communication process. Identity is viewed as reflective self-images constructed, experienced, and communicated by the individuals within a culture and in a particular interaction situation.

The concept *negotiation* is defined as a transactional interaction process (see Chapter 1) whereby individuals in an intercultural situation attempt to assert, define, modify, challenge, and/or support their own and others' desired self-images. At the same time, the communicators attempt to evoke their own desired identities in the interaction; they also attempt to challenge or support the others' identities.

While some individuals are relatively mindless (or act on "automatic pilot") about the identity negotiation process, other individuals are relatively mindful about the dynamics of that process. Mindfulness is, moreover, a learned process of "cognitive focusing" with repeated skillful practice (see the section on "Mindful Intercultural Communication" below). The present section is devoted to (1) the core theoretical assumptions of the identity negotiation theory and (2) an explanation of these key theoretical assumptions.

Core Theoretical Assumptions

In the context of this theory, one of the critical goals of mindful identity negotiation is to explore ways to obtain accurate knowledge of the identity domains of the self and others in the intercultural encounter. In a nutshell, the theory assumes that human beings in all cultures desire both positive group-based and positive person-based identities in any type of communicative situation. How we can enhance intercultural understanding, respect, and mutual support through mindful communication is the essential concern of this approach.

The above theory assumes that while the efforts of both communicators are needed to ensure competent identity negotiation, the effort of one individual can set competent communication in motion. The theory consists of the following *10 core assumptions*, which explain the antecedent, process, and outcome components of intercultural communication:

1. The core dynamics of people's group membership identities (e.g., cultural and ethnic memberships) and personal identities (e.g., unique attributes) are formed via symbolic communication with others.

2. Individuals in all cultures or ethnic groups have the basic motivation needs for identity security, trust, inclusion, connection, and stability on both group-based and person-based identity levels.

3. Individuals tend to experience identity security in a culturally familiar environment and experience identity vulnerability in a culturally unfamiliar environment.

4. Individuals tend to experience identity trust when communicating with culturally similar others and identity distrust when communi-

cating with culturally dissimilar others; identity familiarity leads to trust, and identity unfamiliarity leads to distrust.

5. Individuals tend to feel included when their desired group membership identities are positively endorsed (e.g., in positive in-group contact situations) and experience differentiation when their desired group membership identities are stigmatized (e.g., in hostile out-group contact situations).

6. Individuals tend to desire interpersonal connection via meaningful close relationships (e.g., in close friendship support situations) and experience identity autonomy when they experience relationship separations.

7. Individuals perceive identity stability in predictable cultural situations and detect identity change or chaos in unpredictable cultural situations.

8. Cultural, personal, and situational variability dimensions influence the meanings, interpretations, and evaluations of these identity-related themes.

9. Satisfactory identity negotiation outcomes include the feeling of being understood, respected, and supported.

10. Mindful intercultural communication emphasizes the importance of integrating the necessary intercultural knowledge, motivations, and skills to communicate satisfactorily, appropriately, and effectively.

Drawing from the core assumptions of the identity negotiation theory, the following themes underscore the development of the discussions that follow: identity security–vulnerability, familiarity–unfamiliarity, inclusion–differentiation, connection–autonomy, and stability–change. We turn now in the following subsections to a summary discussion of Assumptions 1–4, then Assumptions 5 and 6, Assumption 7, Assumption 8, and Assumptions 9 and 10. All assumptions are explained and developed in more detail in the rest of the book.

Assumptions 1–4

Assumption 1 has been discussed in the "Primary Identity Domains" section above. The basic idea concerning Assumption 1 is that people in all cultures form their reflective self-images such as cultural identity and ethnic identity via their enculturation process. Through the content of their cultural and ethnic socialization experiences, they acquire the values, norms, and core symbols of their cultural and ethnic groups. Through their identity content and salience levels, their respective group-based and person-based identities influence and shape their thinking, emotions, and communication patterns when interacting with culturally dissimilar others.

Thus, in order to understand the person with whom you are communicating, you need to understand the identity domains that she or he deems as salient. For example, if she strongly values her cultural membership identity and gender membership identity, you need to find ways to validate and be responsive to her cultural and gender identities; or if he strongly values his personal identity above and beyond his cultural or gender group membership, you need to uncover ways to affirm his positively desired personal identity. Through mindful communication, we can discover salient identity issues that are desirable to the individuals in our everyday intercultural encounters.

The identity negotiation perspective posits that individuals in all cultures have similar basic human needs for identity security, trust, inclusion, connection, and stability in their communication with others (J. H. Turner, 1987, 1988). The thematic pairs of the respective needs include identity vulnerability, unfamiliarity, differentiation, autonomy, and change. Since Assumptions 3 and 4 are extensions of Assumption 2, we also discuss these two assumptions here in relationship to Assumption 2.

According to Assumption 3, we often experience insecurity or identity vulnerability because of a perceived threat or fear in a culturally estranged environment. On the other hand, we experience identity security in a culturally familiar environment. Identity security refers to the degree of emotional safety concerning one's sense of both group-based membership and person-based identities in a particular cultural setting. Identity vulnerability refers to the degree of anxiousness or ambivalence in regard to group-based and person-based identity issues.

According to Assumption 4, to the extent that an individual experiences identity trust when interacting with similar others, a predictable or reliable interaction climate is developed. Additionally, when individuals confront a common challenge, say, a group of international students arriving in a new country to study, a sense of shared fate can be cultivated. To the extent that an individual experiences identity distrust when communicating with dissimilar others, an unpredictable or defensive interaction climate is established. While Assumption 3 focuses on emotional security and vulnerability issues, Assumption 4 emphasizes cognitive predictability and unpredictability issues.

We experience identity trust (or a sense of reliability) in interacting with similar others because expected norms and routines occur with a high degree of frequency. Comparatively, we experience identity awkwardness in interacting with dissimilar others because unexpected behaviors (e.g., nonverbal violations behavior) and practices occur frequently and intrusively.

Assumptions 5 and 6

Assumptions 5 and 6 are about intergroup and interpersonal boundary regulation issues. Assumption 5 is about the theme of in-group/out-group-based boundary maintenance issues (see Brewer & Miller, 1996). Assumption 6 is about the theme of relational boundary regulation issues of autonomy and connection in significant close relationships (see Baxter & Montgomery, 1996).

Assumption 5, the identity inclusion and differentiation assumption, refers to membership-based boundary maintenance issues. Identity inclusion is conceptualized as the degree of perceived nearness (i.e., emotional, psychological, and spatial proximity) to our in-groups and out-groups. Identity inclusion is an in-group/out-group boundary maintenance issue in which our self-image is attached with some emotionally significant group membership categories (e.g., racial or ethnic identification). Identity differentiation is defined as the degree of remoteness (i.e., emotional, psychological, and spatial distance) we perceive in regulating our group-based boundary with either in-group or out-group members.

Mindful boundary regulation helps to satisfy ingroup inclusion and intergroup differentiation needs (Brewer, 1991; Brewer & Miller, 1996). To the extent that one's salient in-group (e.g., one's ethnic group) compares favorably with other relevant social/cultural groups, one may consider one's membership group positively. Conversely, to the extent that one's salient ingroup compares unfavorably, one would choose different options. Such options can include changing one's identity group (if possible), changing the comparative criteria dimensions, reaffirming one's own group value, or downgrading the comparative group.

Drawing from the social identity theory, Brewer (1991) argues that "social identity derives from a fundamental tension between human needs for validation and similarity to others (on the one hand) and a countervailing need for uniqueness and individuation (on the other)" (p. 477). The identity needs for both appropriate inclusion and differentiation exist as dualistic motivations to the intergroup communication process. Too much group-based inclusion may cause us to ponder the significance and meanings of our person-based identity. Too much group-based differentiation, however, may cause us to feel unwelcome or excluded.

Assumption 6 concerns the thematic pair of identity autonomy and identity connection. Identity autonomy–connection is defined as an interpersonal relationship boundary regulation issue (e.g., from an autonomy–privacy lens to a relational connection lens) (Baxter & Montgomery, 1996). Cultural values such as individualism and collectivism influence our interpretations and evaluations of concepts such as "autonomy" and "connection."

For example, in an intercultural romantic relationship, an individualistic partner (e.g., an Australian boyfriend) may emphasize personal autonomy or privacy issues, while a collectivistic partner (e.g., a Vietnamese girlfriend) may invest more energy in regulating connection issues with the surrounding family network issues (see Chapter 7).

Furthermore, the theme of identity autonomy–connection is clearly manifested through a culture's language usage (e.g., the frequent mentions of "I" messages in individualistic cultures vs. "we" messages in group-oriented cultures). It can also be observed in nonverbal actions and architectures that emphasize household privacy or household/communal plaza connectedness (see Chapters 4 and 5).

In order to understand more in depth the relational theme of autonomy–connection, we need to have a strong grasp of the value orientations that frame the motif of autonomy and connection (see Chapter 3). We also need to pay mindful attention to the verbal and nonverbal message styles of people in different individualistic and collectivistic communities.

Assumption 7

Assumption 7 is concerned with identity stability and change issues over time. Identity stability refers to a sense of identity continuation or consistency through time—whether it is through cultural, ethnic, gender, or personal identity preservation or rituals. Identity change refers to a sense of identity dislocation or transformation in the intercultural contact journey (see Chapter 9).

The more an individual experiences or cultivates an optimal level of identity security and stability, the more she or he is likely to be open to constructive identity change. The more an individual experiences identity threats (e.g., identity differentiation and disconnection), the more he or she is likely to cling to identity stability. Overall, there exists a tolerable range of identity stability (or rootedness) and identity change (or rootlessness) in an intercultural transformation process.

Too much identity rootedness will turn a person into a highly ethnocentric being. Too much identity change will turn a person into a highly marginal type with no moral center. However, a self-system without change will also stagnate. A balanced pendulum-like oscillation between identity stability and change will help to promote healthy professional and personal growth. Likewise, a complementary perspective in viewing the identity thematic pairs—security–vulnerability, familiarity–unfamiliarity, inclusion–differentiation, connection–autonomy, and stability–change—will help us to be mindful of the complex identity diversity within ourselves and others.

Overall, J. H. Turner (1987) asserts that failure to meet the basic human needs of security, predictability/trust, and inclusion can lead to diffuse anxiety and frustration in our everyday life. He concludes that our efforts to sustain a coherent self-conception are directly fueled by the three following motivation dimensions of group-based and person-based identity communication process: (1) the need to feel secure that things are as they appear; (2) the need to sense predictability or trust the responses of others; and (3) the need to feel included.

However, how we go about establishing security, trust, inclusion, connection, and stability in ourselves and others depends heavily on culture-sensitive knowledge and competent communication skills. Mindful intercultural communication is achieved via a joint function of both communicators successfully meeting the needs for identity security, trust, inclusion, connection, and stability in the identity negotiation process.

Assumption 8

Cultural beliefs and values provide the implicit standards for evaluating and enacting different identity-related practices. Cultural membership and hence its cultural values direct how we think about our "identities," how we construct the identities of others, and how these interactive identities play out in verbal and nonverbal symbolic interaction.

Situational norms and rules influence the appropriate delivery of identity lines or role enactments (Collier & Thomas, 1988). In "loose" cultures (e.g., Australia and the United States), deviation from situational norms (e.g., crossing against red lights and jaywalking) and proper role performance is tolerated. In "tight" cultures (e.g., Greece and Japan), people are expected to follow closely the situational norms and interaction scripts of the larger culture (Triandis, 1994a). Deviation from appropriate role performance often evokes disapproval and sanctions from others. Factors such as cultural heterogeneity/homogeneity, low/high population density, and geographic mobility shape the "looseness" or "tightness" of a cultural situation.

For example, a sparsely populated society (e.g., New Zealand) has only "loose" norms and rules to regulate the behavior of the people. In comparison, in a densely populated society (e.g., India), the culture has developed many norms, rules, rituals, and an elaborate bureaucracy to "tightly control" the behavior of the people and to reduce conflicts within the society.

Finally, personality factors such as tolerance for ambiguity and personal flexibility also help to promote identity security and inclusion of the self and others. Individuals who have higher degrees of tolerance for ambiguity or risk taking, for example, have less fear in approaching cultural strangers than individuals with lower degrees of tolerance for ambiguity (Ward, 1996). Individuals with personal flexibility are more ready to experiment with new knowledge and new skills in culturally diverse situations.

MINDFUL INTERCULTURAL COMMUNICATION

This section covers the outcomes, criteria, and components of mindful intercultural communication. While the outcomes are listed in *Assumption 9* of the identity negotiation model, the criteria and the components of mindful intercultural communication are presented in *Assumption 10*.

Langer's (1989, 1997) concept of mindfulness encourages individuals to tune in conscientiously to their habituated mental scripts and preconceived expectations. *Mindfulness* means the readiness to shift one's frame of reference, the motivation to use new categories to understand cultural or ethnic differences, and the preparedness to experiment with creative avenues of decision making and problem solving. The concept of mindfulness can serve as the first effective step in integrating our theoretical knowledge with the identity-based outcome dimensions.

Mindlessness, on the other hand, is the heavy reliance on familiar frame of reference, old routinized designs or categories, and customary ways of doing things. It means we are operating on "automatic pilot" without conscious thinking or reflection. It means we are at the "reactive" stage rather than the reflective "proactive" stage. To engage in a state of mindfulness in competent intercultural communication, individuals need to be aware that both differences and similarities exist between the membership groups and the communicators as unique individuals.

To be mindful communicators, individuals need to learn the value systems that influence others' self-conceptions. They need to be open to a new way of identity construction. They need to be prepared to perceive and understand a behavior or a problem from others' cultural and personal standpoints. Mindful communicators need to be on the alert that multiple perspectives typically exist in interpreting a basic phenomenon (Langer, 1989, 1997).

Threefold Outcomes of Mindful Intercultural Communication

According to the identity negotiation theory, satisfactory outcomes include the feeling of being understood, the feeling of being respected, and the feeling of being supported. Together, they serve as the identity outcome dimensions. The accomplishment of a satisfactory identity negotiation process is contingent on the perceptions of the communicators in the interaction scene. It also depends on our willingness to practice mindfulness in our interactions with dissimilar others.

To the extent that communicators perceive desired identities have been mindfully understood, accorded with due respect, and are supported, the involved parties should experience a high sense of identity satisfaction. To the extent that the communicators perceive that desired identities have been mindlessly bypassed, misunderstood, and/or insulted, the involved parties should experience a low sense of identity satisfaction. Thus, the construct of identity satisfaction acts as an essential criterion of intercultural communication competence.

Drawing from the discussion of the identity negotiation theory, the *feel-*

ing of being understood is one of the most powerful means of being validated (Cahn, 1987). The feeling of being understood connotes an echoing voice out there that empathizes with one's thinking, feeling, and behaving. The echoing voice does not necessary have to agree, but it has to have empathetic (i.e., "I know where you're coming from") impact. Identity understanding begins with gathering accurate identity-based information and being culturally sensitive in probing identity-based details in the intergroup negotiation process. It also means the willingness to share facets of our own self-conceptions with others in a culturally sensitive manner.

The *feeling of being respected* connotes that our desirable identity-based behaviors and practices are being deemed as legitimate, credible, and on a equal footing with members of other groups. Identity respect connotes the mindful monitoring of one's verbal and nonverbal attitudes in interacting with dissimilar others. It also means treating others' salient group-based and person-based identities with courteousness, consideration, and dignity.

The *feeling of being supported* refers to our sense of being positively valued or endorsed as "worthwhile" individuals despite having different group-based or idiosyncratic identities. When a person perceives authentic and positive identity endorsement, she or he also tends to view self-images positively. When a person perceives negative identity endorsement, she or he also tends to view self-images negatively.

Positive identity endorsement is typically expressed through verbal and nonverbal confirming messages. *Confirmation* is the "process through which individuals are recognized, acknowledged, and endorsed" (Laing, 1961, p. 83). Confirming communication involves recognizing others with important group-based and person-based identities, responding sensitively to other people's affective states, and accepting other people's experiences as real. *Disconfirmation*, on the other hand, is the process through which individuals do not recognize others, do not respond sensitively to dissimilar others, and do not accept others' experiences as valid (Cissna & Sieburg, 1981). In confirming others on an authentic basis, we use identity-support messages to affirm others' alternative lifestyles, feelings, and experiences. In disconfirming others, we use indifferent messages (e.g., verbally and nonverbally ignoring others) or disqualifying messages (e.g., patronizing language, evaluative language, racist and sexist language) to discount the others' feelings, thoughts, and experiences.

We affirm others by the words and nonverbal actions we use in our communication with them. In communicating mindfully, our messages convey our understanding, respect, and support for dissimilar others on a holistic level. In interacting mindlessly, our messages convey evaluative attitudes, doubts, and mistrust. The positive or negative consequences of the identity negotiation process, ultimately, affect the development of quality intergroup and interpersonal relationships.

Mindful Intercultural Communication: Criteria and Components

Mindful intercultural communication involves the appropriate management of shared meanings and effective achievement of desired goals. Shared meanings involve an acute awareness of meaning encoding and decoding on the content, identity, and relational level during the communication process itself. Interpersonal goals refer to anticipated consequences or outcomes that people desire to achieve. Goals can include instrumental goals, self-presentation goals, and relationship goals (Cupach & Canary, 1997). Instrumental goals are concerned with substantive outcomes or resources that people want to achieve in an interaction (e.g., changing another's attitude, gaining compliance, or asking for help). Self-presentation goals or identity goals refer to the personal or public images we want to sustain (e.g., as intelligent, credible, or powerful) and want others to respect as a consequence of our interaction. Lastly, relationship goals pertain to the relationship status (e.g., more intimate or less intimate) we desire to maintain with another person.

Mindful intercultural communication emphasizes the importance of integrating the necessary intercultural knowledge, motivations, and skills to manage process-based issues satisfactorily and achieve desired interactive goals appropriately and effectively. The necessary knowledge blocks that are facilitative to mindful intercultural interaction are discussed in Chapters 3 through 10. A mindful intercultural communication model is presented in Figure 2.2.

Assumption 10 of the identity negotiation theory emphasizes two ideas: the first is that mindful intercultural communication has three components—knowledge, motivation, and skills; the second is that mindful intercultural communication refers to the appropriate, effective, and satisfactorily management of desired shared meanings and goals in an intercultural episode. Competent intercultural interaction emphasizes the importance of integrating knowledge and motivational factors and putting them into mindful practice in everyday interactions. Together with the criterion of "satisfaction" discussed earlier, two additional criteria guide the evaluation of mindful intercultural communication: perceived appropriateness and effectiveness.

Criteria

Spitzberg and Cupach (1984) propose that communication competence has two criteria: appropriateness and effectiveness. "Appropriateness" refers to the degree to which behaviors are regarded as proper and match the expectations generated by the culture. "Effectiveness" refers to the degree to which communicators achieve shared meanings and desirable outcomes in a given situation. Using these two criteria in evaluating mindful intercultural com-

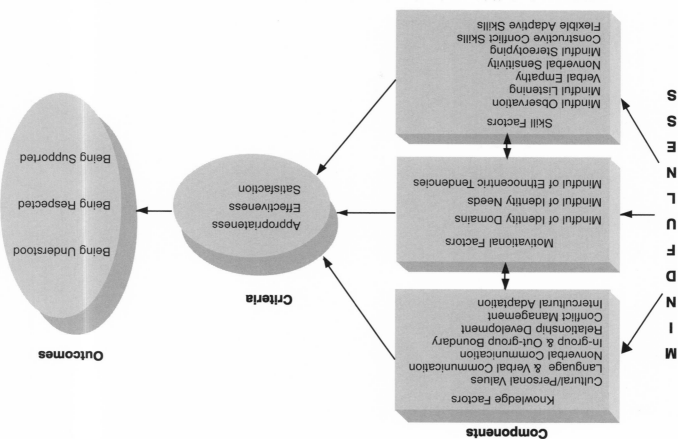

FIGURE 2.2. A mindful intercultural communication model: Components, criteria, and outcomes.

MINDFULNESS

Components

Knowledge Factors
Cultural/Personal Values
Language & Verbal Communication
Nonverbal Communication
In-group & Out-group Boundary
Relationship Development
Conflict Management
Intercultural Adaptation

Motivational Factors
Mindful of Identity Domains
Mindful of Identity Needs
Mindful of Ethnocentric Tendencies

Skill Factors
Mindful Observation
Mindful Listening
Verbal Empathy
Nonverbal Sensitivity
Mindful Stereotyping
Constructive Conflict Skills
Flexible Adaptive Skills

Criteria

Appropriateness
Effectiveness
Satisfaction

Outcomes

Being Understood
Being Respected
Being Supported

petence, we can define *mindful intercultural communication* as the process and outcome of how two dissimilar individuals negotiate shared meanings and achieve desired outcomes through appropriate and effective behaviors in an intercultural situation.

Mindful intercultural communication relies heavily on the perceptions of the communicators in evaluating each other's communicative performance. What may appear effective (e.g., starting a public presentation with a joke) in one cultural context can be viewed as ineffective and inappropriate from another cultural perspective. Likewise, what may appear as appropriate (e.g., speaking apologetically or metaphorically) in one cultural context can be interpreted by another culture as inappropriate and ineffective.

To act appropriately and effectively, individuals have to enhance their cultural knowledge and motivations in applying adaptive interaction skills in the intercultural encounter. Spitzberg and Cupach (1984) identify three components of communication competence: knowledge, motivations, and skills. Knowledge refers to the cognitive understanding one has in order to communicate appropriately and effectively in a given situation. Motivation refers to the cognitive and affective readiness and desire to communicate appropriately and effectively with others. Skills refer to the actual operational abilities to perform those behaviors that are considered appropriate and effective in a given cultural situation. Of all the components of managing intercultural differences, knowledge is the most critical component that underscores the other components of intercultural communication competence.

Knowledge

Without culture-sensitive knowledge, cultural communicators may not be able to match cultural value issues with identity-related behaviors. Knowledge here refers to the process of in-depth understanding of certain phenomena via a range of information gained through conscious learning and personal experiences and observations.

Overall, the knowledge base in this book focuses on how individualists and collectivists (see Chapter 3) negotiate shared meanings, manage different goals, and regulate identity and relational issues. In order to manage cultural differences mindfully, for example, we must take other people's cultural membership and personal identity factors into consideration. If others are collectivists, we may want to pay extra attention to their "process-oriented" (i.e., relationship-based) assumptions to communication. If others are individualists, we may want to be sensitive to their "outcome-oriented" (i.e., instrumental result-based) assumptions to communication. While this book provides culture-general knowledge in explaining identity-based communication differences, it is critical that culture- and ethnic-specific knowledge should be additionally pursued. Both culture-general and culture-specific knowledge can enhance our motivations and skills in dealing with people who are culturally different. A fuller explanation of the various knowledge block factors can be found in subsequent chapters.

To increase our knowledge, we need to be mindful of what is going on in our own thinking, feelings, and experiencing. The concept of "mindfulness" can serve as the first effective step in raising our awareness of our own systems of thinking and judging. Additionally, through mindfulness, we can learn to be more aware of the commonalities and differences that exist between dissimilar individuals and groups. Thich's (1991) concept of "mindful living" (a Buddhist philosophical concept) and Langer's (1989, 1997) concept of "mindful learning" guide individuals to tune in conscientiously to their habitual mental scripts and preconceived categorizations (e.g., rigid stereotypes). According to Langer (1989), if mindlessness is the "rigid reliance on old categories, mindfulness means the continual creation of new ones. Categorization and recategorization, labeling and relabeling as one masters the world are processes natural to children" (p. 63).

To engage in a mindfulness state, an individual needs to learn to (1) be open to new information and ideas, (2) be aware that multiple perspectives typically exist in viewing a situation, and (3) learn to create (or integrate) different standpoints, categories, and contexts to interpret an encounter (Langer, 1989, 1997). As Thich (1991) notes, "All systems of thought are guiding means; they are not absolute truth. . . . Learn and practice nonattachment from views in order to be open to receive others' viewpoints. Truth is found in life and not merely in conceptual knowledge. Be ready to learn throughout your entire life and to observe reality in yourself and in the world at all times" (p. 127).

New information concerning intercultural communication can be acquired through multiple means of learning—attending intercultural classes, readings, interacting more in depth with dissimilar colleagues and classmates, daily mindful observations, and traveling. Being aware that multiple perspectives exist means we come to the realization that there are multiple truths and multiple realities in framing any "bizarre" intercultural situation. Creating or combining different standpoints means we should apply divergent thinking (i.e., looking at things from different angles) and integrative, systems-level thinking (i.e., a creative synthesis of different cultural approaches and resources) in solving an intercultural problem (see Chapter 8).

Lastly, intercultural communication competence can be conceptualized along the following stages: (1) *unconscious incompetence*—the ignorance stage in which an individual is unaware of the communication blunders he or she has committed in interacting with a cultural stranger; (2) *conscious incompetence*—the stage in which an individual is aware of his or her incompetence in communicating with a cultural stranger but does not do anything to change his or her behavior or situation; (3) *conscious com-*

petence—the stage when an individual is aware of his or her intercultural communication "nonfluency" and is committed to integrate the new knowledge, motivations, and skills into effective practice; and (4) *unconscious competence*—the phase when an individual is naturally or spontaneously practicing his or her intercultural knowledge and skills to the extent that the intercultural interaction process flows smoothly and "out-of-conscious awareness" (Howell, 1982) (see Figure 2.3). The third, "conscious competence" stage is the "full mindfulness" phase in which communicators are fully aware of their own systems of thinking, reacting, and experiencing *and simultaneously* attending to the systems of thinking, feelings, and behaviors of their interaction partners. The fourth, "unconscious competence" stage is the "mindlessly mindful" phase in which communicators move in-and-out of spontaneous mindfulness and *"reflective mindlessness"* in communicating with dissimilar others. Competent transcultural communicators often rotate between the conscious competence stage and the unconscious competence stage—for the purpose of refreshening and sharpening their knowledge and motivations in dealing flexibly with dissimilar strangers.

Motivations

Motivations in intercultural communication competence refer to our readiness to learn about and interact with people who are different. Motivations, in the context of the identity negotiation theory, are viewed as identity domain issues and identity needs' issues. From the identity negotiation perspective, we believe that in each intercultural encounter process (e.g., ranging

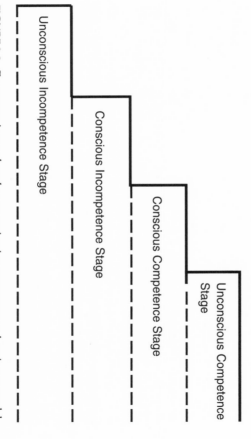

FIGURE 2.3. Four-stage intercultural communication competence: A staircase model.

(Staircase labels, top to bottom:)
Unconscious Incompetence Stage
Conscious Incompetence Stage
Conscious Competence Stage
Unconscious Competence Stage

from a basic greeting ritual of "Hi, how are you?" to a prolonged diplomatic negotiation session) identity dynamics play a critical role in our interaction. A simple "Hi, how are you?"—"Fine!" interaction sequence reflects a cultural greeting ritual. It also evokes a short identity affirmation process: I see you—I greet you—and I affirm your existence.

In order to understand the role of "motivation" in culture-sensitive terms, we need to understand how primary identities and situational identities intersect and affect our intercultural communication process. We also should be mindful that the locus and focus of our different identity needs (e.g., security, inclusion, trust, connection, and stability) are influenced by our cultural membership and personal preference factors. In committing ourselves to deal with culture-based and individual-based differences mindfully, we should have a good grasp of the assumptions presented by the identity negotiation theory.

We need to understand the reasons behind each assumption and be able to apply each flexibly in a diverse range of intercultural situations. We need to analyze systematically our identity needs and those of others in an encounter situation. We need to be attuned to the identity domains and companion values that influence our and others' interactive behavior (see Chapter 3). We need to pay close attention to the identity needs of individuals on both group-based and personal levels. We also should be reflexively aware of our own ethnocentric tendencies that we bring into an intercultural encounter situation. While our primary identities give us guidance and direction in our everyday lives, they also delimit our thinking and behaving. We tend to use our ethnocentric standards in evaluating dissimilar others' performance. A detailed explanation of the various motivational factors can be found in subsequent chapters.

Skills

Skills in this context are our operational abilities to integrate knowledge and motivations with appropriate and effective intercultural practice. Adaptive interaction skills help us to communicate mindfully in an intercultural situation. Many interaction skills are useful in promoting appropriate and effective intercultural communication.

Some of these, for example, are values' clarification skills, mindful observation skills, mindful listening skills, verbal empathy skills, nonverbal sensitivity skills, identity support skills, reframing skills, facework management skills, collaborative dialogue skills, and transcultural competence skills (see the "Recommendations" section at the end of Chapter 3–10). These skills will be discussed as they pertain to the different topics in later chapters.

Of all the operational skills, identity valuation is a major skill to master in mindful intercultural communication. For example, by paying attention to the cultural stranger and mindfully listening to what she or he has to say, we signal our intention of wanting to understand the identity of the dissimilar stranger. By conveying our respect and acceptance of group-based and person-based differences, we encourage interpersonal trust, inclusion, and connection. Lastly, by verbally and nonverbally confirming the desired identities of the cultural stranger, we reaffirm the intrinsic worthiness of the dissimilar other. Identity valuation skill can be conveyed through a word, a glance, a gesture, or responsive silence.

The feelings of being understood, respected, and intrinsically valued form the outcome dimensions of mindful intercultural communication. Mindful intercultural communication emphasizes the appropriate, effective, and satisfactory negotiation of shared meanings and desired goals between persons of different cultures. Mindful intercultural communicators are resourceful individuals who are attuned to both self-identity and other-identity negotiation issues. They are mindful of the antecedent, process, and outcome factors that shape the dynamic interplay of the intercultural communication process. They are also able to adapt to intercultural differences, flexibly and creatively, in a diverse range of communicative situations.

II

THE INTERCULTURAL COMMUNICATION PROCESS: DISSIMILAR ASSUMPTIONS

3

Value Orientations and Intercultural Encounters

Classical Value Orientations 58
    Basic Assumptions 59
    People–Nature Value Orientation 60
    Temporal Orientation 61
    Human Nature Orientation 63
    Activity Orientation 64
    Relational Orientation 65
Cross-Cultural Organizational Value Dimensions 66
    Individualism–Collectivism: The Core Dimension 66
    The Power Distance Dimension 69
    The Uncertainty Avoidance Dimension 71
    The Masculinity and Femininity Dimension 72
    The Confucian Dynamism Dimension 74
    Loose and Tight Social Structures 75
Values, Self-Conception Consequences, and Interaction 76
    Independent and Interdependent Self-Construal 76
    Personal and Collective Self-Esteem 80
    Universalistic-Based versus Particularistic-Based Interaction ... 81
    Summary 82
    Recommendations 82

When we come into contact with strangers from a different culture, we often experience culture shock. Culture shock can occur when we travel overseas for a global assignment and stay there for a period of time. We can also experience interaction shock right here at home because of working or studying along side of peers from different countries or immigrant groups. From unspoken nonverbal differences to language differences, our symbolic identities are constantly being challenged when we work in diverse cultural situations. Nonverbal and language differences are underscored by intercultural value differences.

Kluckhohn and Strodtbeck (1961) conceptualize *cultural value orientations* as "complex but definitely patterned principles . . . which give order and direction to the ever-flowing stream of human acts and thoughts" (p. 4). Cultural value orientations form the basic lenses through which we view our own actions and the actions of others. They set the background criteria for how we should communicate appropriately with others. They also set the emotional tone for how we interpret and evaluate cultural strangers' behaviors. Value orientations influence our overall self-conception, and our self-conception, in turn, influences our behavior.

This chapter is divided into four main sections: the first reviews Kluckhohn and Strodtbeck's (1961) work of classical value orientations; the second examines Hofstede's (1980, 1991) cross-cultural work-related value dimensions; the third explores the relationships among values, self-conception, and communication; finally, the fourth presents a set of recommendations for communicating mindfully with dissimilar others.

CLASSICAL VALUE ORIENTATIONS

Based on the comparative studies of a wide range of cultures throughout the world, specific value patterns in different cultures have been uncovered by researchers in the areas of anthropology, cross-cultural psychology, sociology, international management, linguistics, and intercultural communication. Despite the difficulties in generalizing about the diverse values in heterogeneous cultures such as India and the United States, it is possible and in fact imperative to engage in such cultural value assessments.

Cultural value analysis acts as an organizational grid in mapping the relationships among cultural variability, self-conception, and communication. It highlights both possible differences and similarities of practices between cultural groups. It also helps us to understand our own implicit beliefs and values through looking into the mirror of another culture. Mindful value comparison acts as a critical step toward better understanding of people of diverse cultural backgrounds.

The following subsections explain the basic assumptions and the five value orientations developed by Kluckhohn and Strodtbeck (1961). These five value orientations include people's relationship with their environment, people's concept of time, their concept of human nature, their concept of activity, and their concept of interpersonal relationship. Examples from both national cultures and ethnocultures are given. Ethnocultures are ethnic groups (e.g., African Americans, Irish Americans, Mexican Americans) within a national culture (e.g., the United States) whose members share certain similar sets of values based on their ancestral ties or common heritage. However, these groups also share some of the norms and rules of the larger culture for everyday effective coordination and functioning purposes.

Cultural value orientations serve many functions, including the identity function, group solidarity function, evaluative function, adaptational function, and explanatory function. Within the boundary of our own culture, a clear set of value orientations guide the content (e.g., whether we tend to be more individualistic or group based) of our identity and moral development (i.e., the identity function). Our social and personal identities are formed and reinforced via our intense and frequent interaction with culturally similar others. Additionally, cultural values pave the way to ingroup solidarity and membership affiliation (i.e., the solidarity function). Members who identify strongly with their culture or ethnoculture share perceived partnership ties and often have a common way of living. Furthermore, value orientations regulate in-group consensus and set evaluative standards concerning what is "valued" or "devalued" within a culture (i.e., the evaluative function). They offer us a set of principles by which to function adaptively in a changing cultural milieu (i.e., the adaptive function). Lastly, they help us to explain or "make sense" of events or people's behaviors around us without too much information processing (i.e., the explanatory function). We can "fill in the blank" of why people behave the way they do in our culture because we can draw from our implicit values and scripts in predicting in-group members' actions.

We live and breathe our own cultural values every day through the norms and rules we have consensually developed within our culture. However, if we never venture away from our milieu, we may not detect its importance to us until we, like fish in a pond, are removed from our familiar and comfortable surroundings. This chapter examines several different approaches in understanding values across different cultural groups.

Basic Assumptions

Kluckhohn and Strodtbeck (1961) observe that human beings in all cultures face a set of basic human problems or existential questions. Based on their research on Navajo Indians, Latino(a)s, and European Americans in the Southwest, they list the following five questions to which people in all cultures try to seek answers or solutions:

1. What is the relationship of people to nature (and supernature)? (people–nature orientation)
2. What is the temporal focus of human life? (time sense orientation)
3. What is the character of innate human nature? (human nature orientation)
4. What is the modality of human activity? (activity orientation)
5. What is the modality of a human's social relationship to other human beings? (relational orientation)

The value orientations' approach assumes that the above five questions are universal ones that human beings consciously or unconsciously seek to answer. The answers to these questions are available in all cultures. However, some cultures have a stronger preference for one particular set of solutions than for others. The solutions represent the "deposits of wisdom" of a particular culture passed from one generation to the next. The range of potential solutions to these five questions is shown in Figure 3.1.

People–Nature Value Orientation

The people–nature value orientation asks this question: Is the relationship between people and the natural (or supernatural) environment one of control, harmony, or subordination? While many middle-class European Americans believe in mastery and control over the natural environment, many ethnocultural groups (such as African, Asian, Latino/a, and Native Americans) in the United States tend to believe in living harmoniously with nature.

Many Native American groups, for example, believe that what is human, what is nature, and what is spirit are all extensions of one another: we are all part of the universal continuum, and hence we should learn to live harmoniously with one another. Buddhist cultures such as those of Bhutan, Laos, Thailand, and Tibet also tend to subscribe strongly to the harmony-

ORIENTATION	RANGE		
People & Nature	Subordination to Nature (Yielding)	Harmony with Nature (Flow)	Mastery over Nature (Control)
Time Sense	Past-Oriented (Tradition-Bound)	Present-Oriented (Situation-Bound)	Future-Oriented (Goal-Bound)
Human Nature	Basically Evil Mutable/Immutable	Neutral or Good & Evil Mutable/Immutable	Basically Good Mutable/Immutable
Activity	Being (Expressive/Emotional)	Being-in-Becoming (Inner Development)	Doing (Action-Oriented)
Social Relations	Lineality (Authoritarian Decisions)	Collaterality (Group Decisions)	Individualism (Autonomy)

FIGURE 3.1. The Kluckhohn model: Five value orientations and possible solutions. From Kluckhohn and Strodtbeck (1961) and Kohls (1996).

with-nature belief. In comparison, many Polynesian cultures subscribe to the subjugation-to-nature value solution. Natural disasters such as earthquakes, volcano eruptions, and floods may have contributed to their belief that nature is a powerful force that is beyond the control of individuals. The best way to deal with nature is to pay respect to it and act humbly in the face of cataclysmic external forces.

The implication of this value orientation is that while some individuals believe in gaining control over their environment, others believe in the importance of living harmoniously or submissively in relationship to their natural habitat. People who tend to believe in controlling nature would have a stronger sense of the "self-over-nature" approach in dealing with their surroundings. People who tend to subscribe to the "self-with-nature" or "self-under-nature" viewpoint would have a more harmonious or submissive approach (respectively) in dealing with their environment.

For example, Trompenaars (1994, p. 138) asked managers in 38 different countries to choose between the following two statements: "(A) What happens to me is my own doing," or "(B) Sometimes I feel that I do not have enough control over the directions my life is taking." He found that 89% of U.S. managers and 82% of German managers selected option A, whereas only 56% of Japanese managers and 35% of Chinese managers selected that same option. Overall, most European countries scored high on option A, whereas most African, Middle Eastern, and Asian countries scored low on option A. People who believe in individuals as controllers of nature are "inner directed" or internally driven; people who believe in nature as the controller of humans are "outer directed" or externally driven.

When individuals from different "people–nature" solutions come together, intercultural problems may arise. While individuals from one cultural group are eager to "fix up" the environment with huge projects by building dams, levees, and reservoirs, another cultural group may be deeply offended because the action may provoke the anger of the spirits that inhabit the river being dammed or the terrain being inundated.

Temporal Orientation

The time sense orientation asks this question: Is the temporal focus in the culture based on the past, present, or future? The past-oriented time sense means honoring historic and ancestral ties. The present-oriented time sense means valuing the here and now, especially the interpersonal relationships and activities that are unfolding currently. The future-oriented time sense means planning for desirable short- to medium-term developments and setting out clear objectives to realize them.

Asian immigrants (e.g., Vietnamese Americans) and Native Americans tend to revere the past. African Americans tend to have a strong sense of both past and present references. Latino/a Americans tend to have a strong response to the present experience. European Americans tend to emphasize concern for the immediate future. More specifically, for example, many Vietnamese Americans believe in the Buddhist precepts of karma and rebirth. They believe that "an individual life cycle is predetermined by good and bad deeds from a previous life. The goal is eventually to achieve spiritual liberation. . . . Ancestors are worshiped for four generations after death" (Locke, 1992, pp. 105–106). Thus, for many Vietnamese American immigrants, their past profoundly influences their present identities.

Many Mexican Americans, in contrast, prefer to experience life and people around them fully in the present. This outlook may be derived from the influence of a traditional cultural belief "in the concept of 'limited good.' In fact, this is the belief that there is only so much good in the world and, therefore, only so much good is possible in any one person's life" (Locke, 1992, p. 140). Experiencing life with the fullness of the five senses is prized much higher than "work for the sake of work" itself. Work should never be an end in itself. Living life fully and helping families and friends through meaningful work make more sense to many traditional-oriented Mexicans or Mexican Americans (Hecht, Sedano, & Ribeau, 1993).

Furthermore, many Africans and African Americans tend to embrace a combination of past-present focus. For example, for many Africans and African Americans, people and activities in the present assume a higher priority than an external clock schedule (Asante & Asante, 1990). As Pennington (1990) observes, "Time for Africans does not exist in a vacuum as an entity which can be conceptually isolated. Time is conceived only as it is related to events, and it must be experienced in order to make sense or to become real. The mathematical division of time observed by Westerners has little relevance for Africans" (p. 131). Locke (1992) similarly notes that Africans have a different concept of time from that found in cultures of the Western world: "[The] difference is that in traditional African societies, people [tend to] emphasize something is done only at the present moment . . . In becoming African Americans, the Africans had to develop a new framework capable of holding their beliefs, values, and behavior" (p. 26). For traditional Africans, the actual event that is happening forms the essence of temporal interaction. Furthermore, the past and the ancestors "were indispensable in giving meaning to one's present existence. In regard to the historical . . . sense of time, events were filed as they happened. . . . [T]here was always a conscious awareness and respect for the causal factors linking events among traditional Africans" (Pennington, 1990, p. 137).

On a broader level of interpretation, our sense of developmental identity is closely fused with the temporal value orientation. Those who subscribe to the past-present focus tend to believe in the importance of understanding historical factors and background contexts that frame the "self." In order to understand the present self, it is important to understand the historical contexts that pave the way to it. Those who subscribe to the future focus (e.g., middle-class European Americans), however, tend to deemphasize the past, move forward boldly to the immediate future, and strongly emphasize the importance of "futurism" (e.g., the glorification of the "youth" culture and devaluation of "aging"). The larger French culture, for example, has been classified as "past–present oriented," whereas the larger U.S. culture has been identified as "future oriented." In French culture, "the past looms far larger and is used as a context in which to understand the present. Past, present, and future overlap synchronously so that the past informs the present, and both inform the future" (Trompenaars, 1994, p. 127). However, in the larger U.S. culture, its view of the future is that the individual can control it by personal achievement and inner-directed accountability (Kohls, 1996).

Potential clashes can exist between members of business groups with different time orientations: for example, between members who favor a "past–present" focus and members who favor a "future" focus. While business members from the first group want to view everything from the company's history and traditions, members from the latter group want to bypass the past and plan ahead efficiently for an immediate future. Individuals with a "past–present" focus have a long-term view of time, whereas individuals with a "future" focus have a short- to medium-term view of time.

Human Nature Orientation

The human nature orientation asks this question: At birth, is human nature considered good, neutral, evil, or a mixture of good and evil, and is it changeable? Individuals who believe in the basic goodness of human nature tend to be more trusting of others. Individuals who believe in the inherent evilness of human nature tend to be more skeptical and suspicious when interacting with dissimilar others. Individuals who believe in the neutrality of human nature tend to believe in the role of the environment in shaping their intrinsic nature.

While middle-class European Americans and African Americans tend to perceive human nature as neutral, many Native American groups tend to emphasize the inherent goodness of human nature (Sue & Sue, 1990). Many European Americans tend to believe in the individual's personal willpower to shape the development of human nature, whereas many African Americans tend to believe in the importance of the environment in shaping the nature of a person. For European Americans, human nature can be a mixture of good and evil, depending largely on the individual self-motivation effort. For African Americans, the environment (e.g., family or society) or a spiritual force (e.g., God) plays a critical role in the cultivation of the goodness or evilness of human nature. For many traditional Africans and African Americans, "God is believed to be the creator, the sustainer, and the ultimate controller of life. . . . This belief in God's intervention and ultimate control of the affairs of humans can account for an apparent resignation to fate or to higher forces observed on the part of traditional African peoples" (Pennington, 1990, pp. 127–128).

Many Native American groups believe in the innate goodness of human nature. Locke (1992) observes that "[Native Americans] act on this belief through their customs of welcoming strangers, sharing with each other, and helping others before self. People who do bad things are seen as inhabited by bad spirits, or perhaps as having spells put on them" (p. 57). While different Native American tribes engage in different communication modes in welcoming strangers (e.g., with initial silence and a period of observation), they ultimately believe in the goodness of people's intent. For many Native American groups, people are all part of the larger universe—we are all positively interconnected.

Individuals who believe in the essential goodness of human nature tend to be trusting; they leave their doors unlocked and do not usually fear strangers. Individuals who believe in the essential evilness of human nature tend to be less trusting; they tend to bolt their doors and eye strangers with suspicion. People in rural communities tend to be more trusting than people in urban communities.

Activity Orientation

The activity orientation asks this question: Is the human activity in the culture focused on the doing, being, or being-in-becoming mode? The "doing" solution means achievement-oriented activities. The "being" solution means living with emotional vitality. The "becoming" solution means living with an emphasis on spiritual renewal and connection.

While middle-class African Americans, Asian Americans, and European Americans focus on a "doing" or an achievement-oriented solution, Latino/a Americans and Native Americans tend to focus on the "being-in-becoming" mode (Sue & Sue, 1990). However, the "doing" preference is manifested quite differently among the European American, African American, and Asian American groups.

For example, for the African American group, a "doing" mode means to fight against adversity and to combat racism through social achievements and activism for the good of the community. Furthermore, traditional Africans and African Americans also display a "being" mode for living. They value "having a sense of aliveness, emotional vitality, and openness of feelings. . . . African American culture is infused with a spirit (a knowledge that there is more to life than sorrow, which will pass) and a renewal in sensuousness, joy, and laughter. This symbol has its roots in African culture and expresses the soul and rhythm of that culture in America" (Hecht, Collier,

& Ribeau, 1993, pp. 102–103). Likewise, Latino/a Americans also mix the "being" vitality solution with that of "being-in-becoming" spiritual beliefs.

For Asian immigrants in the United States, the "doing" mode is typically associated with working hard and making money in order to fulfill basic obligations toward family and extended family networks. For European Americans, a "doing" mode means focusing on tangible accomplishments for personal gains such as a coveted job promotion or a bigger salary to take care of self and immediate family.

For both the Latino/a and Native American groups, their preferred choice is the "being-in-becoming" mode. Both groups are oriented toward the religious and spiritual. They are concerned with their spiritual well-being more than their material well-being. Spiritual self-actualization is much more important to them than material rewards and gains. In addition, many traditional Latino(a)s also subscribe to the "being" mode of activity, which means enjoying the moment to the fullest. Shared recreations and celebrations with close friends and family members form a critical part of a Latino(a)'s lifestyle.

Relational Orientation

Finally, the relational orientation asks this question: Does the culture focus on individual, collateral, or lineal relationships? Ho (1987) explains that while European Americans value individualistic relationships, many other ethnocultural groups (such as Asian, African, Latino/a, and Native Americans) enjoy collateral relationships. Individualistic-based relationships emphasize autonomy, differentiation, and the unique qualities of the people in the relationship. Collateral-based relationships emphasize role obligations and in-group interdependence, kinship bonds, and extended family bonds. Lineal-based relationship emphasizes relationship that is passed from one generation to the next along a historical trajectory such as social class, caste, or family background (e.g., the traditional caste system of India).

We can conclude that while middle-class European Americans tend to subscribe to the predominant individualistic relationship tendencies, African Americans, Asian Americans, Native Americans, and Latino/a Americans tend to prefer the collateral relationship tendencies or a mixture of both value sets. Because of the proximity between these ethnic groups within the United States, their value tendencies oftentimes take on mixed adaptational functions. Furthermore, Trompenaars (1994), in asking international managers to read the scenario in which "two people were discussing ways in which individuals could improve the quality of life," finds some interesting results. For example, in his research, the respondents can choose either "(A) . . . It is obvious that if individuals have as much freedom as possible and the maximum opportunity to develop themselves, the quality of their lives will improve as a result," or "(B) . . . If individuals are continuously taking care of their fellow human beings, the quality of life will improve for everyone, even if it obstructs individual freedom and individual development" (p. 51). Overall, Canadian, U.S, and Norwegian managers score highest on option A, and Egyptian, Kuwaiti, and Nepalese managers score lowest on option A. The theme of relational orientation as manifested through the individualism–collectivism dimension will be further discussed in the next section.

CROSS-CULTURAL ORGANIZATIONAL VALUE DIMENSIONS

Moving beyond the classical value orientations' approach, Hofstede (1980, 1991) has empirically derived four cultural variability dimensions in his large-scale study of a U.S. multinational business corporation. The corporation has subsidiaries in 50 countries and 3 regions (the Arabic-speaking countries, East Africa, and West Africa). Altogether, 116,000 managers and employees in this worldwide corporation were surveyed twice. Based on the results of this research project, Hofstede (1980, 1991) delineated four organizational value patterns across a diverse range of cultures.

The first and most important dimension is individualism–collectivism. The other three cultural variability dimensions are power distance, uncertainty avoidance, and masculinity–femininity. Later, Hofstede and his colleagues (see the Chinese Culture Connection, 1987) identified a fifth work-related dimension, Confucian dynamism.

We should note that Hofstede's four cultural variability dimensions are related to business organizational values in different cultures. He also argues that ethnic and religious groups, gender, generation, social class, and social structure assert a strong influence on the value patterns within a particular culture. The four value dimensions should be viewed as a first systematic empirical attempt to compare cultures on an aggregate, group level. Each culture also displays different value configurations along the four cultural variability dimensions.

Individualism–Collectivism: The Core Dimension

While there are many dimensions in which national cultures differ, one dimension that has received consistent attention from both intercultural researchers and cross-cultural psychologists is individualism–collectivism. Numerous cross-cultural studies (Fiske, 1991; Gudykunst & Ting-Toomey, 1988; Hofstede, 1980, 1991; Schwartz & Bilsky, 1990; Triandis, 1994a, 1995) have provided theoretical and empirical evidence that the value orientations of individualism and collectivism are pervasive in a wide range of cultures. Individualism and collectivism can explain some of the basic differences and similarities concerning communication behavior between clusters of cultures.

Basically, *individualism* refers to the broad value tendencies of a culture in emphasizing the importance of individual identity over group identity, individual rights over group rights, and individual needs over group needs. Individualism promotes self-efficiency, individual responsibilities, and personal autonomy. In contrast, *collectivism* refers to the broad value tendencies of a culture in emphasizing the importance of the "we" identity over the "I" identity, group rights over individual rights, and in-group-oriented needs over individual wants and desires. Collectivism promotes relational interdependence, in-group harmony, and in-group collaborative spirit (Ting-Toomey, 1988; Triandis, 1995) (see Table 3.1).

Individualistic and collectivistic value tendencies are manifested in everyday family, school, and workplace interaction. Hofstede (1991) explains that individualism pertains to "societies in which ties between individuals are loose; everyone is expected to look after himself or herself and his or her immediate family" (p. 51). Comparatively, collectivism refers to "societies in which people from birth onwards are integrated into strong, cohesive in-groups, which throughout people's lifetimes continue to protect them in exchange for unquestioning loyalty" (Hofstede, 1991, p. 51).

Hofstede's (1991) research in 50 countries and 3 regions reveals that factors such as national wealth, population growth, and historical roots affect the development of individualistic and collectivistic values. For ex-

TABLE 3.1. Major Differences between Individualistic and Collectivistic Cultures

Individualistic cultures	Collectivistic cultures
"I" identity	"We" identity
Individual goals	Group goals
Interindividual emphasis	Ingroup emphasis
Voluntary reciprocity	Obligatory reciprocity
Management of individuals	Management of groups
Examples	Examples
United States	Guatemala
Australia	Ecuador
United Kingdom	Panama
Canada	Indonesia
Netherlands	Pakistan
New Zealand	Taiwan/China
Sweden/France	Japan
Germany	West/East African countries

Note. Data from Hofstede (1991). The cultures listed are based on the *predominant* tendencies in the cultures.

ample, the wealthy, urbanized, and industrialized societies are more individualistic oriented, whereas the poorer, rural, and traditional societies are more collectivistic oriented. However, there are some exceptions, especially in East Asia, where Japan, South Korea, Taiwan, Hong Kong, and Singapore appear to retain collectivism in spite of industrialization.

Hofstede's (1980, 1991) and Triandis's (1988, 1989) research indicates that individualism is a cultural pattern that is found in most northern and western regions of Europe and in North America. Collectivism refers to a cultural pattern common in Asia, Africa, the Middle East, Central and South America, and the Pacific islands. While less than one-third of the world population resides in cultures with high individualistic value tendencies, a little more than two-thirds of the people live in cultures with high collectivistic value tendencies (Triandis, 1989).

More specifically, high individualistic index values have been found in the United States, Australia, Great Britain, Canada, the Netherlands, New Zealand, Italy, Belgium, Denmark, and Sweden. High collectivistic index values have been found in Guatemala, Equador, Panama, Venezuela, Colombia, Indonesia, Pakistan, Costa Rica, and Peru (Hofstede, 1991, p. 53). In intercultural communication research (Gudykunst & Ting-Toomey, 1988; see also Bellah, Madsen, Sullivan, Swidler, & Tipton, 1985), the United States has been consistently identified as a culture high in individualistic value tendencies, while strong empirical evidence clearly identifies the value patterns of China, South Korea, Japan, and Taiwan as those of collectivistic cultures.

In Triandis, Brislin, and Hui's (1988) research, for example, when respondents were asked to give 20 descriptions of themselves by completing 20 sentences that start with "I am . . . ," people from individualistic cultures used only 15% group-related attributes to define themselves, whereas people from collectivistic cultures used 35–45% group-related attributes (e.g., I am the third daughter of my family) to describe their sense of "selfhood." In terms of specific value emphasis, the top individualist values are freedom, honesty, social recognition, comfort, hedonism, and personal equity. The top collectivist values are harmony, face-saving, filial piety (respect and conformity of parents' wishes), equality in the distribution of rewards among peers (for the sake of group harmony), and fulfillment of other's needs (Triandis et al., 1988). Overall, it has been found that different kinds of individualism (e.g., emphasizing personal need in Australia or immediate family need in Sweden) and collectivism (e.g., emphasizing extended family need in Taiwan, work group need in Japan, or caste need in India) exist in different cultures. For each culture, it is important to determine "the group with which individuals have the closest identification. They could be keen to identify with their trade union, their family, their corporation, their religion, their profession, their nation. . . . The French tend to identify with *la France, la famille, le cadre*; the Japanese with the corporation; the former Eastern Bloc with the Communist Party; and Ireland with the Roman Catholic Church" (Trompenaars, 1994, p. 58).

Within each culture, different ethnic communities can also display distinctive individualistic and collectivistic value patterns. For example, first-generation Asian Americans and Latino/a Americans in the United States tend to retain more group-oriented values than individualistic values. Native Americans also tend to subscribe to group-oriented beliefs more than to individualistic beliefs. African Americans, Middle Eastern Americans, and certain Americans of southern European origin (e.g., Greek Americans) have been found to emphasize extended family solidarity above and beyond individualistic values.

In addition, gender differences exist in adherence to individualistic or relational-based values. U.S. females generally have been found to subscribe to relational-oriented values (however, compared to females in other collectivistic societies such as Japan and Thailand, U.S. females are still fairly individualistic oriented); U.S. males have been found to adhere more to individualistic values than to relational-based values (Bem, 1993; Tannen, 1990; Wood, 1997). For example, according to the research of Gilligan (1988), while U.S. males tend to subscribe to the ideal of the "morality of justice," U.S. females tend to emphasize the ideal of the "morality of caring." The "morality of justice" reflects individualistic concerns of personal equity. The "morality of caring," on the other hand, reflects a relational orientation of mutual empathy.

In their gender identity formation, U.S. males emphasize identity separation and self-empowerment, whereas U.S. females emphasize identity attachment and connection. Gilligan (1988) notes that "[U.S.] male and female voices typically speak of the importance of different truths, the former of the role of separation as it defines and empowers the self, the latter of the ongoing process of attachment that creates and sustains the . . . community" (p. 156). Different gendered groups in many cultures often appear to differ in their preferences for individualistic or collectivistic value tendencies.

Overall, the dimension of individualism–collectivism provides us with a conceptual grid in explaining why the meaning of self-conception varies across cultures. Additionally, it clarifies our understanding of how the various "I" identity or "we" identity orientations influence our everyday communication behaviors across cultures. Another important value dimension we should take into consideration when we interact in a new culture or with an individual from a different culture is the dimension of power distance.

The Power Distance Dimension

Hofstede and Bond (1984) define power distance as the "extent to which the less powerful members of institutions . . . accept that power is distributed unequally" (p. 419). Small power index values are found, for example, in Austria, Israel, Denmark, New Zealand, Ireland, Sweden, and Norway. Large power index values are found, for example, in Malaysia, Guatemala, Panama, the Philippines, Mexico, Venezuela, and Arab countries (Hofstede, 1991). Hofstede (1991) explains that the country's geographic latitude (higher latitudes being associated with a smaller power distance index), its population size (larger size being associated with a larger power distance index), and its wealth (richer countries being associated with a smaller power distance index) affect the power distance dimension. Specific factors that are associated with national wealth *and* less dependence on others include less traditional culture, more modern technology, more urban living, more social mobility, a better educational system, and a larger middle class (Hofstede, 1991).

In small power distance cultural situations, children can contradict their parents and speak their own minds. They are expected to show self-initiative and learn verbal articulateness and persuasion. Parents and children work toward achieving a democratic family decision-making process. In large power distance cultural situations, children are expected to obey their parents. The value of "respect" between unequal status members in the family is taught at a young age. Parents and grandparents assume the authority roles in the family decision-making process (see Table 3.2).

In small power distance work situations, power is evenly distributed. Subordinates expect to be consulted, and the ideal boss is a resourceful democrat. In large power work situations, the power of an organization is centralized at the upper management level. Subordinates expect to be told

TABLE 3.2. Major Differences between Small Power Distance and Large Power Distance Cultures

Small power distance cultures	Large power distance cultures
Emphasize equal distance	Emphasize power distance
Individual credibility	Seniority, age, rank, title
Symmetrical interaction	Asymmetrical interaction
Emphasize informality	Emphasize formality
Subordinates expect consultation	Expect directions
Examples	Examples
Austria	Malaysia
Israel	Guatemala
Denmark	Panama
New Zealand	Philippines
Republic of Ireland	Arab countries
Sweden/Norway	India
Germany	West African countries
Canada/United States	Singapore

Note. Data from Hofstede (1991). The cultures listed are based on the *predominant* tendencies in the cultures.

what to do, and the ideal boss plays the benevolent autocratic role. While the United States scores on the low side of power distance, it is not extremely low. Hofstede (1991) explains that "U.S. leadership theories tend to be based on subordinates with medium-level dependence needs: not too high, not too low" (p. 42).

People in small power distance cultures tend to value equal power distributions, equal rights and relations, and equitable rewards and punishments based on performance. People in large power distance cultures tend to accept unequal power distributions, hierarchical rights, asymmetrical role relations, and rewards and punishments based on age, rank, status, title, and seniority. For small power cultures, equality of personal rights represents an ideal to strive toward in a system. For large power cultures, respect for power hierarchy in any system is a fundamental way of life.

The Uncertainty Avoidance Dimension

Uncertainty avoidance refers to the extent to which the members of a culture feel threatened by uncertain and unknown situations and the extent to which they try to avoid these situations. The stronger the uncertainty avoidance, the greater the feeling of threat and the inclination toward avoidance in the face of uncertain, novel situations. Weak uncertainty avoidance cultures encourage risk taking, whereas strong uncertainty avoidance cultures prefer clear procedures and guidelines in directing members' behavior in an organization. Weak uncertainty avoidance index values, for example, are found in Singapore, Jamaica, Denmark, Sweden, Hong Kong, Ireland, the United Kingdom, and the United States. Strong uncertainty avoidance index values, for example, are found in Greece, Portugal, Guatemala, Uruguay, Belgium, El Salvador, and Japan. Historical/political change contexts and national wealth are proposed by Hofstede (1991) as two preliminary factors that affect the development of uncertainty avoidance work-related values.

While members in weak uncertainty avoidance family situations prefer informal rules to guide their behavior, members in strong uncertainty avoidance family situations tend to prefer formal structure and formal rules. Rules and laws are established to counteract uncertainties in social interaction. In weak avoidance family situations, roles and behavioral expectations are actively negotiated. Children are given more latitude to explore their own values and morals. In strong uncertainty avoidance family situations, family roles are clearly established and family rules are expected to be followed closely (see Table 3.3).

In weak uncertainty work situations, there is a greater tolerance of innovative ideas and behavior. Conflict is also viewed as a natural part of organizational productivity. In strong uncertainty avoidance work situations, there is a greater resistance to deviant and innovative ideas. Career

TABLE 3.3. Major Differences between Weak Uncertainty Avoidance and Strong Uncertainty Avoidance Cultures

Weak uncertainty avoidance cultures	Strong uncertainty avoidance cultures
Uncertainty is valued	Uncertainty is a threat
Career change	Career stability
Encourage risk taking	Expect clear procedures
Conflict can be positive	Conflict is negative
Expect innovations	Preserve status quo
Examples	Examples
Singapore	Greece
Jamaica	Portugal
Denmark	Guatemala
Sweden	Uruguay
Hong Kong	Japan
United States/Canada	France
Norway	Spain
Australia	South Korea/Japan

Note. Data from Hofstede (1991). The cultures listed are based on the *predominant* tendencies in the cultures.

mobility is high in weak uncertainty avoidance cultures, whereas career stability is a desired end goal in strong uncertainty avoidance cultures. In strong uncertainty avoidance organizations, conflict is viewed as a threat to organizational effectiveness.

Hofstede (1980) uses the following statements to represent the basic characteristics of strong uncertainty avoidance organizations: (1) most organizations would be better off if conflict could be eliminated; (2) it is important for a manager to have at hand precise answers to most of the questions that his or her subordinates may raise about their work; and (3) when the respective roles of the members of a department become complex, detailed job descriptions are essential. Members of strong uncertainty avoidance organizations tend to score high on these statements; members of weak uncertainty avoidance organizations tend to score low on them.

The Masculinity and Femininity Dimension

Distinctive male and female organizational behavior differences are found on the masculinity–femininity dimension (Hofstede, 1998). *Masculinity* pertains to "societies in which social gender roles are clearly distinct (namely, men are supposed to be assertive, tough, and focused on material success whereas women are supposed to be more modest, tender, and concerned with the quality of life)" (Hofstede, 1991, p. 82). *Femininity* pertains to "societies in which social gender roles overlap (i.e., both men and women are supposed to be modest, tender, and concerned with the quality of life"

(Hofstede, 1991, pp. 82–83). Japan, Austria, Venezuela, Italy, Switzerland, Mexico, and Ireland, for example, have high masculinity value indexes. The United States ranks 15th on the masculinity continuum out of the 50 countries and 3 regions studied. Sweden, Norway, Netherlands, Denmark, Costa Rica, Yugoslavia, and Finland, for example, have low masculinity value indexes (implying a high femininity continuum). While "feminine" cultures emphasize flexible sex role behaviors, "masculine" cultures emphasize complementary sex role domains.

Historical roots and family socialization processes concerning gender roles shape the development of the masculine–feminine dimension. In "masculine" families, boys learn to be assertive, tough, and ambitious, and girls learn to be modest, nurturing, and relational oriented. In "feminine" families, both boys and girls learn to be caring and concerned with both facts and feelings. "Masculine" families are achievement and success oriented. "Feminine" families are consensus oriented and stress the importance of quality-of-life issues. A "masculine" workplace differentiates male and female roles clearly. A "feminine" workplace merges male and female roles fluidly. A "masculine" organization also tends to emphasize business performance, whereas a "feminine" organization tends to emphasize environmental issues above and beyond business performance (see Table 3.4).

By implication, when one communicates in a "masculine" organizational culture, one should be mindful of the norms and rules of complementary sex role behaviors in the system. When one communicates in a "feminine" organizational culture, one should be sensitive to the flexible sex role norms and roles in that workplace. In working for a "masculine" culture, one should focus more on business achievements and tangible result-

TABLE 3.4. Major Differences between "Feminine" and "Masculine" Cultures

"Feminine" cultures	"Masculine" cultures
Flexible sex roles	Complementary sex roles
Emphasize nurturance	Emphasize achievements
Quality of work life	Economic growth
Work in order to live	Live in order to work
Environmental issues	Business performance
Examples	Examples
Sweden	Japan
Norway	Austria
Netherlands	Venezuela
Denmark	Italy
Costa Rica	Mexico
Finland	Philippines

Note. Data from Hofstede (1991). The cultures listed are based on the *predominant* tendencies in the cultures.

based performance. In working for a "feminine" organization, one should be more mindful of the importance of quality of work/life balance issues and learn to be more concerned with community and environmental issues.

The Confucian Dynamism Dimension

A separate cultural value dimension, Confucian dynamism, has been used by Bond (1991, 1996) and the Chinese Culture Connection group (1987) to explain some of the distinctive behavioral patterns in East Asian cultures. These East Asian cultures are China, Hong Kong, Taiwan, Japan, and South Korea. Their primary values include a dynamic long-term orientation, perseverance, ordering relationships by status, being thrift centered, having a sense of shame, and emphasizing collective face-saving (Hofstede, 1991). The value of tenacity in pursuing one's goals (i.e., the perseverance value), together with the availability of capital for investment (i.e., the thrift value) help to shape the Five Dragons' (i.e., Hong Kong, Taiwan, Singapore, Japan, and—to a lesser degree right now—South Korea) economic growth in the Pacific Rim. In comparison to the long-term orientation characteristics of the Confucian dynamism dimension, members from cultures such as Pakistan, Nigeria, the Philippines, and Canada score low on this dimension. Some of the characteristics associated with the short-term orientation include short- to medium-term planning, being spending centered, and emphasizing individual face-saving (see Table 3.5).

TABLE 3.5. Confucian Dynamism Dimension: Short-Term versus Long-Term Orientation Characteristics

Short-term orientation characteristics	Long-term orientation characteristics
Personal survival/security	Social order
Personal respect/dignity	Hierarchical respect
Individual face-saving	Collective face-saving
Short- to medium-term planning	Long-term planning
Spending centered	Thrift centered
Short- to medium-term outcomes	Long-term outcomes
Examples	Examples
Pakistan	China
Nigeria	Hong Kong
Philippines	Taiwan
Canada	Japan
Zimbabwe	South Korea
United Kingdom	Brazil
United States	Thailand
Germany	Singapore

Note. Data from Hofstede (1991). The cultures listed are based on the *predominant* tendencies in the cultures.

To better understand the Confucian dynamism dimension, a brief look at Confucian philosophy is helpful. Confucius was a Chinese philosopher of practical ethics who lived from 551 to 479 B.C. His practical code of conduct emphasizes hierarchical societal structure and appropriate family role performance (Bond, 1991, 1996). Confucianism remains the fundamental philosophy underlying Chinese values, attitudes, and behavior. The following two principles guide Confucian philosophy: (1) superiors in the workplace must act with virtue, and those in inferior positions must obey their superior; (2) one should act dutifully toward one's parents and elders, reciprocally in one's obligations, and respectfully in role differentiation. Confucianism includes core values such as "servility, frugality, abstinence, . . . diligence . . . hard work, patriarchal leadership, entrepreneurial spirit, and devotion to family" (Engholm, 1994, p. 30). The Confucian dynamism dimension is reflective of the collectivism and large power distance dimensions. Additionally, Confucian dynamism emphasizes both traditional values and adaptation to economic change in the environment.

Finally, based on Confucian philosophy, the Chinese concept of "face" was derived. Face, in the Chinese context, means projected social image and social self-respect. Group harmony, and thus in-group interdependence, is achieved through the maintenance of everyone's face in the society and trying hard not not to cause any one to "lose face." The theme of "facework" permeates many Asian cultures and profoundly influences how Asian cultures conduct business with their counterparts (Lim & Choi, 1996). The theme of facework is further discussed in Chapter 8.

Loose and Tight Social Structures

Cultures with loose social structures (Boldt, 1978), such as Australia, New Zealand, and the United States, tend to afford individuals with more options to experiment with their identity conceptions. Cultures with tight social structures such as Japan and Korea, in contrast, tend to emphasize stringent cultural norms, rules, and interaction scripts. In loose social structures, people have a high degree of freedom to deviate from the societal norms. In tight social structures, people are expected to conform to the societal values, norms, and rules.

Triandis (1995) notes that a probable antecedent of social looseness is cultural heterogeneity (i.e., a mix of ethnocultures and diverse values). Cultures with loose social structures are more lenient in accepting a wide range of role-deviant behaviors. Loose cultures have multiple, sometimes conflicting norms about what to do. Those who deviate from the norms in such cultures are not necessarily punished. There is also a high probability of looseness for cultures that are located at the intersections of other major cultures (e.g., Thailand at the intersection of India and China; Triandis, 1995). In relatively loose societies like the United States, the process of identity negotiation has a wide range of choices and options. In relatively tight societies like Japan, the process of identity negotiation has a narrow range of options.

VALUES, SELF-CONCEPTION CONSEQUENCES, AND INTERACTION

Of all the value patterns that have been explained in the previous sections, the core dimension of individualism–collectivism, in conjunction with the identity negotiation perspective (as presented in Chapter 2), will guide the conceptual development of this book. The reasons are as follows: (1) this dimension has been researched extensively by eminent researchers from multiple academic disciplines; (2) it is a robust dimension that stands the scrutiny of time; (3) it has accumulated a wealth of empirical information concerning self and social behavior in different cultural regions; and (4) it is a practical dimension that people in a wide range of cultures and ethnic groups can understand.

Self-conception is defined as our views of ourselves. Our views of ourselves are derived from how we perceive ourselves in particular situations and from our views of ourselves as members of various groups (e.g., cultural, ethnic, and gender groups). Self-conception is related to the core value dimension of individualism–collectivism via the following characteristics: independent versus interdependent self-construal, personal and collective self-esteem, and generalized-based and in-group-based interaction.

Independent and Interdependent Self-Construal

The fundamental building block of individualism–collectivism lies in its relative emphasis on how people across a wide variety of cultures view themselves. One such concept is the self-construal image or the distinction between independent and interdependent self-construal (Markus & Kitayama, 1991, 1994). Self-construal is linked to cultural values, norms, and communication. Recent research provides empirical evidence that there are two dimensions of self that exist within each individual regardless of her or his cultural identity (Gudykunst et al., 1996; Singelis, 1994; Singelis & Brown, 1995). The terms *independent self-construal* and *interdependent self-construal* (Markus & Kitayama, 1991, 1994) refer to the degree to which people conceive of themselves as separate or connected to others, respectively.

The independent construal of self involves the view that an individual is a unique entity with an individuated repertoire of feelings, cognitions, and motivations (Markus & Kitayama, 1991). Individuals with high independent self-construals tend to view themselves as distinct and unique from others and the context. They use their own abilities, characteristics, and ideas as motivational bases rather than the thoughts and feelings of others. People who view themselves as independents value individualism, personal achievement, self-direction, and competition. When communicating with others, high independents believe in striving for personal goals, being in control of their external environment, and expressing their needs assertively. Overall, independents tend to be more self-face oriented than other-face oriented. Gudykunst et al. (1996) argue that independent self-construal predominates in individualistic cultures or ethnic groups. Independent self-construal has been linked to such behavior as outcome-oriented conversational constraints (M. S. Kim et al., 1996), task outcomes in groups (Oetzel & Bolton-Oetzel, 1997), and low-context communication style (i.e., upfront, direct communication; Gudykunst et al., 1996).

The interdependent construal of self, on the other hand, involves an emphasis on the importance of relational connectedness (Markus & Kitayama, 1991). Markus and Kitayama (1991) note that "people are motivated to find a way to fit in with relevant others, to fulfill and create obligation, and in general to become part of various interpersonal relationships" (p. 227). People who have an interdependent self-construal want to fit in with others, act appropriately, promote others' goals, and value conformity and cooperation. The self in relation to others guides the behavior of high interdependents in social situations. When communicating with others, high interdependents value other-face and mutual-face concerns. They are eager to appeal to other-face concerns in problematic situations in order to preserve relational harmony and to avoid public embarrassment. Gudykunst et al. (1996) argue that interdependent self-construal predominates in collectivistic cultures or ethnic groups. Interdependent self-construal has been linked to such behavior as other-oriented conversational constraints (M. S. Kim et al., 1996), relational outcomes in groups (Oetzel & Bolton-Oetzel, 1997), and high-context communication styles (i.e., subtle, indirect communication; Gudykunst et al., 1996).

More specifically, Markus and Kitayama (1991) argue that our self-construal influences our cognition, emotion, and motivation for actions. For them, the sense of individuality that accompanies this independent construal of self includes a sense of "oneself as an agent, as a producer of one's actions. One is conscious of being in control over the surrounding situation, and of the need to express one's own thoughts, feelings, and actions to others" (p. 246). In contrast, the sense of self-conception that accompanies an interdependent construal of self emphasizes "attentiveness and responsiveness to others that one either explicitly or implicitly assumes will be reciprocated by these others. . . . One is conscious of where one belongs with respect to others" (p. 246). Independent self-construal emphasizes personal achievements and unique contributions of persons on the individual level. Interdependent self-construal emphasizes ascribed status, role relationships, family reputation, and work group effort. Our sense of "self" serves as an experiential point in terms of how we process self-views, how we relate to others, and by what criteria we evaluate others' behavior.

Indeed, a wealth of empirical data has been accumulated by cross-cultural researchers around the world in the area of culture and self-conception. Miller (1991), for example, in researching interpersonal moral responsibility in India and the United States, observes that the Western cultural premise starts with the view of "persons as inherently autonomous. . . . [T]he individual is regarded as primary, with the social order considered a derivative" (pp. 20–21). However, in the Hindu culture, the cultural premise forwards a more social and holistic view of the person. Persons are regarded as "inherently part of the social body, with relationships of hierarchical interdependence assumed to be both natural and normatively desirable. . . . [T]he dyad rather than the autonomous individual is the most basic social unit" (Miller, 1991, pp. 21–22).

In commenting on the Chinese sense of "self," Gao and Ting-Toomey (1998) observe:

> Based on Confucianism, self is relational in Chinese culture. That is, the self is defined by the surrounding relations. Traditionally, the Chinese self involves multiple layers of relationships with others. A person in this relational network tends to be sensitive to his or her position as above, below, or equal to others. . . . The relations often are derived from kinship networks and supported by cultural values such as filial piety (i.e., obedience to parents and financial support of parents), loyalty, dignity, and integrity. (p. 9)

For the Chinese, the "self" is both a center of relationships and as a dynamic process of development within a network of relationships. In Chinese culture, to be aware of one's relations with others is an integral part of *zuo ren*, or "conducting oneself properly" in getting along with others. In sum, Chinese can never separate themselves from obligations to others and a Chinese sense of self-worth is closely tied with kinship and social networks.

In Colombia, the sense of self is also cast in relational connectedness terms (Fitch, 1994, 1998). Terms such as *palanca* (literally, the word means a lever; symbolically, the word means a connection, a personal contact whose influence, or "pull," enables someone to obtain a desired objective), *vínculos* (interpersonal bonds), and *confianza* (reliance, trust, confidence, camaraderie, and unconditional support) permeate the world of urban Colombian professionals. As Fitch (1998) notes:

> For Colombians in this group, "*una persona es un conjunto de vínculos*" (a person is a set of bonds to others). In other words, the fundamental existence for Colombians is the *vínculo*: the bond between human pair-parts, between a family and its home (*la casa*), and between a human and his or her homeland (*tierra*). This premise cuts across a very wide range of Colombian interpersonal

experience. Many diverse aspects of contexts, situations, institutions, and interpretations of action are made sensible within this view of persons (p. 147)

Understanding the fundamental premise of self in each culture and the core linguistic symbols associated with the conceptualization of "self" and "other" will help us to have a clearer grasp of cultural and communication issues in each culture.

Furthermore, every person's self-conception has three layers: the private self, the collective self, and the public self (Triandis, 1989). The *private self* emphasizes cognitions that involve unique traits, states, or behaviors of the person. The *collective self* refers to cognitions that link self-presentation style to the group. The *public self* concerns how the generalized others perceive the self. These three layers or aspects of self are present for each individual. However, cultural socialization processes and personal life experiences shape the configuration of these layers. Thus, for example, in individualistic cultures, the socialization process emphasizes the development of a private self. In individualistic cultures, members are readily willing to disclose or reveal information (e.g., personal attitudes, self-perceptions) about their private selves and move the private information to the public layer. In comparison, in collectivistic cultures, the socialization process emphasizes the development of the collective self and public self. Members in collectivistic cultures tend to be more guarded concerning information within the private self layer. They are, moreover, very aware of the collective and public self layers that people display to each other (see Table 3.6).

In sum, people of independent self-construals value the ideals, goals, motivations, and identity negotiation process of an "unencumbered self." In comparison, people of interdependent self-construals value the ideals, goals, motivations, and the emotions of a "connected self," which ties in closely with the extended family group, work group, neighborhood, village, or caste group. While the independent self emphasizes the basis of the "individual" as the fundamental unit of interaction, the interdependent self emphasizes "relational connectedness" or the "in-group" as the basic focus of human interaction.

TABLE 3.6. Characteristics of the Independent Self and the Interdependent Self

Independent self	Interdependent self
Self-orientation	Other-orientation
Personal self-esteem	Collective self-esteem
Personal achievement	Group achievement
Relational autonomy	Relational connectedness
Universalistic-based principles	Particularistic-based principles

Personal and Collective Self-Esteem

Self-esteem is viewed as occupying a pivotal role in mindful identity negotiation. Self-esteem or self-worth is grounded in the evaluational criteria of the "ideal persons" in their ideal positive performance in the sociocultural webs of the system. As Harre (1984) observes, "For me, a person is not a natural object, but a cultural artifact. A person is a being who has learned a theory, in terms of which his or her experience is ordered. . . . There are two primary realities in human life: the array of persons and the network of their symbiotic interactions" (p. 20). Learning the cultural theories of what it means to maintain a positive view of self versus a negative view of self serves as a good starting point for mindful identity negotiation work.

While individualism influences the personal self-esteem process, collectivism influences the social self-esteem process. As Markus and Kitayama (1991) comment,

> For those with independent selves, feeling good about oneself typically requires fulfilling the tasks associated with being an independent self, that is, being unique, expressing one's inner attributes, and asserting oneself. . . . Maintaining self-esteem requires separating oneself from others and seeing oneself as different from and better than others. (p. 242)

Markus and Kitayama (1991) note, in comparison, that from a collectivistic perspective in conceptualizing self-esteem the process is quite distinct from that just described:

> The motive to maintain a positive view of the self may assume a somewhat different form, however, for those with interdependent selves. Feeling good about one's interdependent self may not be achieved through enhancement of the value attached to one's internal attributes and the attendant self-serving bias. Instead, positive feelings of the self derive from fulfilling the tasks associated with being interdependent with relevant others: belonging, fitting in, occupying one's proper place, engaging in appropriate action, promoting others' goals, and maintaining harmony. (p. 242)

While the locus of self-esteem stemming from the independent self emphasizes person-based motivations, the locus of self-esteem generated by the interdependent self emphasizes social-based communicative motivations.

From the independent self perspective, managing one's own and other's self-esteem means bolstering one's own personal self-worth and recognizing the other's personal self-worth and unique talents. From the interdependent self perspective, managing self-esteem means bolstering one's own membership self-worth by the standards of the in-groups and recognizing the importance of in-group contributions and accomplishments. Family background and reputation, work group prestige, and membership rank are some of the factors that interdependent-self individuals deem as important. In individualistic cultures, managing personal self-esteem is critical to interpersonal relationship functioning. In group-oriented cultures, managing collective or social self-esteem is essential to effective relationship maintenance.

Universalistic-Based versus Particularistic-Based Interaction

While independent-self people are influenced by "generalized others" in enacting their roles or parts, interdependent-self people are influenced by specific in-group expectations and contexts in carrying out their communicative conduct. Independent-self individuals like to use a "universal" set or a "fair" set of standards to measure others' performance. In comparison, interdependent-self individuals prefer to use a "contextual" or a "particular" set of criteria to evaluate others' performance in different situations.

According to Parson's (1951) work, there are two kinds of societies: "universalistic" and "particularistic." Independent-self individuals tend to be found in universalistic societies, whereas interdependent-self individuals tend to be located in particularistic societies. People in universalistic societies, such as Canada, the United States, Sweden, and Norway, believe that laws and regulations are written for everyone and must be upheld by everyone at all times. In contrast, for people in particularistic societies, such as China, South Korea, Venezuela, and Russia, the nature of the particular relationship in a given situation will determine how you will act in that situation (Trompenaars, 1994).

For members of universalistic societies, the laws or regulations should treat everyone equally. On the other hand, for members of particularistic societies, the laws or regulations can be molded to fit the specific relationship or the in-group needs. Universalistic work practice emphasizes the importance of detailed contracts and penalty clauses in order to conduct business properly; particularistic work practice focuses on developing interpersonal trust and close social ties to maintain work commitment.

The in-group asserts a profound impact, especially in particularistic societies. The concept of an "in-group" can refer to both the actual kinship network to which you belong (e.g., your family group) and the reference groups (e.g., work group, political group) with which you identify closely. On the cultural level of analysis, the definition of the in-group can vary tremendously across cultures. For example, in the United States, the in-group is typically defined as "people who are in agreement with me on important issues and values" (Triandis, 1989, p. 53). For the traditional Greeks, the in-group is defined as "family and friends and people who are concerned with my welfare" (Triandis, 1989, p. 53). For the Western Samoans, the in-group consists of the extended family and the immediate village community (Ochs, 1988). For many of the Latin American groups, in-group refers to the extended family and the immediate neighborhood. For Arab cultures, in-group refers to immediate and extended family networks of parents, spouses, siblings, related cousins, and even honored guests who are unrelated to the host.

In sum, an "in-group" is a group whose values, norms, and rules are internalized by its members. By contrast, an "out-group" is a group whose values, norms, and rules appear to be inconsistent from those of the in-group and are viewed as out-group values or attributes. However, it is important to remember that the categorization process of in-group or out-group and the behavioral treatment of in-group/out-group members vary greatly across cultures. For individualistic cultures, the in-group and out-group share a permeable boundary; for collectivistic cultures, in-group and out-group interaction follows a clear set of prescribed, identity-related behaviors.

Summary

Overall, individualistic value tendencies emphasize the importance of the independent self, personal self-esteem, and universalistic-based interaction. In comparison, collectivistic value tendencies emphasize the importance of the interdependent self, collective self-esteem, and particularistic-based interaction. While both individualistic and collectivistic elements are present in all cultures, relatively clear patterns of individualistic value tendencies or collectivistic value tendencies do emerge to influence people's self-conception and behavior in particular interaction scenes.

In terms of which value set is better, individualism or collectivism, the answer is—it depends. Depending on the situation, the interaction goal, the people, and the choices that are available, it is sometimes wise to follow the collectivistic pathway, sometimes the individualistic pathway, and sometimes both. Individualism and collectivism complement each other. They represent a diverse range of cultural resources to solve problems and help people make decisions.

RECOMMENDATIONS

This chapter has examined Kluckhohn and Strodtbeck's classical value orientations and Hofstede's work-related value dimensions. Additionally, the relationships among values, self-conception, and communication have been explored.

To be a mindful intercultural communicator on the value clarification level, here are some recommendations to enhance your knowledge, motivation, and skills:

1. Understand that on the cultural group membership level, different value preferences exist for memberships in different cultures or ethnocultures.

Different contexts and different personality tendencies also affect the sampling of individualistic and collectivistic elements in a given culture.

2. Develop a culture-relative approach in understanding cultural values' differences. Cultural relativism means understanding a particular set of cultural values from that cultural frame of reference rather than your own cultural frame of reference. Cultural ethnocentrism means evaluating the observed cultural difference based on our own cultural values and norms and concluding that our own cultural behavior is superior to other cultural behavior.

3. Realize the differences between individualistic value tendencies and collectivistic value tendencies and understand how individualism shapes independent self-conception and collectivism directs interdependent self-conception.

4. When entering a new culture, learn to mentally *observe (O)*, *describe (D)*, and *interpret (I)* cultural differences from the other cultural values' perspective. In an unfamiliar culture, patient observation with our five senses can help us to shift value lenses and get ready, emotionally and cognitively, to appreciate and understand the differences. Furthermore, with focused observation, we should work on generating multiple cultural interpretations in viewing a "seemingly deviant" behavior. We should make explicit our own unconscious cultural interpretations in comparison to that of the interpretations from the other cultural viewpoint. In this way, we hope, by mentally walking through the O–D–I steps, we have *suspended (S)* our hastily formed ethnocentric evaluations of the observed behavior. Taken together, this is known as the *O–D–I–S method*: observing, describing, interpreting, and suspending evaluations.

5. Learn to observe a wide range of people in a wide range of situations in the new cultural setting before making any premature generalizations about the people's behavior in that culture.

Cultural values are deposits of wisdom that are passed from one generation to the next. Simultaneously, they also can serve as cultural blinders to alternative ways of thinking, feeling, motivating, and behaving. While cultural values serve many useful functions such as those of identity maintenance and group solidarity, they also reinforce various habitual practices and norms of communicating, as we shall see in the following chapters.

4

Mindful Intercultural Verbal Communication

Human Language: A Coherent System 85
    Arbitrariness 85
    Multilayered Rules 86
    Speech Community 90
Languages across Cultures: Diverse Functions 91
    The Group Identity Function 91
    The Perceptual Filtering Function 94
    The Cognitive Reasoning Function 94
    The Status and Intimacy Function 97
    The Creativity Function 98
Cross-Cultural Verbal Communication Styles 100
    Low-Context and High-Context Communication 100
    Direct and Indirect Verbal Interaction Styles 103
    Person-Oriented and Status-Oriented Verbal Styles 106
    Self-Enhancement and Self-Effacement Verbal Styles 107
    Beliefs Expressed in Talk and Silence 110
Recommendations 111

Language can imprison us. It can also set us free. Language is a taken-for-granted aspect of our cultural lives. It frames our expectations and directs our perceptions. We acquire meaning and its underlying values in the symbolic world of our culture. Intercultural communicators achieve shared meanings, and thus understanding, through the effective exchange of verbal and nonverbal messages.

In this and the following chapter we will explore the relationship between cultural values and verbal/nonverbal communication styles. Our primary identities such as cultural and ethnic identities are often expressed through the symbols and styles we use in our interactions with others. The way we "name" or identify ourselves and the way we "name" or identify others draw our attention to the phenomenon we are "naming." The "labels" we use in our everyday naming process shape our social perceptions. They also highlight particular aspects of social reality that are deemed important in our cultural community. Culture is a symbolically mediated meaning system; naming via language is part of this symbolic system.

Intercultural frictions can easily occur because of the ways we name or "catalog" the different groups of individuals or behaviors around us. For example, how we catalog "outsiders" and "insiders," "strangers" and "hosts" and the proper behaviors associated with each category can profoundly influence our communication with them. While language and verbal communication can easily create misunderstandings, it also fortunately can clarify misunderstandings. Sensitive language usage is a pivotal vehicle in reflecting our mindful attitudes in communicating with dissimilar others.

The chapter is divided into four main sections: the first presents the basic features of human language; the second explores the functions and patterns of languages across cultures; the third examines cross-cultural verbal styles; and the last presents a set of recommendations concerning mindful intercultural verbal communication. In order to understand culture, we have to understand the premium role of language in it.

HUMAN LANGUAGE: A COHERENT SYSTEM

Each human language reflects a logical, coherent system. The term "system" implies patterns, rules, and structure. This section explores the structural features of human language. By understanding the basic features of a language, we can become more mindful of the causes that contribute to verbal frictions across cultures. While broad similarities exist among languages, tremendous variations remain in the sounds, written symbols, grammars, and nuances of meaning of an estimated 6,700 language varieties across cultures.

A *language* is an arbitrary, symbolic system that names ideas, feelings, experiences, events, people, and other phenomena and that is governed by the multilayered rules developed by members of a particular speech community. The three distinctive features of each human language are its arbitrariness, its multilayered rules, and its speech community.

Arbitrariness

All human languages are arbitrary in their phonemic (i.e., sound unit) and graphic representations (i.e., alphabets or characters). As early as at 3 months of age, children have already acquired intonations or sounds similar to those changes in pitch heard in adult exclamations and questions in their own culture. Through continuous reinforcement, children learn to retain the sounds that are most familiar to their ears and tongues and drop off other nonsalient sounds. In any culture, children acquire speaking and comprehending skills first, then reading and writing skills.

While all children have the capacity to utter all the sounds in all languages, this linguistic competence tapers off as they reach puberty. This also explains why the speech of nonnative speakers, even those fluent in English, has a strange quality or "accent." Russians, for example, even though rigorously trained to speak English, will still give themselves away by their pronunciation of *t* in English words. The Russian *t* is pronounced by contact between the tip of the tongue and the upper teeth. Native speakers of English pronounce *t* by making contact "between the tongue, just back of its tip, and the upper gum ridge" (Farb, 1973, p. 292). The younger the children acquire a second language, the more highly they tend to retain the "sound fidelity" of the new language.

The arbitrary feature of language also extends to the written symbols or characters that cultural members use to express their ideas. Individuals' cultural or ethnic identity is affectively infused with the linguistic sounds and written symbols that they grew up with. Even if they are fluent bilinguals, newcomers are often drawn to the sounds and symbols of their native languages. These sounds and symbols can evoke strong emotional ties in these newcomers because symbolic familiarity evokes a sense of safety and membership connection in an alien environment.

Multilayered Rules

Human language appears to be the only communication system that combines meaningless elements into meaningful structures (Chaika, 1989). To the nonnative speakers, the rules of a "foreign language" appear random and nonsensical. To the native speakers, the rules of their language make perfect sense and are naturally more logical than those of any other languages. In fact, most native speakers cannot articulate clearly the rules of their own language because they use it daily on an unconscious competence level. All human languages are structured according to the following sets of rules: phonology, morphology, syntax, semantics, and pragmatics.

The *phonological rules* (or phonology) of a language refer to the different accepted procedures for combining phonemes. Phonemes are the basic sound units of a word. For example, some of the phonemes in English are [k], [sh], and [t]. Native speakers of English, for example, may possess an intuitive sense of how to utter sounds such as "kiss," "shy," and "try"; however, they may not be able to articulate the how and why of the phonetic rules for producing these sounds. While the English language has 45 phonemes, other languages have a range of phonemes spanning anywhere between 15 and 85.

Accents of nonnative language speakers are usually related to phonetic sound problems. Depending on the sounds of a given language, native speakers of that language are habituated to using their vocal instruments (e.g., the mouth, tongue, palatem and vocal cords) in certain ways to produce certain sounds. Similarly, the native speaker of language *J* has an ear that is trained to hear the sounds of language *J*. On the other hand, the native speaker of language *E* may have difficulty articulating or even distinguishing sounds of language *J*. The resulting difference in articulation that nonnative speakers often exhibit is referred to as an accent.

Linguistically speaking, however, everyone who communicates orally speaks with an accent because accent means the inflection or tone of voice that is taken to be the characteristic of an individual. That is to say, there are as many accents as there are individuals because each individual's inflections and tone of voice are unique. For example, law enforcement agencies sometimes use electronic equipment to generate "voiceprints" made from recordings of suspects' speech. These voiceprints can be used to help confirm the identities of the suspects because, like fingerprints, voiceprints are highly individualized.

Members of subcultures who are native speakers of the same language can also be identified as having accents. In such cases, the distinctive accents can be attributed to shared group membership. Many Bostonians, for example, claim that they can differentiate the Italian, Irish, and Jewish groups in their city by the way they articulate their /o(r)/ vowel sound (in words like "short" and "corn"). In casual speech situations, Italian Bostonians are the highest users of the /a(r)/ substitute sound (so that "short" sounds like "shot"—with no *r* sound), next are the Boston Irish, and then Jewish Bostonians. Ethnically distinct speech often indicates group solidarity and bondedness. Thus, to a large degree, our accented speech pattern is reflective of our identity group membership.

Additionally, from the perceivers' standpoint, certain voices are attributed to certain groups because of the mediation of group-based stereotypes. Some individuals can switch into different accent patterns at different times and are proud of their linguistic flexibility. Others may feel ashamed of their accented speech. Individuals' positive or negative evaluations of others often cast a strong impact on others' group membership and personal self-worth level.

Intergroup miscommunication arises when nonnative speakers may not be able to produce the sound fidelity of their newly acquired language. They may also misconstrue the incoming messages based on the different shadings of the vocalic cues that accompany the verbal messages. Lastly, the native speaker may prematurely assume that the message has been accurately decoded when in fact different meanings were attached, and vice versa.

The *morphological rules* (or morphology) refer to how different sounds combine to make up a meaningful word or parts of a word (e.g., "new" and "com-er" form "new-com-er"). Phonemes combine to form morphemes, which are the smallest units of meaning in a language. In English and many other European languages, morphemes that are required by grammar are often put at the end of words as *suffixes* (i.e., "is go*ing*," "is sleep*ing*" contain the morpheme "ing," which indicates that an activity is currently in progress). In Swahili, however, the grammatical information indicating verb tense appears at the beginning as *prefixes* (law = "to go," *nlaw* = "is going"; or "sun = to sleep," *nsun* = "is sleeping"; Chaika, 1989, p. 5). Again, languages develop different rules based on cultural conventions that are passed down from one generation to the next.

The *syntactic rules* (or syntactics) of a language refer to how words are sequenced together in accordance with the grammatical practice of the linguistic community. The order of the words helps to establish the meaning of an utterance. It is also reflective of the cultural notions of causality and order. In English grammar, for example, explicit subject pronouns are used to distinguish self from other (e.g., "*I cannot give you the report because it is not ready*"). In Chinese grammar, however, explicit pronouns such as "I" and "you" are deemphasized. Instead, conjunctive words such as "because" (*yinwei*), "so" (*suoyi*), and "then" (*juo*) appear early in the discourse to pave the way for the rest of the story (e.g., "*Because of so many projects all of a sudden piling up, so the report has then not been handled properly.*" While Chinese syntax establishes a context and contingent conditions and then introduce the main point, English syntax establishes the key point and then lays out the reason (Young, 1994). The syntactic rules of a language assert tremendous power on peoples' thinking, and hence on reasoning patterns within a culture.

The *semantic rules* (semantics) of a language concern the features of meaning we attach to words. Words themselves do not have holistic meanings. It is people within a cultural community that consensually establish shared meanings for specific words and phrases. For example, *pretty* has a feature of [+female], and *handsome* has a feature of [+male]. If we combine *pretty* with the [+male] feature such as "pretty boy" (or "handsome woman"), the concept takes on a whole range of different meanings (Chaika, 1989). Beyond mastering the vocabularies of a new language, language learners need to master the appropriate cultural meaning features that are indicated by different word pairings. Without such cultural knowledge, they may have the right vocabularies but an inappropriate meaning association system. Nonnative speakers may think they are complimenting a boy by saying "What a pretty boy!" without realizing that while the sentence structure is accurate, the semantic field is misconstrued.

In any language, two levels of meaning exist: denotative meaning and connotative meaning. A word's *denotative meaning* is its dictionary definition from an objective, public stance. *Connotative meaning* is the informal grasp that we have of particular words and phrases, and these meanings are relatively subjective and personal. Words such as "commitment," "power," and "compromise" can hold both objective and subjective meanings. For instance, the objective meaning of commitment is "the state or an instance of being obligated or emotionally compelled." Jill's connotation of the word "commitment" in the context of her relationship with Jack may include the presumption of marriage, whereas when Jack says, "I'm committed to you, Jill," his subjective meaning includes an exclusive dating relationship but no intention of marriage. Furthermore, according to Osgood, May, and Miron (1975), the following three dimensions form the *affective features of* meaning: value (i.e., good–bad); potency (i.e., strong–weak); and activity (i.e., fast–slow).

For example, one cultural member concludes after a long business meeting, "I am very much committed to this project" with the affective reactions of "good, strong, *and fast*" (i.e., reflecting future-oriented, doing values) to accompany the word "commitment." The other cultural member echoes the same phrase, but with the affective responses of "good, strong, *but slow*" (i.e., reflecting past-oriented, long-term cultural values) in mind. The former party thinks the business contract will be signed that afternoon and he or she can catch a plane home by the evening. However, the latter party thinks the business negotiation has just barely started—especially when relational trust in that culture takes a long time to develop.

While both business parties have similar reactions concerning the "good and strong" part of the concept concerning "commitment," they differ on the activity dimension of "fast versus slow." The three affective meaning features measure the underlying cultural or personal attitudes we hold for a diverse range of concepts. The more abstract the concepts, the more chances that intended meanings can be lost in the translation process.

Furthermore, translation problems and jokes that involve different semantic understanding are abound on the global level: The English phrase "The spirit is willing but the flesh is weak" has been translated into Russian as "The vodka is good but the meat is rotten." The translation for "Things come alive with Pepsi" has been translated into German as "Pepsi can pull you back from your grave!" General Motors' car "Chevy Nova" has been translated into Spanish as "*No va*," meaning "It doesn't go." Intercultural misunderstandings arise when we decode the literal meanings of the words but not the connotative meanings of the messages.

Lastly, we should also pay close attention to the two-leveled cultural meanings that complicate our understanding of semantics. *Emic meanings* refer to behaviors, concepts, and interpretations (e.g., Chinese indigenous words such as *guan xing* meaning "to show concern for another person's heart" or *yuan* meaning "relational karma"; Spanish words such as *fatalismo* meaning "fatalism" and *personalismo* meaning "personalism") that are culture specific. From an emic interpretive standpoint, for example, *personalismo*, in the context of Mexican culture, can be expressed through hugging as well as shaking hands when greeting someone to show warmth of feeling. *Etic meanings*, on the other hand, refer to ideas, behaviors, concepts, and interpretations that are culture general (Triandis, 1994a). Understanding emic concepts of a culture can help us to see through insiders' lenses. Understanding etic concepts (e.g., showing *personalismo* via an engaging sense of personal warmth and responsiveness) are essential to building intercultural understanding on a general level. Understanding both emic and etic meanings of words in context and their underlying cultural values can help us to practice verbal sensitivity in our intercultural communication process.

We shall consider the pragmatic rules in the next subsection, as they are associated with the concept of a speech community.

Speech Community

The *pragmatic rules* (pragmatics) of a language refer to the situational rules that govern language usage in a particular culture. Pragmatics concerns the rules of "how to say what to whom and under what situational conditions" in a speech community. A *speech community* is defined as a group of individuals who share a common set of norms and rules regarding proper communicative practices (Hymes, 1972; Labov, 1972).

Pragmatics concerns the cultural expectations of how, when, where, with whom, and under what situational conditions certain verbal expressions are preferred, prohibited, or prescribed. For example, the large power distance values found in many of the traditional Latin American families basically dictate that the father must be head of the family, the mother must take care of the children, and the children must respect and obey their father's wishes. There are clear pragmatic rules that shape who says what to whom and how in traditional Latin American dinner table conversations.

A speech community is also concerned with how people forge a shared group-based identity, define and interpret interaction goals, and evaluate the use of proper speech codes (Philipsen, 1992). Speech codes refer to the norms, rules, and premises of the cultural way of speaking. It answers the following questions: What is the meaning of being a "community" in this community? What is the meaning of being a "person" in this context? How are persons and communities linked through communication? In order to understand a speech community, we have to understand the speech codes and the multilayered linguistic rules of a language community (Carbaugh, 1990, 1996; Philipsen, 1987, 1992).

We have identified five features of human language and illustrated these features with some cultural examples. Linguistic features give rise to the diverse functions of languages across cultures and answer the question of why a language plays such a critical role within each culture. Language is, indeed, "an integral part of both a sense of identity and the mindsets that go with it" (Fisher, 1998, p. 43).

LANGUAGES ACROSS CULTURES: DIVERSE FUNCTIONS

Cultural value orientations drive language usage in everyday lives. For example, if a culture has a high individualism value index (e.g., Germany and the United States), words and phrases such as "I," "me," "my goal," "my opinion," "self-help," and "self-service" tend to appear as part of everyday parlance. If a culture has a high collectivism value index (e.g., Japan and Korea), phrases such as "our work team," "our goal," "our unit," "our future together" and "we as a group" are part of the everyday lexicons.

In this section, we identify the diverse functions of languages across cultures as the group identity, perceptual filtering, cognitive reasoning, status and intimacy, and creativity functions (Edwards, 1985, 1994; Farb, 1973; Ting-Toomey & Korzenny, 1989). The inherent feature of a language (e.g., whether the language emphasizes the use of the formal "you" or intimate "you," as in Colombia and Mexico) influences the specific function (e.g., the status and intimacy function) of language usage in a particular situation and in a particular culture (see Figure 4.1).

The Group Identity Function

Language is the key to the heart of a culture. Language serves the larger cultural/ethnic identity function because language is an emblem of "groupness." In speaking a common tongue, members signal group solidarity and connectedness. Language represents "a core symbol, a rallying point. . . . [L]anguage is important in ethnic and nationalist sentiment because of its powerful and visible symbolism" (Edwards, 1985, p. 15). The

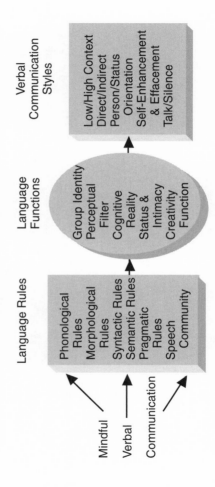

FIGURE 4.1. Mindful verbal communication: Rules, functions, and verbal styles.

historical and the symbolic associations of a language give rise to a shared sense of cultural identity or pride.

For example, the disputes between Anglophones and Francophones over use of English or French in Québec province, the heated debates over whether Ebonics (i.e., Black English) is a language or a dialect in the United States, and the status associations attached to Hindi and English in India all reflect the significant role of the identity membership function of language. The struggle over using Spanish and/or English as a basic language in Puerto Rican schools is also a story of a group-based identity struggle. In the early 1900s, U.S. authorities insisted on the use of English in Puerto Rican schools for the purpose of assimilation. It was not until 1991 that the Puerto Rican legislature finally reversed the law and made Spanish the official language. In 1993 the pro-statehood governor signed legislation restoring equal status to Spanish and English. The struggle of language equity reflects the struggle or claiming of recognition of cultural-based identity.

Since language is learned so early in life and so effortlessly by all children, it permeates the core of our cultural and ethnic identities without our full awareness of its impact. Until we encounter linguistic differences, we may not develop an optimal mindfulness for our cultural-based "linguistic naming" process. Our construction of our own identities and the identities of others are closely tied with the naming or labeling process.

More specifically, for example, in the group-oriented Indian culture, when one asks for a Hindi's name, the person will first give you her or his caste identity, then her or his village name, and finally her or his own name (Bharati, 1985). In the Chinese, Japanese, Korean, and Vietnamese cultures, the family name always precedes the personal name, which signals the importance of family identity over personal identity. Thus, a person named Mei-Ling *Wang* in the Chinese form of address is referred to as *Wang* Mei-Ling in the English form of address. Likewise, in the culture of Bali, a personal name is a nonsense syllable that is almost never used; instead, the name used is related to family role relations (e.g., the second born of family X; mother of Y; grandfather of Z). In sum, individuals construct their identities through "naming," and in turn their naming and labeling process shapes how they view themselves and others.

Finally, while some cultural members develop enormous membership pride in speaking their native tongue, other members derive tremendous flexibility in their ability to code-switch. *Code-switching* means switching to another language or dialect to increase or decrease intergroup distance. For example, many African Americans have developed different verbal strategies to deal with the stigma attached to Black English (or Ebonics) by the dominant group. Black English is "a distinctive language . . . evolving from [a] largely West African pidgin form" and "is governed by rules with specific historical derivations" (Hecht, Collier, & Ribeau, 1993, pp. 84–85). For instance, in Black English, subject nouns are followed by a repeated pronoun ("My sister, she . . . "); statements omit the verb form *to be* ("It dat way") to strategically imply a one-time occurrence, or use it ("It bees dat way") to imply multiple occurrences; questions omit the word *do* ("What it come to?"); and context clarifiers are used instead of a different verb tense ("I know it good when he ask me") (Hecht, Collier, & Ribeau, 1993; Wyatt, 1995). Many African Americans are able to code-switch to use mainstream American English in formal or work-related settings, then switch to Black English with familiar others in casual settings for the purpose of forging group identity and connection.

On *purely* linguistic grounds, all languages are created equal. However, in all linguistic struggles, both within and between languages, a fierce competition exists:

> Not between languages themselves but, rather, between language communities or linguistic "interest groups." It is perhaps a good idea here to remake the point that neither languages nor dialects can be compared in terms of "better" or "worse" and that the strong preferences for given varieties, which have always existed, are based upon sociopolitical considerations; central here are the dominance and prestige of speakers. Matters of power, then, interlock with *perceptions* rather than with any intrinsic qualities of language. (Edwards, 1994, pp. 205–206; emphasis in original)

For example, mainstream American English (AE) is preferred over Black English in work settings because AE is spoken by European Americans who are considered to be the dominant powerholders (i.e., individuals who control corporate or governmental resources) in the U.S. society. The language struggle, in sum, is a sociopolitical power tussle.

The identity issue in language boils down to an affective experience dimension. As G. Fisher (1998) notes,

> Within the mother tongue, the comfort and confidence level is high, the anxiety level low. In consequence, the *affective* worlds of two languages will not equate easily; poetry, for example, often does not translate well. Sentiments can be quite culture-specific; you cannot really separate the feelings that go with being *simpático* from the cultures that go with speaking Spanish. To add to it, [there is] the affective or emotional dimension of communication [which is culture]-specific. How could one be Italian without [using] Italian gestures? (p. 42; emphasis in original)

Language infiltrates so intensely the social experience within a culture that neither language nor culture can be understood without knowledge of both. To understand a culture deeply, we have to understand the culture's language. To understand language in context, we have to understand the fundamental beliefs and value systems that drive particular language usage in particular circumstances.

The Perceptual Filtering Function

Language is more than a communication tool. It reflects the worldviews and the beliefs of the people who speak it. It reflects the important modes of thinking and the salient modes of being in living one's daily life in a culture. It acts as a gatekeeper in selecting and organizing what is considered "news" in our social environment and offers labels to bracket and capture these salient aspects of our perceptual reality.

An everyday language in a culture serves as a prism through which individuals interpret what they perceive to be "out there." For example, in the Mexican culture, Spanish words such as *machismo* (i.e., masculinity, physical strength, sexual attraction), *marianismo* (i.e., a woman's submissiveness, dependence, gentleness, and remaining a virgin until marriage), *respeto* (i.e., showing proper respect for authority such as parents and elders), and *familismo* (i.e., the importance of family and the extended family network) are part of everyday parlance (Paniagua, 1994). These terms infiltrate individuals' perception, and they are used as yardsticks to measure self and others' role performance.

Likewise, in the Chinese culture, words such as *xiao* (i.e., filial piety or the "proper" relationship between children and parents), *han xu* (i.e., implicit communication), *ting hua* (i.e., listening centered), *mian zi* (i.e., facework), *gan qing* (i.e., a multidimensional set of relational emotions), and *ren qing* (i.e., obligations and indebtedness) are used in the everyday language of interaction (Gao & Ting-Toomey, 1998). For the Chinese, individuals who are sensitive to their parents' needs, speak subtly or implicitly, act as good listeners, and are aware of facework and emotional work in developing interpersonal relationships are considered competent communicators. Conversely, individuals who are disrespectful of their parents' needs, speak bluntly or explicitly, and are insensitive to mutual facework issues are considered incompetent communicators. Individuals perceive and simultaneously judge others' proper or improper behaviors via their use of habitual linguistic symbols.

Thus, language permeates our social experience and ultimately shapes our cultured and gendered expectations and perceptions. Individuals' perceptions are closely tied with their symbolically mediated, cognitive reasoning process.

The Cognitive Reasoning Function

Language categorizes the totality of our cultural experience and makes an infinite number of unrelated events appear coherent and understandable—especially in accordance with our cultural frame of reasoning. Benjamin Whorf (1952, 1956), drawing from the work of his mentor Edward Sapir (1921), has tested the "language is a guide to cultural reality" hypothesis.

Focusing on a comparative analysis between the Hopi Indian language and European languages, Whorf (1952) concludes that language is not merely a vehicle for voicing ideas but rather "is itself the shaper of ideas. . . . [T]he world is presented in a kaleidoscopic flux of impressions which has to be organized by our minds—and this means largely by the linguistic system in our minds" (p. 5).

Whorf (1952) emphasizes that it is the grammatical structure of a language that shapes and constitutes one's thought process. This grammatical structure is entirely culture based and, as such, language, thinking, and culture are integral parts of a mindset system.

Whorf cites several examples from the Hopi language to support his point of view: (1) The Hopi language does not possess a discrete past–present–future grammatical system as in most European languages; instead, it has a wide range of present tenses that concern the validity of the verbal statement the speaker is making such as "I know that she is running at this very moment" or "I am told that she is running." (2) The Hopi language does not use a cyclic noun such as "days" or "years" in the same manner as countable quantities such as "five women" or "five men"; instead, it emphasizes the concept of "duration" when conceiving time. Thus the Hopi equivalent for the English statement "They stayed 5 days" is "I know that they stay until the 6th day." (3) While English speakers tend to use many spatial metaphors in their utterances (such as "Your time is *up*," "I feel *elated*," "I feel *depressed*," or "I feel *low*,"), Hopi language tends to emphasize the concept of events that are happening in the here and now (Farb, 1973, pp. 207–208; Whorf, 1952).

To speakers of European languages, time is a "commodity that occurs between fixed points and can be measured. Time is said to be *wasted* or *saved*. . . . [the] Hopi Indian has none of these beliefs about time, but instead thinks of it in terms of events. Plant a seed—and it will grow. The span of time the growing takes place is not the important thing, but rather the way in which the event of growth follows the event of planting. . . . [What is important is] the sequence of events" (Farb, 1973, pp. 208–209; emphasis in original)

In essence, Whorf believes that the grammars of different languages constitute separate conceptual realities for members of different cultures. We experience different cognitions and sensations via our linguistic systems. This idea has been known as the Sapir–Whorf hypothesis or the linguistic relativity hypothesis. For example, the structure of the future tense in the Spanish language tells us a great deal about the Mexican notion of the future. In Spanish, statements made about the future signal probability rather than certainty. For example, a Spanish speaker will say, "I may go to the store" (*"Ire al la tienda"*) rather than "I will go to the store" to indicate the probability of an action in the future rather than the certainty of that action. The future, for many Spanish-speaking people, represents an unknown time and space: many things can happen later this afternoon or tomorrow; it is beyond the control of individuals. (Recall the "present" and "being" value orientations discussed in Chapter 3.) Thus, the use of a "probability" statement seems to fit logically with their overall cultural reasoning schema.

Another example can be seen in the location of a causal referent in a language. The structure of English is concerned with establishing an isolatable agent (e.g., "I did not do it because . . . " or "She or he did it because . . . ") for a given event before providing an explanation. The Chinese language, on the contrary, establish a "field of conditions" first before introducing the agent of the problem (e.g., "It was raining, the parking lot was filled, the post office was crowded with a long line, and closing hour was near; *therefore*, I did not get a chance to mail the package . . . "). In the Chinese language, in order to explain one event, individuals must first consider all the other conditions that are contextually connected to it.

Such different grammatical presuppositions, however, often create serious intercultural distortions. English speakers may presume that the Chinese speakers are acting evasively or deceptively. Reciprocally, Chinese speakers may regard the English speakers as sounding rude and pushy. Both biased attributions stem, in part, from the different causal reasoning rules (which are actually restrained by the grammatical pattern) being applied from their respective linguistic systems. Being mindful of such linguistic and communication rule differences may help us to suspend our snapshot evaluations of dissimilar others' behavior.

Additionally, the vocabularies of different cultures (e.g., the numerous words for coconuts in the South Pacific islands; the many words for snow in the Eskimo culture; the variety of words for rice and tea in Chinese and Japanese cultures; the diversity of words for karma and reincarnation in the culture of India, and for good and evil spirits in many Native American cultures; the many words for expressing gratitude in the Greek and Arab worlds) play a prominent role in people's habitual way of thinking and hence their habitual way of communicating.

After reviewing extensive studies on the Sapir–Whorf hypothesis, Steinfatt (1989) concludes that while the "weak" form (i.e., language *shapes* our thinking patterns) of the linguistic relativity hypothesis receives some support, no conclusive evidence can be drawn to support the "strong" form (i.e., language *determines* our thinking patterns). There is no doubt that the debate on the Sapir–Whorf hypothesis will continue into the next century. The major premise of the Sapir–Whorf hypothesis, however, emphasizes the interpenetrating relationship among language, thoughts, and culture. Edward Sapir and Benjamin Whorf were the trailblazing pioneers in linking language with culture, and as such their work made a major contribution to the study of intercultural communication. Language serves as a mediating link between thoughts and our cultural reality. It acts as a window between the internal mindscape, on the one hand, and the external landscape, on the other.

The Status and Intimacy Function

Language serves the status and intimacy function. For example, cultures (e.g., those of Denmark and Norway) which emphasize small power distance values tend to use language to promote informal, symmetrical interactions. Cultures (e.g., those of Colombia, Mexico, and the Philippines) that emphasize large power distance values tend to use language to accentuate asymmetrical role interactions, especially in formal situations.

We can use language to signify status differences such as the selective use of formal versus informal pronouns in different languages. We can also use language to regulate intimacy through verbal means to signal friendship and relational bonding (Brown & Gilman, 1960). For example, speakers of languages such as French, German, and Spanish have to constantly choose between a more formal or more intimate form of address. For instance, French has *vous* and *tu*, German has *sie* and *du*, and Spanish has *usted* and *tu*.

Garcia (1996) explains that many Mexicans tend to use the Spanish pronoun *usted* in formal situations, and *tu* in familiar, informal situations. It is common for many Spanish speakers to use *usted*, the formal pronoun, to address new acquaintances, older people, professional people, and people of authority. The use of *usted* forges a formal climate of *respeto*, or deference.

Respeto also means honor, respect, and "face" that we accord to the listeners in accordance with their roles and hierarchical statuses. The use of *tu*, on the other hand, fosters a climate of relational intimacy and informality. *Tu* is the informal application of the English pronoun *you*. It is common for speakers of Spanish to use this informal pronoun to address their family members, close friends, or children. Addressing someone by the improper form of "you" can pose serious face-threat problems in Mexican interpersonal interaction. Individuals can also use *usted* and *tu* strategically to change the structure of the relationship, thereby changing the *respeto* climate of the relationship. Similarly, in Colombia, *respeto* is conferred via the following means: (1) by acknowledging hearer status (e.g., through the use of a title); (2) by maintaining interpersonal distance, showing that the speaker does not presume intimacy (e.g., through the use of the first name rather than a nickname); (3) by adhering to a code of conduct named *culto* (well-mannered behavior) and/or staying *formal* in address (e.g., through the use of a title plus the first name, say, Don Pedro, even though the first name alone might be an option); or (4) by recognizing an important connection such as a kinship or quasi-kinship tie (e.g., through the use of *madrina* or *comadre*—terms denoting a godparent relationship—when the first name alone might be an option (Fitch, 1998, p. 60). Thus, well-mannered behavior in the

Colombian culture involves both "knowledge of whom to respect and an expectation that important connections [are] signaled through use of address terms that [call] attention to the symbolic aspects of the relationship (such as the implicit contract involved in godparenting)" (Fitch, 1998, p. 60).

In the Asian cultural context, Lim and Choi (1996) use the concept of *che-myon* to explain how facework identity is employed as a means of social bonding in every aspect of Korean interaction. *Che-myon* refers to the image of "personal self that is claimed and negotiated through social interactions. . . . It is [also] the image of [the] sociological self that is defined by the society and must be protected by passing the normative standards . . . of relevant social values" (Lim & Choi, 1996, p. 124). Most Koreans value *che-myon* dearly. When they "hoist up" their *che-myon*, Koreans do not merely feel good but actually feel more socially desirable. To maintain the cultural construct of *che-myon*, Koreans need to be involved in the activities that are designed to fulfill their face-related social expectations. Such activities include face-honoring behaviors such as showing indebtedness and deference verbally, and playing benevolent or complying social roles in particular situations. Overall, whether a particular linguistic code is selected or evoked in a given situation often depends on the topic, the interaction scene, the relative status of the speakers, and the relational intimacy level.

From intimacy to relational connection function, another interesting trend on the international scene is the issue of language borrowing. Edwards (1994) points out that in Germany, for example, teenagers "wear *die Jeans*" and that "even the French grudgingly acknowledge the appeal of *le drugstore* and *le weekend* . . . [while] English words [are] integrated into Japanese [such as] *hamu tosuto* for a 'toasted ham sandwich,' [or] *apaato* for apartment" (p. 77). Language borrowing can indicate an added status, a necessary convenience, or a signal of in-group intimacy or connection.

The attitudes toward language borrowing also polarize along the line of prestigious borrowing groups versus nonprestigious borrowing groups. Groups of perceived high social status can get away with using borrowed words and phrases, which are viewed as adding flair to their language style, whereas groups of perceived low social status who employ such borrowed terms are often viewed as engaging in "impure" language usage. Thus, the style-shifting ability of the speakers, when viewed through different social status lenses, may well have different evaluative outcomes.

The Creativity Function

Although it is we human beings who have created languages, we are also at times trapped by the habits of our own linguistic systems. While the language of a culture perpetuates that culture's traditions, by changing our language habits we can incrementally transform long-standing cultural norms and attitudes.

For example, the male generic language in English—terms such as *chairman, fireman, businessman,* or *mankind* used in Western society—tends to elevate men's experience as more valid and make women's experience less prominent. While some people may assume that women are included in such male generic terms as *chairman* and *mankind,* research has demonstrated "conclusively that masculine generics are perceived as referring predominantly or exclusively to men. When people hear them, they think of men, not women" (Wood, 1997, p. 152).More specifically, for example, a researcher asked students from the first grade through college to make up a story about an average student. When the instructions referred to "the average student as *he,*" only 12% of students composed a story about a female. However, when the instructions defined "the average student as *he or she,*" 42% of the stories were about females" (Wood, 1997, p. 152).

By mindfully changing some of our linguistic habits (e.g., changing *chairman* to *chairperson, fireman* to *firefighter, mankind* to *humankind,*) we can start transforming our thinking patterns in gender equitable terms. To the extent that the language of a culture makes men appear more visible and concurrently makes women seem invisible, the perceptions generated from such biased language usage create biased thinking. More importantly, language has a carryover effect on our expectations, and hence perceptions, of what constitute proper or improper gendered role behaviors. Research indicates, for example, that "women who use assertive speech associated with masculinity are judged as arrogant and uppity, while men who employ emotional language associated with femininity are often perceived as wimps or gay. . . . Polarized thinking about gender encouraged by our language restricts us from realizing the full range of human possibilities" (Wood, 1997, p. 160). Language can indeed imprison us because it influences our way of perceiving the world "out there."

Fortunately, language can also set us free—that is, if we are willing to mindfully change our language habits and preconceived biased notions about different identity groups. Linguistic sexism occurs when women are devalued and made invisible through the constant use of masculine-based generic words to include both males and females (e.g., using *spokesman* rather than *spokesperson,* and using the generic *he* to imply both female and male). To combat linguistic sexism, here are some suggestions: (1) commit yourself to removing sexist language from all of your communication; (2) practice and reinforce nonsexist language patterns until they become habitual; (3) persuade others to use nonsexist language in their everyday lives; (4) use reconstruction or substitution (e.g., change *founding fathers* to *founders*) to replace verbal sexism; and (5) use your creative capacity to reframe your verbal sexist habits with gender-neutral words in both public and private conversations (Sorrels, 1983, p. 17).

Language creativity is a marvelous achievement of our human species. People in all cultures have the capacity to talk about things far away in time and space (i.e., the displacement feature), to say things they have never said before by a mere reconfiguration of words in their native tongues (i.e., the productivity feature), and to use language (e.g., via oral history, epic poems, parables, or stories) to pass on their heritage and wisdom from one generation to the next (i.e., the traditional transmission feature).

It is remarkable that by the time children with normal language development patterns reach their fourth birthday, they have already internalized the exceedingly complex structures of their native tongues. In only a few more years "children possess the entire linguistic system that allows them to utter and to understand sentences they have not previously heard" (Farb, 1973, p. 9). Individuals can garner their creative potential to use language mindfully for mutual gain and collaboration across gender and cultural groups. Alternatively, they can use language to disseminate hate-filled propaganda, engage in conflict, wage war, and engender destruction. Language can simultaneously be a hacking and a healing instrument: it can be used to "cut down" or degrade others' primary identities; it can also be used mindfully to uplift and support their desired group-based or personal identities.

In this section, we have discussed the diverse functions of languages across cultures: the membership identity, perceptual filter, cognitive reasoning, status and intimacy, and creativity functions. We now turn to a discussion of how our cultural and ethnic identities influence our verbal communication styles. By understanding such differences, we can arrive at mutual clarity, appreciation, and respect.

CROSS-CULTURAL VERBAL COMMUNICATION STYLES

This section examines the low-context and high-context communication framework and its associated verbal interaction dimensions: direct and indirect verbal styles, person-oriented and status-oriented styles, self-enhancement and self-effacement verbal styles, and the importance of talk versus silence.

Low-Context and High-Context Communication

Hall (1976) claims that human interaction, on the broad level, can be divided into low-context and high-context communication systems. By *low-context communication* we emphasize how intention or meaning is best expressed through explicit verbal messages. By *high-context communication* we emphasize how intention or meaning can best be conveyed through the context (e.g., social roles or positions) and the nonverbal channels (e.g., pauses, silence, tone of voice) of the verbal message.

In general, low-context communication refers to communication patterns of direct verbal mode—straight talk, nonverbal immediacy, and sender-oriented values (i.e., the sender assumes the responsibility to communicate

TABLE 4.1. The Low-Context Communication (LCC) and High-Context Communication (HCC) Frameworks

LCC characteristics	HCC characteristics
Individualistic values	Group-oriented values
Self-face concern	Mutual-face concern
Linear logic	Spiral logic
Direct style	Indirect style
Person-oriented style	Status-oriented style
Self-enhancement style	Self-effacement style
Speaker-oriented style	Listener-oriented style
Verbal-based understanding	Context-based understanding

LCC examples		HCC examples	
Germany	United States	Saudi Arabia	Japan
Switzerland	Canada	Kuwait	China
Denmark	Australia	Mexico	South Korea
Sweden	United Kingdom	Nigeria	Vietnam

clearly). In low-context communication, the speaker is expected to be responsible for constructing a clear, persuasive message that the listener can decode easily.

In contrast, high-context communication refers to communication patterns of indirect verbal mode—self-effacing talk, nonverbal subtleties, and interpreter-sensitive values (i.e., the receiver or interpreter of the message assumes the responsibility to infer the hidden or contextual meanings of the message) (Ting-Toomey, 1985). In high-context communication, the listener or interpreter of the message is expected to "read between the lines," to accurately infer the implicit intent of the verbal message, and to observe the nonverbal nuances and subtleties that accompany and enhance the verbal message (see Table 4.1).

When we use low-context communication we stress the importance of explicit verbal messages to convey personal thoughts, opinions, and feelings. When we use high-context communication we stress the importance of multilayered contexts (e.g., historical context, social norms, roles, situational and relational contexts) that frame the interaction encounter. Low-context communication interaction is exemplified by the following dispute between two European American neighbors:

Scene 1

JANE (*knocks on her neighbor's open window*): Excuse me, it is 11 o'clock already, and your high-pitched opera singing is really disturbing my sleep. Please stop your gargling noises immediately! I have an important job interview tomorrow morning, and I want to get a good night's sleep. I really need this job to pay my rent!

DIANE (*resentfully*): Well, this is the only time I can rehearse my opera! I've an important audition coming up tomorrow. You're not the only one that is starving, you know. I also need to pay my rent. Stop being so self-centered!

JANE (*frustrated*): I really think you're being very unreasonable. If you don't stop your singing right now I'm going to file a complaint with the apartment manager and he could evict you. . . .

DIANE (*sarcastically*): OK, be my guest. . . . Do whatever you want. I'm going to sing as I please.

In contrast, the following dialogue involving two Japanese housewives illustrates their use of high-context communication style (Naotsuka et al., 1981, p. 70):

Scene 2

Mrs. A: Your daughter has started taking piano lessons, hasn't she? I envy you, because you can be proud of her talent. You must be looking forward to her future as a pianist. I'm really impressed by her enthusiasm—every day, she practices so hard, for hours and hours, until late at night.

Mrs. B: Oh, no, not at all. She is just a beginner. We don't know her future yet. We hadn't realized that you could hear her playing. I'm so sorry you have been disturbed by her noise.

In Scene 1, Jane and Diane spell out everything that is on their minds with no restraints. Their interaction exchange is direct, to the point, bluntly contentious, and full of face-threat verbal messages. Scene 1 represents one possible low-context way of approaching interpersonal conflict. While the example represents an unproductive conflict dialogue, Jane and Diane might actually turn their dialogue around and obtain a more productive outcome by identifying their common interests (such as urgency of the job search or rent payment due) and exploring other constructive options (such as closing the windows or practicing in another room). They can use the strengths of low-context, "explicit talk" in dealing with the conflict issue openly and nonevaluatively.

In Scene 2, Mrs. A has not directly expressed her concern over the piano noise with Mrs. B because she wants to preserve face and her relationship with Mrs. B. Rather, Mrs. A only uses indirect hints and nonverbal signals to get her point across. However, Mrs. B, correctly "reads between the lines" of Mrs. A's verbal message and apologizes appropriately and effectively before any real conflict can bubble to the surface. Scene 2 represents one possible high-context way of approaching interpersonal conflict. In high-context conflict situations, even minor disagreement is perceived as a major face-threat situation if the "face" or "social self-image" of the contending parties is not upheld. From the high-context communication viewpoint, minor disagreement can easily turn into a major conflict if face-threatening and face-saving issues are not dealt with appropriately and effectively. However, if Mrs. A were the neighbor of Diane in Example 1, Diane might not be able to "read between the lines" of Mrs. A's verbal and, more importantly, nonverbal message. Diane might be clueless that a conflict was already simmering between them. Diane might actually take Mrs. A's verbal message literally and infer her message as a compliment—and thus sing even louder!

While Mrs. A and Mrs. B are practicing the high-context interaction style frequently used in Japanese society, Jane and Diane are using the low-context communication style more commonly employed in U.S. society. Overall, low-context interaction emphasizes direct talk, person-oriented focus, self-enhancement mode, and the importance of "talk." High-context interaction, in comparison, stresses indirect talk, status-oriented focus, self-effacement mode, and the importance of nonverbal signals and even silence.

Direct and Indirect Verbal Interaction Styles

When we refer to the stylistic mode of verbal interaction, according to Katriel (1986), we mean the "tonal coloring given to spoken performance, [the] feeling tone" (p. 7; see also Katriel, 1991). The tone of voice, the speaker's intention, and the verbal content reflect our way of speaking, our verbal style, which in turn reflects our cultural and personal values and sentiments.

Verbal style frames "how" a message should be interpreted. Of the four stylistic modes of verbal interaction (i.e., direct vs. indirect, person oriented vs. status oriented, self-enhancement vs. self-effacement, and talk vs. silence), the research evidence on the direct–indirect verbal interaction dimension is the most extensive and persuasive. This stylistic pair can be thought of as straddling a continuum. Individuals in all cultures use the gradations of all these verbal styles, depending on role identities, interaction goals, and situations. However, in individualistic cultures, people tend to encounter more situations that emphasize the preferential use of direct talk, person-oriented verbal interaction, verbal self-enhancement, and talkativeness. In contrast, in collectivistic cultures, people tend to encounter more situations that emphasize the preferential use of indirect talk, status-oriented verbal interaction, verbal self-effacement, and silence.

The direct and indirect styles differ in the extent to which communicators reveal their intentions through their tone of voice and the straightforwardness of their content message. In the direct verbal style, statements clearly reveal the speaker's intentions and are enunciated in a forthright tone of voice. In the indirect verbal style, on the other hand, verbal statements tend to camouflage the speaker's actual intentions and are carried out with more nuanced tone of voice. For example, the overall U.S. American verbal style often calls for clear and direct communication. Phrases such as "say what you mean," "don't beat around the bush," and "get to the point" are some examples. The direct verbal style of the larger U.S. culture is reflective of its low-context communication character.

By way of comparison, Graf (1994) observes that "Chinese tend to beat around the bush. They are not forthright enough, [so] that Westerners often perceive them as insincere and untrustworthy" (p. 232). For example, in a verbal request situation, U.S. Americans tend to use a straightforward form of request whereas Chinese tend to ask for a favor in a more roundabout and implicit way. This can be demonstrated by the following pair of contrastive "airport ride request" scenes between two U.S. Americans and two Chinese (Gao & Ting-Toomey, 1998, p. 76):

Scene 1

AMERICAN 1: We're going to New Orleans this weekend.

AMERICAN 2: What fun! I wish we were going with you. How long are you going to be there? [If she wants a ride, she will ask.]

AMERICAN 1: Three days. By the way, we may need a ride to the airport. Do you think you can take us?

AMERICAN 2: Sure. What time?

AMERICAN 1: 10:30 P.M. this coming Saturday.

Scene 2

CHINESE 1: We're going to New Orleans this weekend.

CHINESE 2: What fun! I wish we were going with you. How long are you going to be there?

CHINESE 1: Three days. [I hope she'll offer me a ride to the airport.]

CHINESE 2: [She may want me to give her a ride.] Do you need a ride to the airport? I'll take you.

CHINESE 1: Are you sure it's not too much trouble?

CHINESE 2: It's no trouble at all.

Here we see that in the Chinese culture such requests for help are likely to be implied rather than stated explicitly and directly. Indirect requests can help both parties to save face and uphold harmonious interaction. When the hearer detects a request during a conversation with the speaker, the hearer can choose to either grant or deny the request. If the hearer decides to deny it, he or she usually does not respond to it or subtly changes the topic of conversation. Consequently, the speaker discerns the cues from the hearer and drops the request. An implicit understanding generally exists between a speaker and a hearer in Chinese culture that is essential to maintain relational harmony at all costs in everyday social interaction.

Intercultural misunderstanding therefore becomes highly probable when Chinese and U.S. Americans communicate with each other. They each adhere to their habitual verbal styles and carry out their cultural scripts in a relatively mindless fashion. They also rely on their own cultural scripts to inform them of what to expect in the interaction. Let us look at Scene 3 of the "airport ride request" dialogue, this time between a Chinese speaker and a U.S. American hearer (Gao & Ting-Toomey, 1998, p. 77).

Scene 3

CHINESE: We're going to New Orleans this weekend.

AMERICAN: What fun! I wish we were going with you. How long are you going to be there?

CHINESE: Three days. [I hope she'll offer me a ride to the airport.]

AMERICAN: [If she wants a ride, she'll ask me.] Have a great time.

CHINESE: [If she had wanted to give me a ride, she would have offered it. I'd better ask somebody else.] Thanks. I'll see you when I get back.

Thus we see that while the U.S. American verbal model rewards direct assertions and opinions, the Chinese model emphasizes indirect verbal style to cultivate relational harmony and implicit interpersonal understanding.

Similarly, in the context of the Korean culture, Koreans do not make negative responses like "No," or "I disagree with you," or "I cannot do it." Rather, they like to use indirect expressions such as "[I] kind of agree with you in principle; however, please understand my difficulties . . ." or "[I] sympathize with your difficulties; unfortunately . . ." (Park, 1979). The importance of preserving relational harmony with in-group members and the importance of *nunchi* (an affective sense by which Koreans can detect whether others are pleased or satisfied) are the reasons why most Koreans opt for the indirect style of verbal communication. Additionally, *kibun* (respect for others' sense of selfhood that includes their morale and facework support) is shown through indirect verbal behavior.

Cohen (1991), in analyzing diplomatic negotiation processes in China, Japan, Egypt, India, Mexico, and the United States, provides strong evidence that communication patterns differentiate China, Japan, Egypt, India, and Mexico (i.e., the indirect style), on the one hand, and the United States (i.e., the direct style) on the other. For example, Cohen documented that on the eve of the departure of Prime Minister Eisaku Sato of Japan for a crucial summit with President Richard M. Nixon in 1970, Sato released the following remarkable statement to the press: "Since Mr. Nixon and I are old friends, the negotiations will be three parts talk and seven parts *haragei* [belly-to-belly talk, i.e., reading one another's mind]" (p. 117).

Unfortunately for the bilateral relationship, this did not turn out to be true and Prime Minister Sato's faith in a man he considered a close ally and personal friend was misplaced. Nixon declined to give any weight to Sato's domestic difficulties and "insisted [that he agree] to an explicit five-point proposal as the basis for a settlement" (Cohen, 1991, p. 117). The dimension of the direct versus the indirect communication style clearly posed a major barrier to effective diplomatic negotiations between Japan and the United States in that instance. Furthermore, the unwillingness to use "no" as a direct response in many of the collectivistic, high-context cultures often causes international conflicts. For high-context individuals, it is always easier to agree than to disagree. Confronted by a persistent and undesirable request, "they find the 'social affirmative' the best way out of an uncomfortable situation. The fault is not theirs but that of their obtuse interlocutor, who has failed to draw the correct conclusions from the hesitancy and unenthusiastic nature of the reply" (Cohen, 1991, p. 115).

Person-Oriented and Status-Oriented Verbal Styles

The person-oriented verbal style is individual-centered verbal mode that emphasizes the importance of informality and role suspension. The status-oriented verbal style is a role-centered verbal mode that emphasizes formality and large power distance. The former emphasizes the importance of symmetrical interaction, whereas the latter stresses asymmetrical interaction.

The person-oriented verbal style emphasizes the importance of respecting unique, personal identities in the interaction. The status-oriented verbal style emphasizes the importance of honoring prescribed power-based membership identities. Those who engage in status-oriented verbal interaction use specific vocabularies and paralinguistic features to accentuate the status distance of the role relationships (e.g., in parent–child interaction, superior–subordinate relations, and male–female interaction in many Latin American cultures). While low-context cultures tend to emphasize the use of the person-oriented verbal style, high-context cultures tend to value the status-oriented verbal mode.

For example, Okabe (1983), in commenting on the Japanese language, contends that English is a person-oriented language whereas Japanese is a status-oriented language. Okabe (1983) observes that U.S. Americans tend to treat other people with informality and casualness. They tend to "shun the formal codes of conduct, titles, honorifics, and ritualistic manners in [their] interaction with others. They instead prefer a first-name basis and direct address. They also strive to equalize the language style between the sexes. In sharp contrast, the Japanese are likely to assume that formality is essential in their human relations. They are apt to feel uncomfortable in some informal situations" (p. 27). In other words, the Japanese tend to uphold the proper roles, with the proper words, in the appropriate contexts to create a predictable interaction climate.

Similarly, Yum (1988a) notes that the Korean language accommodates the Confucian ethics of hierarchical human relationships. It has special vocabularies for each sex, for different degrees of social status and intimacy, and for different levels of formality depending on the occasion. The use of proper verbal styles for the proper types of relationships and in the proper contexts are sure signs that one is an "educated" person in the Korean culture. In addition, Yum (1988b) argues that the Korean language is a status-based language because the cultural ethos of the Korean interaction style is based on the primary value of *uye-ri* (i.e., righteousness, duty, obligation, a debt of gratitude, and loyalty in accordance with proper relationships between people). Deferential language is used when a Korean communicates with a higher-status person or with a person to whom he or she is indebted.

The style of speaking, in short, reflects the overall values and norms of a culture. The cultural styles of speaking in many speech communities reflect the hierarchical social order, asymmetrical role positions, and power distance values of the different cultures.

Self-Enhancement and Self-Effacement Verbal Styles

The self-enhancement verbal style emphasizes the importance of boasting about one's accomplishments and abilities. The self-effacement verbal style, on the other hand, emphasizes the importance of humbling oneself via verbal restraints, hesitations, modest talk, and the use of self-deprecation concerning one's effort or performance.

For example, in many Asian cultures, self-effacement talk is expected to signal modesty or humility. Japanese, when serving tea, tend to say, "So-*cha desuga . . .*," which means "This is not very delicious, but . . ." Condon (1984) observes that in Japan, when one offers something to another person such as a gift or a meal that one has prepared, verbal self-deprecation is expected. There are set expressions for verbal humility such as "It's not very tasty," and "It's nothing special." The hostess who apologizes to her guests that "There is nothing special to offer you" has probably "spent the better part of two days planning and preparing the meal. Of course the guest should protest such [a] disclaimer" (Condon, 1984, p. 52) and reemphasize her or his gratitude. Self-effacement is a necessary part of Japanese politeness rituals. Here is an example, as seen from the Japanese standpoint:

Two people cannot occupy the same position of precedence at the same time and so a sort of "after you" is required—politeness demands a natural formal assumption of the superiority of the other person, the host being required to politely state his [or her] inferiority to the guest, and the guest in turn being required to politely deny the [host's] self-claimed inferiority. Not to do so would seem arrogant, as if one were replying to a polite "You are superior" with "Yes, I certainly am." (Naotsuka et al., 1981, p. 40)

In the U.S. culture, we encourage individuals to "sell and boast about themselves," for example, in performance review or job interview sessions, or else no one would notice their accomplishments. However, the notion of merchandizing oneself does not set well with the Japanese. In Japan, one does not like to "stand out or be singled out, even by others; it is far worse to promote oneself" (Condon, 1984, p. 51). For example, there are Japanese "personals" in the classified ads in magazines that are similar to those in the United States. However, an American ad might begin, "A handsome, athletic male with a good sense of humor seeks a fun-loving partner . . ."; the comparable Japanese ad might read, "Although I am not very good looking, I'm willing to try my best to work hard. . . ."

In many Asian cultures, individuals believe that if their performance is good, their behavior will be noticed, for example, by their supervisors during promotion review situations. However, from the Western cultural standpoint, if my performance is good, I should document or boast about it so that my supervisor will be sure to take notice. This difference is probably due to the observer-sensitive value of the Asian, high-context communication pattern, as opposed to the sender-responsible value of the Western, low-context interaction pattern.

We should note that the pattern of verbal self-effacement cannot be generalized to many Arab or African cultures. In Egypt, for example, a popular saying is "Make your harvest look big, lest your enemies rejoice" (Cohen, 1991, p. 132). Effusive verbal self-enhancement is critical to the enhancement of one's face or honor in some large power distance Arab cultures. For example,

An Arab feels compelled to overassert in almost all types of communication because others expect him [or her] to do so. If an Arab says exactly what he [or she] means without the expected assertion, other Arabs may still think that he [or she] means the opposite. For example, a simple "No" by a [male] guest to the host's request to eat more or drink more will not suffice. To convey the meaning that he is actually full, the guest must keep repeating "No" several times, coupling it with an oath such as "By God" or "I swear to God." . . . An Arab often fails to realize that others, particularly foreigners, may mean exactly what they say even though their language is simple. (Almaney & Alwan, 1982, p. 84)

The value of large power distance, in conjunction with the nature of Arabic as a rather ornate or demonstrative language, probably contribute to the effect of effusive verbal self-enhancement. Additionally, many Arab hosts feel obligated to engage in effusive other-enhancement talk in communicating with honored guests. The tendency in Arabic to use somewhat charged or even hyperbolic expressions during diplomatic confrontations has possibly caused more misunderstandings between the United States and some Arab countries than any other single factor (Cohen, 1987).

Overall, for many Asian cultures that have a collectivistic outlook, humbling oneself through deferential speech is a preferred mode of ritualized politeness. It signals a willingness to be sensitive to the feelings of other in-group members. It also signals humility or modesty concerning one's self-identity. While a moderate self-enhancement verbal style is reflective of many Western individualistic cultures, a self-effacement verbal style is reflective of many Asian collectivistic cultures.

There are also ethnic verbal style differences in terms of expressive or animated verbal styles. There are, for example, distinctive differences between African Americans' and European Americans' verbal interaction styles. As Kochman (1990) notes,

The differing potencies of Blacks and White public presentations are a regular cause of communicative conflict. Black presentations are emotionally intense, dynamic, and demonstrative; White presentations are more modest and emotionally restrained. Where Whites use the relatively detached and unemotional *discussion* mode to engage an issue, Blacks use the more emotionally intense and involving mode of *argument*. Where Whites tend to *understate* their exceptional talents, Blacks tend to *boast* about theirs. (p. 193; emphasis in original)

The verbal styles of African Americans have been identified as emotionally expressive, assertive, boastful, vigorous, rhythmic, and synchronized (Kochman, 1990). The "animation and vitality of Black expressive behavior is in part owing to the emotional force or spiritual energy that Blacks habitually invest in their public presentations and the functional role that emotions play in realizing the goals of Black interactions, activities, and events" (Kochman, 1990, p. 195). It is critical to note that verbal styles revolving "expressive or enhancement style" and "understated or effacement style" are *relative comparison* issues. For example, in comparison to many traditional Asian American groups, the European American verbal style might well be deemed "boastful." However, in comparison to the African American verbal style, the European American verbal pattern might seem "understated." From the standpoint of the African American group, many Asian immigrant groups sound "extremely understated, distant, or evasive."

Interethnic frictions arise when a group uses its own verbal style yardstick to evaluate another group's verbal output. Even routine conversations can escalate into major conflicts because of our ignorance of each other's preferred verbal styles. More importantly, our ethnocentric evaluations can clutter our ability to listen clearly to ongoing communication from others. Recognizing and respecting verbal style differences requires mindfulness.

Beliefs Expressed in Talk and Silence

Silence can oftentimes say as much as words. While silence occurs in interaction contexts in cultures around the world, how silence is interpreted and evaluated differs across cultures and between persons. Hall (1983) claims that silence, or *ma*, serves as a critical communication device in the Japanese communication pattern. *Ma* is much more than pausing between words; rather, it is like a semicolon that reflects the inner pausing of the speaker's thoughts. Through *ma*, interpersonal synchrony is made possible in many high-context cultures.

While silence may hold strong, contextual meanings in high-context cultures, prolonged silence is often viewed as "empty pauses" or "ignorant lapses" in the Western rhetorical model. From the high-context perspective, silence can be the essence of the language of superiority and inferiority, affecting such relationships as teacher–student, male–female, and expert–client. The process of silencing or refraining from speaking can have both positive and negative effects. In some situations, notably, in many Asian collectivistic cultures, "quiet is demanded by others and by those who must themselves be quiet. Being quiet—effecting a self-imposed silence—is often valued in some social environments. Being quiet is often a sign of respect for the wisdom and expertise of others" (Ishii & Bruneau, 1991, p. 315).

Research studies by Barnlund (1989) and Wiemann, Chen, and Giles (1986) provide strong empirical evidence on the important role of silence in high-context cultures such as those of China, Japan, Korea, and many Southeastern Asian countries. More specifically, Wiemann et al. (1986) have found that European Americans perceive talk as more important and enjoyable than Chinese Americans and native-born Chinese. In addition, European Americans perceive the use of *talk* as being a means of social control, whereas native-born Chinese perceive the use of *silence* as being a conversational control strategy. Finally, native-born Chinese have been found to be more tolerant of silence in conversations than European Americans or Chinese Americans. Ting-Toomey's (1980, 1981) ethnographic studies of Chinese immigrant families in the United States indicates that traditional Chinese parents tend to use talk to elicit obedience and conformity from their children and silence to indicate displeasure and disapproval. Modern Chinese parents, on the other hand, use talk to create closeness and intimacy and silence to signal attentive listening and understanding.

The concept of silence also occupies a central role in the Apache culture in the United States (Basso, 1970). Silence is deemed appropriate in contexts where social relations between individuals are unpredictable and involve high levels of ambiguity. They also prefer silence in situations in which role expectations are unclear. Members of the Navajo and Papago Indian tribes exhibit similar silent behavior under the same conditions as do the Apache (Basso, 1970). Likewise, in France people tend to engage in animated conversations to affirm the nature of their established relationships; in the absence of any such relationship, silence serves as a neutral communication process. This is why "in the elevator, in the street, on the bus . . . people don't talk to each other readily in France. . . . This is a seemingly inexhaustible source of misunderstanding between the French and the [European] Americans, especially since these rules are suspended under exceptional circumstances and on vacation (and therefore on the train, on the plane). . . . [European] Americans often feel rejected, disapproved of, criticized, or scorned without understanding the reason for this hostility" (Carroll, 1987, p. 30). With strangers, the French and many Native American groups generally preserve proper distance by means of silence. In contrast, European Americans tend to use talk to "break the ice" and reserve silence for their most intimate relationship.

Intercultural miscommunication can thus often occur because of the different priorities placed on talk and silence by different groups. Silence can serve various functions, depending on the type of relationship, the interactive situation, and the particular cultural beliefs held. Intercultural clashes arise when we unintentionally use our own culture-bound evaluations in judging dissimilar other's talk and silence. Our mindless versus mindful orientations in interpreting these different verbal communication styles can ultimately influence the quality of our intergroup relationship development with dissimilar others.

RECOMMENDATIONS

This chapter has covered the following major areas: the features of human language, the functions of languages across diverse cultures, the low-context and high-context communication framework, and low-context and high-context verbal style dimensions. Intercultural miscommunications often occur because individuals use cultural-laden habits and assumptions to interpret each other's verbal messages and verbal styles. Unfortunately, individuals are frequently unaware of their ethnocentric-based verbal interpretations and evaluations.

In order to be mindful verbal communicators, we should do the following:

1. Understand the functions and interpretations that are attached to different modes of talk—from the group identity function to the status function of language usage in a particular culture—we should be sensitive to the cultural beliefs and values that underlie the different modes of verbal expressions.

2. Have a basic grasp of the features of the "languaculture" that we will be encountering. The term "languaculture" emphasizes the *necessary* tie between language and culture (Agar, 1994). The features of a particular language, from syntactic rules to semantic rules, reflect a speaker's worldviews, values, and premises concerning different functions and ways of speaking.

3. Develop verbal empathy and patience for nonnative speakers in our culture. We can, for example, (a) speak slowly, in simple sentences, and allow for comprehension pauses; (b) restate what we say in simple words; (c) use probing questions to check whether the message is received accurately; (d) paraphrase and perception check (see Recommendation 5 below) and ask for feedback response; and (e) use visual restatements such as pictures, graphs, gestures, or written summaries to reinforce our points. Likewise, if we sojourn to another country and are using a second language, we should use similar strategies to cross-check for understanding of the *meaning* of the message.

4. Practice mindful listening skills when communicating with nonnative speakers. Mindful listening demands that we pay thoughtful attention to both the verbal and nonverbal messages of the speaker before responding or evaluating. It means listening attentively with all our senses and checking responsively for the accuracy of our meaning decoding process on multiple levels (i.e., on content, identity, and relational meaning). Mindful listening is an important intercultural communication skill for a variety of reasons. First, mindful listening helps us to manage emotional vulnerability between ourselves and dissimilar others. Second, it helps us to minimize misunderstanding and maximize mutual understanding of cocreated meanings. Third, mindful listening helps us to uncover our own perceptual biases in the listening process. By listening mindfully, we are sending the following identity-support message to the other person: "I am committed to understanding your verbal message and the person behind the message." Mindful listening consists of culture-sensitive paraphrasing skills (see Recommendation 5) and perception checking skills (see the "Recommendations" section in Chapter 5).

5. Practice culture-sensitive paraphrasing skills. Paraphrasing skill refers to two major characteristics: (a) verbally restating the content meaning of the speaker's message in our own words, and (b) nonverbally echoing back our interpretation of the emotional meaning of the speaker's message. The verbal restatement should reflect our tentative understanding of the speaker's meaning behind the content message, using phrases such as "It sounds to me that . . . " and "In other words, you're saying that. . . . "

Nonverbally, you should pay attention to the attitudinal tone that underlies your verbal restatement (i.e., it is critical to display a genuine tone of the desire to understand). In dealing with high-context members, your paraphrasing statements should consist of deferential, qualifying phrases such as "I may be wrong, but what I'm hearing is that . . . " or "Please correct me if I misinterpret what you've said. . . . " In interacting with low-context members, our paraphrasing statements can be more direct and to the point than when interacting with high-context members.

6. Understand the fundamental differences of low-context and high-context communication patterns and the ethnocentric tendencies that we assign to evaluating the opposing characteristics. Individuals who engage in low-context patterns of communication prefer direct verbal style, person-oriented language usage, self-enhancement, and talkativeness in order to "get acquainted." In contrast, individuals who engage in high-context patterns of interaction prefer indirect verbal style, status-oriented language usage, self-effacement, and silence in order to gauge the situation and the stranger. To be mindful intercultural communicators, we need the knowledge of both verbal and nonverbal communication in order to communicate sensitively across cultural and ethnic boundaries.

5

Mindful Intercultural
Nonverbal Communication

Nonverbal Communication: Specific Functions and Patterns 115
Reflecting and Managing Identities 117
Expressing Emotions and Attitudes 119
Conversational Management 123
Impression Formation and Attraction 126
Space and Time across Cultures 127
Interpersonal Spatial Boundary Regulation 128
Environmental Boundary Regulation 131
Temporal Regulation 134
Interpersonal Synchrony and Nonverbal Cautions 137
Interpersonal Interactive Synchrony 137
Nonverbal Cautions 139
Recommendations 140

Nonverbal messages serve multiple functions in intercultural interaction. While verbal messages convey content meaning, nonverbal messages carry strong identity and relational meaning. Nonverbal messages can help to complement, emphasize, substitute, and even contradict the meaning of verbal messages. While verbal messages are digital in nature (i.e., using discrete units of sounds), nonverbal messages are analogic in form (i.e, using continuous streams of icons). While the use of verbal messages involves human intention, the use of nonverbal messages can be intentional or unintentional.

Nonverbal messages can be used without verbal messages. Spoken verbal messages, on the other hand, always involve some nonverbal cues (e.g., the tone of voice). Nonverbal messages are the nonlinguistic aspects of the communication that carry powerful emotional meaning. They provide the context for how the accompanying verbal message should be interpreted and understood. They can either create miscommunication or clarify communication (e.g., through the use of facial expressions). But, more often than not, nonverbal messages can create intercultural friction and confusion because (1) the same nonverbal signal can mean different things to different people in different cultures (e.g., the nonverbal OK sign means

114

"victory," "insult," and "money" in the United States, Brazil, and Japan, respectively); (2) multiple nonverbal cues are sent in each interaction, thereby creating interpretive ambiguities; and (3) factors of personality, gender, relational distance, socioeconomic status, and situation create tremendous variations of nonverbal display patterns in different cultures.

Nonverbal communication is, overall, a powerful form of human expression. It is everywhere. It has interaction primacy. That is to say, nonverbal messages are often the primary means of signaling our emotions, attitudes, and the nature of our relationships with others. Nonverbal messages can oftentimes express what verbal messages cannot express and are assumed to be more truthful than verbal messages. In the development of our human species, nonverbal actions predated language. Infants learn to communicate first via nonverbal movements before they master linguistic codes. Many nonverbal experts (e.g., Birdwhistell, 1955; Mehrabian, 1981) estimated that in every social encounter, nearly two-thirds of the interaction meaning is derived through nonverbal messages. Nonverbal messages signify who we are via our artifacts (e.g., the clothes we wear), our vocal cues, our nonverbal self-presentation modes, and the interpersonal spaces we claim for ourselves (e.g., members of southern European cultures prefer closer distances than do northern Europeans).

This chapter is organized in four main sections. First, the specific functions, patterns, and examples of nonverbal interaction across a wide range of cultures are presented. Second, the boundary regulation processes of space and time across cultures are discussed. Third, the concepts of interpersonal nonverbal synchrony and cautions are reviewed. Lastly, recommendations for mindful nonverbal communication across cultures are presented.

NONVERBAL COMMUNICATION: SPECIFIC FUNCTIONS AND PATTERNS

Nonverbal interaction has both cultural-universal and cultural-specific aspects. For example, while all human beings carry the predisposition to express emotions via nonverbal cues, culture shapes the display rules of when, where, with whom, and how these different emotions should be expressed or suppressed (Ekman & Oster, 1979). Nonverbal display rules are learned within a culture. Cultural value tendencies (e.g., individualism–collectivism and power distance), in conjunction with many relational and situational factors, influence cross-cultural nonverbal behaviors.

Nonverbal communication is defined as the nonlinguistic behaviors (or attributes) that are consciously or unconsciously encoded and decoded via multiple communication channels. Multiple channels refer to how the meaning of nonverbal messages can be simultaneously signaled and interpreted through various nonverbal mediums such as facial expressions, bodily gestures, spatial relationships, and the environment (physical and psychological) in which people are communicating. Nonverbal communication shares many features with verbal communication; nevertheless, nonverbal messages have the following distinctive characteristics: (1) they are analogic messages that carry continuous meanings (e.g., via various ranges of tone of voice); (2) they are sent via multiple interaction channels; (3) they have sensory immediacy, appealing to our senses of sight, smell, taste, hearing, and touch; (4) they can be simultaneously decoded (e.g., decoding facial expressions and the tone of voice together); and (5) from a perceiver-centered perspective, nonverbal communication takes place both intentionally and unintentionally.

Nonverbal communication is a rich, complex field of study. This section examines the basic functions of cross-cultural nonverbal communication and uses examples from the study of kinesics (facial and bodily movements), oculesics (eye contact), vocalics (e.g., tone of voice, volume), proxemics (spatial distance), haptics (touch), environment (e.g., decor, architecture), and chronemics (time) to illustrate the diverse nonverbal functions (see Figure 5.1).

Based on previous nonverbal research (e.g., Altman & Gauvain, 1981; Hall, 1976, 1983; Matsumoto, 1989, 1992; Matsumoto & Kudoh, 1993), the following nonverbal functions are identified: (1) reflecting and managing identities; (2) expressing emotions and attitudes; (3) conversational management; and (4) impression formation and attraction.

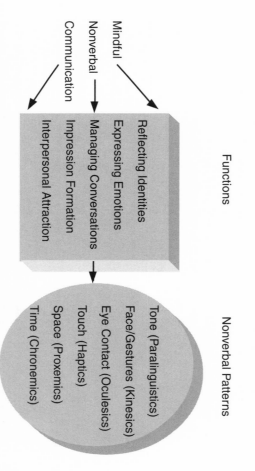

Functions

Mindful
Nonverbal
Communication

Reflecting Identities
Expressing Emotions
Managing Conversations
Impression Formation
Interpersonal Attraction

Nonverbal Patterns

Tone (Paralinguistics)
Face/Gestures (Kinesics)
Eye Contact (Oculesics)
Touch (Haptics)
Space (Proxemics)
Time (Chronemics)

FIGURE 5.1. Mindful nonverbal communication: Functions and patterns.

Reflecting and Managing Identities

Nonverbal cues serve as the markers of our identities. The way we dress, our accent pattern, our nonverbal way of gesturing tell others something about ourselves and how we want to be perceived. Likewise, we rely on nonverbal cues as "name badges"—to discern what groups they [or others] belong to and whether they appear similar or dissimilar to us. This process of identification is at the heart of our self-concept and is a driving force behind our feelings of belonging to valued or stigmatized groups" (Burgoon et al., 1996, p. 215).

Thus, nonverbal cues serve as our identity badges and the identity badges through which we place others into categories (e.g., in-group and out-group). Whenever we come into contact with others, our sex, race, age, face, hair, clothing, body shape, and overall physical attractiveness are visually displayed and then interpreted through the mediation of stereotypes (Smith & Bond, 1993). Our accents, posture, and hand gestures further give our group membership away. According to social perception research, sex and race are the two primary or "primitive" categories that are immediately processed in the first few minutes of an intergroup encounter (Brewer, 1988).

Factors that affect such categorical slotting include the following: (1) contrastive physical cues (such as skin color and facial features); (2) a person's "typicality" as mediated through our stereotypic lenses that she or he "looks like someone from that group"; and (3) nonverbal speech patterns such as contrastive accents, grammar, and manner of speaking (Smith & Bond, 1993). In initial intergroup encounters, the communicators typically perform their nonverbal identity habits (e.g., the use of a habitual tone of voice) without conscious processing. Likewise, we tend to respond to others via our stereotypic group images and expectations rather than responding to personal contact characteristics.

For example, many devout Muslim women wear clothing that is at least ankle length and partially sleeved. They also veil their faces, "wholly or partially, in conservative countries such as Saudi Arabia, Kuwait, the Arabian Gulf states, Yemen and Libya, and to some degree in Morocco, Algeria, and Tunisia . . . as an appropriate acknowledgment of the status and nature of women . . . providing protection for women [from] possible indignities found in outside society. Some women, however, view their situation otherwise and have begun pressing for greater social, legal, and personal freedom" (Nydell, 1996, p. 63).

Thus, adornment features such as clothing, jewelry, cosmetics, and accessories in different cultures also reflect a complex reality—with respect to enhancing, asserting, or reflecting identities. Based on our stereotypic knowledge of a particular group, we look for validation of our expectations via nonverbal cues and surface adornment features.

Surface adornment features such as the use of traditional face painting techniques (e.g., via traditional Asian, African, and American Indian face painting and masks) are thought to be the forerunners of modern cosmetics (Burgoon et al., 1996). In today's society, the cosmetics industry is a multibillion-dollar business engaged in enhancing or "making over" our faces, and thus our symbolic identities, in public. Body tattoos and flesh piercing (e.g., of the ears or nose), which are again in vogue, have occurred at various times in history and serve as identity markers of the individuals and/or the normative practices of the larger culture.

Furthermore, the uniforms that people wear—for example, doctors, nurses, police officers—also connote different identity markers. Uniforms in Japan, for example, worn by students, businesspeople, entertainers, and even vacationers, among others, reflect the individual's special relationship to a specific identity group. Japanese tourists typically wear the resort hotel's *yukata* (a lightweight kimono) and stroll around town wearing these "identity badges" signifying that they are guests of that particular hot springs resort.

Beyond adornment features, another area that gives our cultural, ethnic, or gender identity away is in our use of vocalics. Vocalics refer to the use of voice qualifiers and vocalizations (Trager, 1958). *Voice qualifiers* include vocalic behavior related to speech, such as accent, pitch range (high to low, wide to narrow inflection), pitch intensity (emotional involvement–uninvolvement), volume (loud to soft), articulation (precise to slurred), resonance (rich to thin), and tempo (fast to slow). Each of these characteristics represents a vocalic continuum. For example, U.S. Americans often interpret the clipped speech of some Britons as "arrogant" and "pompous," whereas some Britons would consider U.S. Americans' speech style as "too casual" and as having "no class." Cultural group members often tend to use their own vocal qualifiers and rules to evaluate others' vocalic signals.

Furthermore, *vocalizations* refer to specific vocal sounds or noises that are independent from speech such as the use of vocal characterizers (e.g., sounds of laughing, crying, moaning, groaning, yawning, or belching; belching in public, for instance, can be considered as acceptable in some Asian cultures but is deemed rude in many northern European cultures) and vocal segregates (e.g., pauses, "uh-huh" for yes, "um, uh" for hesitation, and "sh" for silence) (Burgoon et al., 1996). From cultural and regional to social class identities, perceivers form attitudes and impressions based on their ethnocentric evaluations of different vocalic markers.

As the communication accommodation theory (Gallois, Giles, Joyes, Cargile, & Ota, 1995) explains, we tend to view people who sound like us as more friendly and attractive and people who sound different from us as strange and distant. Individuals, however, can monitor their use of vocalics to achieve different interaction results. If low-power individuals, for example, desire to achieve positive intergroup contact with high-power individuals, they might converge their speech pattern toward that of their partners. In contrast, if they desire to maintain their in-group identity via their distinctive speech pattern, they might maintain or deliberately diverge their speech pattern from that of their out-group partners.

Many intergroup relation factors promote the maintenance of diverse vocalic or dialect varieties within a culture. Based on the members' preferred identity orientations, some individuals (with multiple vocalics competencies) can code-switch their speech patterns toward the partner's pattern, maintain their own distinctive speech patterns, or shift to some other speech patterns.

In sum, from adornments to the use of vocalics, we encode our sense of self via different nonverbal features and behaviors. Perceivers also tend to use ethnocentric evaluations to construct and decode others' identities via their use of different nonverbal signals. While some of these identity markers can be intentionally sent (e.g., wearing ethnic clothes), others can be unintentional identity cues (e.g., use of personal space). The following subsections expand this identity theme further by examining how nonverbal behaviors serve multiple nonverbal functions across cultures.

Expressing Emotions and Attitudes

It is through nonverbal messages that we infer the feelings and attitudes of the stranger in the interaction. Feelings and attitudes are typically inferred through the nonverbal systems of kinesics and vocalics. The term *kinesics*, derived from the Greek word *kinesis* ("movement"), encompasses all forms of facial, bodily, and gestural movement. According to Birdwhistell (1970), the face is capable of producing some 250,000 expressions. There are two well-known ways to study emotional facial expressions: the cultural universal approach and the cultural relative approach (Ekman & Friesen, 1975).

Cultural universalists believe that emotional facial expressions are innate and serve basic human adaptation functions. They argue that infants do not actually acquire facial expressions from adults; rather, they hold, infants know how to use facial expressions instinctively or intentionally to get what they want. Children who are born blind or deaf also appear to be able to manifest emotional expressions like laughter or resentment (Darwin, 1872/1965; Izard, 1980).

Cultural relativists, on the other hand, believe that culture shapes emotional facial expressions. They hold that culture provides the basic rules that govern the when and how of what emotions should be expressed or concealed (Birdwhistell, 1970; Hall, 1981). Infants and children learn the social roles, rules, and proper nonverbal emotional displays on an unconscious level. Through a continuous cultural reinforcement process, individuals internalize the nonverbal rules in their culture without conscious effort. They can perform "spontaneously" with the proper nonverbal cues in accordance to particular situational requirements.

Ekman and Friesen (1975) seek to integrate both the above positions and argue for the *neuroculture theory* of facial expression of emotions. According to this theory, while human beings are predisposed to make the connection between certain emotional states and facial muscles, it is through the continuous socialization, reward–sanction process within their culture that human beings acquire nonverbal display rules. Individuals soak up nonverbal cues in a saturated nonverbal environment without needing to check a nonverbal dictionary for correspondent meanings. If language is the key to the core of a culture, nonverbal communication is indeed the *heart of* each culture. Nonverbal communication is omnipresent throughout a culture—it is everywhere. *Cultural display rules* shape when, how, what, and with whom certain nonverbal expressions should be displayed or suppressed within a specific cultural context. Cultural values influence the latitude of emotional expressions under particular situational conditions in different cultures. Drawing from the values of individualism–collectivism and power distance (Hofstede, 1991), for example, it seems reasonable to propose that individualists will tend to value spontaneous emotional expressions with less censorship and collectivists will tend to monitor their nonverbal emotional expressions more carefully because of their concern for relational harmony and in-group reactions.

Individualists often think it is their right to freely express their personal ideas and feelings, whereas collectivists tend to be more concerned with other people's opinions and reactions. Thus, they guard their emotions more cautiously, especially with in-group members. Furthermore, when perceiving threats in the interaction, individualists tend to be more concerned with expressing and repairing self-focused emotions (e.g., personal anger, frustration, or resentment), whereas collectivists generally are more concerned with other-focused emotions (e.g., relational shame, hurt, or embarrassment).

People from small power distance cultures (e.g., in Australia and Canada) tend to use nonverbal emotional cues to establish equal-status relationships. People from large power distance cultures (e.g., in many Latin and Middle Eastern cultures) tend to use nonverbal emotional cues (e.g., the proper tone of voice) to signify asymmetrical-status relationships. However, misunderstandings or frustrations often occur because cultural members fail to observe and decode the subtle (or not so subtle) nonverbal cues in intercultural episodes. Cultural members tend to use their nonverbal cultural frame of reference to judge the other's "miscued" performance.

While both individualists and collectivists may experience a wide spectrum of types of emotions, they may internalize certain types of emotions with varying intensity in response to different situational conditions (e.g., a collectivist might tend to experience a higher intensity of shame for the wrongdoings of a close relative than an individualist would). They may also choose to disintensify, neutralize, or dramatize different types of facial expressions to achieve specific interaction outcomes or goals in their particular culture.

Nonverbal researchers have generally agreed that there is relative universality in the decoding of basic facial emotions (Ekman et al., 1987; Izard, 1980). These basic facial emotions are anger, disgust, fear, happiness, sadness, and surprise. These facial emotional expressions (e.g., facial photographs as portrayed by U.S. Americans and Papua New Guineans) have been consistently recognized or decoded by members of different cultures (e.g., from Estonia, Germany, Greece, Hong Kong, Italy, Japan, Scotland, the Indonesian island of Sumatra, Turkey, and the United States).

The more similar the cultures (i.e., from the same geographic region), the more accurate is the nonverbal decoding process. Further studies (with pictures of both Japanese and U.S. American male and female faces) indicate that U.S. students are better at identifying anger, disgust, fear, and sadness than are Japanese students. A possible explanation for the U.S. students' greater aptitude for identifying these emotions is that the Japanese students have been socialized to suppress the overt expression of such emotions, as such expression could be face threatening to others. If a great majority of Japanese suppress the expression of these emotions, members of the Japanese culture would then tend to have less exposure to them. Therefore, they would have less practice in identifying these "negative" emotions. Both groups, however, are equally adept at recognizing happiness and surprise (Matsumoto, 1989, 1992).

In a study probing the emotional experience of generic "feel good" emotions (such as feeling relaxed, elated, and calm), some interesting cross-cultural differences emerge (Kitayama & Markus, 1994). U.S. college students perceive the generic "feel good" emotions as associated with socially disengaged emotions (such as feelings of pride and superiority). Japanese college students, on the other hand, equate the "feel good" emotions with socially engaged emotions (such as friendly feelings and feelings of respect). It appears that while the decoding of the six facial emotions can be pancultural, the meaning, the circumstances, and the associated tasks that are related to generate such emotions are culture specific. For individualists, the successful achievement of goals that bring personal recognition and pride makes them feel generally good about themselves. For collectivists, the effective achievement of goals that makes the group members feel good about one another generates the general feelings of well-being.

In addition, the meaning of smiles can carry different connotations in different cultures. Within the U.S. culture, a smile can mean joy or happiness. In the Japanese culture, while a smile can be used to signal joy, it can also be used to mask embarrassment, hide displeasure, or suppress anger. In Russia, facial expressions serve as important negotiation cues. U.S. Americans are taught to "open conversations with a smile and to keep smiling.

Russians tend to start out with grim faces, but when they do smile, it reflects relaxation and progress in developing a good relationship. Winks and nods are also good signs" (Richmond, 1996, p. 136).

Overall, culture appears to play a powerful role in terms of the types of emotions that should be displayed or suppressed in different interactive situations (Gudykunst & Ting-Toomey, 1988). Individualistic cultures tend to encourage the display of a wide range of positive and negative emotions, and members are also able to accurately decode a wide range of positive and negative emotions. In contrast, collectivistic cultures tend to encourage the display of modest "positive" emotions (e.g., friendly and agreeable emotions) while suppressing the display of extreme "negative" emotions (e.g., anger and disgust) in everyday lives. Collectivists also tend to have a harder time reading negative facial expressions, perhaps because of their lack of experience in dealing with them on a day-to-day basis. Furthermore, collectivists make a stronger distinction in terms of what facial emotions should be displayed or suppressed with respect to in-group and out-group members.

Along with facial expressions of emotions, the human voice carries powerful emotional meaning. In the U.S. culture, soft emotions such as grief and love are expressed through pitch variations. Harsh emotions such as anger and contempt are expressed by changes in volume (i.e., loudness vs. softness). Neutral emotions such as indifference are expressed through tempo changes (Costanzo, Markel, & Costanzo, 1969). Overall, while anger has been found to be an easy vocal emotion to decode (Davitz & Davitz, 1959), fear and love are found to be the most difficult vocal emotions to recognize (Zuckerman, Lipets, Kolvumaki, & Rosenthal, 1975).

Cultural norms also greatly influence our conversational volume and intensity. While many Southern European cultures (e.g., Greece and Italy) and Arab cultures (e.g., Saudi Arabia and Yemen) tend to value an emotionally engaged, expressive tone of voice when important issues are discussed, many East and Southeast Asian cultures (e.g., Malaysia and Thailand) tend to value a moderating, soft tone of voice for both females and males. According to Nydell (1996), one of the most commonly misunderstood aspects of Arab communication involves the "display of anger. Arabs are not usually angry as they appear to be. Raising the voice, repeating points, even pounding the table for emphasis may sound angry, but in the speaker's mind, they merely indicate sincerity. A Westerner overhearing such a conversation may wrongly conclude that an argument is taking place. Emotion connotes deep and sincere concern for the substance of the discussion" (p. 44).

While members of the German and U.S. cultures, for example, tend to perceive the tone of voice of the Arabs as aggressive and pushy, Arabs oftentimes evaluate the nonexpressive style of Germans and U.S. Americans as "cold," "distant," and "harsh." In contrast, from the Filipino standpoint, U.S. Americans tend to speak in a louder voice than Filipinos do.

When an American thinks "he or she is merely talking in a normal voice while offering a comment on the work of a Filipino colleague, the Filipino may feel the criticism is being shouted for all to hear. Probably no other rule is as simple and yet effective for Americans dealing with Filipinos than to speak calmly, quietly, and sensitively" (Gochenour, 1990, p. 62).

Thus, nonverbal cultural differences exist on a scale of relative differences: from the Arab point of view, the U.S. American tone of voice sounds "cold" and "emotionally disengaging"; from the East Asian point of view, the same voice tone can sound "too heated" and "harsh." Members of different cultures use their own cultural nonverbal standards as guidelines for proper or improper ways of "sounding" and evaluating others. It is also important to realize that, within the broader labels of what constitute "individualistic" and "collectivistic" nonverbal patterns, diverse nonverbal rules (with subtle variations) exist in different regions of individualistic and collectivistic cultures.

In sum, different cultural socialization processes contribute to the display of various facial and vocalic emotional expressions. Consensual meanings of such nonverbal behaviors are perpetuated and reinforced through ongoing cultural activities and interactions. Intercultural nonverbal strains may occur when individualists cannot accurately decode or interpret collectivists' nonverbal expressive style. Likewise, tensions may arise when collectivists cannot fathom the implicit norms and rules that govern individualists' nonverbal expressive mode.

Conversational Management

People generally use kinesics (e.g., hand gestures and body posture) and oculesics (i.e., eye gaze and face gaze) to manage their conversation with others. Hand gestures and body postures have been categorized as emblems, illustrators, regulators, and adaptors (Ekman & Friesen, 1969). Each of these categories emphasizes some specific communication functions. The categories, however, are not mutually exclusive—a single hand gesture can be classified as serving both illustrative and regulative functions, etc.

Emblems are hand gestures that hold specific meanings for members within a culture. They have a direct verbal referent and can substitute for the words that they represent (e.g., the nonverbal peace sign, the hitchhike sign, etc.). They are most often gestures or movements with intentional meanings (e.g., lifted shoulders with palms turned up meaning "I don't know," a common U.S. emblem). They can be recognized by in-group members even when displayed out of context. Emblems typically carry special meanings for members of the in-group. Greeting rituals, beckoning gestures, peace or insult gestures, gang signs, and head movements to indicate "yes" or "no" are all examples of emblems.

Every culture has a rich variety of emblems with specific meanings and rules of display. However, emblems can contribute to intercultural misunderstandings or conflicts. For example, misusing nonverbal greeting rituals can create bad first impressions. The beckoning "come here" gesture observed in many Asian cultures (e.g., China and Japan) with the palm down and the fingers waving toward the body can signal "go away" to most North Americans. Filipino colleagues in the workplace first meet each other every day by shaking hands and exchanging spoken greetings. Later in the day, it is enough for them to acknowledge each other with just an upward movement of the eyebrows. Nothing need be said, and nothing impolite or unfriendly has taken place. But failure to exchange this "eyebrow-greeting or a little wave of the hand would constitute unfriendliness" (Gochenour, 1990, p. 65).

Many emblems across cultures also hold contradictory meanings in different cultures. For example, a single hand gesture signifying OK to U.S. Americans in which one raises one's hand and makes a circle between the thumb and forefinger can mean "money" to the Japanese, a sexual insult in Brazil and Greece, a vulgar gesture in Russia, or "zero" in French. The Bulgarian turn of the head sideways from left to right, which indicates "yes," means "no" for many other cultures. The "V-for-victory" sign is done by extending the forefinger and index finger upward and apart—the palm may face in or out in the United States; however, in Britain the "V" sign with the palm turned inward (but not outward) connotes an insult. The "thumbs-up" gesture used in Canada and the United States to signify approval or encouragement is offensive throughout the Arab world (e.g., in Egypt and Kuwait; Morrison, Conaway, & Borden, 1994). Thus, inaccurate and insensitive encoding and decoding of emblematic nonverbal gestures can create intercultural misunderstanding or strife.

Illustrators are nonverbal hand gestures that are used to complement or illustrate spoken words. They are less arbitrary than emblems. They are the most "pictorial" of all kinesic behaviors, being hand gestures that accentuate a word or phrase. They can also be used to illustrate directions or "draw" a picture of the intended verbal meaning.

Italians have been found to use more broad, full-arm gestures to illustrate their conversations than do U.S. Americans. They also like to "talk with their hands," and most hand gestures are expressive and innocuous. Many Spaniards also use a variety of hand illustrators, and many of these illustrators are region specific (Morrison et al., 1994). Generally southern Europeans tend to employ more animated hand gestures than do northern Europeans.

In contrast, Asians tend to use fewer and more restrained hand gestures to complement their conversations than do either U.S. Americans or southern Europeans. They prefer to focus on the interactions and consider that the use of too many hand gestures is distracting, rude, and undisciplined.

While southern Europeans (e.g., Italians and Greeks), Arabs (e.g., Egyptians and Saudis), and Latin Americans (e.g., Chileans and Venezuelans) tend to use animated hand illustrators, many Asians and northern Europeans (e.g., Belgians, Finns, and Swedes) prefer "quiet gestures" when speaking. Furthermore, the left hand is considered unclean in the Arab world: it is wise not to gesture too much with the left hand, and it is strictly taboo to eat with it. Additionally, the head is considered to be the seat of the soul by many Asian Indians; therefore, individuals should refrain from touching or patting the head of a child during conversations. U.S. Americans occupy the middle position in using moderate degrees of nonverbal illustrators—somewhere between the southern Europeans and the northern Europeans.

Regulators include the use of vocalics, kinesics (especially nonverbal gestures and head movements), and oculesics to regulate the pacing and flow of the conversation. Next to emblems, regulators are considered as culture specific nonverbal behaviors. They are also the most rule-governed kinesic behaviors. They act as the nonverbal traffic signs to control the flow and pauses of conversations.

For example, in international business negotiations, it has been found that Brazilians tend to interrupt twice as much as either Japanese or U.S. Americans during conversations. In addition, Japanese negotiators tend to use silence most, U.S. Americans use it a moderate amount, and Brazilian negotiators almost none at all (Graham, 1985). Like the Brazilians, the French are inclined to use interruptions to create "fireworks" in their "serious" conversations, especially in established relationships. The French interruption–punctuation pattern signals "interest in the other's remark, which merits a commentary, a word of appreciation, denial, protest, or laughter—in short, a reaction without which the remark would 'fall flat.' The ball is tossed to be caught and tossed back. Where there is no 'interruption,' when each person speaks sedately in turn (as in American conversation, according to the French), the conversation never 'takes off'; it remains polite, formal, cold" (Carroll, 1987, p. 37). The interruption pattern reflects interaction spontaneity, enthusiasm, and a source of stimulation. However, the continuous interruption pattern in French conversation often baffles U.S. Americans.

Regulators are vocalic and kinesic behaviors that we learn at a very young age. We use them at a very low level of awareness. The use of regulators with different rhythms and punctuations often cause intercultural distress and misunderstandings. However, while individuals from contrastive cultures may experience such interaction frustrations, they may not be able to articulate the reasons for them. Regulators are the most rule-governed nonverbal interaction category, unconsciously reflecting the norms of the larger culture.

Additionally, vocal segregates such as "*hai, hai*" in Japanese and "uh-huh" in English can be classified as nonverbal regulatory devices. For the Japanese, vocal pause-filler cues such as "*hai, hai*" mean "I'm hearing you"; however, the literal translation of "*hai*" means "yes" to Westerners. Intercultural misunderstanding can easily occur when, for instance, Westerners think the Japanese have actually signaled "yes" to a contract agreement by saying "*hai, hai*" while the Japanese think they have merely acknowledged hearing the speaker's statement.

Moreover, changing body posture, using terminating gestures, and breaking off eye contact are some examples of turn-yielding cues in typical U.S. conversations. Within the U.S. culture, however, ethnic groups such as African American, European American, Latino/a American, and Asian immigrant groups have been found to follow different eye contact norms in regulating conversations. For example, it has been found that African Americans tend to maintain eye contact when speaking and break off eye contact when listening; European Americans tend to break off eye contact when speaking and maintain eye contact when listening (LaFrance & Mayo, 1978). Interethnic expectancy violations exist when African Americans expect the European Americans to look them in the eyes when speaking but instead receive "nonresponsiveness" or "indifference" cues. European Americans, on the other hand, may view the direct eye gaze during speaking as "confrontational" or "aggressive." Of the four groups, Latino/a Americans appear to engage in more intense and prolonged eye contact during conversations than do European American, African American, and Asian immigrant groups, in that order. Furthermore, Asian immigrants and Native Americans have been taught to show respect, especially when conversing with elderly or high-status persons, by averting eye contact (i.e., in order to signal self-effacing status). Status position, gender role, and situational norms strongly influence the various uses of nonverbal cues. Within a pluralistic society, we should pay mindful attention to the ethnic diversity of nonverbal communication styles.

Finally, *adaptors* are nonverbal habits or gestures that are reactions to internal or external stimuli and are used to satisfy psychological or physical needs. Some are learned within a culture (such as covering the mouth when we cough, or blowing the nose using a handkerchief) and others are more automatic (such as scratching an itch). Most are not intended to communicate a message. However, some of these habits can be considered rude in the context of another culture (e.g., never chew gum in public in France; whistling under any circumstances in India is considered impolite; pointing a finger in the Arab world is considered a rude gesture; and winking may be considered an insult or a sexual proposition in India and Pakistan). Using adaptors in the wrong context or at the wrong time can create great distress and confusion in cultural strangers who are unaccustomed to the display of these nonverbal habits.

Impression Formation and Attraction

When we manage our impressions on the nonverbal level, we are concerned with creating a favorable impression in the presence of others so that they can either be attracted to us or at least find us credible. Impression formation and interpersonal attraction are closely intertwined. Perceived physical attractiveness has been consistently associated with positive impression formation. Cultural values and norms, however, influence the implicit criteria we hold for what constitutes perceived attractiveness or unattractiveness.

Research in the United States, for example, indicates that physical appearance is closely associated to perceived attractiveness. Perceived attractiveness, in turn, is closely related to perceived desirable personality characteristics such as appearing more sensitive, kind, sociable, pleasant, likable, and interesting than those who are perceived as unattractive (Dion, 1986; Patzer, 1985). Attractive people are also evaluated as more competent and intelligent in the United States (Ross & Ferris, 1981).

In comparing U.S. and Japanese perceptions of attractiveness, U.S. college students have consistently rated smiling faces (both American and Japanese faces) as more attractive, intelligent, and sociable than neutral faces. Although the Japanese students have rated smiling faces as more sociable than neutral faces, they have evaluated neutral faces as more intelligent. Additionally, the Japanese students do not perceive smiling faces as being more attractive than neutral faces (Matsumoto & Kudoh, 1993).

In terms of the perceived credibility aspect, facial composure and body posture appear to influence our judgments of whether individuals appear to be credible (i.e., have high social influence power) or not credible (i.e., have low social influence power). In some Asian cultures (e.g., South Korea and Japan), influential people tend to maintain restrained facial expressions and postural rigidity. In the U.S. culture, however, relaxed facial expressions and posture are associated with credibility and giving positive impressions (Burgoon et al., 1996).

Overall, we can conclude that perceived attractiveness and credibility are two culturally laden phenomena whose meaning reflects social agreements that are created and sustained through cultural nonverbal practices.

SPACE AND TIME ACROSS CULTURES

Space and time are boundary-regulation and identity-protection issues because we, as humans, are territorial animals. Our primary identities are tied closely with our claimed territories. When our territories (e.g., extending from our home down to our personal space) are "invaded," our identities perceive threats and experience emotional vulnerability. Protective territory or sacred space satisfies our needs for human security, trust, inclusion, connection, and stability. In this section we shall consider the following three themes: interpersonal spatial boundary regulation, environmental boundary regulation, and temporal regulation.

Interpersonal Spatial Boundary Regulation

Interpersonal spatial boundary regulation of interpersonal space can be discussed in relation to two nonverbal classification systems: proxemics and haptics.

Proxemics

Proxemic studies examine the functions and regulation of interpersonal space in different cultures. Claiming a space for oneself means injecting one's sense of identity or selfhood into a place. For instance, we often use object markers such as books, coats, and umbrellas to "mark" or "claim" our favorite chair or table in a classroom or library.

According to Hall's (1966) proxemic theory, the use of interpersonal space or distance helps individuals regulate intimacy by controlling sensory exposure. Hall observes that middle-class European Americans typically use the following four spatial distances: (1) *intimate distance*—from body contact to 18 inches, a distance for lovemaking, comforting, whispering secrets, and the like; (2) *personal distance*—from 18 inches to 4 feet, a distance that enables personal to casual conversations to take place and in which people carry an invisible "space bubble" surrounding them; (3) *social distance*—from 4 to 12 feet, a distance reserved for formal business transactions or formal social interaction; and (4) *public distance*—from 12 to 25 feet, a suitable distance for public lectures or performances. Intercultural irritations most often occur in defining what constitutes intimate space as opposed to personal space.

What constitutes appropriate personal distance for one cultural group can be perceived as crowding by another group. The average conversational distance or personal space for European Americans is approximately 20 inches. For some Latin American and Caribbean cultural groups (e.g., Costa Ricans, Puerto Ricans, Bahamians, and Jamaicans), however, the average personal space is approximately 14–15 inches. For the Saudi, the ideal conversational distance between two Arabs is approximately 9–10 inches (Ferraro, 1990). When Arabs overstep the personal space boundary of European Americans, they are often considered "rude" and "intrusive." On the other hand, Arab negotiators frequently find European Americans to be "aloof," "cold," and "standoffish." Personal space often serves as a "hidden dimension" of intercultural misunderstanding and discomfort (Hall, 1966). Personal space is our unconscious protective territory that we carry around with us and deem sacred, nonviolable, and nonnegotiable.

While members of all cultures engage in the claiming of space for themselves or for the collective effort, the experience of spaciousness and crowdedness and the perception of space violation and space respect vary from one culture to the next.

The key mediating variable appears to be associated with the need for sensory exposure and contact in different cultures. Sensory exposure means the need for tactile (touch) and olfactory (smell) modes of communication. People in high-contact cultures appear to have high tactile and olfactory needs in their communication process with others; those in low-contact cultures appear to have more visual needs than the other two needs (Hall, 1966).

People in cultures favoring high sensory exposure require much personal contact. Those in cultures favoring low sensory exposure require little personal contact. The French, Italians, Latin Americans, Russians, Arabs, and Africans are members of high-contact cultures. U.S. Americans, Canadians, northern Europeans, New Zealanders, and Australians are members of moderate-contact cultures, as are, to a lesser degree, Germans and Danes. East Asians such as Chinese, Japanese, and Koreans are members of low-contact cultures (Barnlund, 1975; Hall, 1976; Watson, 1970).

In a high-contact culture communicators face one another directly, often look one another in the eye, interact closely with one another, often touch one another, and speak in a rather loud voice. In a low-contact culture, in contrast, interactants face one another more indirectly, interact with a wider space between them, engage in little or no touching, prefer indirect eye glances, and speak in a soft-to-moderate tone of voice (Watson, 1970). As moderate-contact culture has a mixture of both high-contact and low-contact nonverbal interaction characteristics. Andersen (1997) argues that high-contact cultures tend to be located in warmer climates or regions whereas low-contact cultures tend to be located in cooler climates or regions. He concludes that cultures in warmer climates tend to be more socioemotional oriented than task oriented, and cultures in cooler climates tend to be more task oriented than socioemotional oriented. A possible explanation is that survival in warmer climates is far less dependent on task collaboration: people can focus more on sensual pleasures and touch, and enjoy one another more on the socioemotional level. In extremely cold climates, however, human survival depends on the development of task solutions to solve the climatic problems. The heavy layers of clothing that individuals must wear to protect themselves from the cold may also tend to interfere with frequent close contact.

Beyond climate, many factors, of course, influence the use of interaction space and touch behaviors. For example, in testing the proxemic theory of sensory exposure, researchers examined the use of personal distance in Japanese, Venezuelan, and U.S. American students. Results indicate that (1) when speaking their native languages, Japanese students sit further apart than do Venezuelan students, with U.S. American students sitting at an intermediate distance; (2) females tend to sit closer together than males do in all three groups; and (3) when speaking English, students from Japan and Venezuela use personal distances more closely approximating U.S. American spatial distance norms (Sussman & Rosenfeld, 1982). While Venezuela has been identified as a high-contact culture, the United States has been deemed a moderate-contact culture and Japan has been deemed a low-contact culture. Apparently, when individuals converse in their native language, its use triggers a broader package of culturally appropriate behaviors.

Other research indicates that the Japanese prefer greater interaction distances with their professors, friends, and fathers than do Japanese Americans in Hawaii and European Americans on the U.S. mainland (Engebretson & Fullman, 1972). Nonverbal studies also reveal that while African American children exhibit closer interaction distances than do European American children, by the fifth grade these differences are minimized (e.g., Halberstadt, 1991; Scherer, 1994). By age 16, however, African Americans tend to maintain greater conversational distances with adolescent European Americans than with adolescents of their own race. Latino(a) Americans tend to interact at closer distances than do European Americans or African Americans.

In terms of spatial violation behavior, several studies suggest that members of individualistic cultures tend to take an active, aggressive stance when their space is violated, whereas members of collectivistic cultures tend to assume a passive, withdrawal stance when their personal space is intruded upon (Gudykunst & Ting-Toomey, 1988). Cultural values, language usage, gender difference, age, and context are all key factors to watch for in attempting to understand the complex proxemic behaviors in various situations in different cultures.

Haptics

Haptic studies investigate the perceptions, functions, and meanings of touch behavior as communication in different cultures. Different cultures encode and interpret touch behavior in different ways. Touch is used to fulfill five communicative functions: (1) ritualistic interaction such as shaking hands or bowing; (2) expressing affect such as kissing and kicking; (3) playfulness such as flirtatious stroking and poking; (4) a control function such as grabbing someone's arm; and (5) a task-related function such as a nurse taking a patient's pulse at the wrist (Jones & Yarborough, 1985).

Different cultures have different expectations as to who should touch whom in different interaction scenes. For example, while Chinese view opposite-sex handshakes as acceptable, Malays and Arabs view contact by opposite-sex handshakes as taboo. Furthermore, different cultures uphold different gender norms for embracing and handholding. The friendly full embrace between males is much more acceptable in many Latin American cultures than in Britain or the United States. Likewise, the friendly arm link pattern between two males in Arab and Latin American cultures is a commonplace practice. The friendly handholding pattern between two females in many Asian cultures is also common nonverbal practice (Barnlund, 1975). As Nydell (1987) observes,

In general, Arabs tend to stand and sit closer and to touch other people (of the same sex) more than Westerners do. It is common to see two men or two women holding hands as they walk down a street, which is simply a sign of friendship. A Westerner must be prepared for the possibility that an Arab will take his hand, especially when crossing the street.... Kissing on both cheeks is a common form of greeting (again, only with members of the same sex), as is embracing. (p. 44)

Arab and Western cultures differ considerably on the nonverbal norms of haptics. These norms, however, are often out of their conscious awareness. The tendency for North Americans to remain outside the appropriate haptic zone of Arabs often leads to the Arabs suspecting the speakers' intentions. Arabs tend to see such distancing nonverbal acts as "insincere" and "cold." Conversely, the need for close contact of Arabs often constitutes a violation of the personal space and privacy of most North Americans, who tend to consider such nonverbal intrusive acts as "aggressive" and "belligerent."

Comparative haptic studies on touch behaviors in Latin American cultures and U.S. and Canadian cultures also indicate that Latino(a)s tend to engage in more frequent touch behaviors than do U.S. Americans and Canadians (Engebretson & Fullman, 1972; Mayo & LaFrance, 1977; Shuter, 1976). However, it is important to remember that the touch behaviors in both the Arab and the Latin American cultures are usually confined to same-sex touching rather than opposite-sex touching. Furthermore, while Latin Americans and southern Europeans view kissing and hugging as spontaneous expressions of their positive feelings, many Asian cultures do not subscribe to such overt display of affection. The French, for example, like to kiss acquaintances on both cheeks. In comparison, Britons practice "vacuum kisses" and not actual kisses.

Different cultures uphold different standards and expectations concerning the amount of touching permitted, what areas of the body is it proper and improper to touch, and whom one should or should not touch. Finally, the rules of appropriate and inappropriate touch behaviors are much more stringent in collectivistic cultures than in individualistic cultures. Similarly, rules of respect and deference as expressed through proper nonverbal behaviors are much more exacting in large power distance cultures than in small power distance cultures.

Environmental Boundary Regulation

We will discuss environmental boundary regulation in two parts: physical boundary regulation, and psychological boundary regulation.

Physical Boundary Regulation

Our claimed primary territories (e.g., homes, farms, community properties) offer us a sense of security, interaction trust or predictability, and inclusion.

Primary territories are places or locations that are central to our lives and to which we have a strong emotional attachment; secondary territories are places such as neighborhood markets or bars to which we feel less connected (Altman & Chemers, 1980).

It is important to keep in mind, however, that how people define primary and secondary territories can be culturally and subjectively based. A neighborhood bar, for some people, may be their second home or "turf," and hence would be their primary territory needing to be defended from outsiders. Concepts of territory and identity are intertwined because we usually invest lots of time, effort, emotion, and self-worth in places that we claim as our primary territories. Our home territory or immediate environment asserts a strong influence on our everyday lives.

Lewin (1936), for example, focuses our attention on the importance of environment in influencing human behavior. He introduces the following formula for human behavior: $B = f(P, E)$, where B = behavior, P = person, and E = environment. Simply put, Lewin believes that human behavior is defined by the persons interacting as well as the environment in which the communication takes place. For example, the middle-class home environment in Canada and the United States is very different from the middle-class home environment in many Latin American and Asian cultures.

In the United States, for example, the middle-class home environment typically is separated from the community at large by fences with gates and by yards with lawns in the front and back. In contrast, in Mexico, the middle-class home environment is developed in such a way that the architectural design of the house is integrated with that of a central plaza possibly containing a community center and a church. While U.S. middle-class homes appear to reflect individualistic values, Mexican middle-class homes appear to promote collectivism and group-based interaction.

Overall, North American homes often symbolize the desire of the owners to assert their individual identities and separate themselves from one another. They create boundaries in both the external and internal environments of their homes. These boundaries are exercised through the use of gates, lawns, living rooms, separate bedrooms, private bathrooms, and many locks. Similarly, Hall (1983) observes that in Germany homes, like offices, have heavy soundproof doors and double-locks. It is considered rude to enter someone's room in Germany without knocking. Elaborate laws also govern German gardens such that trees must be planted at a prescribed distance without shading the neighbor's property (i.e., not even a shadow may intrude upon the other's garden). In Norwegian homes, in comparison, the use of high shrubbery, trees, fences, and large carved doors shield the homes from public sight. While the issue of privacy is critical for both German and Norwegian homes, the means to protect or express such privacy differs between cultures.

Furthermore, different cultural assumptions are attached to the diverse ways guests or outsiders should be entertained: at home versus in public places. Cultural members hold different expectations concerning the specific functions of different rooms in the house. For example, in some Asian cultures such as China, Korea, and Japan, the proper way to entertain guests is in a formal restaurant, because of self-effacement cultural values (i.e., home is a humble habitat for the family). In contrast, many Arabs, like U.S. Americans and Canadians, do not mind entertaining guests in their homes. The difference is that while many Arab homes reserve a specific formal room (with exquisite heirlooms and furnishings) to entertain guests and the guests may not see any other part of the house (until the relationship is trusted), many American hosts may take their guests on a tour around the entire house before settling in. In many Arab homes, separate quarters are also reserved for male and female activities.

Interestingly, in many traditional Japanese homes, families and close friends usually sit in a multipurpose room to chat, eat, and drink. Traditional Japanese homes do not make clear distinctions between the living room, dining room, and bedroom. Thus, when close friends are invited over, it is critical for them to remove their shoes before entering the multipurpose space, the floor of which is covered with straw mats, or *tatami*. While many of these Japanese homes do not separate eating from sleeping areas, they make a strong distinction between the bathroom (*ofuro*), used solely for bathing, and the toilet room (*otearai*). From the Japanese cultural perspective, to mix up bathing (a cleaning function) and toileting (a dirtying function) is against their code of civility and personal hygiene.

To put it simply, many individualistic cultures foster personal identity-type home environments whereas many collectivistic cultures encourage communal-type home settings. In our early childhood homes we all have acquired, on an unconscious level, our cultural norms of how to deal with space and boundary issues through social roles, furniture arrangements, and proper interaction etiquettes to be performed in each room. We turn now to psychological space and privacy regulation issues.

Psychological Boundary Regulation

On the psychological level, privacy regulation refers to the selective monitoring of closedness and openness or access to the self or to one's group (Altman, 1975, p.18). While privacy regulation can be achieved by carving out spacious areas for home in uncrowded countries like New Zealand or Australia, population density and crowded environmental conditions make it virtually impossible for people in many Asian countries (e.g., China, India, Indonesia, and Japan) to maintain personal privacy or intrapersonal space.

Intrapersonal space refers to the need for information privacy or psychological quietness between the self and others. While privacy regulation is a major concern in many Western social environments, the issue may not be perceived as very critical in many collectivistic-oriented cultures. In fact, the concept of privacy carries heavily negative connotations in many collectivistic cultures. For example, the Chinese words that closely correspond to the concept "privacy" are "secretive" and "selfishness," both with heavy pejorative meanings. This is not to say that Chinese do not need personal privacy or space. It just implies that many Chinese believe that relational interconnection should override the importance of personal privacy in everyday interactions.

Likewise, for many Arab cultures, the concept of privacy is baffling at best because in translation the Arabic word that comes closest to the concept "privacy" means "loneliness" (Nydell, 1996, p. 29). The following example illustrates the Arab's construction of the meaning of "privacy": When an exhausted American guest, after 3 hours of partying and loud music, decided to step onto the balcony for some fresh air, her worried Cairo host immediately followed after her and asked, "Is anything wrong? Are you angry at someone?" (Nydell, 1996, p. 30).

If a culture does not emphasize linguistic categories such as "privacy" and "solitary" to guide everyday interactions, then such categories may not be a critical part of the everyday social reality. Language, in conjunction with myriads of nonverbal cues, directs our perceptions and attitudes toward the functions of space and time.

Drawing from the identity negotiation theory presented in Chapter 2, psychological and physical boundary regulation serves to satisfy human needs for balancing identity safety and vulnerability, trust and unfamiliarity, and inclusion and differentiation. To the extent that we perceive territorial safety, we feel comfortable in our interaction with others. To the extent that we perceive identity threat, we build up defenses via physical or symbolic means. Spatial regulation is, indeed, a powerful means of marking in-group and out-group boundaries, and of differentiating "self" versus "others" in diverse intergroup contact settings.

Temporal Regulation

Temporal regulation is reflective of our spiritual, relational, and task-oriented attitudes toward the time frame in which communication is taking place. We all know that time flies when two friends are enjoying themselves and having a good time. Time crawls, however, when two ex-friends are staring at each other with nothing to say to one another.

The study of time is referred to as the study of chronemics. Chronemics concerns how people in different cultures structure, interpret, and understand the time dimension. Our developmental identities (i.e., at different age-linked stages) are closely tied in with the sense of time. Our conceptions of birth, development, aging, and death are related to the consciousness of time dimension. Our religious or spiritual beliefs, in terms of where the universe begins and ends, and where life begins and ends are also two temporal-related worldview questions.

On the cultural-specific level, Kluckhohn and Strodtbeck's (1961) value orientation of time indicates that some cultures (e.g., many African cultures) emphasize the past–present time continuum whereas other cultures emphasize the future time continuum (e.g., Australia, Canada, and the United States). Cultural temporal patterns designate when and how we should start the day, and when we should eat, work, play, sleep, even die, and reincarnate.

Hall (1983) distinguishes two patterns of time that govern different cultures: the *monochronic time schedule* (M-time) and the *polychronic time schedule* (P-time). According to Hall and Hall (1987), the M-time and P-time are empirically quite distinct: people in M-time cultures pay attention to clock time and do one thing at a time; people in P-time pay attention to relational time and may be involved in many simultaneous activities. They elaborate:

In monochronic cultures, time is experienced and used in a linear way—comparable to a road extending from the past to the future. M-time is divided quite naturally into segments; it is scheduled and compartmentalized, making it possible for a person to concentrate on one thing at a time. In a monochronic system, the schedule may take on priority above all else and be treated as sacred and unalterable. (p. 16)

For Hall and Hall (1987), the United States, Germany, and Switzerland represent classic examples of M-time cultures. As to P-time cultures, they comment,

P-time is characterized by the simultaneous occurrence of many things and by *a great involvement with people*. There is also more emphasis on completing human transactions than on holding to schedules. For example, two polychronic Latins conversing on a street corner would likely opt to be late for their next appointments rather than abruptly terminate the conversation before it came to a natural conclusion. (pp. 17–18; emphasis in original)

For Hall and Hall (1987), Arab, African, Latin American, Asian, and Mediterranean cultures are representatives of P-time patterns. For example, according to Pennington (1990), for many Africans, time is viewed in the context of

establishing a complexity of balanced relationships: . . . time [is] used [1] to establish a relationship with the Supreme Being; [2] to establish a relationship of continuity between the present and past generations; [3] to establish a relationship with nature and the forces of one's environment (nature); and [4] to create group harmony and participation among the living. This sense of temporal synchronization and group connectedness can be seen in the performing arts of Africans, such as dance and drumming. Time for traditional Africans, has been organic, rather than mechanical. (p. 137)

People that follow M-time patterns usually engage in one activity at a time. They compartmentalize time schedules to serve personal identity needs, and they tend to separate task-oriented time from socioemotional time. For M-time people, time is a tangible commodity. On the other hand, people that follow P-time tend to engage in multiple activities at the same time (e.g., in China, the doctors can simultaneously be treating their patients while talking with visiting relatives about unrelated medical topics). P-time people tend to hold more fluid attitudes toward time schedules and appointments, and they tend to blend socioemotional need with task accomplishment. For P-time individuals, time is a relational issue rather than a clock time issue (Tung, 1994; Ting-Toomey, 1994a).

Members of individualistic cultures tend to follow the M-time pattern, whereas members of collectivistic cultures tend to follow the P-time pattern. Members of individualistic cultures tend to view time as something that can be controlled and arranged. Members of collectivistic cultures tend to view time as experientially based (i.e., living and experiencing time fully rather than monitoring clock time mechanically).

Beyond M-time and P-time, Hall (1959) also differentiates five time zones for arriving late for appointments in accordance with European American reflections: (1) mumble something time (5–10 minutes late, approximately); (2) slight apology time (10–15 minutes late); (3) mildly insulting or serious apology time (15–30 minutes late); (4) rude time (30–45 minutes late); and (5) downright insulting time (45–60 minutes late). For people who follow M-time schedules stringently (e.g., many northern Europeans and European Americans), their working unit of time is the 5-minute block. If they are 5-minutes late for an appointment, they mumble something. If they are 15 minutes late—a block of time representing three significant units—they are expected to make a block of time representing three significant late, they are expected to offer a serious apology with a persuasive reason for their lateness.

For other cultures, such as some of the Arab and Latin American cultures, a historical time perspective is important. Arab culture, for example, has a 6,000-year history, and many Arabs will "address the historical aspects of a situation before addressing the current issue. The working unit of time for many Arabs is also a much larger block of time than that of European Americans—about 15 minutes" (Cushner & Brislin, 1996, p. 285). Thus, if Arab visitors are 30 minutes late, their mindset may indicate "2 units" of delay time. They may not even "mumble something" to express an apology, especially when the reason concerns taking care of family or kinship affairs. They will expect understanding from those who are waiting for them. The Arabic word *ma'alish* means "never mind, or it doesn't matter . . . it's not that serious. You will hear this said frequently when someone has had a delay, a disappointment, or an unfortunate experience. . . . Arabs often react to . . . adversity with resignation and, to some extent, an acceptance of their fate" (Nydell, 1996, p. 71).

In sum, individualistic cultures are clock time oriented and short-term goal oriented. Collectivistic cultures are relationally oriented in their time attitude and historically oriented in terms of long-term goal planning. Individualists tend to protect their individual identity via exacting use of clock time, and collectivists tend to mark their communal identities by treating time from a relational standpoint. Intercultural frictions occur frequently because people in different cultures have different time orientations (see Table 5.1).

A synergistic, common ground can be developed when individuals from contrastive M-time and P-time schedules come to some common point of understanding such that M-time people can learn to establish a wider window of appointment time (e.g., "I'll wait for you from 11:00 to 11:30") or deadline schedule (e.g., "The delivery date is between Wednesday and Friday") and P-time people learn to honor deadlines because of such flextime orientation from the other parties. Culture serves as the normative frame in which expectations concerning appropriate or inappropriate nonverbal behaviors are defined and interpreted.

INTERPERSONAL SYNCHRONY AND NONVERBAL CAUTIONS

Two areas that give us additional insights into the nonverbal dynamics between people from the same or different cultures are interpersonal interactive synchrony and nonverbal cautions.

Interpersonal Interactive Synchrony

Interpersonal synchronization is needed to function appropriately and effectively within and between cultures. According to Hall (1983), interper-

TABLE 5.1. Characteristics of Monochronic Time (M-Time) and Polychronic Time (P-Time)

M-time	P-time
Clock time	Situational time
Appointment time	Flextime
Segmented activities	Simultaneous activities
Task-oriented perspective	Relationship-oriented perspective
Achievement tempos	Experiential tempos
Future-focused approach	Past/present-focused approach
Tangible outcome orientation	Historical orientation

sonal synchrony refers to convergent rhythmic movements between two people on both the verbal and the nonverbal levels. Every facet of human behavior is involved in the rhythmic process. As Hall asserts, "It can now be said with assurance that individuals are dominated in their behavior by complex hierarchies of interlocking rhythms. Furthermore, these same interlocking rhythms are comparable to fundamental themes in a symphonic score, a keystone in the interpersonal processes between mates, co-workers, and organizations of all types on the interpersonal level within as well as across cultural boundaries" (p.153). Based on kinesic and proxemic film research, results indicate that the interpersonal synchronization between individuals within the same culture displays incredible synchrony or mirroring effect. The process appears rhythmic, and the individuals are locked together in a "dance" that functions almost totally out of awareness.

Hall (1983) observes that people in African and Latin American cultures seem to be more conscious of these rhythmic movements than are people in northern European, U.S., and Canadian cultures. The fact that synchronized rhythmic movements are based on the "hidden dimensions" of nonverbal behavior might explain why people in African and Latin American cultures (with emphasis on high-context nonverbal modes) display more sensitivity toward nonverbal synchronous rhythms than do people in U.S. and Canadian cultures (with emphasis on low-context verbal modes). As Kochman (1990) notes,

[For some African Americans,] the hand-to-hand exchange that they call *giving skin* is invigorated by its connection to inner impulses and feelings and one's spiritual connection with others in the group. The genuineness and strength of both connections act as a catalyst to ignite the sensibilities and actions of others who respond by giving skin in return. The integrated structuring of elements within call and response means that giving is getting and getting is giving, in a rhythmic, interlocking, escalating, synergistic go-around. (p. 197)

African Americans' habitual use of the call and response pattern on both verbal and nonverbal levels has often led to miscommunication with European Americans, who do not use the pattern. African Americans tend to infer from the absence of a response that "the Whites to whom they are speaking are not listening. White speakers tend to infer from the various responses like 'Dig it!' or 'I hear you!' which Blacks consider necessary and appropriate interpolations . . . as that Blacks are constantly *interrupting* them" (Kochman, 1990, p.199; emphasis in original).

Furthermore, collectivists appear to have a higher need to fully complete the rhythmic pattern of a conversational episode (i.e., beginning, middle, and ending action chains) than do individualists. An action chain is defined as a rhythmic sequence of events in which people alternately "release appropriate responses in each other in order to achieve an agreed-upon or predictable goal. The steps or links in the chain . . . vary from culture to culture" (Hall & Hall, 1987, p. 183). For example, it often takes Arabs a longer time to complete a nonverbal greeting ritual, to display hospitality, to introduce a topic, to maintain a topic, and to end a conversation. The common Arabic greeting ritual includes "*Ahlan wa Sahlan or Marhaba*"—meaning "welcome"—repeated several times during a guest's visit. In addition, the following action components are followed: "A guest is often given a seat of honor (this is particularly common as a gesture to a foreigner), and solicitous inquiries are made of the guest's comfort during the visit . . . [as well as] offering something to drink" (Nydell, 1996, pp. 68–69). All these greeting activities must be accomplished before the host and the visiting guest can be fully satisfied with the entire initial interaction.

In contrast, individualists (e.g., from Australia and Canada) have a relatively low need to complete an action chain on the nonverbal level. They tend to approach greeting, maintenance, and goodbye rituals at a faster pace than is used in many collectivistic cultures. Whatever members of individualistic cultures do not accomplish on the nonverbal level, they can rely on words to complete the interaction ritual. However, for collectivists, nonverbal rhythm is an intangible but important aspect of interaction. This is because "nature's cycles are rhythmic, it is understandable that rhythm and tempo are distinguishing features of any culture. Rhythm ties the people of a culture together and can also alienate them from members of other cultures" (Hall & Hall, 1987, p. 18).

In some cultures people move very slowly and subtlety. In other cultures, people move with energy and vitality. When people from two such cultures meet, they are apt to have difficulty relating because they are not "in sync." Synchronized action chain is vital to all collaborative efforts. Synchrony—the ability to move together with a mirror effect—can be observed and achieved through synchronized breathing, synchronized attentiveness, and synchronized other-orientation.

Interpersonal synchrony or convergence is achieved when the nonverbal behavior between two individuals moves toward smoothness, responsiveness, and spontaneity. Interpersonal divergence occurs when the nonverbal behavior between two individuals moves toward difficulty, rigidity, and awkwardness. Interpersonal synchrony signifies increased rapport and trust, whereas interpersonal divergence signifies increased distance and mistrust.

Nonverbal Cautions

Members from similar identity groups typically display rhythmic synchrony; members from dissimilar identity groups often experience interaction awkwardness. However, while cultural differences assert a strong influence on nonverbal patterns across cultures, tremendous within-culture variations also exist in any given system.

In discussing cross-cultural nonverbal differences, our emphasis is on "differences"—which means that the differences between cultures are exaggerated and the similarities between them are downplayed. Furthermore, within-culture variations are also glossed over. Thus, the following three factors should be taken into serious consideration when interpreting any nonverbal behaviors across cultures (Burgoon et al., 1996, pp. 216–217):

1. *Overgeneralization*—Variations within entire cultures, subcultures, age groups, genders, regions, or personality types are enormous. Within-culture differences are often glossed over or simplified because of their complexity.

2. *Mythical "average person"*—The "average person" of a culture is a hypothetical construct. It must be remembered that group norms represent an amalgamation of characteristics possessed by a majority of individuals. The phrase "a majority of individuals" is a projective statistic or a generalized image of what is going on in a culture based on selective empirical data.

3. *Viewing cultural norms as static*—Just as people constantly change over a lifetime, norms associated with various classes of people in different cultures are also dynamic. Thus nonverbal identity markers and nonverbal behaviors are subject to change based on a variety of group membership and personal identity factors.

In attempting to understand within-culture and across-culture nonverbal variations, interpersonal sensitivity, respect, and patience in dealing with such differences serve as a good first step in gaining nonverbal entrance to a culture.

RECOMMENDATIONS

To communicate mindfully on the intercultural nonverbal message exchange level, individuals should learn to do the following:

1. Identify the appropriate nonverbal display rules in different cultures. They have to use a situational analysis approach in patiently observing the matching of social role identities, statuses of performers, intimacy distance, social expectations, norms, scripts, props, proper language usage, and appropriate nonverbal behaviors—all in particular situations.

2. Understand the cultural values and attributions that are attached to different nonverbal norms and rules. Surface understanding of nonverbal differences does not offer the depth of explanation for day-to-day nonverbal operation in a given culture.

3. Realize that the fundamental functions and interpretations of any

nonverbal cues are tied closely to identity, emotional expression, conversational management, impression formation, and boundary regulation functions. Understanding what nonverbal behavior and cues serve primarily what functions in what situations will facilitate nonverbal interaction effectiveness.

4. Convey acknowledgment and culture-sensitive respect in regard to different nonverbal norms and behaviors in different ethnic and cultural communities. If individuals do not feel comfortable in nonverbally adapting, at a minimum they should mindfully monitor their ethnocentric interpretations and evaluations of "alien" nonverbal patterns (e.g., as arrogant or rude).

5. Deepen the complexities of their understanding of nonverbal behaviors within each culture along multiple dimensions such as ethnicity, gender, age, region, social class, relational variations, language usage, and situations. Different configurations of different dimensions impact the functions and interpretations of nonverbal cues in different cultural contexts.

6. Use culture-sensitive perception checking statements. Perception checking skill helps individuals make sure they are interpreting the speaker's nonverbal behavior accurately. It is a skill that can be used anytime when they are unsure they are understanding the meaning of the nonverbal behavior. Perception checking involves the use of clear, perceptual eyewitness statements and perceptual verification questions. For example, statements such as "From your tired facial expression, I can see that you need a break right now. Do you?" and "You have a confused look and seems like you want me to slow down. Should I?" are clear perception checking statements. Perception checking is part of mindful observation and mindful listening skills.

Mindful verbal and nonverbal communication requires the application of flexible, adaptive interaction skills. Appropriate verbal and nonverbal adaptation creates positive interaction synchrony. Positive interaction synchrony, in the long-run, facilitates quality intercultural relationship development. Communicative adaptability requires cognitive, affective, and behavioral flexibility. It signals our willingness and commitment to learn from culturally dissimilar others. It reflects our ability to change mindsets, behaviors, and goals to meet the specific needs of the people and the situation. It signals our desire to understand, respect, and support the other's cultural identity and way of communicating—and to do so with sensitivity and mindfulness.

III

BOUNDARY REGULATION AND INTERGROUP–INTERPERSONAL RELATIONSHIP DEVELOPMENTS

6

Identity Contact and Intergroup Encounters

Social Identity Theory and Its Associated Constructs: 146
   A Boundary-Regulation Approach 147
   Social Identity Theory 149
   Social Categorization 150
   Social Comparison 152
Intergroup Attribution: A Sense-Making Process 152
   Attribution Theory 154
   Intergroup Attribution Theory 156
Mindsets: Affective and Cognitive Filters 156
   Intergroup Perception 157
   Ethnocentrism and Communication 161
   Stereotypes and Communication 164
   Prejudice and Communication 169
   Reduction of Prejudice and Discrimination 171
Recommendations 171

Individuals often experience greater emotional vulnerability in their initial interactions with people from other cultural groups than with people from their own groups. This is due to the fact that with in-group cultural members they can use habitual scripts and interaction styles to communicate. However, with out-group members, the habitual scripts and styles do not appear to operate effectively.

Furthermore, since cultural strangers have limited norms and rules to guide their communication process, they often fall back to using stereotypes of other people's groups to bolster their predictions of cultural strangers' actions. While some of the stereotypes have kernels of approximate truth, many of the group-based stereotypes are inaccurate and so perpetuate further intergroup misunderstandings and prejudice.

An intergroup encounter can be an informative, cultural learning journey—if both parties are willing to open their eyes, ears, and mindsets. It can also, however, be an identity-threatening experience. Encountering strang-

145

ers in a culturally unfamiliar environment conjures emotional vulnerability and interaction unpredictability. It is a testing ground for boundary-regulation and identity-contesting issues.

This chapter examines some of the factors that contribute to in-group/out-group mindsets and how these mindsets affect the perceptual lenses we use to evaluate an intergroup encounter. In particular, the identity negotiation perspective in conjunction with social identity theory (Tajfel, 1981; Tajfel & Turner, 1986) and intergroup attribution theory guide the development of this chapter.

The chapter is organized in four main sections. First, the core ideas of social identity theory in relation to the identity negotiation perspective are discussed. Second, drawing from the bases of social identity theory and the identity negotiation perspective, intergroup attribution theory is presented. Third, intergroup mindsets of ethnocentrism, stereotyping, and prejudice are examined. Fourth, specific recommendations for breaking stereotypes and reducing prejudices are proposed.

SOCIAL IDENTITY THEORY AND ITS ASSOCIATED CONSTRUCTS: A BOUNDARY-REGULATION APPROACH

Initial intergroup encounters are typically fraught with anxiety and awkwardness. Even if the strangers are interacting via a common language, there are many complex perceptual factors at work that influence the intergroup impression formation process. This section discusses social identity theory and its associated constructs, social categorization and social comparison. Before we examine social identity theory, let us review identity negotiation theory briefly (it is discussed in detail in Chapter 2).

According to the identity negotiation perspective, our cultural or ethnic identity *consciousness* becomes more salient under the following conditions: (1) when we encounter an interaction threat and experience emotional vulnerability on the group membership level (e.g., prejudiced remarks); (2) when we encounter an identity valuation that leads to group membership pride (e.g., "Your country must be very proud of you in winning this Olympic gold medal!"); (3) when our membership identity is negatively stigmatized (e.g., "The X people are all tardy and unreliable!"); or (4) when our membership identity is stigmatized on a positive stereotypical level (e.g., "The Y people have such great musical rhythm!").

When one of these conditions is heightened, we oftentimes experience cultural or ethnic/racial identity distinctiveness. Communicating with strangers from another identity group involves the interplay processes of group-based differentiation and inclusion. Group-based differentiation and inclusion serve as the two "powerful social motives" for understanding the in-group and out-group boundary-regulation process (Billig, 1987; Brewer & Miller, 1996).

Out-group-based differentiation or contrast can be achieved by separating the self and the dissimilar other on salient group-membership dimensions (e.g., skin color, language, religion). In-group-based loyalty can be attained by identifying the self with salient in-group memberships (e.g., by ethnicity or race). Through intergroup comparative processes, individuals draw in-group/out-group membership boundaries. Such in-group/out-group membership boundary issues are related to the province of social identity theory. Boundary regulation also satisfies the basic human needs for group-based security, inclusion, and connection.

Social Identity Theory

Social identity theory informs us that people practice in-group favoritism and out-group differentiation (i.e., contrast) for the purpose of enhancing their social and personal identities. An enhanced social identity increases social self-esteem and self-worth. An increased sense of social self-esteem (e.g., self-worth based on group membership) also bolsters positive personal self-esteem (i.e., self-worth based on personal attributes in comparison to other individuals).

According to social identity theory, people can improve their membership self-image in two ways: by enhancing their in-group identity or by bolstering their personal identity (Tajfel, 1981). Both identity types are interdependent—enhancing one identity type can increase the attraction of the other. In-group identity refers to the emotional attachments and shared fate (i.e., perceived common treatment as a function of category membership) that we attach to our selective cultural, ethnic, or social group categories. Out-groups are groups to which we remain emotionally detached and that are cognitively distrusted by us. However, out-groups serve as the bases for social comparison in terms of group values, norms, behaviors, and achievements (Brewer & Miller, 1996).

From a social identity negotiation standpoint, it seems reasonable to argue that members of particular social groups often prefer to perceive their in-group attributes in a more positive rather than negative light, especially in comparison to other groups (e.g., Israelis vs. Palestinians). The more they view their salient in-group values and norms as desirable and rewarding, the more they tend to see their own membership identity as desirable and rewarding. Moreover, individuals often tend to assume that fellow in-group members are more similar to them than out-group members. The essential characteristics of the self and in-group relationship appear to be loyalty and preference.

Loyalty is defined as "adherence to [in-group] norms and trustworthiness in dealings with fellow [in-group] members" and *preference* is defined as "differential acceptance of [in-group] members over members of [out-groups] and positive evaluation of [in-group] characteristics that differ from those of [out-groups]" (Brewer & Miller, 1996, p. 24). Ethnocentric loyalty and preference upgrade social and personal self-esteem. Thus, in-group loyalty and preference lead to the principle of in-group favoritism.

The *in-group favoritism principle* states that there is positive attachment to and predisposition for norms and behaviors that are related to in-group categories more than to out-group categories. In-group favoritism ultimately enhances our desired in-group and personal identities. Personal identity refers to the individual attributes that we use to conceptualize our sense of "unique self" (e.g., individual motivation, intelligence, attractiveness) in comparison to other individuals. Overall, the experiments under the Minimal Group Paradigm project (in which subjects are arbitrarily divided into two groups) and other related studies show that participants consistently favor in-group members in rewarding points (or money) and attempt to maximize in-group/out-group contrast (Hogg & Abrams, 1988; Tajfel, 1981; Tajfel & Turner, 1986).

In addition, high-status groups whose perceived position is secure show less in-group bias in comparison to low-status groups. However, when the perceived status differences (i.e., the perceived power dimension) are threatened, both identity groups are motivated to establish in-group favoritism and out-group differentiation (Brewer & Kramer, 1985). In-groups can be of many different types, ranging from small, face-to-face groupings of family and friends to "large social categories such as gender, religion, and nationality. . . . [In-group] membership is more than mere cognitive classification—it carries emotional attachment as well. Attachment to [in-groups] and preference of [in-groups] over [out-groups] may be a universal characteristic of human life" (Brewer & Miller, 1996, p. 23).

If we evaluate our in-groups positively, we also view our own membership identities positively. This viewpoint is congruent with the identity negotiation perspective in this book: people in all cultures desire positive identities in their everyday interactions with others. One of the many ways to bolster their desired positive identities, especially in perceived identity threat situations, is to engage in positive in-group evaluations and negative out-group ratings.

Positive in-group evaluations can satisfy our needs for group-based identity security, trust, inclusion, and connection. Our need to trust (i.e., others act predictably or consistently) and our need to be trusted (i.e., to be viewed as acting consistently or honorably) drive us to stick with people whom we view as similar or familiar. With similar others, we assume we share similar values and outlooks. With dissimilar others, we experience identity threat and emotional vulnerability.

The in-group favoritism principle can also translate to our understanding of why people behave ethnocentrically in different cultures (see the "Ethnocentrism and Communication" section below). When we behave ethnocentrically, we are basically protecting our group membership boundaries and, more fundamentally, our habitual ways of thinking, feeling, and responding. Countless research studies across cultures (see, e.g., Devine, Hamilton, & Ostrom, 1994; Leyens, Yzerbyt, & Schadron, 1994) indicate that people in all cultures tend to behave with in-group favoritism and outgroup prejudice. The core construct, intergroup boundary regulation, together with two other constructs, social categorization and social comparison, lay the foundations of social identity theory.

Social Categorization

Social categorization is a fundamental quality of cognition. It offers us a way to manage our chaotic environment in a predictable and efficient fashion. It is also a function of human language—as a categorical organizing system reflecting our highly abstract thoughts. The consequences of social categorization lead to certain expectation states of how others should or should not behave in a certain way. These expectancy states are closely related to our stereotypes of dissimilar others.

A stereotype is a "broad generalization about an entire class of phenomena based on some knowledge of some members of the class" (Wood, 1997, p. 159). For example, when we stereotype French people as arrogant and rude, we may be basing our stereotypes on two to three incidents of interaction with a handful of French people. Conversely, we may not even have had any direct contact with French people at all; however, we might still have formed our mental images through selective media exposure or indirect sources such as hearsay.

Additionally, our social categorization process also frames our expectations and meanings we attach to people's behavior or action. For example, when we learn that someone is a "lesbian," we tend to be instantly guided by this linguistic category of "lesbian" and start perceiving this individual's every word and action as stemming from her sexual orientation identity. Sadly, her unique or other group-based identity tends to completely vanish or is unperceived.

Our linguistic categories also start to create polarized boundaries between me and you, us and them, females and males, Blacks and Whites, etc. Engaging in polarized thinking of good or bad, beautiful or ugly, and right or wrong can reduce our anxiety of dealing with gray areas between two polarities. It reduces interpretive and interaction complexities. It bolsters stability and predictability, especially if we are functioning in an unfamiliar environment. Unfortunately, polarized thinking also leads to a unidirectional view of the "correct" or "incorrect" way of behaving. For example, according to Wood (1997), "women who use assertive speech associated with masculinity are judged as arrogant and uppity," while "men who employ emotional language associated with femininity are often perceived to be wimps or gay" (p. 160).

Social categorization influences our tendency to accentuate the differences between membership categories and minimize variations within each of the categories. As Wood (1997) observes insightfully,

> In truth, of course, most of us have a number of qualities, some of which our society designates as feminine and some of which it defines as masculine. Polarized thinking about gender encouraged by our language restricts us from realizing the full range of human possibilities. By being aware of the tendencies to stereotype and think in polar terms, we enhance our capacity to question and resist limiting conceptions of masculinity and femininity. (pp. 160–161)

Generally, preconceived social categories help to frame our expectations and make our social world more predictable and meaningful in accordance with *our own cultural and personal frames of reference*. They also simultaneously delimit our thinking and perceptual capabilities. By being mindful of our own categorical and hence expectancy formation system, we may start debunking some of the myths or negative images we form about out-group members.

Social Comparison

In addition to the social categorization process, social identity theory posits that individuals strive for a positive social identity in social comparison to other groups (J. C. Turner, 1987). We compare the standing of our in-group with that of other groups in order to bolster our positive social identities. Or in-group is made up of those people who are emotionally close to us and with whom we experience identity security and trust. We can call upon members of our in-group in times of need.

Out-groups, on the other hand, consist of those people who are avoided or excluded as much as possible from our everyday experiences. Out-groups contain "people who are avoided, who are actively discouraged from seeking membership in [our in-group], and who are often distrusted" (Cushner & Brislin, 1996, p. 336).

Through comparison with other relevant social groups, the value of one's identity group is assessed and established. The need for positive social identities prompts individuals to compare their salient identity groups with other relevant social groups. The criteria for social comparison are situational specific, that is, dependent on the interaction task, conversation topic, and context that triggers the identity consciousness level. Oftentimes, social comparison can involve three comparative bases: lateral comparison, downward comparison, and upward comparison (Wills, 1991).

Lateral comparison refers to comparing one's identity group with other social or cultural groups who "should be" at essentially the same level. *Downward comparison* refers to comparing one's identity group with groups perceived as less powerful. *Upward comparison* refers to comparing one's identity group with groups perceived as more powerful than one's own. Research indicates that individuals most often engage in either lateral or downward comparison rather than upward comparison. Lateral or downward comparison bolsters individuals' membership and personal self-esteem level (Wills, 1991). The more one feels good about one's identity group, the more one experiences positive sentiments concerning one's social and personal selves.

Positive social comparison, in brief, enhances our sense of desired social and personal identities. In addition, social comparison is stage linked and motivation linked. For example, while new immigrants may initially compare their identity group with other recent immigrant groups, they may well engage in upward comparisons at a later adaptation stage when they feel capable of closing the gaps between their own group and the upward comparative groups.

What happens if group members experience negative social or cultural identities because of negative comparisons? Several options exist for such negative comparisons. Individuals can, for example, maintain a distancing posture from their in-group and not mingle with its members. They can deemphasize the importance of their social identities and maximize the importance of their personal identities (e.g., "The important thing about me is not that I'm a member of group X but that I'm an honest and hardworking person").

Individuals can also enhance their personal identities by allying themselves with members of high-status groups (e.g., "Although I wasn't chosen for membership in any of the country clubs, I now have several close friends who are members of the most prestigious country clubs—so I guess I have a likeable personality after all"). They can, conversely, downgrade the comparative group via biased intergroup attributions (e.g., "Who would ever want to join these boring country clubs—with all these boring people talking about boring topics"). They can also engage in an active social change process (e.g., push for new laws) to change the criteria for membership admission or, alternatively, create innovative options (e.g., start their own ethnic country clubs) (van Knippenberg, 1989; see also Orbe, 1998).

Lastly, when perceived group boundaries are permeable, individuals with negative social identities can switch group memberships (e.g., they can sometimes engage in "passing" as members of a more powerful racial group if their physical characteristics permit such a strategy). When perceived group boundaries are impermeable, individuals may not have many membership-switching options. They may also turn their frustrations to intergroup anger, hostility, and hatred. Through either positive or negative social comparisons, individuals' identities are impacted: positive social comparisons evoke positive social identities; negative social comparisons, in conjunction with many complex sociohistorical factors, induce negative social identities.

Thus, social identity theory emphasizes the importance of the reciprocal reinforcement of social identity and personal identity. A positive membership self-worth evokes a desirable personal identity. A positive personal identity, in turn, induces positive membership self-worth. In order to satisfy the various layers of identity needs, individuals engage in an in-group/out-group boundary-regulation process. While an optimal level of in-group identification satisfies individuals' security needs, an extreme level of in-group identification evokes rigid ethnocentrism, stereotypes, and intergroup prejudice.

INTERGROUP ATTRIBUTION: A SENSE-MAKING PROCESS

From the social categorization process to social comparison differentiations, intergroup attribution is a natural by-product of these interactive processes. The intergroup attribution process helps us to make sense of our intergroup encounters. It helps us to interpret and evaluate our in-group membership status and out-group membership role in our interactions. Together with the social identity process, the attribution process influences the formation of our in-group/out-group stereotypes and our prejudiced attitudes.

Attribution Theory

Attribution theory has been around ever since the publication of the seminal work of Fritz Heider in the mid-1940s (Heider, 1944, 1958). We shall first discuss the basic ideas of attribution theory and then examine the specifics of attribution errors and intergroup attribution biases.

The fundamental premise of attribution theory is that every human being is a naive psychologist with implicit assumptions, beliefs, and social categorizations of what human nature or human behavior is all about. In trying to "make sense" of other people's behavior, the perceiver is viewed as performing the important role of a causal attributor (E. Jones, 1990). We are motivated to attribute meanings or causes to people's behavior by some very practical concerns, such as managing our complex environment more predictably and with a sense of closure. Thus, we often use our implicit assumptions and built-in social categories to explain behaviors or events occurring around us. Generally, we interpret and explain human behavior either by attributing causation to the perceived disposition of the person under scrutiny (i.e., personality traits) or to environmental influences (i.e., situational factors) (Heider, 1958).

Attribution Biases

Kelley (1967) identified three inherent biases in the human attribution process. First, perceivers have a tendency to *overestimate* the influence of negative dispositional factors in explaining a stranger's negative performance and underestimate situational factors. This is known as the "fundamental attribution error." For example, if a stranger walks into a class late, we (as perceivers) might well attribute his or her behavior to "laziness and tardiness." However, if we walk into a class late, we would readily explain our negative behavior via situational factors such as car trouble, no parking space, or a sick friend needing our help at the last minute. Overall, when we engage in negative behavior, we protect our own social or personal identities by invoking justifiable situational causes. We tend, however, to be more stringent in explaining a stranger's negative behavior because we may not be aware of situational factors that frame her or his behavior. Furthermore, it is cognitively more efficient to engage in snapshot dispositional judgments rather than time-consuming, situational reasoning.

The second attribution bias stems from the fact that perceivers typically use the principle of negativity to explain a stranger's negative action. The *principle of negativity* refers to the tendency of individuals to attend to negative information as more salient than positive information (Kanouse & Hanson, 1972). Under the conditions of interpersonal competition or anonymity (i.e., we are not in direct contact with the strangers), we place a higher emphasis on negative information concerning strangers or members of out-groups than we place on positive evidence. In other words, the negative news catches our eyes more than the positive news does because of the accentuated "extraordinariness" of the negative news. Additionally, in-group/out-group interactions are anxiety provoking because of interaction uncertainty (i.e., a lack of information needed to predict others' behavior) (Gudykunst, 1995, 1998).

Given the heightened anxiety and uncertainty toward out-group-based interactions, we often fall back on negative stereotypes when interacting with out-group members. Negative stereotypes are the ones that most likely justify our perception of an identity threat in interacting with dissimilar strangers. Our perceived identity threat or fear also causes us to experience vulnerable defensive emotions (Pettigrew, 1979).

With preconceived negative stereotypes, we also look for negative out-group behaviors to confirm our negative expectations. Furthermore, we tend to subscribe to the *negative correlation principle* according to which if one out-group member engages in a negative action, we typecast the entire out-group as behaving in a similar negative manner because of our ignorance or overgeneralization.

The third attribution bias arises from the use of different types of attribution in accounting for positive or negative acts. This concerns attributions for our own behavior versus a stranger's behavior. For example, if we get a promotion (a positive act) in our organization, we will tend to attribute it to positive dispositional traits such as hard work and perseverance on our part. However, if a stranger gets a promotion, we would more likely attribute the promotion to luck or situational pressure. Similarly, if we get fired from our job, we might well attribute our misfortune to the bad economy or a budget cut in the organization. However, if a stranger gets fired, we would tend to use negative dispositional attributions such as "inertia and incompetence" to account for her or his being fired from the organization.

As perceivers, we engage in self-serving bias in coming up with positive dispositional reasons for desirable events that bolster our self-image while attributing situational reasons for pleasant events that happen to dissimilar others. This same sort of self-serving attributional bias is manifested in our use of situational reasons for undesirable events that unfold in our own lives while using negative dispositional reasons to explain undesirable events that befall dissimilar others.

The finding concerning positive self-serving bias is more applicable in individualistic than collectivistic cultures. For example, in comparing how U.S. students and Japanese students attribute success in recalling details of slides of scenes in unfamiliar countries, researchers have uncovered some interesting differences. The U.S. students tend to explain their successes more (i.e., remember accurate details) in terms of their ability than they did their failures. Japanese students, in contrast, tend to attribute their failures to lack of ability, which reflects a "self-effacement bias" (Smith & Bond, 1993; Kashima & Triandis, 1986).

Intergroup Attribution Theory

In extending attribution theory to the intergroup attribution process, Hewstone and Jaspars (1984) explain that this process is essentially social in nature. This is because (1) the process is to a large extent filtered through social interaction and is influenced by social information; (2) most attributions are social categorical in nature rather than interindividually based; (3) we typically share similar attributions with in-group members about out-groups' attributes; and (4) shared social attributions with in-groups enhance our positive social identities, and hence reinforce our social solidarity and identity inclusion with in-group members.

Hewstone (1989) refers to intergroup attribution in discussing how members of different social groups "explain the behavior, outcomes of behavior, and the social conditions that characterize members of their own [the in-group] and other [out-group] social groups" (p. 25). Using the same examples of job promotion and demotion as we did before, if an in-group member were to get a promotion, we would tend to attribute it to positive dispositional traits such as "hard work and determination." However, if an out-group member gained such a promotion, we would likely attribute this desirable event to any of the following possibilities: (1) external luck or a special quota advantage; (2) her or his manipulation of the system by networking with the right people; or (3) her or his being an exception to the group rather than reflective of the larger out-group norm (Pettigrew, 1978). Conversely, if an in-group member received a demotion, we might criticize it as an instance of unfair treatment or attribute the incident to an economic downsizing problem. However, if out-group members got demoted, we would likely use negative dispositional attributions to explain it (e.g., "They deserve it because they are always tardy and irresponsible") (see Figure 6.1).

Note that the intergroup attribution phenomenon is particularly reflective of individualistic Western cultures rather than collectivistic cultures. Cross-cultural research evidence indicates that for some Asian collectivistic cultures (e.g., China, India, and Japan), the intergroup attribution error works, but to a lesser degree. For example, people in India and Japan attribute more situational factors concerning out-group members' failed performance (e.g., demotions) and less reference to negative dispositional factors than do people in the United States (Kashima & Triandis, 1986).

The values of individualism and collectivism reinforce the notion that, overall, individualists tend to use dispositional attributions to explain the social world around them and collectivists tend to be more sensitive to situational features that frame behavior. Furthermore, the content of dispositional attributions (positive or negative) reflects the underlying values and norms of the cross-cultural perceivers. The nature of intergroup attributions directly affects the intergroup relationship formation process.

	Positive Event	Negative Event
In-group	Positive Dispositional Attributions	Situational Attributions
Out-group	Situational Attributions	Negative Dispositional Attributions

Attribution Process

FIGURE 6.1. In-group and out-group attribution differences.

MINDSETS: AFFECTIVE AND COGNITIVE FILTERS

Affective and cognitive filters refer to our reactive emotions and the perceptual lenses that we use in interpreting and evaluating out-group members' behaviors. They form part of our mindsets—a complex of mental outlooks on how to deal with in-group and out-group members. Affective and cognitive lenses include perceptions, ethnocentrism, stereotypes, and prejudice. While the in-group favoritism principle of social identity theory has helped to explain biased in-group behavior, the assumptions of intergroup attribution theory have shaped our understanding of prejudiced attitudes. Attitudes are cognitive and affective predispositions—learned via education, experience, and cultural programming—in responding toward individuals or groups of individuals.

Intergroup Perception

Human perception is the process of selecting cues from the social environment, organizing them into some coherent pattern, and interpreting that pattern. The selective perception, organization, and interpretation process is influenced profoundly by our cultural socialization. Our cultural beliefs and values have "programmed" us to attend to cues that are deemed valuable in our culture, and our language also directs us to aspects of social reality that are deemed important in our culture. We attach meanings to these incoming stimuli or behaviors based on our expectations, including preconceived categories, stereotypes, and personal attitudes. Our expectations influence the way we perceive and interpret cultural strangers' behavior, and likewise their reactions to us are based on their expectations and preconceptions.

Human perception and, more importantly, intergroup perception function in accordance with the following principles: (1) perception is a largely subjective phenomenon—we generally construct the reality of what we want to perceive, and this is basically a biased process; (2) perception is categorical—we use social or linguistic categories to guide our expectations in actual intergroup interactions; (3) perception is selective—we select information that fits our expectancy categories and ignore other incoming stimuli in our information-loaded environment; (4) perceptual patterns tend to be consistent—once we see something a certain way, we tend to continue to see the same pattern despite contradictory evidence; (5) perception is largely a learned process—to a great extent, it is learned through our cultural socialization; and (6) intergroup perception accentuates differences between identity groups.

The need to sustain a valued social or personal identity, the need to ward off identity threat, the need to protect our in-group boundaries, and the subjective nature of human perception lead to the development of ethnocentrism, stereotypes, and prejudice. Taken together, these three perceptual filters act as major barriers to effective intercultural communication. Ineffective communication between cultural groups often occurs because we assume that we perceive and interpret other people's behavior in an unbiased way. The reality, however, is that our perceptions of others are highly biased and selective. By understanding the forms and processes of how ethnocentrism, stereotypes, and prejudice operate, we can tune in to our biased preconceptions with a mindful analysis.

Ethnocentrism and Communication

Ethnocentrism is derived from the two Greek words *ethnos*, meaning nation, and *kentron*, meaning the center of a circle. "Ethno" is the prefix denoting cultural, ethnic, or racial groupings; "centrism" refers to the centrality of our own group. Ethnocentrism means that we hold views and standards that are "own group/centric" and make judgments about other groups based on our own group's values and beliefs. In the context of the Greek culture in the Golden Age, for example, those who spoke the Greek language were viewed as the "cultured" and "eloquent" people, while those who did not speak the language of Greece were labeled as *barbarikos*, or "barbarians" (i.e., those "aliens" whose language was incomprehensible and sounded like a repeated babbling "barbar" noise). When rigidly held views take on an in-group favoritism stance, the sentiments of in-group superiority and out-group inferiority are reinforced.

Another example of this ethnocentric tendency can be found in the Chinese characters for "China" (or "Middle Kingdom"). The characters or pictographs for "China," first written more than 4,000 years ago during the Hsia dynasty, meant "the center of the universe." This example is also reminiscent of the concept of "Manifest Destiny" that prevailed in the United States during the 19th century. Finally, we need only to look at any world atlas, as produced by each nation, to understand the ethnocentric perspective: every nation shows itself in a central position on the map, with neighboring states depicted as peripheral.

Ethnocentrism is our defensive attitudinal tendency to view the values and norms of our culture as superior to other cultures, and we perceive our cultural ways of living as the most reasonable and proper ways to conduct our lives. Consequently, there is the expectation that all other groups should follow our civilized ways of thinking and behaving. Ethnocentrism is bolstered through our own cultural socialization process. It can consist of both implicit and explicit attitudes toward out-group members' customs or behavior. Sumner (1940) summarizes ethnocentrism as the "view of things in which one's own group is the center of everything, and all others are rated and scaled with reference to it" (pp. 27–28). Triandis (1990) explains that all human beings display the ethnocentric tendencies to (1) define what goes on in their cultures as "natural" and "correct" and what goes on in other cultures as "unnatural" and "incorrect"; (2) perceive in-group values, customs, norms, and roles as universally valid—that is, what is good for us is good for everybody; (3) act in ways that favor the in-group and exalt it; and (4) experience relational distance from the out-group especially when one's membership identity is threatened or under attack.

While all human beings carry a certain degree of ethnocentric tendency in them because of their needs for identity security, in-group inclusion, and predictability, a rigidly held ethnocentric mindset creates a superior-inferior gap in intergroup relations. The degree of ethnocentric tendency in an individual can range all the way from the basic need for valued social identity to the identity defensive need for power or dominance. Additionally, people can be ethnocentric about different aspects of their culture (e.g., language, food, architecture). Under conditions of a perceived out-group threat of competition for scarce resources, members of various identity groups can oscillate between high ethnocentrism and low ethnocentrism depending on the changing circumstances.

In fact, Lukens (1978) uses the communicative distances of indifference, avoidance, and disparagement to discuss the differential degree of ethnocentrism. The *distance of indifference* (i.e., low ethnocentrism) reflects the lack of sensitivity in our verbal and nonverbal interaction in dealing with dissimilar others. From the use of insensitive questioning approaches to the use of "foreigner talk" (i.e., exaggeratedly slow speech or a dramatically loud tone of voice, as if all foreigners are deaf), the speech pattern serves as a reminder that these strangers are somehow "exotic" and "quaintly different." The *distance of avoidance* (i.e., moderate ethnocentrism) reflects attempted linguistic or dialect switching in the presence of out-group members, and with displayed nonverbal inattention (e.g., members of the dominant group only maintain eye contact with members of their group) to accentuate in-group connection and avoidance of out-group members. Finally, the *distance of disparagement* (i.e., high ethnocentrism) refers to the use of verbal sarcasms, racist jokes, hate-filled speech, and physical violence to marginalize or obliterate the existence of out-group members (Zanna & Olson, 1994).

In counterbalancing the concept of ethnocentrism, we can draw from the identity negotiation theory in discussing the concept of *ethnorelativism* (M. Bennett, 1993). Ethnorelativism emphasizes the concept of out-group members' cultural frame of reference in interpreting their behaviors. Like ethnocentrism, ethnorelativism comes in various gradations (see Figure 6.2).

The *interaction understanding* stage, for example, refers to the use of appropriate and responsive verbal and nonverbal messages to fully comprehend the out-group members' identity experience, in addition to content-based issues. It is a combined cognitive—behavioral process. Individuals use culture-sensitive paraphrasing and perception checking skills (e.g., paraphras-

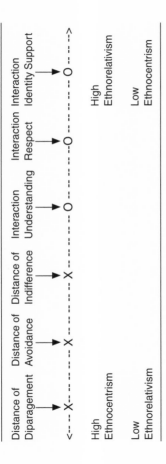

FIGURE 6.2. Degrees of ethnocentrism and ethnorelativism via communication.

ing the others' words or using probing clarifying questions) to make sure that their interpretations of the others' behavior are what they intended. Perception checking helps to reduce unpredictability and promote interaction trust.

Cultural strangers who use perception checking skills signal to each other their desire for a shared understanding of the communication process itself. Beyond verbal perception checking, nonverbal perception checking via mindful observation is a critical skill. Individuals observe and listen mindfully to the content, identity, and relational messages that are being exchanged in the process. They are attentive and patient in their listening process. They listen in order to understand rather than to judge.

Additionally, they are willing to share their cultural and personal identity stories with out-group members. They do that with appropriate timing and pacing, in accordance with the particular situation. Through their newly acquired knowledge, they also practice *isomorphic attribution*, which means trying to cognitively interpret the behaviors of members of the other group from that group's cultural frame of reference (Triandis, 1994a, 1994b). When interacting members of different groups engage in isomorphic attribution, their conflicts are likely to decrease because they understand each other's interpretations of behavior. They refrain from rushing into negative evaluative judgments based on their own ethnocentric frames.

In the *interaction respect* stage, members of different cultural or ethnic groups display a strong sense of respect and empathy for the others' cultural frame of reference. Respect implies giving particular attention and empathetic consideration to the standpoints of dissimilar others. At this stage, individuals are able to move from respecting others to empathizing with their experience. Empathy refers to a strong affective resonance component, the ability to "temporarily set aside one's own perception [or experience] of the world and assume an alternative perspective. Self-interest and [self-focused] purposes are held in check as one attempts to place oneself in the immediate situation and field . . . of the other" (Stewart & Bennett, 1991, p. 152; see also M. Bennett, 1993). While by *understanding* we mean accurate cognitive comprehension, *empathy* is a state of affective transformation in which we transpose ourselves to the field of the other's cultural context. In other words, through empathy we are willing to imaginatively place ourselves in the dissimilar other's cultural world and to experience what she or he is experiencing.

Lastly, *interaction support* reflects an open mindset of commitment to affirm the "identity worthiness" of members of diverse identity groups. Individuals endeavor to decrease the psychological and emotional distance between in-group and out-group members. They try to convey identity support rather than arouse interaction defensiveness in the communication process. Interaction defensiveness refers to anticipating or perceiving threat in the interaction climate. The use of inclusive communication skills signals recognition of the other's presence. Some characteristics of inclusive interaction skills are (1) using inclusive language such as "we as a community" or "we as a team" (vs. exclusive language usage such as "you people" or "you, the oppressed group"); (2) using nonverbal recognition signals such as appropriate eye contact and nonverbal responsive sounds such as "mmmhuh" and "awww" to members of diverse groups; (3) promoting the search for superordinate goals, that is, searching for or creating common goals that are desired by members of all groups and whose fulfillment requires the efforts of everyone involved; and (4) encouraging feedback from dissimilar others—using nonverbal and verbal encouragements such as smiles, head nods, appropriate silence, and culture-sensitive open-ended questions such as "How do you think we should proceed?" or "Any suggestions on how we can help each other to solve this problem?"

In addition to inclusive interaction skills, *identity confirmation skills* include (1) recognition of the other's existence (i.e., "To me, you exist"); (2) acknowledgment of a relationship of affiliation with the dissimilar other (i.e., "We are relating on an equal level"); (3) expressed awareness of the significance or worth of the dissimilar other (i.e., "To me, you are significant"); and (4) endorsement or acceptance of the other's self-experience, particularly emotional experience pertaining to a person's self-conception (i.e., "Your way of experiencing the world is valid") (Cissna & Sieburg, 1986, p. 232).

In contrast, when we *disconfirm someone's identity*, we tend to engage in the following: (1) denial of the other's presence—without even a minimal display of interpersonal recognition (e.g., "To me, you don't exist"); (2) avoidance of genuine interaction involvement—individuals try nonverbally (e.g., by avoiding natural eye contact) or verbally (e.g., by neither hearing or acknowledging what the speaker says or by only engaging in a self-interest monologue) to cut short the conversation or monopolize the interaction;

(3) use of displacements—that is, there is a lack of accurate awareness of the dissimilar other's perceptions or self-expressions (e.g., "You don't really mean that . . ." or "You're only saying that because . . ."; and (4) use of disqualifications—that is, condescending remarks, sarcasm, harsh criticism, blame, and hostile attacks (e.g., "What would you know about being a White male in this society?" or "Here we go again—guess we're all sexists!" or "We heard you the first time—why do you keep repeating yourself?" (Cissna & Sieburg, 1986).

In disconfirming communication, we are basically stating that "Your way of experiencing the world is invalid—you're an unworthy individual." On the other hand, confirming communication is "dialogic in structure; it is a reciprocal activity involving shared talk and sometimes shared silence. It is interactional in the broadest sense of the word. . . . Confirming response . . . is not something one does, it is a process in which one shares" (Cissna & Sieburg, 1986, p. 238). Confirming communication can be a powerful affective experience sometimes causing a shift in the mindset of participants.

Mindful intercultural communicators are willing to experiment with new paradigms of experiencing, communicating, and confirming. They are willing to admit their ethnocentrism and reframe their mindsets through ethnorelative thinking. They are willing to "struggle *with*" rather than "struggle *against*" dissimilar others.

Stereotypes and Communication

Stereotyping is an exaggerated set of expectations and beliefs about the attributes of a group membership category (such as "Californians," "New Yorkers," "lawyers," and "doctors"). A stereotype is an *overgeneralization* about an identity group without any attempt to perceive individual variations within the identity category.

Stereotyping can refer to subconsciously held beliefs about a membership group. The content of stereotypes can convey both positive and negative information (e.g., "Chinese are good in math" or "Koreans are too aggressive"). They are exaggerated "pictures in our head" (Lipmann, 1936; Stephan & Stephan, 1992, 1996) about a class or group of individuals based on the principle of group homogeneity.

There are different kinds of stereotype. The term *autostereotype* refers to what insiders think of themselves as a group (e.g., what Californians think of Californians); *heterostereotype* refers to what one group thinks of another group (e.g., what Californians think of New Yorkers). When stereotypes have a high degree of external validity (e.g., 90% agreement with empirical evidence from research), they become known as *sociotypes* (Triandis, 1994a). Furthermore, a distinction can be made between normative stereotypes and personal stereotypes.

Normative stereotypes result when we make guesses based on generalized knowledge we have acquired concerning another group via information from mass media or books. Normative stereotypes can have accurate or inaccurate aspects. If social science research has established that "90% of some group have a trait, if we think that a member of that group has that trait . . . we would do better using the sociotype than saying—I know nothing about this person." (Triandis, 1994a, p. 138). *Personal stereotypes* are formed as the result of our personal experiences and limited contacts with the other group. However, personal stereotypes can also be faulty because our contact experiences might well be based on a very skewed sample.

The process of heterostereotyping occurs as follows: (a) individuals are categorized, usually on the basis of easily identifiable characteristics such as gender or ethnicity; (b) features or attributes are ascribed to all or most members of that category—that is, individuals belonging to the stereotyped group are assumed to be similar to each other; and (c) the preconceived attributes are applied to individual members belonging to that category (Cox, 1994; Hewstone & Brown, 1986). From the social categorization principle to the illusory correlation principle, members of the out-groups are often "stigmatized" as behaving and thinking in the same undesirable way.

Furthermore, group members can engage in an autostereotyping process by taking on other's stereotyped images that are imposed on them. This is also reflective of the *principle of self-fulfilling prophecy*. For example, a group member is consistently perceived by other out-group members as a "lazy dropout." If this image is bolstered by institutional backing (e.g., the mass media), this "dropout" image can feed back to the self-perception schema of this group member. Such negative self-stereotyping can create a negative self-image, which in turn can induce negative self-expectations in the individual. Self-fulfilling prophecies occur when we think something is true about ourselves and then behave accordingly.

A classic study by Rosenthal and Jacobson (1968) illustrates the power of other-perception on self-perception. Students were randomly assigned to the intellectual "bloomer" group and the regular student group. The teachers were told that the test scores of one group were significantly higher than those of the other group. After a year, the experimenters found that the "bloomer" group showed more dramatic gains in IQ than did the "regular" group.

The teacher's preconception of this "bloomer" group and the students' positive self-perception were explained as the key factors that led to the dramatic increase in IQ gains. Thus, the power of positive versus negative stereotypes holds tremendous promise in influencing group and individuals' desired identities. To the extent that we use negative stereotypes in interacting with out-group members, our relationships only end up in unproductive interaction spirals. To the extent that we use neutral-to-positive stereotypes in interacting with out-group members, intergroup relationships can be improved substantially.

Since it is inevitable that all individuals stereotype their own identity groups and other groups, the key to dealing with the issue is to learn to distinguish between mindless stereotyping and mindful stereotyping. The characteristics of *mindless stereotyping* are as follows: (1) holding our preconceived, negative stereotypes rigidly and operating on automatic pilot in exercising such negative stereotypes; (2) presuming that the out-group stereotypes are valid and ignoring all new incoming information and evidence; (3) using emotionally laden evaluative categories to guide our "typecasting" process; (4) employing a polarized, cognitive mode to engage in ingroup favoritism and out-group bias; (5) engaging in mental distortions to "force" members' behaviors into preconceived categories; (6) presuming that one member's behavior is reflective of all members' behaviors and norms; and (7) maximizing intergroup distance with exaggerated, contrastive categories with no productive outcome (see Table 6.1).

In comparison to mindless stereotyping, the characteristics of *mindful stereotyping* are as follows: (1) holding the stereotypes consciously or mindfully—that is, being meta-cognitively aware that we are stereotyping members of an entire group; (2) assuming that the stereotypes we use are merely first best guesses rather than definitive answers (Adler, 1997); (3) using loose, interpretive categories rather than evaluative categories; (4) employing qualifying, contextual statements to frame our perceptions and interpretations; (5) being open to new information and evidence and redefining the preconceived social categories accordingly; (6) getting to know, in depth, the group membership and personal identities of the individuals within the group and sampling a variety of sources within the group; and (7) recognizing valid and meaningful differences and similarities between the self and others, and between one's own group and the other group.

While mindful stereotyping evokes an open-minded attitude in dealing with others, mindless stereotyping reflects a closed-ended mindset. Mindless stereotyping refers to our tightly held beliefs concerning a group of individuals. Mindful stereotyping, on the other hand, refers to our consciously held beliefs about a group of individuals, with a willingness to change our loosely held images based on diversified, firsthand contact expe-

TABLE 6.1. Mindless and Mindful Stereotyping

Mindless stereotyping	Mindful stereotyping
Rigid categories	Open-ended categories
Premature closure	First best guesses
Polarized evaluations	Loose interpretations
Delimiting contexts	Creating contexts
Information distortion	Information openness
Unwilling to change categories	Willingness to change categories
Maximizing intergroup distance	Minimizing intergroup distance

riences. Mindful stereotyping relies heavily on a receptive communication process in observing, listening, and attending to the new cues and signals sent by strangers from other groups.

Prejudice and Communication

An individual learns prejudice against out-group members via the family socialization process, education, the peer group, the mass media, and other such influences. Prejudice, strictly speaking, can refer to either negative or positive predispositions and feelings about out-group members; for the most part, however, the concept has taken on negative connotations in the literature of intergroup relations.

The word *prejudice* means "prejudging" something or someone based on biased cognitive and affective preconceptions. The word *discrimination* refers to antagonistic, degradational treatment and behavior aimed at members of an out-group.

Prejudice

More precisely, prejudice is defined by Allport (1954) as "an antipathy based on faulty and inflexible generalization. It may be felt or expressed. It may be directed toward a group as a whole, or toward an individual because he [or she] is a member of that group" (p. 7). Such an antipathy stems from an aversive or negative feeling toward out-group members based on hasty and inflexible overgeneralizations above and beyond existing evidence.

Individuals can hold prejudices against others based on their skin color, foreign accent or local dialect, cultural or religious practices, and the like. Four theories have been posited to account for the development of prejudice: exploitation theory, scapegoating theory, the authoritarian personality approach, and the structural approach (Schaefer, 1990).

Exploitation theory views power as a scarce resource and explains that in order to keep one's valued status and power one has to suppress the social mobility of the underclass to bolster one's own group position and security.

Scapegoating theory suggests that prejudiced individuals believe that they are the victims of society. In fact, the term *scapegoat* comes from "a biblical injunction . . ., telling the Hebrews to send a goat into the wilderness to symbolically carry away the people's sins" (Schaefer, 1990, p. 61). Scapegoating theory holds that the scapegoaters often first perceive themselves as victims; then, rather than accepting the basic responsibility for some failure (e.g., defeat in a war) they typically shift the locus of responsibility for it to some vulnerable group.

The *authoritarian personality approach* emphasizes the personality features of rigid adherence to conventional norms, uncritical acceptance of authority, and concern for power as the composites of a personality type that inclines toward prejudiced attitudes and discriminatory behavior (Schaefer, 1990). Harsh discipline inflicted in childhood shapes the authoritarian personality syndrome, and later such individuals tend to treat vulnerable others as they were treated when young and powerless. Of course, other mediating variables such as an individual's motivational level, educational environment, peer group networks, and his or her role models can serve to enhance or dilute the authoritarian personality profile.

The *structural approach* to prejudice emphasizes the social climate in promoting cultural and ethnic tolerance or intolerance. The societal norms of either cultivating genuine equality among all groups or promoting a "pecking order" between majority–minority group statuses are deemed to have a profound impact on the prejudiced attitudes held by group members.

Beyond these four broad approaches to prejudice, prejudice serves some specific functions: (1) the ego-defensive function; (2) the value-expressive function; (3) the knowledge function; and (4) the utilitarian function (Brislin, 1993).

The *ego-defensive function* of prejudice is to protect people's view of themselves on both personal and social identity levels. If some individuals are not good businesspeople, they can put down others in order to protect their egos as compared to spending time analyzing their own business incompetence. They can also be quick to protect in-group identity image by asserting that other groups are behaving unethically or unfairly.

The *value-expressive function* refers to people's need for value and behavioral consistencies in viewing their own cultural values, norms, and practices as the proper and civilized ways of thinking and behaving.

The *knowledge function* refers to the way information is learned and organized. Since it takes time and energy to acquire new knowledge, people tend to want to defend their knowledge base and view others who lack such knowledge as ignorant or deficient. For example, if one's in-group has attained proficiency through the use of computer technology, then one may see out-group members who have not learned to master this new technology as backward and unintelligent.

The *utilitarian function* of prejudice refers to how people impose preexisting categories or biased expectations on others to simplify their information-overload environment. They can also collect rewards from their own group by sharing in the consensual prejudiced beliefs of their in-group. For example, some middle managers, in order to appease top management expectations (e.g., that certain minority groups cannot "rise to the top" because of their "laid-back" or loafing lifestyle) and to make "efficient" decisions (e.g., in dealing with more than 250 job applicants) can casually drop minority group applications onto the rejection pile, thereby making the entire screening process much easier on themselves.

Discriminatory Practices

While prejudice refers to antagonistic feelings and biased attitudes toward out-group members, discrimination refers to both verbal and nonverbal actions that carry out such prejudiced attitudes. According to Feagin (1989), four basic types of discriminatory practices exist in a society: (1) isolate discrimination; (2) small-group discrimination; (3) direct institutional discrimination; and (4) indirect institutional discrimination.

Isolate discrimination refers to harmful verbal and nonverbal action taken intentionally by a member of a group toward an out-group member without the outright support of the larger organizational or community network. This refers to discriminatory activity on an individual basis, from the use of racist slurs to violent physical actions.

Small-group discrimination refers to a band of individuals from an identifiable group engaging in hostile and abusive actions against members of an out-group. However, these actions do not have the normative support of the larger organizational or community network. Activities of groups like the Ku Klux Klan might be viewed as exemplifying this type.

Direct institutional discrimination refers to community-prescribed endorsements of discriminatory practices. These practices are not isolated incidents but are carried out routinely by a large number of individuals protected by the laws of a large-scale community. For example, the Alien Land Law in 1913 passed in California forbade "aliens" to own land. A blatant institutional discriminatory practice against Japanese Americans was carried out in the World War II incarceration of 110,000 Japanese Americans in internment camps. Other historical examples include African Americans being segregated in schools, segregated in seating arrangements on public buses, segregated in the use of drinking fountains, and segregated in the use of restrooms up until the mid-1960s.

Indirect institutional discrimination consists of practices having a negative impact on group members even though the original intent of the established guidelines of the institution bore no malice. For example, educational IQ tests such as the WISC-R, WAIS-R, and Stanford IQ tests, the verbal dysfluency diagnostic test, etc., serve an indirect discriminatory function in practice. The use of a "homogenized" standard (with a strong White middle-class orientation) to test the intelligence or verbal fluency level of all children in a pluralistic immigrant culture is an example of indirect institutional discrimination. The improper use of such "standardized" instruments in diverse ethnic and immigrant populations in the United States can lead to an exclusion of group members seeking better educational opportunities and job promotions. Thus, even without hostile intent, the institution has, through ignorance, discriminated against these group members.

Moving beyond the kinds of discrimination that exist in a society, Merton (1957) presents a model that links the relationship between prejudice and discrimination (see Figure 6.3). From the continuum of low to high prejudiced attitudes, and from the continuum of low to high discriminatory practices, Merton (1957) develops a typology of prejudice–discrimination types. Under certain conditions, individual members can be identified as (1) prejudiced discriminators, or "active bigots"; (2) prejudiced nondiscriminators, or "timid bigots"; (3) nonprejudiced discriminators, or "fair-weather liberals"; and (4) nonprejudiced nondiscriminators, or as I term this category "proactive change agents."

Individuals of the first type, *active bigots*, hold prejudiced attitudes and actively discriminate against out-group members. Groups like the Ku Klux Klan and the Nazis serve as exemplars of this type. Individuals of the second type, *timid bigots*, hold prejudiced attitudes toward out-group members but learn to sublimate their hostility or resentment because of social pressures or norms. However, these individuals do engage in covert discriminatory practices. For example, a timid bigot acting in a hiring capacity might pay lip service to the rightness of nondiscriminatory hiring practices but might turn down perfectly suitable out-group candidates due to covert discrimination. The third type, *fair-weather liberals* do not harbor strong hostilities toward out-group members. However, because of the fact that surrounding peer group members talk in a prejudiced manner or engage in racist jokes, these individuals feel compelled to either join in or to maintain silence for social expediency purposes. The fourth type, *proactive change agents*, take an activist stance in promoting true equality between all cultural, ethnic, and gender groups. These individuals are committed to eliminate unfair racial, gender, and social practices. They are likely to speak up when they perceive discriminatory practices in their surrounding environment. They also advocate a nonviolent approach to achieve peace-building

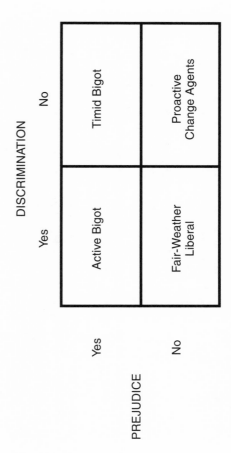

FIGURE 6.3. A prejudice–discrimination typology. Data from Merton (1957).

goals. Mohandas K. Gandhi, Martin Luther King, Jr., Nelson R. Mandela, the Dalai Lama, Aung San Suu Kyi, and Mother Teresa are some examples. They can also be "ordinary people" who intervene directly or indirectly (and appropriately to the situation) when they hear or observe a discriminatory remark or sexually harassing action directed by a perpetrator to a victim.

While some individuals can be identified as belonging to one of these four prejudice–discrimination categories, most individuals typically oscillate in their dealing with such in-group and out-group feelings. Some individuals may display favorable attitudes toward one minority group but show strong racist attitudes against another. Some individuals may harbor no deep resentments against out-groups until their identity status is seriously threatened or challenged by other members' intrusions. Other individuals may engage in "arm's-length prejudice" or "symbolic racism" (Brislin, 1993).

Arm's-length prejudice refers to individuals who engage in cordial, positive behaviors toward out-group members in semiformal social situations (e.g., the work setting or a business party setting) while treating the same out-group members at arm's-length when the contacts involve intimate situations (e.g., a within-home dinner invitation, dating, or more intimate friendship development). These individuals are uncomfortable in sharing personal thoughts or feelings and treating out-group members as true equals. Arm's-length prejudice differs from "tokenism-type" prejudice in that in the former individuals do engage in friendly relations with out-group members in social settings whereas in the latter, individuals "harbor negative feelings about an out-group but do not want to admit this to themselves or to others. . . . By engaging in relatively effortless behaviors [e.g., small money donations], people can persuade themselves and others that they are unprejudiced and can then later refuse to perform more difficult and important intergroup behaviors" (Brislin, 1993, p. 189).

Symbolic racism, on the other hand, refers to the perceived threat viewed by a group of individuals who believe that out-group members are interfering with the *symbols* of their culture. These symbols can be "abstract or concrete. Abstract symbols include (a) the belief [in hard work] as the backbone of society and (b) the importance of standing on one's own two feet and solving one's own problem. Concrete symbols include (c) the classroom as a place for learning the basics, not a place to deal with everyone's social problems, and (d) the job interview as a 'level playing field' where some people should not have an advantage because they are from a minority group" (Brislin, 1993, pp. 186–187). Symbolic racism is different from "intense racism" in that people who engage in symbolic racism believe that out-group members are seriously interfering with important aspects of their culture, whereas people who engage in intense racism believe that "virtually all members of [out-groups] are inferior in various ways and are not able to fully benefit from society's offerings. . . . [T]hose individuals are inferior on dimensions such as intelligence, morals, and an ability to interact in 'decent' society" (Brislin, 1993, p. 185).

Reduction of Prejudice and Discrimination

People have prejudiced attitudes and engage in discriminatory practices because of many factors. One such factor is the fundamental emotion of fear. Fear gives rise to emotional vulnerability and identity insecurity and exclusion. Individuals are worried that their cultural or social habits, and hence identities, are being attacked because of the influx of outsiders or immigrants whom they perceive to be fragmenting a nation.

Individuals are apprehensive of losing power or domination because all these newcomers compete for scarce resources in an institutionalized setting. They are scared because out-group members bring in with them alternative values, norms, and lifestyles, thereby directly challenging their fundamental way of existence. This fundamental fear triggers a package of other feelings such as resentment, frustration, anger, and anxiety. While some of these feelings may be legitimate, others are probably completely groundless.

To reduce prejudice and discriminatory practices effectively, we should conduct a mindset analysis along the following lines:

First, we must be honest with ourselves—confront our own biases and ethnocentric attitudes. We should question where we have learned our biases about out-group members. We should also question how strongly or rigidly we buy into this set of preconceived stereotypes about others.

Second, we should question the contents of our stereotypes and check against our actual interactions with out-group members. In sum, we should practice mindful, rather than mindless, stereotyping.

Third, we should understand how our negative images concerning out-group members affect our biased attitudes and unfavorable interactions with them. In harboring prejudice against out-group members, we are locked into using the principle of homogeneity against an entire group of individuals. We are, in fact, treating everyone from that group in a prejudiced manner as if all its members are made from the same mold.

Fourth, we should work on deepening the complexity of our intergroup perceptions, that is, use the principle of heterogeneity to break down the broad social categories (e.g., Asian Americans) into subunits (e.g., recent Asian immigrants vs. native-born Asian Americans), and with finer distinctions (e.g., Korean Americans, Vietnamese Americans, Japanese Americans) and multifaceted variations (e.g., generation, age, social class, hobbies, unique personality traits). We should be willing to spend time to really get to know members of an out-group on an individual basis: their real likes and dislikes, their fears, and their dreams.

Fifth, we should use mindful, qualifying language (e.g., "From my contacts with several Vietnamese American students, they appear to be on the "quiet side" in describing dissimilar others' behaviors. We should strive to use "neutral" language in our descriptions or analysis. We should strive to use "situated language" in qualifying or "contexting" our understanding.

Lastly, we should put ourselves in frequent intergroup contact situations to be comfortable with group-based differences. We can gain more realistic and accurate information based on increased positive contacts with a variety of individuals from a wide spectrum of the identity group. At the same time we should learn to honor group-based differences; we should not totalize the differences and forget about genuine human commonalities.

On a more specific level of dealing with racism in our society, Auletta and Jones (1994) suggest the following: (1) Recognize racism as existing on a continuum (e.g., on dimensions such as conscious–unconscious, overt–covert, little impact–great impact); viewing racism thus allows us to think about perceived racism from both the victim's and the perpetrator's standpoint. (2) Recognize that racism occurs on multiple levels—personal, institutional, and cultural. *Personal racism* involves the belief that certain physical traits are the determinants of social, moral, and intellectual character so that skin color, for example, would signal inferior moral character. *Institutional racism* is an extension of personal racism and includes those institutional practices that operate to restrict groups of individuals on a low power status level. *Cultural racism* combines elements of personal and institutional racism to perpetuate the belief in the cultural superiority of one race and the cultural inferiority of all others. Racism, in sum, is not an all-or-none phenomenon. (3) Recognize that racism always occurs within a context—all individuals are inextricably linked to complex web of influences. Racism is perpetuated because it is allowed and nurtured within the context in which it occurs (Auletta & Jones, 1994, pp. 169–170).

Additionally, to approach racism mindfully, we must strive to do the following:

1. Be able to get mad, to feel angry about the injustices that peoples have suffered and are still suffering. Be willing and able to express that indignation at the pain, humiliation, anguish, frustration, and despair to which many people are subjected. This is particularly essential for those who are not members of the victimized group. Knowledge brings the power of sight, but affect brings the power of insight; no *affect* yields no *effect*.

2. Be empathetic, able to reach deep down and feel the experiences, and traumas of others; but be sensitive without being excessively so (thus, being overwhelmed by our emotions to the point of inaction).

3. Be willing to be uncomfortable—uncomfortable with the limited extent of our knowledge about others and their experiences.

4. Be able to recognize that others may have experiences that we may not be able to grasp fully. With our passion must come humility.

5. Understand ethnicity as a phenomenon that many diverse peoples experience within common parameters but for different lengths of time, based on different historical events, and with different degrees of intensity and commitment. Shared characteristics of ethnicity do not mean an equality or sameness of experiences (Barkan, 1994, pp. 184–185).

Auletta and Jones (1994) observe that "Racism can be reduced, but it cannot be eliminated in our lifetime. Racism is so intricately woven into our personal and collective unconscious that only constant vigilance will reduce it in our lifetime" (p. 170). Knowledge, together with insight, may help to reduce our ignorance and increase our sensitivity and responsiveness to prejudice and racism issues. As Barkan (1994) concludes,

In the process of this [multicultural] instruction, we must also be working to empower students by enhancing their self-esteem and their ethnic group pride as well as their respect for others and their willingness and ability to understand, tolerate, and appreciate ethnic differences. We must make them realize that knowledge instills pride (and sometimes anger) but also awareness; group consciousness but also less fear of others; and greater self-understanding but also a new (or renewed) visibility for those long overlooked. (p. 187)

RECOMMENDATIONS

To be mindful intergroup communicators, we have to understand the basic assumptions that undergird the formation of our cultural or social identities, and how these identities, in turn, impact our desired personal identities. The need for identity security, inclusion, and interactive trust leads us to engage in in-group favoritism and out-group bias. When our identities perceive threats from out-group members, we often tighten our in-group boundaries and reinforce in-group solidarity and loyalty. Additionally, mindset filters such as ethnocentrism, stereotypes, and prejudice create cognitive and affective distortions.

To become mindful intergroup communicators, we need to do the following:

1. Recognize the fact that all human beings are ethnocentric to certain degrees and at different levels. We should be aware of where we learn our ethnocentric tendencies. We learn them from our cultural upbringing, religious practices, educational system, mass media, government, and peer influence.

2. Acknowledge that the concept of "power" underscores many of the interplays between "dominant" and "nondominant" group relations within the larger society. It is typically the case that members of a dominant group hold more power and occupy more status control than members of a less privileged group in any system. In willing to promote quality and equality-based intergroup relations, both groups need to learn to share power and assert power productively. Sharing power can be manifested through willingness to listen and readiness to incorporate the other group member's point of view; willingness to delegate and let others take on more task-oriented responsibilities; the honesty to give useful, critical feedback when necessary for improving task-oriented and relationship-oriented issues; and willingness to mentor, motivate, and act as role models of members of diverse groups.

3. Express responsible power via learning to act affirmatively through asserting one's viewpoint responsibly *and* at the same time respecting the different voices of members of diverse groups; learning to separate constructive feedback from group membership identity issues (i.e., not every comment is intended to be a "racist" or "antiracist" comment); learning to develop identity security in the self and others within and across diverse groups via supportive identity work; and willingness to assume leadership roles and take chances in improving oneself.

4. Monitor our mindless stereotyping of out-group members. We have to realize that we cannot not stereotype in social interaction. In stereotyping out-group members, we are categorizing the behavior of a large group of individuals under generalized labels or categories. Since stereotyping is an inevitable process, we have to monitor our typecasting process of out-group members (and that of our own groups). We have to engage in mindfully "minding" our own social categorization process.

5. Understand the basic functions of prejudice and discrimination. Prejudice and discrimination are oftentimes developed through ignorance and identity-defensiveness functions. We need to increase our cultural and ethnic literacy regarding different ethnic groups within different cultures. Additionally, we should articulate our concern for members of an identity group as individuals with unique experiences, attributes, and competencies. While members of an identity group share many similar values, norms, and characteristics, no two individuals are ever alike in all attributes, likes, and dislikes. We should learn to honor and affirm both group membership and personal identities of the individuals in the communication process. We should learn to understand the historical conditions that frame the marginalization experiences of "minority" group members. Only by assuming an inclusive stance and an equality mindset can intergroup racism be reduced.

6. Practice ethnic-sensitive identity confirmation skills. We should address members of different cultural and ethnic groups by their preferred

titles and names. Addressing people in that way conveys to others our recognition of their existence and the validity of their experiences. For example, individuals sometimes may identify strongly with their ethnic-based membership or religious denomination (e.g., as African Americans, Cuban Americans, or Italian Americans, or as Jewish, Lutherans, Buddhists, Amish, or Quakers) and sometimes their person-based identities. By being sensitive to people's self-images in particular situations and according due respect to their desired identities, we confirm their self-worth. Calling others what they want to be called and recognizing group memberships that are important to them are part of supporting their self-images.

7. Practice using inclusive language rather than exclusive language (e.g., "you gay people") and using situational language rather than polarized language as part of identity support skills. Inclusive language means that we are mindful at all times of our use of verbal messages when we converse with both in-group and out-group members in a small group setting. We should cross-check our own verbal habits and make sure that we are directing our comments to both in-group and out-group members on an equitable basis. Inclusive language usage also includes the use of inclusive nonverbal behavior (e.g., eye contact is evenly spread out to both in-group and out-group members and not just to in-group members). Situational language means that when we observe out-group members' behavior we are willing to take situational contingencies into account in understanding that behavior and accord out-group members the same courtesy as we accord in-group members. In sum, we honor the identities of out-group members as if they are members of our in-group rather than overemphasize in-group/out-group circles.

Thus, we confirm and disconfirm dissimilar others by the words we choose to address them and by the attitude behind the words with which we "name" them. Sometimes we may want to downplay group-based identities because members who belong to dissimilar groups do not necessarily identify strongly with their groups. However, we may also be interacting with dissimilar individuals who value their group memberships enormously. To communicate mindfully on an intergroup level, we must pay close attention to people's identity affiliation process in particular relationships and situations.

7

Intercultural Personal
Relationship Development:
Identity- and Relational-Based Themes

Personal Relationship Developments:
Membership and Contextual Conditions.............................175
Cultural and Ethnic Membership Values 176
Gender Expectations and Norms 177
Individual Personality Attributes......................................178
Situational Contact Conditions 179
Four Identity- and Relational-Based Themes 181
The Identity Vulnerability and Security Theme 181
The Identity Autonomy and Connection Theme 184
The Relational Dissimilarity and Similarity Theme 186
The Relational Openness and Closedness Theme 188
Summary 192
Recommendations 192

To understand how our intercultural personal relationships develop, we need to recognize the conditions and patterns that underlie our interpersonal relationship formation process. Understanding these relational patterns or themes can help us to demystify stereotypes and manage ethnocentric attributions mindfully. Such knowledge can help us to improve the quality of our personal relationships such as friendships, dating relationships, and marital relationships across cultural boundaries.

There are many reasons why we should understand intercultural personal relationship development within the U.S. context and on a global level. First, the changing demographic trends of the U.S. population indicate that within the next 50 years one in every three Americans will be a person of non-White heritage (Thornton, 1992). The chance of developing diverse types of intercultural personal relationships is increasing rapidly. Second, research indicates that friendship formation between people of different cultures greatly facilitates intergroup understanding and dispels outgroup-based stereotypes. Third, intergroup marriage rates within the United States have increased dramatically by 53% between 1980 and 1995 (e.g., 50% of all Jewish marriages are intermarriages, and 60% of all Japanese American marriages are intermarriages). Intergroup marriage is an experimental testing ground for direct culture clash, on the one hand, or relational harmony between intimate partners from two contrastive cultures, on the other.

By probing deeply into the different cultural ways of dealing with personal relationship issues, we may gain new insights into managing our own current intimate relationships. Overall, the purpose of this chapter is to call attention to the central role in which culture plays in our attitudes and expectations toward voluntary personal relationship developments. The chapter is divided into three main sections. First, the contextual conditions (e.g., group membership values) that influence the formation, the expectations, and the norms we have regarding personal relationships will be addressed. Second, based on the identity negotiation theory, four identity-based relational themes and relevant research findings in intercultural personal relationships will be discussed. Third, recommendations for managing personal relationship development between individualists and collectivists will be presented.

PERSONAL RELATIONSHIP DEVELOPMENTS: MEMBERSHIP AND CONTEXTUAL CONDITIONS

To understand our communication in intercultural personal relationships, we have to first define what we mean by "personal relationships." A personal relationship in the present context is defined as any close relationship that exhibits a certain degree of voluntary engagement, relational interdependence, affective sentiments, and personalized understanding. Voluntary engagement means that the partners clearly want to be involved in the relationship. Relational interdependence means that the partners influence each other on cognitive, emotional, and/or behavioral levels. Affective sentiments refer to the positive and/or negative feelings the partners have for each other. Lastly, personalized understanding means that the symbolic exchange process involves some disclosure of unique personal information.

A quality relational culture is formed when contrastive cultural partners perceive positive relational interdependence, express responsive positive sentiments, and experience a depth of personal understanding. According to Wood (1995), the term *relational culture* refers to "processes, structures, and practices that create, express, and sustain personal relationships and the identities of partners" (p. 150). A quality relational culture takes time and commitment to develop. It is a "privately transacted system of understandings that coordinate attitudes, actions, and identities of the participants in a relationship" (Wood, 1995, p. 150). In comparison, an ineffective relational culture occurs when the partners consistently perceive negative interdependence, express negative sentiments, and complain of recurring cultural or personal misunderstandings (Cahn, 1990, 1992).

The membership and contextual conditions that affect the development of relational culture in any type of intercultural personal relationship include cultural and ethnic membership values, gender expectations and norms, individual personalities, and situational contact conditions. We begin by examining cultural and ethnic membership values.

Cultural and Ethnic Membership Values

Cultural values such as individualism and collectivism shape our interpretations of concepts such as "autonomy" and "connection" in a close relationship. In a capsule description, the core building block of individualism–collectivism lies in its relative emphasis on the importance of the "I" identity and the "we" identity (see Chapter 3). "I" identity cultural members (e.g., Germans and U.S. Americans) tend to emphasize personal privacy issues and privatized relationship issues. In contrast, the "we" identity cultural members (e.g., Filipinos and Mexicans) tend to emphasize relational and family network connection issues and in-group network activity issues.

From an individualism–collectivism values' approach in explaining close relationships, three observations can be gleaned. First, cultural and ethnic values of individualism and collectivism undergird many of the themes (see the "Identity- and Relational-Based Themes" section below) in close relationships. From an individualistic perspective, the emphasis is on how the private relational culture influences the individual's selfhood actualization process. From a collectivistic perspective, the study of the relational culture often emphasizes how the social network context shapes the development of relationship intimacy. From the collectivistic viewpoint, a relational culture is closely intertwined with the fate of others in the in-group networks. Thus, gaining approval from families and close friends (e.g., in cultures such as India and Indonesia) acts as a critical stage in an intercultural attraction process.

Furthermore, it appears that while passionate love is treasured where kinship ties are weak (as in the larger U.S. culture), passionate love is diluted where kinship ties are strong (e.g., in China and Korea). Romantic, passionate love has been found to be a critical component in the "falling in love" stage of individualists. However, research (Gao, 1991) indicates that many collectivists value companionate love (i.e., companion comfort and support) more than passionate love in heterosexual romantic relationships.

Lastly, individualists often use a low-context, direct verbal approach in initiating and ending close relationships. In comparison, collectivists generally use a high-context, indirect approach in dealing with relational initiation and disengagement issues (see the "Identity Autonomy and Connection Theme" section below). Despite some individualistic and collectivistic cultural differences, in nearly all of 37 cultural samples studied (Buss et al., 1990), both females and males endorsed *mutual attraction–love, dependability, emotional stability, kindness–understanding,* and *intelligence* as top-ranked mate-selection criteria. Overall, the greatest cultural variation is found in the attitude toward premarital chastity. Respondents in China, India, Nigeria, Iran, and Zambia (reflective of collectivistic values) differ from those of the continental United States and western Europe (reflective of individualistic values) in placing a premium value on premarital chastity.

Gender Expectations and Norms

The concept of gender identity is something individuals learn within the larger context of cultural values and institutional practices. It is an interpretive system of "social meanings that specify what is associated with men and women in a given society at a particular time. . . . To understand what gender means and how meanings of gender change, we must explore cultural values and the institutions and activities through which those are expressed and promoted" (Wood, 1997, p. 41).

One such institution in which individuals learn the values of "masculine" and "feminine" attributes is the family. Children learn appropriate gender roles through rewards and punishments they receive from their parents in performing the "proper" or "improper" gender-related behaviors. In the United States, masculine-based tendencies such as independence, competition, and verbal assertiveness are often promoted in boys, whereas feminine-based tendencies such as interdependence, cooperation, and verbal relatedness are often rewarded in girls.

Maltz and Borker (1982; see also Tannen, 1990, 1994) observe that young boys and girls learn their gender-related behaviors in the home and school, and in childhood games. For example, in the United States, boys' games (e.g., baseball, football) typically involve fairly large groups and have clear objectives, distinct roles and rules, and clear win–lose outcomes. In comparison, girls' games (e.g., playing house, jump rope) tend to involve either pairs or small groups. The girls' games often involve fluid discussion about who is going to play what roles in the "playing house" game, for example, and usually promote relational collaboration. The *process* of playing, rather than the win–lose outcome, predominates in girls' games in the larger U.S. culture.

From such research observations, Wood (1997) concludes that games enable U.S. males to form the expectations that "communication" is used to achieve some clear outcomes, attract and maintain an audience, and compete with others for the "talk stage." In comparison, games enable U.S. females to form the expectations that "communication" is used to create and maintain relationships, respond to others' feelings and nonverbal nuances, and foster relational connectedness rather than individual competitiveness.

Furthermore, based on her findings, Gilligan (1988), argues that in approaching interpersonal relationships U.S. males tend to follow the "norm of justice" whereas U.S. females tend to follow the "norm of caring." From the justice perspective, relationships are organized in terms of personal equity and self-esteem. From the caring perspective, relationships are organized in terms of mutual responsiveness, engagement, and network connectedness.

While the norm of justice is grounded in an individualistic belief system, the norm of caring is enmeshed in a collectivistic belief system. In the cross-cultural arena, research by Stimpson, Jensen, and Neff (1992) reveals that females in China, South Korea, Thailand, and the United States prefer a more caring morality than do males. Both males and females can subscribe to either the morality of justice or the morality of caring or both—depending on the influence of culture, the family socialization process, and individual personality conditions.

Individual Personality Attributes

Two personality attributes stand out when we are considering the development of close intercultural relationships: high versus low tolerance for ambiguity and the independent versus the interdependent self. In the intercultural adaptation literature (see Chapter 9), tolerance for ambiguity refers to our ability to deal appropriately and effectively with an unfamiliar situation (Ruben & Kealey, 1979). High tolerance for ambiguity means that when we are faced with an ambiguous situation we are able to manage our emotional vulnerability constructively—without being overly threatened by the unfamiliar situation. Low tolerance for ambiguity, on the other hand, means when we are faced with an ambiguous situation we are overwhelmed by the unfamiliar situation to such an extent that we cannot function appropriately or effectively.

People who are highly tolerant of ambiguity are more likely to initiate close interpersonal ties with culturally dissimilar others than people who are low in such tolerance. Highly tolerant individuals tend to be more emotionally creative or resourceful than are individuals who have little tolerance in dealing with unfamiliar experiences. The former are also more likely to use a diverse range of adaptive relational strategies (e.g., culture-sensitive requests, qualifiers, and questions) in their intercultural close relationships than are the latter.

Additionally, the personality factor of whether one has an independent or an interdependent self (Markus & Kitayama, 1991) plays a critical role in how individuals regulate relational boundary issues. While independent-self concepts are predominant in individualistic cultures, interdependent-self concepts are predominant in collectivistic cultures. Independent people view themselves as unique individuals with unique attributes and with clear boundaries that separate them from others. In contrast, interdependent people view themselves as part of an interlinked social network, tending to define themselves in terms of their relationships with their immediate family and extended family, close friends, and in some cases clans and villages (e.g., many native-born Southeast Asians and Africans).

While independent-self individuals tend to value personal freedom and commitment in close relationships, interdependent-self individuals tend to value relational connectedness and social role commitment in close relationships. For independents, voluntary relational choices and activities are critical to their close relationship. For interdependents, relational choices are often made in view of the larger kinship context. Many obligatory role activities are attached with labels such as "close friendships" or "marital relationships." For independents, it is easy to compartmentalize role-based social relationships (e.g., work relationships) from intimate, personal relationships (e.g., close friendships). For interdependents, however, the boundary between role-based social relationships and personalized relationships is blurred. For example, in the Thai workplace, many working colleagues can also be included in one's close friendship circle. Finally, males (across many cultures) tend to be socialized to define themselves as independents, and females (across many cultures) tend to define themselves as interdependents. We should note that females and males (across ethnic and cultural boundaries) have both independent and interdependent self-construal attributes. Particular situations evoke particular personality tendencies. In individualistic cultures there are more situations that call for "effective" independent-based responses, whereas in collectivistic cultures there are more situations that call for "appropriate" interdependent-based responses.

Situational Contact Conditions

Contact conditions can either impede or induce favorable intergroup interaction. For example, a prior history of intergroup contact and actual intergroup contact experience (positive or negative) serve as barometric indicators of either intergroup attraction or rivalry. Geographic/spatial proximity is a precondition for intergroup interaction. Linguistic similarities can also help to promote direct intergroup dialogue (Brewer & Campbell, 1976).

Brewer (1996, p. 107; see also Cook, 1985) identifies the following situational contact conditions that can produce favorable intergroup or intercultural attitudes:

1. The situation promotes *equal status* interactions between members of the ethnic/cultural groups.
2. The interaction encourages behaviors that *disconfirm stereotypes* that the groups hold of each other.
3. *Cooperative interdependence* among members of both groups is involved.

4. The situation must have high "acquaintance potential," promoting *intimate contact* over an extended period between participants.
5. The *social norms* in the situation must be perceived as favoring intergroup acceptance.

Moreover, researchers have found that it is not the frequency of contact alone but the quality of contact in cooperative intergroup conditions that induce positive intergroup attitudes. For example, in looking closely at the contact conditions between Hindu and Muslim religious groups in Bangladesh, researchers (Islam & Hewstone, 1993) have concluded that the role of anxiety mediates between contact condition and contact outcome.

Anticipated contact with out-group members in a competitive task situation arouses intergroup anxiety. Intergroup anxiety reinforces group-based stereotypes and prejudice. On the other hand, anticipated contact with out-group members in a cooperative task situation reduces intergroup anxiety. Reduced anxiety enhances favorable intergroup attitudes and attraction. Thus, anxiety or identity threat is aroused when contact conditions foster unequal status treatments and competition, and reinforce intergroup stereotypes.

In comparison, emotional vulnerability is reduced when contact conditions foster equal status interactions and common-interest goals' cooperation (e.g., different teams merging their separate identities to create a common identity and work for positive interdependent rewards). Additionally, it is critical that members of each team be exposed to members of the other team over multiple cooperative opportunities (Brewer, 1996). For example, in a collaborative learning classroom environment, teachers can assign students from diverse ethnic backgrounds to work in mixed-ethnic teams. Teachers can also use motivational strategies of group grades and praise in encouraging students to work collaboratively and creatively to solve a problem. Teachers might give part of the lesson to each team (e.g., one part of five-step solution to a math problem) and ask each team to coach all the other teams. Research has shown that students can learn as much from this collaborative learning approach—while learning about each other on a personalized level—as from a traditional, teacher-centered lecturing format (Brislin, 1993).

This section has covered membership and contextual conditions such as cultural and ethnic values, gender expectations and norms, personality attributes, and situational contact conditions that shape the intercultural relationship development process. We now turn to a discussion of four identity- and relational-based themes. Identity memberships and contextual conditions frame the meanings, interpretations, and interpersonal behaviors we engage in—in different types of intimate intercultural relationships (see Figure 7.1).

Identity Membership and
Contextual Conditions

Identity- and
Relational-Based Themes

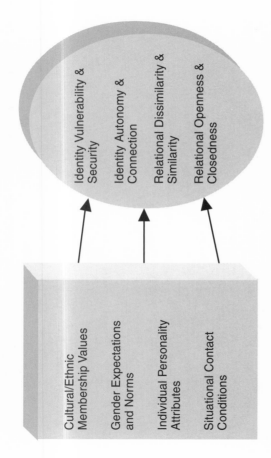

Cultural/Ethnic
Membership Values

Gender Expectations
and Norms

Individual Personality
Attributes

Situational Contact
Conditions

Identity Vulnerability &
Security

Identity Autonomy &
Connection

Relational Dissimilarity &
Similarity

Relational Openness &
Closedness

FIGURE 7.1. The influence of contextual conditions on identity- and relational-based themes.

FOUR IDENTITY- AND RELATIONAL-BASED THEMES

An identity-based thematic approach emphasizes the recurring themes or patterns that all partners must face in dealing with their intercultural close relationships. These recurring themes are identity vulnerability and security, identity autonomy and connection, relational dissimilarity and similarity, and relational openness and closedness (Baxter & Montgomery, 1996; Collier, 1996; Ting-Toomey, 1986, 1989a, 1989b, 1993, 1997a).

Cultural values, gender role expectations, personality attributes, and contact conditions influence our attitudes and treatments of these identity- and relational-based themes. We will first discuss the identity vulnerability and security theme.

The Identity Vulnerability and Security Theme

When strangers encounter one another in a new situation (e.g., at a party), they typically experience identity vulnerability and awkwardness. The term *identity vulnerability* refers to the degree of stress or perceived threat individuals experience in an unfamiliar situation. In any unfamiliar situation or in any situation that involves two complete strangers, identity-based fragility and emotional vulnerability are inevitable. The term *identity security* refers to a sense of confidence or resourcefulness in approaching the unfamiliar situation (Ting-Toomey, 1993).

While identity vulnerability connotes fear of the unfamiliar, identity security connotes a comfortable sense of safety in relating to a stranger. Many interesting things can happen in an intercultural relationship development journey. For example, let us consider the following incident. Michael and Mae are classmates in the basic intercultural communication class. Michael is an European American from the United States, and Mae is from China.

Based on positive classroom interactions and exchanges of pleasant smiles, after 3 weeks Michael was thinking of asking Mae out for a date. One evening, right after the intercultural class, Michael finally plucked up the courage to broach the subject with Mae. He stopped Mae and said, "Mae, I would really like to take you out for a date this weekend. Will you have time?" Mae was dumbfounded.

As a newly arrived Chinese international student on campus, Mae had somewhat limited English proficiency. She understood the word "date" as meaning either "the fruit of a palm tree" or "duration." She was unfamiliar with the sense of the word in this context. Even had she understood it, this date request—from Mae's collectivistic perspective—might well have come at too early a stage of their acquaintance. She felt embarrassed and hesitated in her response. Meanwhile, Michael felt that he had made a fool of himself.

Both Michael and Mae experienced emotional vulnerability and discomfort in this interaction episode. Mae, looking at Michael's facial expression, realized that somehow he was hurt. Michael, on the other hand, did not realize that Mae was having verbal decoding problems with the word "date." He just felt that he had put his self-esteem foolishly at risk. Both parties experienced anxiety and uncertainty.

Gudykunst and his associates have been testing the anxiety/uncertainty management (AUM) theory for the last 15 years (see Gudykunst, 1988, 1993, 1995). The AUM theory basically posits that effective intergroup communication is a function of the amount of anxiety and uncertainty individuals experience when communicating with others. Anxiety refers to the feelings of discomfort when two cultural strangers try to relate to one another. Uncertainty refers to the interaction unpredictability of an intergroup encounter situation. Thus, in the Michael and Mae encounter, both experienced anxious feelings and information uncertainty. Due to cultural unfamiliarity, both parties behaved awkwardly.

Gudykunst and Shapiro (1996) have found that greater amounts of anxiety and uncertainty are experienced in intergroup (i.e., interethnic and intercultural) encounters than in intragroup encounters. As intergroup contact increases under positive contact conditions, anxiety and uncertainty tend to decrease over time (Hubbert, Guerrero, & Gudykunst, 1995). At a minimum, to reduce initial anxiety significantly, the two cultural strangers need to be proficient in a shared language or the native language user must develop cultural sensitivity to the difficulties of the nonnative language user in the interpersonal scene.

Additionally, to increase relational security in their interaction, the two cultural strangers need to have some positive regard for each other's cultural or ethnic background. In fact, Stephan and Stephan (1992) argue that the amount of anxiety we experience in an initial encounter is, in part, due to our attitudes. Individuals with rigid ethnocentric attitudes report a higher degree of intergroup interaction anxiety than individuals with open-minded attitudes. Moreover, the cultural values of individualism and collectivism may influence what constitutes an identity threat in such situations.

For example, for Michael, coming from an individualistic culture, the identity threat often involves scenes threatening his self-esteem such as date rejections, or criticisms directed toward his credibility and competence. In contrast, for Mae, coming from a group-oriented culture, the identity threat is more likely to be associated with social self-esteem issues. Threatening social self-esteem episodes can include disrespect for her cultural heritage or family background, criticisms directed toward her close network members, or embarrassing scenes causing her to "lose face" and look unpoised in front of others. Even if she had understood it, Michael's dating request might still have seriously embarrassed Mae because of its up-front nature. She might have felt obliged to uphold the traditional Chinese female role of reticence (saying something like "Let me think about it and let you know later") and not appear too eager.

Thus, beyond a shared language and an open-minded attitude, knowledge of the other's culture and communication style (e.g., how to ask someone for a date in the proper way and with the right timing) would greatly help Michael to manage his feelings of emotional vulnerability. Then, if Michael developed an understanding of facework sensitivity issues in the Chinese culture, he might reframe his date request into a more tactful, task-oriented question such as "Mae, if you have time, can we get together this weekend and compare our lecture notes before the coming midterm exam?" Mae would thus be offered a wider range of options, enabling her to say "yes," "no," or "maybe" without embarrassment.

In any intercultural personal relationship, the effective balancing of the identity-based thematic pair of vulnerability–security can lead to a satisfying relationship rather than a frustrating one. To move such a relationship from the vulnerable stage to the security stage, individuals need to increase their intercultural acumen and sensitivity as well as their relational communication competence.

The Identity Autonomy and Connection Theme

In developing a relational culture between individuals from two contrastive cultures, friends or partners often face the choice of how to manage autonomy and connection issues competently. Cultural values (e.g., individualism or collectivism) and personality attributes (e.g., the independent self or the interdependent self) underlie the identity-based thematic pair *autonomy–connection* (Baxter & Montgomery, 1996).

Here autonomy means the need for privacy, personal space with definite boundaries while connection means the need for relatedness, overlapping space with indistinct or merging boundaries. For independent-self individualists, the autonomy–connection theme is often viewed by intimate partners as a delicate high-wire act, balancing "me–we" dialectical forces. For interdependent-self collectivists, autonomy and connection are often viewed as a quadrangular contest, a "me–we–they–they" juggling act between the two partners and both their kinship networks.

Identity-based and relational-based needs consist of satisfying both autonomy and connection expectations of both intimate partners (Cupach & Imahori, 1994). Dion and Dion (1988; see also Dion & Dion, 1996), in reviewing the cultural perspectives on romantic love, conclude that the high divorce rate that "characterizes [U.S.] American society is due in good part to the culture's exaggerated sense of individualism" (p. 286). They observe that U.S. Americans, in their keen subscription to "expressive individualism," face the following dilemmas in romantic relationships:

First, one can "lose" one's self and the feeling of personal autonomy in a love relationship, feeling used and exploited as a result. Second, satisfying the autonomous needs of two "separate" individuals in a love relationship obviously becomes a difficult balancing act. Third, the spirit of American individualism makes it difficult for either partner in a relationship to justify sacrificing or giving to the other more than one is receiving. Finally, and inevitably, Americans confront a fundamental conflict trying to reconcile personal freedom and individuality, on the one hand, with obligations and role requirements of marital partner and parent, on the other. (p. 286)

Thus, for many U.S. Americans, romantic love often poses major relational paradoxes. While intimate partners desire to "lose" themselves in a love relationship, many of them also struggle with their desires for personal autonomy and freedom. For example, in interviewing more than a hundred U.S. individuals, Baxter (1990) finds that the "me–we pull" dialectic, that is, a desire "to be with the partner" and a desire to want "autonomy, separation, and independence to be their own person and do their own thing" (p. 76) is the most salient dialectic in the context of U.S. romantic relationships. Comparatively, for many traditional collectivists, the meaning of being "in love" is constructed within social network contexts (e.g., the immediate family and extended family; clan relationships) (Jankowiak, 1995). Romantic or "passionate" love, in sum, may not be perceived as a vital experience for traditional collectivists. In a related line of studies (Simmons, Vom Kolke, & Shimizu, 1986; Simmons, Wehner, & Kay, 1989), for example, research reveals that German and U.S. respondents score higher in their attitudes of valuing romantic love than do Japanese respondents. Likewise, Ting-Toomey (1991) notes that U.S. respondents report more "love commitment" in their heterosexual dating relationships (i.e., they invest more time and energy in their relationships) and more "relational ambivalence" (i.e., they are less certain where their relationship is heading) than Japanese respondents.

In individualistic cultures, most individuals typically "fall in love" first (which sometimes involves intensive dating procedures) and then either get married or move on to another dating partner. However, for members in many traditional, collectivistic cultures (e.g., in India, Iran, and northern Nigeria, in which arranged marriages are still the norm), they first get married and then learn to "fall in love" while carrying out gender-based husband and wife obligations. Individualists tend to look at the thematic pair of autonomy–connection as consisting of contrastive, oppositional forces. Collectivists tend to view autonomy–connection as *complementary* factors that contribute to the relational whole.

In terms of relational commitment, we can also speculate that individualists would value personal commitment from their partners in the close relationships more than collectivists do. In contrast, collectivists might well weigh structural commitment as an important factor in continuing the close relationships (e.g., marital relations) more than individualists do. Here *personal commitment* means the individuals' desire or intent to continue the relationship based on their subjective feelings and experiences; *structural commitment*, on the other hand, means the individuals take into consideration various external social reactions and alternatives in deciding to either continue or terminate a relationship (Johnson, 1991).

Individualists tend to focus on managing the relational struggles of the autonomy and connection theme in their private domain. Collectivists, in comparison, may expend more energy in dealing with the autonomy–connection theme internal and external to the intimate relationship. In an individualistic culture, the relational boundary between the two intimate partners revolves between the "self" and "us." In a collectivistic culture, the relational boundary encompasses crosscutting circles that spill over from immediate to extended families' worries and concerns (see Table 7.1).

For individualistic and collectivistic partners, knowing the cultural meanings and interpretations concerning autonomy and connection issues in a close relationship will help to pave the way to a quality relationship. Understanding the individual expectations and thresholds of the autonomy and connection theme will also clarify individual and relational boundary

TABLE 7.1. Identity- and Relational-Based Themes: Individualistic and Collectivistic Orientations

Individualistic orientation	Collectivistic orientation
Person-based vulnerability	Network-based vulnerability
Autonomy	Connection
"Me"–"We" dialectic	"We"–"Them" dialectic
Personal commitment	Structural commitment
Relational novelty	Relational stability
Private-self openness	Private-self guardedness
Unique relational culture	Conventional relational culture

issues. Lastly, communicating with culture-sensitive relational competence (see the "Recommendations" section below) will greatly help in moving the close relationship to a deeper level.

The Relational Dissimilarity and Similarity Theme

The relational dissimilarity-similarity theme refers to the degree to which people think others are dissimilar or similar to themselves. The term *relational dissimilarity* implies perceived differentiation in beliefs, values, attitudes, and/or interests; its thematic opposite, *perceived similarity*, implies perceived shared views in beliefs, values, attitudes, and/or interests.

The similarity-attraction perspective (Byrne, 1971) has received intense attention in intergroup-interpersonal attraction research for the last three decades. The argument behind this perspective (with a distinct individualistic-based focus) posits that individuals are motivated to maintain or increase their positive self-evaluations by choosing to associate with others that reinforce dimensions relevant to the self. We turn now to a synoptic review in this area.

Research on the *similarity-attraction hypothesis* has provided us with strong evidence supporting this postulate: a positive relationship exists between perceived similarity and interpersonal attraction (Berscheid & Reis, 1998; Berscheid & Walster, 1969; Byrne, 1971; Gudykunst & Nishida, 1984; Lee & Boster, 1991; Snyder & Cantor, 1998). Three plausible explanations exist for the perceived similarity-attraction phenomenon: (1) we experience cognitive consistency if we hold similar attitudes and outlooks in our relationship; (2) cognitive consistency is ego reinforcing and provides identity rewards and affirmations; and (3) with similar others, we tend to invest less time and energy in managing relational vulnerable feelings, and hence similarity bolsters interpersonal attraction.

In the context of intergroup-interpersonal attraction, perceived similarity takes on multifaceted aspects. For example, in intergroup attraction situations, perceived similarity aspects can include cultural/racial similarity and attitudinal similarity. There is considerable research that directly tests the "racial versus attitudinal similarity" controversy (Byrne, 1971; H. K. Kim, 1991).

For example, Byrne (1971) concludes that for low-prejudiced individuals, race is a nonissue in intergroup attraction. Rather, physical attractiveness serves as the decisive factor for intergroup attraction. In contrast, for high-prejudiced individuals, racial dissimilarity is viewed as creating barriers to intergroup attraction. Recent evidence also indicates that while physical attractiveness is critical to initial attraction, there exist cultural differences of attribution. For example, U.S. Americans perceive attractive persons to be high in potency (i.e., high energy and enthusiasm); however, Koreans perceive attractive persons to be high in integrity and concern for others (Wheeler & Kim, 1997). Interestingly also, Cunningham, Roberts, Barbee, Duren, and Wu (1995) report that Asian and Latino/a students newly arrived in the United States and European American students arrive at very similar attractiveness judgments of facial photos of African, Asian, European, and Latina American females.

In examining linguistic similarity, H. K. Kim's (1991) research suggests that perceived attitude similarity acts as a stronger predictor of intercultural attraction than either cultural similarity or in-group language similarity. Hubbert and associates' (1995) research reveals that perceived attitude similarity tends to increase over time in intergroup relationship developments because of the enhanced quality of communication that gradually takes place. In this context *perceived attitude similarity* means that both partners hold similar attitudes and viewpoints concerning salient issues that are essential to the relationship (e.g., attitudes toward religion, marriage, family, work, bringing up children, friends, and leisure time activities). Attitude similarity fosters a sense of familiarity, and a sense of familiarity reinforces our identity security and safety.

Relationship frictions occur because cultural partners often cannot or will not put forth the energy and commitment to work out a consensus concerning core attitudinal issues. Broome (1983) has shown that in the context of the "dissimilar other" attraction process, the variables of positive interaction expectations (i.e., a positive attitude) and direct message openness (i.e., being honest and open) tend to cultivate a deeper intercultural relationship development process.

In sum, people may be attracted to dissimilar strangers if they have repeated chances to interact with them under favorable contact conditions and with a positive mindset. With repeated interaction opportunities, individuals uncover core belief/attitude similarity issues (and also dissimilarity issues) via quality communication. From a relational thematic approach, we believe that individuals desire both some similarity and some complementarity (i.e., mutually enhancing other's limitations) in their close relationships. The complementarity dimensions are essential to the relationship breadth of interaction. The belief/attitude similarity dimensions (e.g., core moral beliefs and work/family attitudes), however, are critical for the development of depth or intimacy in any close relationships. Both breadth and depth of relational communication requires culture-sensitive treatment on the theme of openness and closedness.

The Relational Openness and Closedness Theme

In any relationship, openness and closedness act as critical gatekeepers in moving a relationship to greater or lesser intimacy. Here *openness* refers to the disclosure of information concerning the different facets of the public self (e.g., interest, hobbies, political opinions, career aspirations) and private self (e.g., family issues, self-image and self-esteem issues). The term *public self* refers to those facets of the person that are readily available and are easily shared with others; the term *private self*, on the other hand, refers to those facets of the person that are potentially communicable but are not usually shared with others (Barnlund, 1975). The meanings of public self and private self are culture and gender loaded with variable interpretations.

For example, Barnlund (1975) finds that Japanese tend to have a relatively small layer of public self and a relatively large layer of private self. In contrast, his research reveals that U.S. Americans have a larger layer of public self and a smaller layer of private self. The sharing of information concerning either the public or private self is conducted through relational openness. The Japanese are found to be more guarded as to disclosing their inner attitudes and private feelings and desires. In comparison, he found that U.S. Americans are more responsive in disclosing information of a personal, private nature.

Thus, in this context, *closedness* refers to the cautious regulation of information flow between the self and the outer world (Baxter & Montgomery, 1996; Ting-Toomey, 1986, 1993). Study of the openness-closedness thematic pair is related to the line of research on social penetration theory and self-disclosure (Altman & Taylor, 1973).

In its most general form, the social penetration theory posits that interpersonal exchange usually progresses from superficial, nonintimate self-disclosure to more deep-layered, intimate self-disclosure. This developmental process also involves the "breadth" (number of topics we are willing to disclose to reveal our dynamic self) and "depth" (intimate layers that reveal our emotionally vulnerable self) of self-disclosure. Deep-layered self-disclosure, as a hallmark of intimacy, is defined as an individual's willingness to reveal exclusive private information about her- or himself—usually to a "significant other" (Altman & Taylor, 1973).

Self-disclosure and intimacy are interdependent: appropriate self-disclosure can increase intimacy, and increased intimacy prompts more self-disclosure. Self-disclosure also opens up the vulnerable self to pain, disappointment, and manipulation. However, without the risk of self-disclosure, intimate partners cannot learn to protect each other's vulnerable spots. Thus, self-disclosure entails a trust–risk dilemma: to trust, one has to learn to risk; and to risk, one has to learn to trust. This dilemma applies to many close relationships within and across cultures.

In fact, research has established three important links between self-disclosure and interpersonal attraction in the U.S. culture (Collins & Miller, 1994): (1) people who engage in intimate disclosure tend to be liked better than people who self-disclose less; (2) people tend to disclose more to people whom they initially like; and (3) people like others more as a result of their own disclosure/trusting process. Self-disclosure is obviously one way to reduce uncertainty between two cultural strangers.

The uncertainty reduction disclosure process between strangers often follows three information-seeking routes: a passive strategy, an active strategy, and an interactive strategy (Berger, 1979). *The passive strategy* entails reflective observations concerning the verbal and nonverbal performance of the individual whom you are interested in getting to know. The *active strategy* refers to seeking out information from a third person about the interests and hobbies of the individual of interest. Lastly, the *interactive strategy* refers to the direct interaction between yourself and that person. We can speculate that while collectivists would likely tend to use the passive and active strategies in collecting the needed information, individualists would probably tend to use more direct, interactive strategies to get to know those to whom they are attracted face to face.

Furthermore, three classes of information acquisition strategies between strangers have been delineated: interrogation, self-disclosure, and deception detection (Berger & Kellerman, 1983). *Interrogation strategy* refers to the use of questions to solicit cultural-and personal-background information. *Self-disclosure strategy*, as already discussed, refers to revealing personal and exclusive information about oneself. *Deception detection strategy* refers to the careful decoding process used to infer whether a person is lying or telling the truth. According to deception research in the United States, deceivers often unconsciously give off *leakage cues* reflecting that they are lying. Deceivers are least likely to give off leakage cues in nonverbal areas they can easily control, for example, their facial expressions. Rather, leakage cues are mostly likely to occur in body motions such as nervous twitches and in the eyes (pupil dilation, eye blinking) (Knapp & Hall, 1992). Across cultural lines, we can also speculate that individualists will tend to use more direct deceptive messages in their relationships because of their preference for low-context communication, and collectivists will tend to use more ambiguous deceptive messages because of their preference for high-context communication. Moreover, the reasons for lying or deception may differ across cultures: individualists may engage in relational lying to protect self-esteem and hide incompetence, whereas collectivists may engage in relational deception to protect family secrets or save face.

Gudykunst (1983), in examining the uncertainty reduction process in a collectivistic culture (Japan) and an individualistic culture (the United States) notes that collectivists are typically more cautious in the use of interrogation strategies at the initial encounter stages than are individualists. Collectivists also tend to spend more time in seeking out normative, sociocultural background information at these initial stages than do individualists. More specifically, Barnlund (1989) observes that the most frequently asked question by the Japanese he studied was the occupation of the stranger; as for his U.S. American sample, the most frequently requested information was the name of the interaction partner, closely followed by her or his personal activities and interests. Furthermore, the Japanese respondents said that their chance encounters with strangers were usually on public transportation or in other public settings. The U.S. respondents, on the other hand, said they were more likely to meet strangers at work or while shopping.

Moving beyond the use of verbal questioning strategies in initial attraction, a well-regulated self-disclosure process is critical to managing emotional vulnerability and developing interpersonal trust. Overall, individualists have been found to engage in more active self-disclosure than collectivists (Barnlund, 1975, 1989) across topics of self-disclosure and different "targets," or receivers, of self-disclosure (e.g., parents vs. friends). However, Barnlund (1975) also found a high degree of general similarity between U.S. and Japanese college students in the following self-disclosure topics: interests/tastes, work/studies, opinions on public issues, financial matters, personality, and physical condition. Both cultural groups viewed interests, work/studies, and opinions as the most appropriate topics for self-disclosure, whereas personality traits and physical attributes were preferred least. Interestingly, both U.S. and Japanese groups also agreed on their preferences of self-disclosure "targets" in the following order: same-sex friend, opposite-sex friend, mother, father, stranger, and untrusted acquaintance. Ting-Toomey's (1991) and Chen's (1995) research also indicates that the amount of self-disclosure is higher for U.S. Americans than for Japanese and Chinese groups. Overall, females report a significantly higher degree of self-disclosure than do their male cohorts in Japan and the United States (Ting-Toomey, 1991).

In the area of ethnic self-disclosure, Gudykunst and Hammer (1987) report that European Americans tend to self-disclose more with people they do not know than do African Americans. However, in close friendship situations, African Americans tend to self-disclose more and at a deeper level than do European Americans (Hammer & Gudykunst, 1987; Hecht & Ribeau, 1984). Collier (1991), in comparing close friendships in three ethnic groups, observes that African American interviewees repeatedly emphasized the importance of "acceptance," "problem-solving," and "lifetime support" in close friendships; in comparison, European Americans emphasized "trust," "confiding in each other," and being "free to be myself"; Mexican American interviewees emphasized terms like "supportiveness," "mutual sharing," and "mutual understanding" in explaining close friendships.

In sum, relational openness helps us to gain insight into our own thoughts and feelings. It also helps our intimate partners to understand our culture-based and unique-based self. Self-disclosure helps to create identity familiarity and increase relational safety and trust. While some of the functions of self-disclosure are universal, the means, the meanings, the rhythms, the timing, and the situations in which we exchange self-disclosure may differ from one culture to the next.

Interpreting the existing findings from a relational thematic framework, we can conclude that both relational openness and closedness are critical to the development of an intimate relationship in any cultural or ethnic group. Too much information openness may leave no relational mystery. Too much information closedness, on the other hand, may lead to no relational depth and growth. From a cultural level of interpretation, we can safely state that independent-self individuals would tend to value more verbal openness and honesty than would collectivists. Interdependent-self collectivists, on the other hand, would tend to value more verbal restraint and guardedness than would individualists. Such differences are more prominent in initial experimentation stages of relationship development than in later, more integrated stages of disclosure exchange.

Furthermore, while individualists would be inclined to draw a clear line of privacy between themselves and the external world with regard to their disclosure process, collectivists might well opt to blur that distinction between the private world and the family kinship world with regard to the information disclosed. While individualists would tend to see self-disclosure as an emotional venting process, collectivists would likely see it as a reaching out process for empathy and advice from trusted friends or close network members (perhaps from wise family elders).

Lastly, there are three dimensions of relational involvement competence that cuts across ethnic and cultural differences: attentiveness, responsiveness, and perceptiveness (Cegala & Waldron, 1992; see also Collier, 1996). *Attentiveness* means paying close attention to what our intimate partner is saying or hinting, observing mindfully, listening carefully, and focusing our full attention on the content, relational, and identity meanings of the exchanged message. *Responsiveness* means knowing our role (e.g., an empathy role or an advising role) in that particular situation, understanding the culture-sensitive role expectations, knowing what to say and how to say it, and how to respond with culture-sensitive timing and nonverbal gestures. Finally, *perceptiveness* means the extent of role taking and our ability to see behavior through our intimate partners' cultural and personal lenses. Taken together, high levels of attentiveness, responsiveness, and perceptiveness will convey our support for the worldviews and life experiences of our intimate partners from different cultural shores.

Summary

Four identity- and relational-based thematic pairs in intercultural close relationships have been identified: vulnerability–security, autonomy–connection, dissimilarity–similarity, and openness–closedness. All four influence the fluctuations and movements of close relationship developments across cultures. In gaining knowledge and familiarity of these four themes, individuals need to incorporate the relational knowledge component with culture-sensitive relational practices. Greater depth of culture-based and person-based knowledge can enhance relational involvement competence.

RECOMMENDATIONS

Several general observations can be gleaned from the previous discussions. In order to deal with collectivists competently in the intimate relationship arena, individualists should pay mindful attention to the following:

1. The emotional vulnerability of collectivists concerning their role statuses, in-group membership identities, and in-group and family reactions concerning the particular close relationship development.

2. The relational connectedness needs of collectivists, especially in terms of how each of the partners fit in with family and close friendship network circles and activities.

3. The importance of structural "role-based" commitments in carrying out basic cultural duties and obligations (e.g., taking care of aging parents and grandparents) in addition to the personal commitment in the close relationship.

4. The idea that the more the individualists increase their knowledge and understanding concerning the collectivists' family and close network circles, the more relational harmony and balance may be attained.

5. The subtle and indirect self-disclosure style of collectivists, which can be highly informative if mindful attention is paid to their verbal and nonverbal hints, suggestions, expressions, and gestures.

6. The polychronic rhythms of collectivists in developing close relationships—it takes time, patience, and tactfulness to develop interpersonal trust and intimacy in collectivistic cultures.

In order to deal with individualists competently in the intimate relationship arena, collectivists should pay mindful attention to the following:

1. The emotional vulnerability of individualists concerning their personal self-esteem issues, personal identity attributes, and high individual expectations of personalized meanings of an "intimate relationship."

2. The autonomy needs of individualists, especially for personal time, private space, and relational nonintrusion from family or close friends.

3. The importance of personal commitment and choices in staying in the voluntary relationship, which means certain degrees of personal ownership, accountability, and proactive management of relational problems by the intimate partners themselves.

4. The idea that the more collectivists increase their knowledge and understanding of the individualists' likes and dislikes, personal tastes and preferences, individual dreams and fears, the more relational satisfaction and balance may be attained.

5. The direct verbal self-disclosure style of individualists—and the need for collectivists to reciprocate expressively regarding their own emotional vulnerability, anger, and relational hopes and fears.

6. The monochronic, fast-paced rhythms of individualists in developing close relationships—overt actions or explicit signals should be shown if a collectivist is attracted to an individualist.

Understanding the general themes and patterns of how our intercultural–interpersonal relationships develop can help us to be more mindful of the ebbs and flows of different relationships. Reciprocal self-concept confirmation, through supportive identity messages on both group-based and person-based identity levels, helps to promote quality intercultural and interpersonal relationships. Lastly, the way we manage conflicts in our relationships will have profound positive or negative consequences on our relationships with dissimilar others.

8

Constructive Intercultural Conflict Management

Intercultural Conflict: Definitional Characteristics 195
Conflict Goal Issues 195
Conflict-Related Characteristics 198
Contributing Factors Affecting Intercultural Conflict 201
A Cultural Variability Perspective 202
Cultural-Based Conflict: Different Lenses 210
Intercultural Conflict Management Skills 219
Operational Skills Needed for Constructive
Conflict Management 219
Collaborative Dialogue and Communication Adaptability 224
Recommendations 227

Intercultural miscommunication and misattributions often underscore intercultural conflict. Individuals coming from two contrastive cultural communities bring with them different value assumptions, expectations, verbal and nonverbal habits, and interaction scripts that influence the conflict process. Intercultural conflict is defined as the *perceived or actual incompatibility of values, norms, processes, or goals between a minimum of two cultural parties over content, identity, relational, and procedural issues.* Intercultural conflict often starts off with different expectations concerning appropriate or inappropriate behavior in an interaction episode. Expectation violations, in turn, often influence the effectiveness of how two cultural members negotiate their goals in the conflict process. If the different cultural members continue to engage in inappropriate or ineffective negotiation behavior, the miscommunication can very easily spiral into a complex, polarized conflict situation.

While everyday intercultural conflicts are often based on cultural ignorance or misunderstanding, it is obvious that not all intercultural conflicts are based on miscommunication or lack of understanding. Some intercultural conflicts are based on deep-seated hatred and centuries-old antagonism often arising from long-standing historical grievances (e.g., as in

Northern Ireland, Bosnia, or Kosovo). However, a majority of everyday conflicts that we encounter can be traced to cultural miscommunication or ignorance. As cultural beings, we are socialized or "programmed" by the values and norms of our culture to think and behave in a certain way. Our families, peer groups, educational institutions, mass media, political systems, and religious institutions are some of the forces that shape and mold our cultural and personal values. Our learned values and norms are, in turn, expressed through the way we communicate.

With immigrants (many of whom are non-English speakers), minority group members, and women representing more than 50% of the present workforce in the United States, the study of constructive conflict management is especially critical in today's society. Managing intercultural conflict constructively means managing cultural-based conflict differences appropriately and effectively.

This chapter examines some of the cultural background factors that influence face-to-face intercultural conflict. It is developed in four main sections. First, the definitional characteristics of intercultural conflict are presented. Second, some underlying factors that contribute to intercultural conflict processes are identified. Third, a competence-based approach to intercultural conflict management is discussed. Finally, some recommendations are given as to how to deal with such conflict constructively.

INTERCULTURAL CONFLICT: DEFINITIONAL CHARACTERISTICS

Intercultural conflict revolves around diverse cultural approaches people bring with them in expressing their values, norms, rhythms, and styles in managing conflict. Conflict is a well-nigh inevitable part of any relationship. However, how we perceive the conflict, how we choose to engage in or disengage from it, and how we attribute meanings to the different goals in an intercultural clash can vary tremendously across cultural lines. The perceived or actual differences often rotate around the following goal issues: content, identity, relational, and conflict process or procedure (Wilmot & Hocker, 1998). This section explores conflict goal issues and other conflict-related characteristics.

Conflict Goal Issues

People experience conflict in intimate and nonintimate relationships across a diverse range of cultures. Conflict is a well-nigh inevitable part of any relationship. However, how we perceive the conflict, how we choose to engage in or disengage from it, and how we attribute meanings to the different goals in an intercultural clash can vary tremendously across cultural lines.

By *content goals* we mean the substantive issues that are external to the individuals involved. For example, an interfaith couple might argue as to whether they should raise their children to be Buddhists or Catholics or whether they should raise their kids as bilinguals or monolinguals. Intercultural business partners might argue about whether they should hold their business meetings in Mexico City, Tokyo, or Los Angeles. Content conflict goals also affect the perceptions of identity and relational goals (Fisher & Ury, 1981).

By *identity-based goals* we mean face-saving and face-honoring issues in a conflict episode. They revolve around self-image and other-image issues via the use of respect or disrespect messages. For example, while the above interfaith couple is arguing about which religious faith they should instill in their kids, they are also engaged in evaluating the "worthiness" of their beliefs and the respect quotients they are receiving from their partners. To the extent the couple can engage in a constructive dialogue about this important issue, the conflict can act as a catalyst for their personal and relationship growth. To the extent that the interaction spirals into negative loops (e.g., the more the wife wants to talk about it, the more the husband seeks to avoid the topic), the conflict can be detrimental to both individuals' sense of self-worth.

Likewise, in the case of deciding where the aforementioned business meeting should take place, the conflicting parties may be arguing over a concrete topic such as a location site; however, they are also each testing their "self-image" or "face" in front of others. The decision to hold the business meeting in country X may mean enhanced face power or increased status for the business representative of that country. Face images or identity goals are also closely tied to relational conflict goals.

By *relational conflict goals* we refer to how individuals define the particular relationship (e.g., intimate vs. nonintimate, informal vs. informal) or would like to define it in that interactive situation. For example, in Chapter 7, we suggested that individualists generally crave more privacy and collectivists generally desire more connectedness in an intimate relationship. The struggle to define "independence" and "interdependence" can cause chronic relationship problems in many intercultural (and also intracultural) couples. In the business setting, while one business partner, say, from the United States might opt to scribble a note and fax it to another international partner, say, from Japan, the latter might well view this hastily prepared communication as a cavalier gesture signaling disregard of the formal business partnership and disrespect for him- or herself. For the Japanese partner, face threat and relationship threat may have been perceived and experienced. However, the U.S. business partner may not even realize that he or she has committed a faux pas by sending this offhand message. He or she was actually signaling "friendliness" and "closeness" to minimize the formal relationship distance.

Identity-based and relational conflict goals undergird content-based conflict goals. On the overt level, people may be arguing or disagreeing over content issues. However, beneath the surface lie relational and identity goal problems. From the collectivistic cultural perspective, relational and identity conflict goals usually supersede content goals. The reasoning from the collectivistic point of view is that if the relationship is in jeopardy and mutual face images have been threatened, there is no use spending time talking about substantive issues. The reasoning from the individualistic point of view is that content goals (especially in a task-oriented conflict) are often separated from relationship goals and that, once business is taken care of, people can then attend to their relationship and enjoy each other's company. Identity goals, however, are paramount to both individualists and collectivists.

Identity goals, or face-saving and face-honoring goals, are related to an individual's personal and collective self-esteem issues. These personal and collective self-esteem issues also drive our focus and locus of face images. While "face" is concerned with how we want others to view our public images, "facework" is concerned with how our public images come across with the use of particular verbal and nonverbal messages. All individuals in all cultures have a need for face respect and face consideration as well as face approval and face competence. However, how we go about conveying our respect and face approval needs in a conflict episode differ from one culture to the next (Ting-Toomey, 1988; Ting-Toomey & Kurogi, 1998). For individualists, face-saving and face-defensive needs may be expressed through a direct mode of conflict. For collectivists, face saving and face protection needs may be signaled through an indirect mode of conflict (see the subsection on "Conflict Styles and Facework Strategies" below).

By *process conflict goals* we refer to procedural and stylistic differences in how to manage the conflict problem. For example, individualists may prefer to use a step-by-step, linear mode to dissect the problem, generate criteria, brainstorm some solutions, and select the best one in line with these criteria. Collectivists, on the other hand, prefer to use a spiral mode in probing for all the contextual conditions that contribute to the problem, looking at the "big picture," then deciding on how to resolve the issue. Individualists are good at generating solutions, and collectivists are good at analyzing the holistic contexts that contribute to the problem.

Additionally, individualists and collectivists have different cultural approaches to handling a conflict situation: individualists often prefer to use a direct approach in dealing with the conflict problem, whereas collectivists generally prefer to use an indirect approach. The use of particular conflict styles, however, is contingent on many factors such as the type and severity of the conflict and various resources being contested for. Here *resources* refer to tangible or intangible rewards and advantages that people strive for in the contest. Tangible rewards might be a salary increase, a promotion, or a good grade in a group project. Intangible advantages might be enhanced, for example, safety, attention, affection, understanding, respect, support, self-esteem, and power.

Some tangible commodities are indeed limited (e.g., only one person can get the promotion), as are some intangible commodities (e.g., there is limited time to juggle between schoolwork and family), which can create a highly tense situation. Other perceived scarce resources can be redistributed or managed constructively. A scarce resource situation occurs, for example, when a teacher only directs eye contact at the boys in the elementary classroom and pays more attention to them than to the girls. The situation can be rectified if the teacher is made aware of his or her "unintentional" nonverbal behavior. In other conflict situations, the scarcity of an intangible (or tangible) reward is really based on the *perception* of the conflict party concerning the problematic issue (e.g., an individualistic husband feels left out because his wife goes frequently to visit her collectivistic family). By mindfully changing our own perceptions (and also behaviors) or by persuading the other party to combine his or her interest with our own (see the section on "Constructive Conflict Management Skills" below), the conflict parties may move closer to resolving their conflict differences.

Conflict-Related Characteristics

Conflict involves both perception and interaction. It is an intense disagreement process between two interdependent parties over incompatible goals and the interference each perceives from the other in her or his effort to achieve those goals (Folger, Poole, & Stutman, 1997). The major characteristics of intercultural conflict are the following: (1) *conflict involves intercultural perceptions*—perceptions are filtered through our lenses of ethnocentrism and stereotypes (see Chapter 6), and perceptions color our conflict attribution process; (2) *conflict involves interaction*—conflict is sustained and managed via verbal and nonverbal behaviors, and verbal and nonverbal behaviors are culture-bound concepts (see Chapters 4 and 5); (3) *conflict involves interdependence*—for a conflict to arise, the behavior of one or both parties must have consequences for the other, for otherwise the conflict parties can walk away from each other easily; (4) *conflict involves both self-interest and mutual-interest goals*—conflict is a mixed-up and incomplete jigsaw puzzle, with both parties needing something from each other in order to complete the entire picture; and (5) *conflict involves the protection of intergroup images*—in an intercultural or intergroup conflict situation, conflict parties have to worry about protecting both individual and group-based images (e.g., the sense of group identity as an "African American," as a "Christian," or as a "Democrat").

Recall that *ethnocentrism* is defined as our tendency to view our cultural practices as the "correct" ones and to rate all other cultural practices with reference to our standards (see Chapter 6). Similarly, when members of a culture believe that their own approach is the only "correct" or "natural" way to handle conflict, they tend to see the conflict management behaviors of other cultures as "deviant" from that standard.

A rigidly held ethnocentric attitude promotes a climate of mistrust in intergroup conflict and serves as a hidden barrier to constructive conflict management. Individuals often practice ethnocentric behaviors and biased attributions without a high degree of awareness. They have internalized the standards of their culture as the "proper" and "right" ways of behaving. They tend to use their own cultural or ethnic expectations to attribute meaning to a conflict scene. A conflict scene is often sustained through particular styles of verbal and nonverbal interaction. We often engage in familiar conflict styles as the "natural way" to handle a conflict. For example, the following dialogue between Ms. Gumb (an African American supervisor) and Mr. Lee (a recent Chinese immigrant) in a U.S.–China joint venture firm illustrates the different conflict styles and attribution processes:

Scene 1

Ms. GUMB (*in the main office*): Lee, where is your project report? You said you'd get it done soon. I need your part of the report so that I can finish my final report by the end of this week. When do you think you can get it done? [Attribution: Lee is very irresponsible. I should never have trusted him. I thought I was giving him a break by putting him in charge of this report.]

Mr. LEE (*hesitantly*): Well . . . Ms. Gumb . . . I didn't realize the deadline was so soon . . . I will try my best to get it done as soon as possible. It's just that there are lots of details I need to cross-check . . . I'm really not sure . . . [Attribution: Ms. Gumb is sure a tough lady. Anyway, she is the supervisor—why didn't she tell me the exact deadline early on? Just last week, she told me to take my time on the report. I'm really confused. In China, the supervisor always tells the workers what to do.]

Ms. GUMB (*frustrated*): Lee, how soon is soon? I really need to know your plan of action right now. You cannot be so vague in answering my questions all the time. I believe I've given you plenty of time to work on this report already. [Attribution: Lee is trying to be sneaky. He does not answer my questions directly at all. I wonder if all Chinese are that sneaky? Or maybe he is not comfortable working for a Black female? Anyway, I have to press him to be more efficient and responsible. He is in America—he has to learn the American way.]

Mr. LEE (*a long pause*): Well . . . I'm really not sure, Ms. Gumb. I really don't want to do a bad job on the report and disappoint you. I'll try my best to finish it as soon as possible. Maybe I can finish the report next week. [Attribution: Ms. Gumb is sure a pushy boss. She doesn't seem to like me, and she is causing me to lose face in front of all my peers. Her voice sounds so harsh and loud. I have heard that American people are hard to work with, but she is especially rude and overbearing. I'd better start looking for a new job tomorrow.]

In this scene, while, Ms. Gumb uses an assertive, emotionally expressive verbal style in dealing with the conflict, Mr. Lee uses a hesitant, indirect verbal style in answering her questions. Ms. Gumb uses a "straight talk" low-context approach in dealing with the work problem, whereas Mr. Lee uses a "face talk" high-context approach in dealing with the issue.

If both had a chance to understand concepts such as low-context and high-context communication styles, they might arrive at a better understanding of each other's behavior. Conflict style differences between cultural or ethnic group members also profoundly influence the meanings we attach to each other's behavior. We typically use our own habitual scripts as a baseline to judge the other's behavior. While Mr. Lee uses his high-context scripts to evaluate Ms. Gumb's behavior. While Mr. Lee uses his high-context script to evaluate Ms. Gumb's behavior as "rude and overbearing," Ms. Gumb is using her low-context (e.g., "Lee is trying to be sneaky") attribution and historical script (e.g., "Maybe he is not comfortable working for a Black female" to "make sense" of Mr. Lee's high-context approach. If Ms. Gumb and Mr. Lee understood the cultural/historical conditioning process of their own and the other's behavior, they might learn to be more culturally sensitive in their attribution process. They might also learn to be more respectful of each other's distinctive styles and work more adaptively in achieving a common goal in their interaction.

Then Ms. Gumb might learn to talk privately to Mr. Lee rather than engage in such direct face-threat behavior in public. Mr. Lee might learn to be more direct and open in answering his supervisor's questions and use fewer pauses and hedges in his interaction style. It appears that on the conflict strategy level, individualists often tend to prefer direct verbal assertions, direct verbal questioning, direct requests for clarifications and answers. In contrast, collectivists prefer to use qualifiers (e.g., *"Perhaps we should meet this deadline together"*), tag questions (e.g., *"Don't you think you'll feel better if you finish it and get it out of your way?"*), disclaimers (e.g., *"Maybe I don't understand what's going on here . . ."*), and indirect requests (e.g., *"If it isn't too much trouble, let's try to finish this report together"*) to convey a "softened" approach to working out differences.

Any intercultural conflict also involves certain degrees of interdependence between the two conflict parties. For example, in Scene 1, Ms. Gumb is dependent on Mr. Lee to finish his report before she can put her final report together. Ms. Gumb's final report to the senior management can mean a year-end bonus for her. On the other hand, Mr. Lee is dependent on Ms. Gumb to give him a good performance review or, ultimately, a good recommendation.

They both have personal and mutual interests in resolving the conflict. Unfortunately, oftentimes the cultural-based conflict styles and behaviors lead to cross-purposes and collisions in the interaction process. With their views of the situation distorted by ethnocentric lenses and mindless stereotypes, both parties' conflict may be stuck in their polarized positions and perceptual views. They need to learn new interactive skills (see the "Intercultural Conflict Management Skills" section below) to get "unstuck" and freed from their negative conflict loops.

CONTRIBUTING FACTORS AFFECTING INTERCULTURAL CONFLICT

There are many factors that affect the escalation or deescalation of intercultural conflict negotiation, some of which are different conflict norms, styles, and rhythms (see Figure 8.1).

In order to explain these factors, we need a perspective to organize and relate ideas in a coherent fashion. We use a cultural variability perspective to illustrate how some of the factors stem from our conceptions of cultural, personal, and communication self-images. A cultural variability perspective emphasizes the four dimensions of: individualism–collectivism, power distance, construal of self, and low- or high-context communication. These four dimensions influence the values we hold in approaching or avoiding

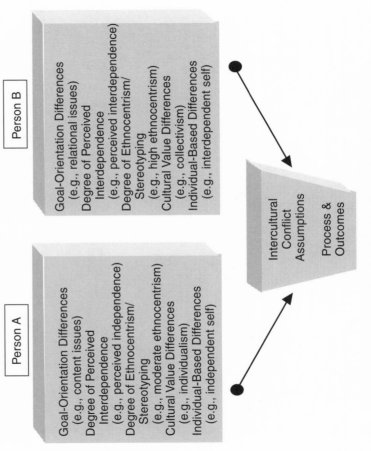

FIGURE 8.1. Factors that influence an intercultural conflict episode.

conflict, the way we attribute meanings to conflict events, and the way we communicate in specific conflict episodes. This section is organized in two parts: first, we look at conflict from a cultural variability perspective with examples, and then we consider some of the specific factors contributing to intercultural conflicts.

A Cultural Variability Perspective

A value-based dimension, such as individualism-collectivism, can provide us with a more in-depth understanding of why members of two contrastive cultures (e.g., those of Germany and Thailand) approach conflict differently. Power distance, as a value dimension, also influences our expectations of how we should be treated and how we treat others. In addition to these two value dimensions, the dimension of self-construal helps us to understand individual distinctions. While the construal of self dimension explains individual-level approaches to conflict, the difference between low- and high-context communication explains conflict style differences between cultures and individuals.

Individualism–Collectivism Values

Basically, as we saw earlier, *individualism* refers to the broad value tendencies of people in a culture to emphasize the individual identity over group identity, and individual rights over group obligations. In contrast, *collectivism* refers to the broad value tendencies of people in a culture to emphasize the group identity over the individual identity, and in-group-oriented concerns over individual wants and desires (Hofstede, 1980, 1991; Triandis, 1995; see also Chapters 3 and 6).

Individualism is expressed in interpersonal conflict through the strong assertion of personal opinions, the display of personal emotions, and the importance of personal accountability for any conflict problem or mistake. Collectivism, on the other hand, is manifested in interpersonal conflict through the representation of collective opinions or ideas, the restraint of personal emotional expressions, and the protection of in-group members, if possible, from being held accountable for the conflict problem. To illustrate, let us look at the following conflict example between a supervisor (Ms. Shapiro, an American Jewish woman) and a supervisee (Mr. Kim, a recent Korean immigrant). The conflict takes place at an international firm in Los Angeles:

Scene 2

Ms. Shapiro: David, is the new computer procedure working yet?

Mr. Kim: There were some minor problems.

Ms. SHAPIRO: How soon will it be ready?

MR. KIM: It's hard to tell, Ms. Shapiro. We need to look into it more carefully.

Ms. SHAPIRO (*impatiently*): Whose idea was this new procedure anyway?

MR. KIM (*with apologetic smile*): Well . . . we'll definitely be more careful next time. We've learned from this lesson.

Ms. SHAPIRO (*decisively*): It came from Peter Lee's division, didn't it?

MR. KIM (*hesitantly*): Well . . . many people worked on this project, Ms. Shapiro. It's hard to say . . .

Ms. SHAPIRO (*frustrated*): All right, just give me a definite timeline when the procedure can be up and running. I've got to run to the next meeting. I don't have time to waste.

While in this scene Ms. Shapiro is operating from an "I"-oriented mode of conflict behavior, Mr. Kim is operating from the "we"-oriented mode. Ms. Shapiro expects two pieces of information from her line of questioning, namely, to find out who is responsible for the problem and when Mr. Kim can fix it. However, Mr. Kim appears "fuzzy" on both issues. From Mr. Kim's Korean group-oriented values' perspective, he feels extremely uneasy to single out a culprit for the computer mistake. From Mr. Kim's attribution process, he perceives that many people have contributed to the oversight. In addition, since Mr. Kim perceives the situation as a team effort, he really has to consult the opinion of the entire group before he can offer his supervisor a feasible timeline for completion of the work.

On the other hand, Ms. Shapiro feels the need to confront Mr. Kim for more information and a specific timeline because she wants to get to the bottom of the situation—the "truth." She is eager to identify a particular person with the mistake so that she can reward the good workers and sanction the bad ones. From her attribution process, Ms. Shapiro wants to be an effective supervisor and wants to deal with the problematic situation equitably and fairly. She does not want to blame the entire work team for one person's mistake. In sum, while Ms. Shapiro has been socialized into an individualistic mode of thinking and behaving, Mr. Kim has been influenced by his cultural conditioning process of group orientation.

In order to preserve the appearance of group harmony or group "face" (i.e., a social self-image issue), Mr. Kim feels he has answered Ms. Shapiro appropriately and perhaps even effectively. On the other hand, Ms. Shapiro walks away from the conflict scene with a sense of frustration because she perceives Mr. Kim's response to be neither effective nor appropriate. She feels "betrayed" by Mr. Kim because he has not leveled with her openly and honestly. Communication openness and honesty are two qualities that Ms. Shapiro prizes deeply. In brief, both Mr. Kim and Ms. Shapiro have been "programmed" by their cultural beliefs and values to think and act in a certain manner. However, both remain unconscious of the underlying value assumptions (such as individualism and collectivism) that "drive" their behavior.

In intercultural communication research, British, French, German, Scandinavian, Swiss, Australian, Canadian, and the U.S. cultures have been identified consistently as cultures high in individualistic value tendencies (Hofstede, 1991). In contrast, strong empirical evidence has shown that many East Asian (e.g., China, Japan, and Korea), Southeast Asian (e.g., Thailand and Vietnam), Mediterranean (e.g., Greece and Italy), Latino (e.g., Brazil and Mexico), Middle Eastern (e.g., Iran and Saudi Arabia), and African (e.g., Ghana) cultures can be identified clearly as group-based cultures (Hofstede, 1991). Various degrees and forms of individualism and collectivism (see, e.g., Triandis, 1995) exist in different cultures.

Nevertheless, we can also find both individualistic and collectivistic elements in *all* of these countries, in different combinations (Triandis, 1995). Additionally, considerable within-culture differences have also been uncovered in many of the pluralistic societies. For example, within a pluralistic society (such as Canada or the United States), different ethnic communities can also display distinctive individualistic and group-oriented value tendencies. For example, ethnic groups that follow their ethnic traditions such as African Americans, Asian Americans, Latino/a Americans, and Native Americans tend to subscribe to some forms of collectivistic values more than do many European Americans. Cultural and ethnic miscommunication and conflicts often arise because of our ignorance of different value priorities in different ethnic communities and cultures. In addition to individualism–collectivism, in order to mindfully manage intercultural conflicts, we should pay close attention to the value dimension of power distance.

Power Distance Values

Let us start off with a critical incident (Cushner & Brislin, 1996)—The Immigration Officer Incident:

Felipe Cordova is a senior official in the Philippines Ministry of Communication. He is proud of the fact that he has been invited to the United States to attend an international conference and is excited at the prospect of his first trip there. Upon entering the United States, he has to pass through immigration and customs. The immigration officer subjects him to a long series of questions concerning how long he intends to stay, how much money he has, whether he intends to visit relatives, whether he understands the visa regulations, and so on. Felipe grows increasingly irritated and finally refuses to answer any more questions. . . . He suffers all this with repressed indignation, but swears to himself that he will never return to this uncivilized country. (pp. 137–138)

How would you explain Felipe's obstinate and uncooperative attitude toward the immigration authorities? (1) He is fatigued and irritable because of the long plane ride. (2) He feels he is being singled out as a suspicious person and is insulted. (3) His expectations as to his status and treatment in the United States have been strongly violated. (4) He feels the officer's questioning is too personal and resents having to disclose such information (Cushner & Brislin, 1996, p. 138). If your choice was answer 3, congratulations!

Felipe, as a senior official representing the Philippines, believes that his invitation to the international conference in the United States reflects his high-status position in his country. He expects to be treated as an honored guest upon his arrival. As such, he expects his path through the bureaucracy to be smooth and unhindered. His expectations as to his high status are strongly violated when he is treated like any Filipino immigrant or common visitor. He feels both outraged and humiliated. His group-based identity (i.e., as a high-status Ministry of Communication functionary from the Philippines) and "face" identity (i.e., his pride and self-esteem) have experienced a sharp insult and severe degradation.

The Philippines, together with Malaysia, Korea, Japan, Guatemala, Panama, Mexico, and many Arab countries, have been identified as large power distance cultures (Hofstede, 1991) whose members give priority treatment and asymmetrical respect to people who are in high-status positions. Subordinates know their "humble" roles, whereas supervisors and managers know their "superior" role scripts. In comparison, in small power distance cultures such as Denmark, Norway, Australia, New Zealand, and the United States (to a moderate degree), members in either high-status or low-status positions strive to foster informal, symmetrical interaction. Subordinates expect to be respected and valued based more on personal attributes than on their position or titles. Supervisors tend to play consultative roles more than authoritarian roles.

Intercultural expectancy violations and miscommunications are commonplace when a supervisee subscribes to small power distance values and a supervisor subscribes to larger power distance values in an international corporation. The small power distance supervisee wants more personal respect from his or her supervisor, and the large power distance supervisor expects more deference and humility from the supervisee. Moving beyond the general discussion of culture-level differences, we next examine individual-level differences within and across cultures.

Construal of Self

An alternative way to understand individualism—collectivism and power distance focuses on how individuals within a culture conceptualize the sense of "self." Markus and Kitayama (1991) argue that our self-conception within our culture profoundly influences our communication with others: individuals with a strongly *independent sense of self* tend to see themselves as autonomous, self-reliant, unencumbered, and as rational choice makers; individuals with a strongly *interdependent sense of self* tend to see themselves as in-group-bound, obligatory agents, and as harmony seekers. Both types of self-construal exist within a culture. Overall, however, whereas independent concepts of self are more common in individualistic cultures, interdependent concepts of self are more common in collectivistic cultures. Let us look at the following dialogue between a Japanese American (with a strongly independent self-concept), Ms. Sueda, and a Japanese national (with a strongly interdependent self-concept), Mr. Ota. Ms. Sueda is an executive vice-president of the accounting department of a joint-venture U.S.-Japanese firm. Mr. Ota is the head of the marketing department based in Tokyo. The following dialogue takes place there at a staff meeting (with Japanese and American staff members):

Scene 3

Ms. Sueda (*enthusiastically*): Since we're all here today in the meeting, I would like to discuss with you my opinion on renewing our contract with the Fuji advertising firm. But before I do that, Ota-san, what do you think of the Fuji firm?

Mr. Ota (*taken by surprise*): Ms. Sueda, what about the Fuji firm?

Ms. Sueda: Ota-san, I don't think they are working out for us. I don't think they are being aggressive enough in pushing our spring water products. I seriously think we should switch to a new firm. Their ads did not seem to have any impact on generating new sales for us.

Mr. Ota (*after a long pause*): Ms. Sueda, Have you discussed this with others in our department?

Ms. Sueda (*looking around*): Not really. That's why I'm sounding you out right now.

Mr. Ota: Well . . . it is a good idea to get as many people's opinions as possible on this important decision. Why don't we wait . . .

Ms. Sueda (*impatiently*): But I'm really not satisfied with the Fuji's "soft sell" approach to our products. If you have any opinion, now is a good time to speak up. So what do you think?

Mr. Ota: Um . . . we really have to give this some more thought. . . . After all, we've cultivated a good relationship with the people in the Fuji firm . . . Maybe I'll check around with other people in the department after the meeting to get their input.

Ms. Sueda: Well, all your department people are here in this room. Why don't we ask them right now? Okabe-san, what do you think?

Mr. Okabe (*taken by surprise*): Well . . . (*a long pause*) . . . we should spend more time thinking together . . .

Ms. Sueda (*very frustrated*): All right, everyone, wasted time is wasted effort. Ota-san, back to you. What do you really think?

Mr. Ota (*glancing around the room and sensing tension*): Well . . . (*a very long pause*) . . . I couldn't really say right now . . . It takes time to make such an important decision.

While Ms. Sueda is direct and forthright in her approach in dealing with a problematic issue, Mr. Ota is cautious and circumspective. For Mr. Ota, from his interdependent self-perspective, he perceives major problems in changing from an old advertising firm to a new one. It takes time to cultivate reliable, reciprocal social and business ties in Japan. It will take a long time for him and his staff to nurture network relations with a new firm. In addition, Mr. Ota also resents the fact that he is being singled out so suddenly by Ms. Sueda for his personal opinion in a group setting. It causes him to "lose face" in front of his colleagues because he is underprepared to respond to the sudden question. He wishes Ms. Sueda had consulted with him before the staff meeting. He does not want to state his opinion in the public setting for fear that his opinion will go against the opinion of his in-group members. Also, in front of other staff members (which include both Americans and Japanese), he does not want to raise all the issues openly with Ms. Sueda because that may cause her to "lose face" (e.g., issue such as that "soft-sell" advertising works better in Japan than "hard-sell" advertising) and appear incompetent (see Imahori & Cupach, 1994).

Anyway, if Ms. Sueda were listening attentively to both the verbal and nonverbal nuances conveyed by Mr. Ota, she would realize that Mr. Ota's answer to her initial question is a "no—maybe" response. By remarking that "After all, we've cultivated a good relationship with the people in the Fuji firm," Mr. Ota is implicitly saying "No . . . but let's talk about this issue later, maybe privately, and maybe we can work something out." Ms. Sueda, on the other hand, perceives herself as being a very consultative colleague. From her independent self-perspective, Ms. Sueda assumes that everyone else in the room will feel free to speak up openly. In soliciting everyone's input in the staff meeting, she views herself as very respectful of staff members working in this joint-venture operation. By asking Mr. Ota's opinion, Ms. Sueda thinks she is being "face sensitive" to the status position of Mr. Ota as head of the marketing department in Tokyo. She is baffled and frustrated by Mr. Ota's hesitant and elusive speech style. She is starting to think that maybe her Japanese colleagues do not like working with a woman executive officer, especially one who is a *sansei* (third-generation) Japanese American.

In sum, whereas independent-self people tend to "make sense" of their environment through "autonomous self" lenses, interdependent-self people tend to "make sense" of their surrounding through "in-group self" lenses. Independent-self individuals tend to worry about whether they present their "individualistic self" credibly and competently in front of others. Interdependent-self individuals tend to be more reflective of what others think of their projected "face image" in the context of in-group/out-group relations.

Finally, while independent-self individuals tend to practice direct verbal communication in expressing thoughts and feelings, interdependent-self individuals tend to practice responsive communication in anticipating the thoughts and feelings of the other person. Direct, verbal communication reflects a low-context way of communicating, and responsive communication reflects a high-context way of communicating (Hall, 1976, 1983).

Parallel to the above self-construal idea, we can examine power distance from a personal variation dimension. Individuals and their behaviors can be conceptualized as either moving toward the "horizontal self" spectrum or the "vertical self" spectrum. Individuals who endorse horizontal self construal prefer informal, symmetrical interactions (i.e., equal treatment) regardless of people's status or the occasion. In comparison, individuals who emphasize vertical self-construal would prefer formal, asymmetrical interactions (i.e., differential treatment), with due respect to people with high-status positions, titles, and the special occasion. As Triandis (1995) observes,

> This means that people will seek different kinds of relationships and when possible "convert" a relationship to the kind that they are most comfortable with. Thus, a professor [with] a horizontal-based [self-construal] may convert a professor–student relationship to a friend–friend relationship, which may well confuse a student [with] a vertical-based [self-construal]. Conversely, a friend [with] a vertical-based [self-construal] might convert a friend–friend relationship to a counselor–client relationship and provide all sorts of unrequested and unexpected advice. (p. 164)

While horizontal selves tend to be predominant in small power distance cultures, vertical selves tend to be predominant in large power distance cultures.

Low-Context and High-Context Communication

Low-context communication emphasizes how intention or meaning can be best expressed through the explicit verbal message. High-context communication emphasizes how intention or meaning can be best conveyed through the context (e.g., social roles, positions) and nonverbal channels (e.g., pauses, silence, tone of voice) of the verbal message (Hall, 1976). In general, low-context communication refers to communication patterns of direct verbal mode, straight talk, nonverbal immediacy, and sender-oriented value. In low-context communication, the speaker of the message is expected to be responsible for constructing a clear, persuasive message that the listener can decode easily. In contrast, high-context communication refers to communication patterns of indirect verbal mode, ambiguous talk, nonverbal subtleties, and interpreter-sensitive value (Ting-Toomey, 1985). In high-context communication, the listener or interpreter of the message is expected to read "between the lines," to accurately infer the implicit intent of the verbal message, and to observe the nonverbal nuances and subtleties that encircle or "wrap" the verbal message.

Low-context communication emphasizes the importance of explicit verbal messages to convey personal thoughts, opinions, and feelings. High-context communication emphasizes the importance of multilayered contexts (e.g., historical context, social norms, roles, situational and relational contexts) that frame the interaction encounter. As Barnlund (1989) observes, in commenting on the communication style differences between Japanese and U.S. Americans,

Conflict is far less common in Japanese society for a number of reasons. First, the emphasis on the group instead of the individual reduces interpersonal friction. Second, an elaborate set of standards emphasize "obligations" over "rights," what one owes to others rather than deserves for oneself. Third, the value attached to harmony cultivates skill in the use of ambiguity, circumlocution, euphemism, and silence in blunting incipient disputes. The ability to assimilate differences, to engineer consensus, is valued above a talent for argument. (p. 39)

Individualism and independent self-construal in the United States promotes the need for verbal self-assertion, and verbal self-assertion often promotes individual differences and competition. In contrast, collectivism and interdependent self-construal in Japan promote the need for verbal circumspection, and verbal circumspection often promotes face preservation and relational harmony.

While independent-self individualists engage in low-context styles of conflict management, interdependent-self collectivists engage in high-context styles of conflict negotiation. Overall, the cultural variability dimensions of individualism versus collectivism, large or small power distance, independent or interdependent self, horizontal or vertical self, and low- or high-context communication patterns help to guide us toward a general understanding of conflict process between members of individualistic and collectivistic cultures.

Cultural-Based Conflict: Different Lenses

Drawing from the key ideas of a cultural variability perspective, the following subsections identify the different lenses that create intercultural frictions and conflicts between individuals and collectivists. These lenses include different conflict assumptions, conflict rhythms, conflict norms, conflict styles, and ethnocentric lenses. Culture-based lenses can distort our perceptions and interpretations of exchanged messages in conflict episodes like Scenes 1–3 (see Table 8.1).

Different Conflict Assumptions

The values of individualism versus collectivism, and how these are linked to individual self-construals and low-/high-context communication, affect our assumptions about conflict. Cultural assumptions about conflict color our attitudes, expectations, and behaviors in a conflict episode. Different cultural assumptions toward conflict serve as the first set of factors that contribute to intercultural miscommunication and antagonism.

For individualists, interpersonal conflict resolution follows an "outcome-oriented" model. However, for collectivists, interpersonal conflict management follows a "process-oriented" model. An outcome-oriented model emphasizes the importance of asserting "I"-identity interests in the conflict situation and moving rapidly toward the phase of reaching tangible outcomes or goals. A process-oriented model, in contrast, emphasizes the importance of the management of "mutual or group face" interests in the conflict process before any tangible outcomes or goals can be discussed. As earlier, "face," in this context, refers to the orientation of upholding a claimed

TABLE 8.1. Individualistic and Collectivistic Conflict Lenses

Individualistic conflict lens	Collectivistic conflict lens
Outcome focused	Process focused
Emphasis on factual details	Emphasis on holistic pictures
Content goal oriented	Relational goal oriented
Emphasis on tangible resources	Emphasis on intangible resources
Work at monochronic pace	Work at polychronic pace
Use of personal equity norms	Use of communal or status-based norms
Reliance on linear inductive or deductive reasoning	Reliance on spiral and metaphorical reasoning
Facts and evidence are most important data	Intuition and experience are most important data
Competitive/controlling behaviors	Avoiding/accommodating behaviors
Direct conflict styles	Indirect conflict styles
Self-face concern	Other-face concern
Emphasis on conflict effectiveness	Emphasis on conflict appropriateness

sense of positive public image in any social interactive situations (Ting-Toomey, 1994c). From the collectivistic perspective, face is not about what one thinks of oneself but about what others think of one's worth, especially within the context of one's in-group and out-group. For individualists, effective conflict negotiation means settling the conflict problem openly and working out a set of functional conflict solutions conjointly. Effective conflict resolution behavior (e.g., emphasizing the importance of addressing incompatible goals or outcomes) is *relatively* more important for individualists than is appropriate facework behavior. For collectivists, on the other hand, appropriate conflict management means the subtle negotiation of in-group/out-group face-related issues—pride, honor, dignity, insult, shame, disgrace, humility, trust, mistrust, respect, and prestige—in a given conflict episode. Appropriate facework moves and countermoves are critical for collectivists before tangible conflict outcomes or goals can be addressed.

In commenting on face issues in the collectivistic cultures, Cohen (1991) observes, "For the representatives of interdependent cultures the experience of international negotiation is fraught with considerations of face. The very structure of the situation, in which competing parties pit their wills and skills against each other, is uncongenial to societies that see social harmony, not confrontation, as the desired state of affairs" (p. 132).

To summarize, independent-self individualists tend to operate from the following "outcome-oriented" model of conflict assumptions:

1. Conflict is perceived as closely related to the goals or outcomes that are salient to the respective individual conflict parties in a given conflict situation.

2. Communication in the conflict process is viewed as dissatisfying when the conflict parties are not willing to deal with the conflict openly and honestly.

3. Conversely, communication in the conflict process is viewed as satisfying when the conflict parties are willing to confront the conflict issues openly and share their feelings honestly (i.e., assertively but not aggressively).

4. The conflict outcome is perceived as unproductive when no tangible outcomes are reached or no plan of action is developed.

5. The conflict outcome is perceived as productive when tangible solutions are reached and objective criteria are met.

6. Effective and appropriate management of conflict means individual goals are addressed and differences are being dealt with openly, honestly, and properly in relation to timing and the situational context.

Interdependent-self collectivists follow the conflict assumptions of a "process-oriented" model:

1. Conflict is weighed against the face threat incurred in the conflict negotiation process; it is also being interpreted in the webs of in-group/out-group relationships.

2. Communication in the conflict process is perceived as threatening when the conflict parties push for substantive issue discussion before proper facework management.

3. Communication in the conflict interaction is viewed as satisfying when the conflict parties engage in *mutual* face-saving and face-giving behavior and attend to both verbal *and* nonverbal signals.

4. The conflict process or outcome is perceived as unproductive when face issues are not addressed and relational/group feelings are not attended to properly.

5. The conflict process or outcome is defined as productive when both conflict parties can claim win-win results on the facework front in addition to substantive agreement.

6. Appropriate and effective management of conflict means that the mutual "faces" of the conflict parties are saved or even upgraded in the interaction and they have dealt with the conflict episode strategically in conjunction with substantive gains or losses.

Thus, whereas individualists are concerned with conflict problem-solution closure, collectivists are concerned with in-group/out-group face dynamic issues. These implicit conflict assumptions are, in turn, superimposed on the rhythms and pacing of intercultural conflict resolution.

Different Conflict Rhythms

The consciousness of conflict management rhythms also varies along the individualism-collectivism divide. This operates as the second set of factors contributing to the intercultural conflict process between individualists and collectivists. Individualistic value tendencies tend to foster monochronic time (M-time) rhythms, and collectivistic value tendencies tend to cultivate polychronic time (P-time) rhythms. While the "I"-identity individuals tend to subscribe to an M-time orientation, the "we"-identity individuals tend to value a P-time orientation (see Chapter 5).

As Hall and Hall (1987) explain: "In monochronic cultures, time is experienced and used in a linear way—comparable to a road. . . . M-time is divided quite naturally into segments; it is scheduled and compartmentalized, making it possible for a person to concentrate on one thing at a time" (p. 16). Hall and Hall identified Germany, the Scandinavian countries, Switzerland, and the United States as prime M-time examples. In contrast, they note, "[P-time] systems are the antithesis of M-time systems. P-time is characterized by the simultaneous occurrence of many things and by a great involvement with people. There is also more emphasis on completing human transactions than on holding schedules. . . . P-time is experienced as much less tangible than M-time, and can better be compared to a single point than to a road" (pp. 17–18). Many African, Asian, Latin American, eastern European, Caribbean, and Mediterranean cultures are prime examples of P-time.

M-time people prefer to deal with conflict from a linear-sequential approach (either via inductive or deductive means); P-time people prefer to handle conflict from a spiral-holistic viewpoint. For M-time individuals, conflict management time should be filled with problem-solving or decision-making activities. For P-time individuals, time is a "being" idea governed by the smooth implicit rhythms in the interaction between people. When conflict occurs between two P-time individuals, they will be more concerned with restoring the disjunctive rhythms in the interaction than in dealing head on with discussion of substantive issues.

M-time people tend to emphasize agenda setting, objective criteria, and precise schedules to accomplish certain conflict goals. P-time people, in contrast, tend to work on the relational atmosphere and the contextual setting that frame the conflict episode. For M-time individuals, effective conflict negotiation means reaching and implementing tangible conflict outcomes within a clearly established timetable. For P-time individuals, the arbitrary division of clock time or calendar time holds little meaning for them if the relational rhythms between people are "out of sync." For M-time people, a signed contract or written agreement signals joint explicit agreement to the solution of the conflict. However, for P-time people, once the appropriate level of relational rhythm (or rapport and trust) is established, their pledged words can mean more than a signed contract. Likewise, if they perceive that the relational rhythms are disjunctive, then renewed facework negotiation might well be needed to restore that delicate face-honoring point.

M-time people tend to define conflict in terms of a short- to medium-term timeline; P-time people tend to view time as a long-term, historical process. For P-time members, a "deadline" is always subject to renegotiation and should be dealt with flexibly and patiently. People thus can move with different rhythms in conflict negotiation encounters. Intercultural conflict between individualists and collectivists is magnified when the implicit rhythm of time plays a decisive factor in the encounter process.

M-time individuals want to move faster to address substantive problem and conflict resolution issues, whereas P-time individuals prefer to deal with relational or contextual issues before concrete, substantive negotiation. M-time people want to establish a clear timetable to achieve specific conflict goals and objectives; P-time people want to spend more time building up trust and commitment between the conflict parties. Different M-time and P-time rhythms thus can further polarize individualists and collectivists in the intercultural misattribution process.

Different Conflict Norms

The use of different norms in conflict interaction serves as a third set of factors compounding intercultural clashes. Norms are standards or guidelines for behavior. They are reflected via our expectations of what constitute "proper" or "improper" behavior in a given setting.

According to past research (Leung & Bond, 1984; Leung & Iwawaki, 1988), individualists tend to prefer use of the equity norm (i.e., the self-deservingness norm) in dealing with reward allocation (e.g., in dealing with group project points) in conflict interaction. In comparison, collectivists prefer use of the communal norm (i.e., the equal distribution norm—divid-ing the group project points evenly) in in-group conflict, thereby preserving in-group harmony. The equity norm emphasizes the importance of *indi-vidual* reward and cost calculations and the importance of obtaining equi-table rewards in resolving the problematic issue. The communal norm, in contrast, stresses the importance of taking *in-group* expectations into the calculation and of determining how to satisfy the face needs of the in-group members involved in the conflict.

While the equity norm reflects the individualistic, outcome-oriented model of conflict resolution, the communal norm reflects the collectivistic, process-oriented model. In addition, it is critical to remember that in col-lectivistic cultures, different norms govern conflict interaction with in-group and out-group members. Recall that, according to Triandis (1995), in-groups are groups of individuals "about whose welfare a person is concerned, with whom that person is willing to cooperate without demanding equitable re-turns, and separation from whom leads to anxiety" (p. 9). In-groups are usually characterized by members who perceive a "common fate" or shared attributes among them. Out-groups are groups of individuals "with which one has something to divide, perhaps unequally, or are harmful in some way, groups that disagreed on valued attributes" (Triandis, 1995, p. 9).

According to research findings (Leung & Iwawaki, 1988), for highly important conflicts collectivists (like individualists) prefer the use of the equity norm when competing with out-group members (e.g., people from another company) for needed resources. However, for less important con-flicts collectivists prefer the use of the communal, smoothing norm with either in-group or out-group members. We should also remember that each culture has different rules and meanings for proper or improper conflict behavior in dealing with in-group/out-group members in different situa-tions.

In regarding norms of emotional expression, conflict is essentially an emotionally distressing experience. In two extensive, detailed reviews (Mesquita & Frijida, 1992; Russell, 1991) of culture and emotions, clear cross-cultural emotional expression and interpretation differences are un-covered. Based on these reviews, we can conclude that cultural norms do exist in conflict which regulate displays of "aggressive" or "negative" emotional reactions such as anger, fear, shame, frustration, resentment, and hostility in different cultures. For example, in many individualistic Western cultures, open expressions of emotions are viewed as honest, engaging signals in dealing with a conflict. However, in many collectivistic Asian cultures, maintaining restrained emotional composure is viewed as the self-disciplined, mature way to handle the conflict. Triandis (1994b) also observes that

The collectivist concern with the possible disruption of [in-group] harmony will press individuals to avoid the expression of negative emotions and to avoid assigning responsibility for negative events to others. Individualists, on the other hand, are more likely than collectivists to engage in actions that may cause anger in others. . . . Most cultures (about 85% of known cultures . . .) also specify that some role relationships (e.g., mother-in-law/son-in-law, father-in-law/daughter-in-law) must be marked by avoidance–respect–formality, which has the effect of avoiding disruptions of the [in-group]. (pp. 301–302)

This does not mean, however, that collectivists deal with each other harmoniously all the time. As Triandis (1994b) concludes,

In collectivist cultures . . . norms are very powerful regulators of behavior. . . . [Japanese returnees] after spending some time abroad are frequently criticized, teased, and bullied by their peers, and even by authorities such as teachers, for "non-Japanese behaviors" such as having a [suntan] or a permanent-wave hairstyle or for eating Western food. Thus, negative emotions will occur in collectivist culture when *minor* norms are violated to a greater degree than in individualistic cultures. The threat of ostracism is an especially powerful source of fear in collectivist cultures. (p. 302; emphasis in original)

We must also remember that within-cultures variations exist in each culture. In individualistic cultures, there are interdependent-self individuals who act just like the collectivists. Likewise, in collectivistic cultures, there are independent-self persons who behave just like individualists. We must also keep in mind that behavior is only a partial indicator of a person's identity. To understand a "full-fledged" independent or interdependent person, we must also examine the thinking and affective pattern of this individual.

Overall, while basic emotions such as anxiety, shame, and fear can be viewed as pancultural conflict emotions, *cultural display rules* of when to express what nonverbal emotions (to whom and in what context) differ from one cultural community to the next. For example, for collectivists, the masking of "negative" emotions is critical to maintaining a harmonious front during conflict. As noted earlier, when collectivists feel embarrassed or perceive face threat in a conflict situation, they may sometimes smile to cover up their embarrassment or shame.

Different norms and rules govern the way individualists and collectivists deal with specific conflict issues. When an individualist prefers to use the equity norm to deal with a conflict issue and when a collectivist prefers to use the equality norm, the hidden factor of normative expectations further splinters the intercultural miscommunication process. In addition, the nonverbal/verbal dimension of emotional expression in conflict can vary along the individualism and collectivism schism, creating further conflict tensions and gaps.

Conflict Styles and Facework Strategies

Findings in many past studies also indicate that people do exhibit quite consistent cross-situational styles of conflict in different cultures. Each culture assumes the primary role of conditioning certain conflict styles or facework behaviors in preference to others (Ting-Toomey, 1994a, 1994b, 1997a). Different conflict styles serve as a fourth set of factors impinging on intercultural negotiations. Different cross-cultural conflict styles further generate different intergroup attribution errors and biases.

In fact, research across cultures (e.g., in China, Hong Kong, Japan, Korea, Taiwan, Mexico, and the United States) clearly indicates that individualists tend to use more self-defensive controlling/dominating and competitive styles in managing conflict than do collectivists. In comparison, collectivists tend to use more collaborative/integrative and compromising styles in dealing with conflict than do individualists. Furthermore, collectivists tend to use more obliging and avoiding styles in task-related conflicts than do individualists (Chua & Gudykunst, 1987; Ting-Toomey et al., 1991; Trubisky, Ting-Toomey, & Lin, 1991).

In addition, the use of silence is also a critical strategy in dealing with both in-group and out-group conflicts in collectivistic cultures. Silence can signal either approval or disapproval in collectivistic conflict interaction. In silence, there is no incurrence of obligations by the parties to the conflict. Silence can also be interpreted as an ambiguous "yes" or "no" response. On the other hand, in individualistic cultures, silence may well be viewed as an admission of guilt or a sign of incompetence.

In examining facework strategies in saving self-face or giving consideration to the other's face, research by Ting-Toomey and associates (Cocroft & Ting-Toomey, 1994; Ting-Toomey, 1994b; Ting-Toomey et al., 1991) indicates that while individualists tend to use more self-oriented face-saving strategies in conflicts, collectivists tend to use more other-oriented face-saving strategies in such situations. In addition, individualists (e.g., U.S. respondents) tend to use more direct, face-threatening conflict behaviors, whereas collectivists (i.e., Taiwan and China respondents) tend to use more indirect, mutual face-saving conflict behaviors.

In cross-ethnic conflict situations, it has been found that the philosophy of Confucianism strongly influences proper facework management in Asian American immigrants (Ting-Toomey et al., in press). For Asian Americans who subscribe to their traditional ethnic values, meeting the vital needs of the other person or avoiding the conflict situation altogether enables both conflict parties to "give face" and also "save face."

In the context of traditional Latino/a Americans' conflict practices, tactfulness and consideration of others' feelings are considered to be important norms in interpersonal confrontation situations (Casas & Pytluk, 1995; Garcia, 1996; Padilla, 1981). Tactfulness and consideration of others' feelings are conveyed through the use of accommodating and other-concern facework rituals. In commenting on the cultural values and norms of Mexican Americans, for example, Locke (1992) observes that "Whereas members of the dominant culture of the United States are taught to value openness, frankness, and directness, the traditional Mexican-American approach requires the use of much diplomacy and tact when communicating with another individual. Concern and respect for the feelings of others dictate that a screen be provided behind which an individual may preserve dignity" (p. 140).

In terms of African Americans' conflict styles, Kochman (1981) notes that in most confrontation situations, African Americans and European Americans are divided not only over the content but also over the engagement process. According to Kochman (1981), the "Black mode" of conflict is "high-keyed: animated, interpersonal, and confrontational" whereas the "White mode" of conflict is relatively "low-keyed: dispassionate, impersonal and non-challenging" (p. 18). African Americans tend to prefer emotionally expressive self-face assertion modes, while European Americans often prefer logically inductive self-face defensive modes.

The explanation for these African American conflict modes can be explained by many factors, including the importance of oral artistry of traditional African culture and the ethnic socialization experiences of African Americans. Spontaneous affective expressions and rich storytelling are highly prized in many traditional African societies. Additionally, the ethnic socialization experiences of African Americans within the larger U.S. culture may well contribute to their emotionally expressive conflict style. As Locke (1992) comments, from that ethnic lens "future successes for their sons [and daughters] hinges on an ability to be alternatively assertive and acquiescent. . . . [T]he environment of African-American children is an ambiguous and marginal one in which they live simultaneously in two worlds—the African-American world and the world of the dominant culture" (p. 21).

In investigating ethnic socialization by parents of ethnic minority adolescents, researchers have found that African American parents reported more frequent discussion of prejudice issues with their children than did Japanese American and Mexican American parents (Phinney & Chavira, 1995). Thus, self-face protection via emotionally expressive facework styles may be one method for African Americans to uphold self-pride and handle interpersonal conflicts.

Several research studies (e.g., Cohen, 1991; Leung, 1987, 1988; Ting-Toomey, 1985, 1988) indicate that collectivists tend to prefer an *informal* third-party conflict mediation procedure (such as seeking help from relatives or wise teachers or gurus) more than do individualists. While individualists prefer objective advice and facilitation from an impartial formal (certified) third-party mediator, collectivists prefer to seek help from someone who already is informed as to the conflict situation and whom they can trust and respect.

Different cross-cultural conflict styles and facework behaviors create different attribution biases and tensions. In attributing meanings to collectivistic, indirect conflict styles, individualists tend to view collectivists in the conflict as trying to sidestep genuine issue discussions. Conversely, collectivists would tend to perceive individualists as too pushy, rude, and overbearing because of their confrontative, direct conflict style.

Different Ethnocentric Lenses

In dealing with intercultural conflict situations mindfully, we must first recognize just what ethnocentric lenses we look through to evaluate a conflict situation. In perceiving unfamiliar conflict behaviors, we use our culture-based scripts to evaluate whether the behavior is "proper" or "improper," "nonthreatening" or "threatening." Ethnocentrism colors our perceptions and attitudes in any intergroup-based conflict situation. As Stewart and Bennett (1991) comment,

Participants in a cross-cultural situation need to consider first the possibility that a negative evaluation might be based on unrecognized cultural difference rather than the result of astute cross-cultural analysis. Each person needs to be aware that he or she is evaluating the other, often on similarly ethnocentric grounds, and [should] seek to suspend these kinds of evaluations until the potential spiraling effects of the action have been considered.... [S]wift evaluation is likely to be ethnocentric and detrimental to effective intercultural communication. (p. 167)

Acknowledging our own ethnocentric biases and suspending our reactive evaluations are critical in managing the intercultural misattribution process. By withholding our gut-level negative judgments concerning unfamiliar behavior, we are giving ourselves and others a chance to understand the cultural nuances that exist in a problematic situation.

Summary

Thus, different cultural conflict assumptions, rhythms, norms, styles, and ethnocentric lenses act as the many invisible barriers that often widen the gap of intercultural disputes. Individualists and collectivists typically collide over their use of an "outcome-oriented" model or a "process-oriented" model. They also collide over the rhythms, the norms, and the styles of how to approach conflict appropriately and effectively. Finally, ethnocentric lenses may well be distorting the attribution process and creating further evaluative biases and binary mindsets (i.e., "My way is the *right way*, and your way is *wrong*").

INTERCULTURAL CONFLICT MANAGEMENT SKILLS

Constructive and destructive intercultural conflict management depends on many factors. One of the key factors is the ability to apply flexible communication skills in managing both culture-based and individual-based differences. Constructive intercultural conflict management is defined as the use of culture-sensitive communication skills to manage the process of conflict productively and reach important conflict goals of all parties amicably. By contrast, destructive conflict means the parties are engaging in inflexible thinking and inflexible conflict patterns that lock them into prolonged cycles of defensiveness and mutual dissatisfaction leading to escalation or total impasse.

In constructive conflict resolution, the parties are mindful of culture-based factors that contribute to the different approaches to the dispute. They are mindful of the different goals that underlie the issue between them. They are also willing to experiment with different constructive conflict management skills and to draw on cultural resources to reach a synergistic common ground. This section is divided into two parts: first, constructive conflict operational skills, and second, suggestions for how individualists and collectivists can deal with conflicts productively.

Operational Skills Needed for Constructive Conflict Management

Skills refer to the actual abilities to perform those behaviors that are considered effective and appropriate in a given situation. Operational skills enable us to put our culture-based knowledge into practice. Such skills also depend heavily on our motivation or commitment to working out the conflict peacefully and productively together with our opponents.

A major problem exists, however, when individualists and collectivists hold different notions of what constitute effective and appropriate practices in conflict resolution. For individualists a conflict is *effectively* resolved when personal opinions are voiced and acknowledged, interests are defined and clarified, each side's goals are either reached or compromised, and action plans are drawn up for avoiding trouble in the future. In addition, individualists perceive themselves to have acted *appropriately* when they display sensitivity to the background and causes of the conflict. Conversely, for collectivists a conflict is *effectively* resolved when both parties help to attain mutual face saving while reaching a consensus on substantive issues between them. In addition, a conflict is *appropriately* managed when both sides acknowledge the expectations of the relevant in-groups and give honor and attention to the in-groups' needs. To collectivists, a conflict solution has group-based and long-term implications. It entails fulfilling mutual face needs during disagreement and repaying any incurred "face" debts and obligations from a long-term, historical perspective.

Overall, the individualistic, outcome-oriented model promotes the criterion of effectiveness over that of appropriateness. Conversely, the collectivistic, process-oriented model emphasizes the criterion of appropriateness over that of effectiveness. Moreover, achieving one criterion may help achieve the other. For individualists, by effectively resolving the substantive issues in conflict, appropriate and cordial interaction between the parties can follow naturally. However, from a collectivist point of view, acting appropriately (in accordance to one's status and position) in the conflict situation and inducing facework cooperation can ultimately bring about effective outcomes. For collectivists, making strategic face moves and incurring face debts from the other party are often much more important than "winning" or "losing" a conflict. From a collectivist perspective, "losing" a given conflict in the moment can be interpreted as "winning" key advantages in the long-term facework obligatory process. Of course, the facework negotiation sequence would vary according to individualistic and collectivistic value tendencies. To manage intercultural conflict constructively, we *must* take other people's cultural perspectives and personality factors into consideration. If others are interdependent-self collectivists, we may want to pay extra attention to their "process-oriented" assumptions as to the negotiation. If others are independent-self individualists, we may want to be sensitive to their "outcome-oriented" assumptions as to the negotiation. The following are some skills that both individualists and collectivists can practice during their conflict negotiation process (see Figure 8.2).

Mindful Listening

Acquiring new information in conflict negotiation means both parties have to learn to listen mindfully to each other even when they are disagreeing. In an intercultural conflict situation, disagreeing parties have to learn to listen attentively to the cultural assumptions that are being expressed in the interaction. They have to learn to listen responsively (*ting*, the Chinese word for "listening," means attending closely with our "ears, eyes, and a focused heart") to the sounds, tones, gestures, movements, nonverbal nuances, pauses, and silence in a given situation.

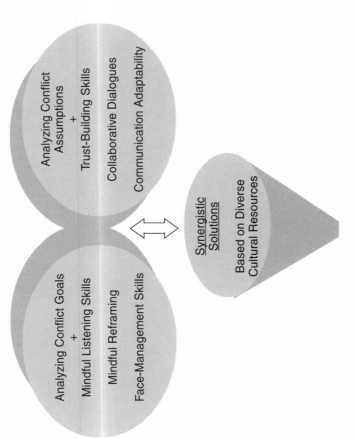

FIGURE 8.2. Constructive intercultural conflict management skills.

The parties have to learn to mindfully notice the verbal, nonverbal, and meta-nonverbal contexts that are being conveyed in the negotiation process. It is also important to create new categories or contexts in "minding" our listening process. Creating new categories in conflicts means learning to apply culturally sensitive concepts such as low- or high-context communication styles in making sense of conflict variation behaviors. Finally, being aware that multiple perspectives exist means individuals can apply different frameworks (such as *both* individualistic and collectivistic perspectives) in analyzing and interpreting a conflict situation and come up with a creative, synergistic solution.

Mindful Reframing

Mindful reframing means that both individualists and collectivists need to learn how to "translate" the other's verbal and nonverbal messages from the context of the other's cultural viewpoint. Reframing also means conflict parties need to reprioritize their goals after mindfully observing and listening to the viewpoints and expectations of their opponents. For example, after listening to the complaint from a collectivist, an individualist may realize that the friction lies not in content goal issues but in identity respect/disrespect issues. Conversely, after understanding the complaint from an individualist, a collectivist may realize that an individualist really wants solution closure and is in no way trying to "slight" the face image of the collectivist. Both parties should also remember that many of these conflicts are based on out-of-awareness cultural habits and scripts.

Face-Management Skills

Intercultural conflict parties should learn to cultivate face-management skills in dealing with intergroup negotiations competently. Face-management skills basically address the fundamental core issue of social self-esteem. All human beings like to be respected and be approved of in their daily interactions. However, how they behaviorally show such self-respect needs and concerns as well as how others accord them respect and dignity very likely differ from one culture to the next.

Individualists may want to learn to "give face" to the collectivists in the conflict negotiation process. *Giving face* means not humiliating others, especially one's opponents, in public. Here it also means acknowledging collectivists' in-group concerns and obligations. Collectivists, on the other hand, may want to reorient facework concerns and learn to pay more attention to the substantive issues at stake. Collectivists may also want to recognize that individualists often separate substantive issues from socioemotional issues in conflict. Conversely, individualists may want to pay more attention to the interlink between substantive issues and facework/relational issues when negotiating disagreements with collectivists. Thus, although the concern for face maintenance is universal, how we manage face issues is a cultural-specific phenomenon.

Trust-Building Skills

Another skill that is critical in intercultural negotiation competence is that of trust building. If conflict parties do not trust each other, they tend to move away (cognitively, affectively, and physically) from each other rather than struggle side by side with each other in the negotiations. Trust is often viewed as the single most important element of a good working relationship (Fisher & Brown, 1988). When we do not trust someone's words or actions, we also tend to automatically turn off our listening devices. We may hear the words, but we are not taking them in. Trust building is both a mindset and a communication skill. Especially in intercultural conflict situations, when we are experiencing high anxieties with unfamiliar behavior (e.g., accents, nonverbal gestures), we may automatically withhold our trust. Well-founded trust is critical in any effective and appropriate management of intercultural conflicts.

To develop trust, we have to understand the cultural meanings behind the words "trust" and "trustworthiness." Trust means to rely on the consistency of someone's credibility, words, behaviors, actions, or network support. Trustworthiness means to make our own behaviors or actions worthy of the trust of others. In small power distance cultures, trust is often based on charismatic personality traits, personal credibility, reliability, persuasive words, and decisive actions. In comparison, in large power distance cultures, trust is usually based on credible roles in a reputable organization, dependable family and kinship networks, and consistency between words and actions from a long-term perspective. For example, Lederach (1997), in working with many peace-building projects in Central America (e.g., El Salvador, Guatemala), observes that the following three key terms are vital to the conflict resolution process in this region: *confianza, cuello,* and *coyuntura.* In brief, *confianza* refers to "trust" or "confidence." It refers to individuals who "inspire my confidence" and in whom "I can deposit my trust." *Confianza* emphasizes sincerity, reliability, and continuous support across time. *Cuello* literally means

neck, the connection of head and heart, but is one of many vernacular metaphors in Spanish for "connections" that help get things done. In other words, *cuello* is the strategic use of my network. When faced with everyday problems and conflicts, Central Americans are more likely to think first of "who" than of "what" in order to get out of the problem. *Coyuntura* is often translated as "juncture" and/or "timing," but it really represents a metaphor for placing oneself in the stream of time and space and determining at any given moment what things mean and therefore what should be done. *Coyuntura* is "timing" to the degree that timing contemplates the fluidity and art of [the] possible. In practical conflict resolution terms, it means being present and available on an ongoing basis. (Lederach, 1997, p. 96)

Thus, the trust, networking, and timing (TNT) approach is essential to foster confidence in the peace-making process in the Central American region.

Understanding core metaphors, terms, and cultural premises and meanings behind these "linguistic categories" sensitize us so we can glimpse part of the social reality from cultural insiders' standpoint. In fact, *"xin ren,"* the Chinese words for "trust," mean a person keeping his or her word consistently, in a dependable manner, and one who will deliver them properly in a functional context. In many high power distance cultures, the pledged words of high-status individuals are their "face." When the words are spoken, the actions will be carried out and promises will be diligently kept. Thus, people in high power distance cultures tend to be verbally cautious in their conflict negotiations. They tend not to trust people who are too "wordy" or "verbally persuasive." They also shun written contracts and documents. For members of large power distance cultures, a handshake between two high-status individuals, a trustworthy relationship, or a long-term face gain perspective is often much more important than a signed piece of paper.

Trusting someone, however, entails certain risks. In emphasizing the importance of developing a good working relationship as a base, Fisher and Brown (1988) recommend that we should learn to be "trustworthy" but not necessarily "wholly trusting." Being trustworthy means we need to understand the cultural preferences of the strangers concerning the concepts of trust and trustworthiness. We need to understand the expectations they have of our trust-based behavior. We also need to strive to match their expectations with our behavior on a consistently dependable basis. Engaging in trustworthy behavior can lead to a supportive, trusting climate of interaction (rather than a defensive climate) in the conflict negotiation process. Unfortunately, when we are experiencing fear or threat concerning unfamiliar behavior (e.g., accents, nonverbal gestures), we often automatically withhold our trust. Well-founded trust is critical in any effective and appropriate management of facework interaction.

Collaborative Dialogue and Communication Adaptability

The last two sets of constructive conflict management skills are collaborative dialogue and communication adaptability.

Collaborative Dialogue

In collaborative dialogue sessions with collectivists, individualists may want to (1) practice patience and verbal restraint in articulating their personal interests, goals, and wants; (2) use vocal segregates or back-channeling cues such as "uhm, uhm" or "uh-huh" to signal listening attentiveness; (3) be open to the expressions of stories, proverbs, metaphors, analogies, and understatements; (4) use self-effacing questions to encourage the others to coach you or show you the way; (5) address the conflict problem to general team members rather than singling out one person; (6) accept longer turn-taking pauses and reflective silences; (7) use appropriate head nods to indicate identity affirmation; and (8) listen to the identity and relational meanings that underscore the conflict content messages.

In collaborative dialogue sessions with individualists, collectivists may want to (1) practice verbal assertiveness in articulating their personal interests, goals, and wants; (2) use direct verbal responses to indicate agreements, negotiable points, and disagreements; (3) articulate clearly the reasons behind the disagreement from either an inductive mode (i.e., from specific reasons to general conclusions when dealing with, say, U.S. Americans) or a deductive logical mode (i.e., from a general framework to specific reasons when dealing with, say, western Europeans); (4) use direct, specific questions to cross-check facts, interests, and unclear goals; (5) target the questions to a specific individual; (6) learn to engage in overlap talks and faster turn-taking verbal behavior; (7) use verbal paraphrasing to summarize what you have heard in your own words so as to prevent misunderstanding; (8) use perception check questions to clarify whether you have interpreted the nonverbal messages accurately; and (9) listen to content messages and action plans, as well as identity and relational meanings that underlie content messages.

Collaborative dialogue is based on a culture-sensitive, respectful inquiry process in which conflict parties try to suspend their own assumptions regarding the conflict situation. Rather, they work on inviting the other conflict parties to tell their stories, expectations, and needs. In the inquiry stage, new dimensions of thinking, feeling, and seeing are explored. Cultural dimensions of inquiry can include the following questions: (1) What are their cultural identity tendencies—individualistic-based or group-based? (2) What are their power value tendencies—horizontal-based or vertical-based? (3) What are their facework assumptions—the "I"-identity or "we"-identity facework model? (4) What are their preferred interaction styles—direct, low-context or indirect, high-context styles?

Personal dimensions of inquiry can include the following questions: (1) What activates their personal motivations—independent-self or interdependent-self motivations—and what is the extent of discrepancy between the personal-self and the cultural-self motivations? (2) How would they like to be respected—on an equal basis or a deferential basis? (3) What would it take to satisfy their face needs—approval face (self vs. other) and/or boundary respect (personal privacy vs. group-based regulation) issues? (4) What are the most effective ways to practice appropriate facework interaction in this particular situation?

Collaborative dialogue, in a long-term negotiation session, aims to unfold common identity-need issues such as safety, honor/dignity, boundary, approval, competence, and meaning issues. The more we learn to display a genuine, inquiring attitude, the more we may uncover deep-level common interests and common ground. Collaborative dialogue also emphasizes inclusivity in terms of drawing from local cultural resources in mediating or managing the historical, intergroup conflict problem. To engage in genuine collaborative dialogue, the international community needs to adopt a paradigm shift: "that we move beyond a simple prescription of answers and modalities for dealing with conflict from outside the setting and focus at least as much attention on discovering and empowering the resources, modalities, and mechanisms for building peace that exist [within] the context" (Lederach, 1997, p. 95).

Many examples of cultural resources' inclusivity can be identified. From Somalia, we have the extraordinary example of "women functioning as forerunners in rebuilding interclan communication, which prepared the way for clan conferences—guided by elders and massaged by poets—that led to local and regional peace agreements. From Mozambique is the . . . example of the UNICEF-funded 'Circus of Peace,' built on traditional arts, music, and drama, which targeted and incorporated children at the village level in conflict resolutions and peacebuilding activities" (Lederach, 1997, p. 95). While the roads to peace are diverse, the ultimate goal of universal peace without violence remains a common vision.

After understanding the different angles on all issues (e.g., cultural premises toward conflicts, face/identity, relational, and process issues), the two cultural teams can then use the following substantive problem-solving sequence: differentiation, mutual problem description, and integration (Papa & Papa, 1997). *The differentiation phase* refers to the important stage of clarifying conflict positions, interests, and goals, and pursuing the underlying reasons that underscore the positional differences. *The mutual problem description phase* refers to the stage wherein the conflict problem is described in specific, mutually understandable terms. Each party tries to use neutral-toned language to describe the conflict situation and its related dilemmas. Individuals refrain from any evaluative comments or intrusive interruptions. Individuals also focus on peace-building outcomes rather than on assigning blames. Lastly, the *integration* phase includes (1) displaying cooperative, mutual-interest intentions via culture-sensitive verbal and nonverbal acknowledgment and supportive messages; (2) generating creative solutions via a wide range of cultural approaches such as traditional dramas, storytelling, naming cultural metaphors, proverbs, visualization or sculpting techniques (i.e., using people as nonverbal living sculptures to role-play the solutions), and Western "brainstorming"; (3) evaluating the positive and negative aspects of each solution and making sure that all cultural members are committed and involved in the selection process; (4) combining the best of different solutions that members of both teams help to blend together; (5) selecting the best synergistic solutions that are applicable (i.e., desirable and feasible) to both cultural teams; and (6) establishing a monitoring system (e.g., a timeline and criteria for successful implementation) to determine if the solution or action plan is culturally workable.

Communication Adaptability

All the skills already mentioned cannot be applied prescriptively. Depending on the context, the conflict issue, the people, relationship, resources, and timing, no conflict resolution relies primarily on collaborative dialogue or mindful reframing alone. Even in the best of negotiations, there will be a mixed pattern of competitive and collaborative exchanged messages. The key in any constructive conflict management is to be flexible and adaptable and not be locked into one set of thinking patterns or behavioral patterns.

Communication adaptability is one of the key skills to constructive intercultural conflict negotiation. Communication adaptability refers to our ability to change our conflict goals and behaviors to meet the specific needs of the situation (Duran, 1985, 1992). It signals our mindful awareness of the other person's perspectives, interests, and/or goals, and our willingness to modify our own interests or goals to adapt to the conflict situation. It can also imply behavioral flexibility in dealing with the intercultural conflict episode. By mindfully observing what is going on in the intercultural conflict situation, both parties may modify their nonverbal and verbal behavior to achieve a more synchronized interaction process. In modifying or tailoring our behavioral styles, polarized views on the conflict content problem may also be depolarized or "softened."

In sum, constructive intercultural conflict management requires us to communicate effectively and appropriately in different intercultural situations, which necessitates adaptation. Constructive conflict management requires us to be knowledgeable and respectful of different worldviews and multiple approaches to dealing with a conflict situation. It requires us to be sensitive to the differences and similarities between individualistic and collectivistic cultures. It also demands that we be aware of our own ethnocentric biases and cultural-based attributions when making snapshot evaluations of other people's conflict management approaches.

Constructive conflict negotiation promotes flexible, adaptive behaviors in attuning to both the process and the outcome of an intercultural conflict episode. While the study of intercultural conflict is a complex phenomenon, understanding conflict along the individualism–collectivism continuum and the personal variation continuum (e.g., the independent and interdependent self across a spectrum) serves as the beginning step in understanding conflict variations among different clusters of cultures.

RECOMMENDATIONS

Some specific recommendations can be made based on differences in individualistic and collectivistic styles of conflict management. These recommendations, however, are not listed in the order of importance. In order to deal with conflict constructively in the collectivistic culture, individualists need to do the following:

1. Be mindful of the mutual face-saving premises in a collectivistic culture. Strategic skills of managing the delicate balance of humiliation and pride, sincerity and appropriateness, shame and honor are critical. Culture-sensitive face-protecting and face-honoring moves, the use of same status negotiators, and the proprieties of gracious "face fighting" have to be strategically staged with the larger group audience in mind.

2. Be proactive in dealing with low-grade conflict situations (such as by using informal consultation or "go-between" methods) before they esca-

late into runaway escalatory conflict spirals. Individualists should try to realize that by helping their opponent to save face, they may also enhance their own face. Face is intrinsically an interdependent/relational connectedness concept in many collectivistic cultures.

3. "Give face" and try not to push their opponent's back against the wall with no room to maneuver face loss or recovery. They should learn to let their opponent find a gracious way out of the conflict situation if at all possible (i.e., without violating the basic principle of fundamental human rights). They should also learn self-restraint and try not to humiliate their opponent in the public arena or slight her or his public reputation if at all possible. For collectivists, "giving face" typically operates from a long-term historical perspective.

4. Practice patient, mindful observation. Individualists need to be mindful of the past events that bear relevance to the present conflict situation. They also need to restrain themselves from asking too many "why" questions. Since collectivists typically focus on the nonverbal "how" process, individualists need to learn to experience the conflict process on the implicit, nonverbal rhythmic level.

5. Practice attentive listening skills. Attend to the sounds, movements, and emotional experiences of the other person. Patient and attentive listening indicates that one person is attending to the other person's identity and relational expectation issue. Individualists should remember that the word "listen" can become "silent" by rearranging the letters.

6. Discard the Western model of effective communication skills in dealing with conflict situations in high-context cultures. Individualists should learn to use qualifiers, disclaimers, tag questions, and tentative statements to convey their thoughts. In refusing a request, they should learn not to use a blunt "no" as a response, as that word is typically conceived as carrying high face-threat value in high-context cultures. They should also learn to use self-effacing accounts (e.g., "Perhaps someone else is more qualified than I am in working on this project") or conditional statements (e.g., "I'm honored by your invitation, but I think someone else is more suitable to present this report . . .") to signal a refusal.

7. Let go of a conflict situation if the opposite side does not want to deal with it directly. A cooling period sometimes may help to mend a broken relationship and deescalate the intensity of a dispute. Individualists should remember that avoidance is part of the integral conflict style that is commonly used in high-context cultures. Avoidance does not necessarily mean that collectivists do not care to resolve the conflict. In all likelihood, avoidance is being strategically used to avoid a face-threatening process and is meant to maintain face harmony and mutual face dignity.

Some specific recommendations also can be made for collectivists in handling conflict with individualists. When encountering a conflict situation in an individualistic culture, collectivists need to do the following:

1. Be mindful of the outcome assumptions of the conflict situation. The ability to separate the relationship from the conflict problem is critical to constructive conflict negotiation in an individualistic culture. Collectivists need to learn to compartmentalize the task dimension and the socioemotional dimension of conflict.

2. Focus in resolving the substantive issues of the conflict, and learn to openly express their opinions in a conflict scene. Collectivists should try not to take the conflict issues to the personal level, and they should learn to maintain distance between the person and the problem. They should also try not to take offense by the up-front, low-context conflict style.

3. Engage in an assertive style of conflict behavior emphasizing the right of both parties to speak up in the conflict situation and to respect each other's right to defend his or her position. Collectivists need to learn to open a conflict dialogue with a clear thesis statement, and then to develop the key point systematically—with evidence, examples, figures, or a well-planned proposal. They also need to accept criticisms and suggestions for modification as part of the ongoing dialogue.

4. Acknowledge being individually accountable for the conflict decision-making process, which means using "I" statements in expressing their opinions, in describing their feelings, and in actively sharing their thought process. Collectivists should assume a sender-responsible approach to managing the conflict constructively. They should also learn to ask more "why" questions and probe for clear explanations and details.

5. Provide active verbal feedback and engage in active listening skills. Active listening skill means collectivists have to engage in active verbal paraphrasing and perception checking skills and to ensure that the other person is understanding their points thoroughly. Collectivists have to learn to occasionally disclose their emotions, attitudes, and experiences within the conflict process itself. They cannot rely solely on nonverbal signals and count on other people to "intuit" their reactions.

6. Learn to "grab the floor" faster if they have something to say in the conflict negotiation process. Collectivists also may not want to engage in too many silent moments, as individualists will infer that as inefficient use of time.

7. Commit to working out the conflict situation with the other party. Collectivists should learn to use more active task-based inquiry strategies and be more outcome-oriented in thinking of the consequences of an unresolved conflict. They can also work on managing the defensive climate and learn to build up trust and bring down their fear concerning dissimilar others.

Both individualists and collectivists need to be mindful of the cognitive, affective, and behavioral blinders that they bring to a conflict encounter. They need to continuously develop new visions and ideas in dealing with differences. They need to be provided with enough space, a contact place for a true encounter. Reconciliation of any group-based or person-based differences must be "proactive in seeking to create an encounter where people can focus on their relationship and share their perceptions, feelings, and experiences with one another, with the goal of creating new perceptions and a new shared experience" (Lederach, 1997, p. 30).

In managing conflicts constructively, all cultural members need to possess flexible intercultural conflict negotiation skills in managing diversities and uncovering common interests. By pooling their cultural and personal resources, different cultural and ethnic members can learn to engage in the peace-building process together—and to create a more just and harmonious human society.

IV

IDENTITY TRANSFORMATION AND TRANSCULTURAL COMPETENCIES

9

Identity Change
and Intercultural Adaptation

Intercultural Adaptation: Antecedent Factors 234
   Systems-Level Factors 235
   Individual-Level Factors 239
   Interpersonal-Level Factors 241
Intercultural Adaptation: The Identity Change Process 245
   Managing the Culture Shock Process 245
   Sojourners' Adjustment Models 247
   Minority and Immigrants' Identity Change Models 254
Intercultural Adaptation: Effective Outcomes 257
   Systems-Level and Interpersonal-Level Outcomes 257
   Personal Identity Change Outcomes 258
Recommendations 259

International business people with overseas assignments, international students, government personnel, immigrants, and refugees are some of the people who need to learn how to cross cultural boundaries effectively. In addition, members of the host culture need to be mindful of their stances and attitudes in welcoming the newcomers. As a result of sustained first-hand contact with persons from the host culture, individuals often undergo external and internal changes in their adventurous adaptive journey.

The intercultural adaptation process is defined as the degree of change that occurs when individuals move from a familiar environment to an unfamiliar one. It involves an intercultural boundary-crossing journey—from security to insecurity, and from familiarity to unfamiliarity. The journey can be a turbulent or exhilarating process. The route itself has many ups and downs, twists and turns, so that the journeyer's movements are often erratic, sometimes tumbling forward, sometimes propelled backward. In such a long, demanding journey, an incremental process of identity change is inevitable. The longer the sojourning experience, the more likely a person's cognitive, affective, and behavioral outlook will change.

Intercultural adaptation, however, does not happen overnight. It is a gradual transformation process. Many factors influence the intercultural adaptation process—from systems-level factors (e.g., receptivity of the host culture), to individual-level (e.g., individual expectations) and interpersonal-level factors (e.g., formation of social networks).

Indeed, in conceptualizing the intercultural adaptation process, the theme of *identity being-and-becoming* can best serve as the metaphor that reflects the oscillating movements of the newcomer's identity change process. Immigrants, for example, have to constantly negotiate the theme of identity being-and-becoming as they learn to acquire new roles and new adaptive skills in their newly adopted homeland. The larger the cultural distance or difference between the two cultures, the higher the degree of identity vulnerability immigrants will experience in the new culture. For most individuals, as Anderson (1994) comments, adaptation is "not only a cyclical process where ends fade out into new beginnings, it is also often a . . . roller-coaster ride, with depression and elation, successes and failures in overcoming obstacles providing the hills and valleys" (p. 307). With identity stress comes possible identity stretch and resourcefulness (Lazarus, 1991; Ting-Toomey, 1993). Many complex factors, of course, influence this identity tug-and-pull experience.

This chapter is developed in four main sections. The first section examines the antecedent factors that influence the newcomers' adaptation process. The second section explores the identity change process in sojourners' and immigrants' adaptational experience. The third presents some of the findings related to adaptation outcomes. The last comprises a set of recommendations of how hosts and newcomers can help each other to facilitate the optimal learning process.

INTERCULTURAL ADAPTATION: ANTECEDENT FACTORS

Strangers come to a new land in different roles—visitors, sojourners, immigrants, or refugees. Generally, tourists play the visitor roles with an anticipated short span of stay. Sojourners (e.g., businesspersons, military personnel, peace corp volunteers) play the visitor-resident roles with a medium span of stay. In comparison, immigrants and refugees play the long-term inhabitant roles whereby they have uprooted and transplanted themselves to their adopted homelands.

While the immigrant group comprises those who generally have voluntarily moved across cultural boundaries, those in the refugee group often have involuntarily done so (for reasons of political, religious, or economic oppression). Unlike tourists and sojourners, immigrants and refugees usually aim for a permanent stay in their adopted country. While there are some similar adaptation patterns (e.g., initial stress and culture shock) in these diverse groups, there are also very different motivational patterns in these newcomers' means and goals of adaptation.

Due to continuous, first-hand contact with people in the new culture, individuals learn to adapt and change. The term *intercultural adaptation* refers to the incremental identity-related change process of sojourners and immigrants in a new environment (Redfield, Linton, & Herskovits, 1936). Much less attention, however, has been paid to the changing fabric of the host society due to the influx of immigrants and refugees. In this chapter, we shall emphasize the need and responsibility of both the host society and the newcomers to learn from each other—in order to create an inclusive, just community.

More specifically, the term, *adjustment* has been used to refer to the short-term and medium-term adaptive process of sojourners in their overseas assignments. Sojourners are typically individuals who have a transitional stay in a new culture as they strive to achieve their instrumental goals (e.g., an international student wanting to achieve her or his MBA degree) and/or socioemotional goals (e.g., making friends with U.S. students).

In contrast, the term *acculturation* has been employed in the intercultural literature to describe the long-term change process of immigrants or refugees in adapting to their new homeland. The change process of immigrants (hereafter, the term "immigrants" will also include refugees) often involves subtle change to overt change. Acculturation involves the long-term conditioning process of newcomers in integrating the new values, norms, and symbols of their new culture, and developing new roles and skills to meet its demands. *Enculturation*, on the other hand, often refers to the sustained, primary socialization process of strangers in their original home (or natal) culture wherein they have internalized their primary cultural values. Three sets of *antecedent factors* typically influence newcomers' adaptation process: systems-level factors, individual-level factors, and interpersonal-level factors (see Figure 9.1).

Systems-Level Factors

Systems-level factors are those elements in the host environment that influence newcomers' adaptation to the new culture (Y. Y. Kim, 1988, 1991, 1995). Based on the findings of existing adaptation research, the following five observations are gleaned.

First, the host culture's *socioeconomic conditions* influence the climate of adaptation (Puentha, Giles, & Young, 1987). When the host culture is operating under economically affluent conditions, its members appear to be more tolerant and hospitable toward newcomers. When the socioeconomic conditions are poor, strangers become the scapegoats for local economic problems. For example, newcomers are often perceived as competing for scarce resources such as new jobs and promotion opportunities and taking away the job opportunities of cultural insiders.

Second, a host culture's *attitudinal stance* on cultural assimilation or

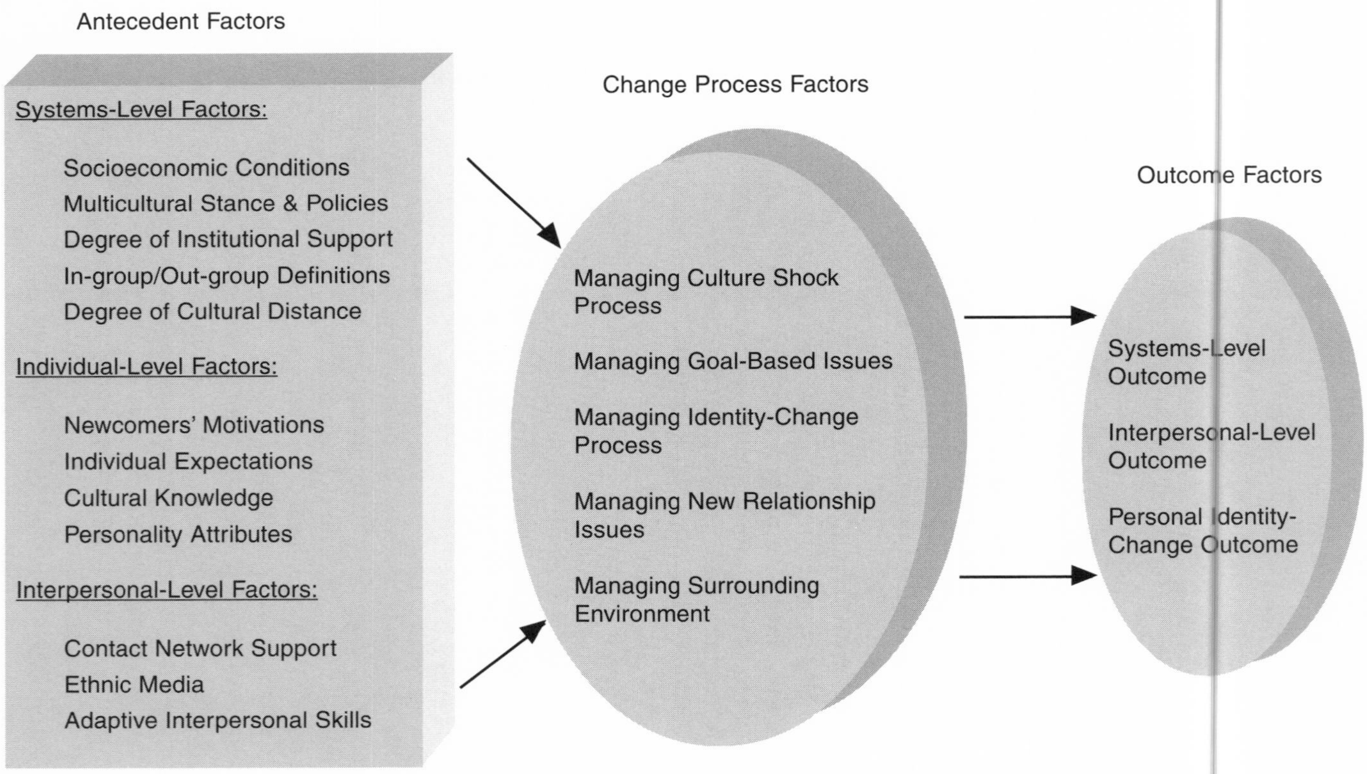

Antecedent Factors

Systems-Level Factors:

Socioeconomic Conditions
Multicultural Stance & Policies
Degree of Institutional Support
In-group/Out-group Definitions
Degree of Cultural Distance

Individual-Level Factors:

Newcomers' Motivations
Individual Expectations
Cultural Knowledge
Personality Attributes

Interpersonal-Level Factors:

Contact Network Support
Ethnic Media
Adaptive Interpersonal Skills

Change Process Factors

Managing Culture Shock Process

Managing Goal-Based Issues

Managing Identity-Change Process

Managing New Relationship Issues

Managing Surrounding Environment

Outcome Factors

Systems-Level Outcome

Interpersonal-Level Outcome

Personal Identity-Change Outcome

FIGURE 9.1. An intercultural adaptation model: Antecedent, process, and outcome factors.

cultural pluralism produces a spillover effect on institutional policies (as well as on attitudes of the citizenry) toward newcomers' adaptation process (Berry, Kim, & Boski, 1987; Kraus, 1991). The cultural assimilationist stance demands higher conformity from strangers in adapting to the host environment (e.g., as urged by the U.S. "English Only" movement) than does the cultural pluralist stance. In contrast, the cultural pluralist stance encourages a diversity of values (as supported by Canadian "multicultural" policies) and hence provides strangers with a wider latitude of norms from which to choose in their newfound homeland.

In an assimilationist society, ethnic identity formation is strongly influenced by the dominant group values. In a pluralistic society, ethnic identity formation rests on the choices between maintaining the customs of the heritage culture, on the one hand, and inventing a new identity, on the other. As Berry et al. (1987) comment, "In culturally plural societies, individuals and groups must confront two important issues. One pertains to the maintenance and development of one's ethnic distinctiveness in society, deciding whether one's own . . . [ethnic] identity and customs are of value and should be retained. The other issue involves the desirability of interethnic contact, deciding whether relations with the larger society are of value and should be sought" (p. 65). In an assimilationist society, immigrants are often expected to conform quickly to the local cultural practices. In a pluralistic society, immigrants are given more leeway to acquire the fund of knowledge and skills needed in adapting to the new culture. Societies with an assimilationist stance tend to be more intolerant of newcomers' retention of traditions and customs of their own heritage. Societies with a pluralist stance tend to display more tolerant attitudes and acceptance toward immigrants' ethnic traditions and practices. Overall, host nationals also tend to show a more lenient attitude to sojourners' nonconforming behavior (e.g., that of executives from multinational corporations) than to that of immigrants because of the "transitory visitor" role of the former versus the "permanent resident" role of the latter.

Third, *local institutions* (such as school, place of work, social services, and mass media) serve as firsthand contact agencies that facilitate or impede the adaptation process of sojourners and immigrants (Mortland & Ledgerwood, 1988). Following the prevailing national policies, local institutions can either greatly facilitate strangers' adaptation process (e.g., via language help programs or job training programs) or produce roadblocks to the newcomers' adaptive experience.

For example, at schools varying degrees of receptivity and helpfulness of teachers toward immigrant children can either help the children to feel "at home" or leave them to "sink or swim" by themselves in their adopted homeland. Whether the attitudes of local children in the classrooms are favorable or unfavorable can also produce a pleasant or hostile climate for these immigrant children during their vulnerable adaptive stages. Getting used to a strange language, unfamiliar signs, and different expectations and norms of a new classroom can be overwhelming for recent immigrant children.

Fourth, the host culture's *meaning definition* concerning the role of "strangers" can profoundly influence sojourners' and immigrants' initial adaptation process. Whether members of the host culture perceive strangers as nonpersons, intruders, aliens, visitors, guests, or adopted family members will greatly influence their attitudes and behaviors toward the strangers. Members of host cultures that view outsiders as "intruders" are likely to be hostile to them, whereas host nationals that use an adoptive family metaphor for the incorporation of newcomers are likely to display positive sentiments toward them. Thus, some host nationals may offer proactive help, as opposed to reactive resistance, to the adaptation process of newcomers.

While some cultures make greater distinctions between insiders and outsiders, some groups have built-in mechanisms to facilitate the socialization of newcomers (Anderson, 1994). Sojourners and immigrants are marginalists to a new culture. They often need help and coaching to learn the inner working of a culture. To the extent that the newcomers are treated with dignity and respect by insiders of a new culture and a trusting climate is developed, they experience identity validation and inclusion. To the extent that newcomers (including second- or third-generation families) are long treated as borderline persons (e.g., by asking third-generation Japanese Americans where did they come from and when will they return "home"—when their home culture is right here in the United States), they experience resentments, frustrations, and identity exclusion.

Finally, the *cultural distance* between the two cultures—that of the newcomers and that of the host—has a strong impact on the newcomers' adaptation. Cultural distance refers to the degree of psychological adjustment that is needed to bridge the dissimilarities between the culture of origin and the culture of entry (Ward, 1996; Ward & Searle, 1991). As cultural distance increases, newcomers need to use greater affective, cognitive, and behavioral resources to cope with such differences. Cultural distance dimensions can include differences in cultural values, in self-conceptions, in language and communication styles, as well as in religious, economic, and political systems. The larger the cultural distances, the more efforts and supportive resources the individuals will need to transcend such differences.

The combined systems-level factors can create either a favorable or unfavorable climate for the newly arrived strangers. Obviously, the more favorable and receptive the cultural climate toward the arrival of strangers, the easier it is for the strangers to adapt to the new culture (Y. Y. Kim, 1988, 1995). The more help the newcomers receive during the initial cultural adaptation stages, the more positive are their perceptions of their new environment. Lastly, the more realistic expectations the newcomers have concerning the new environment, the more they are psychologically prepared to handle the external and internal pressures of their new adventure.

Individual-Level Factors

The following individual-level factors have been found to influence intercultural adaptation: individual motivations, expectations, cultural and interaction-based knowledge, and personal attributes.

Newcomers' *motivational orientations* to leave their home countries and enter a new culture have a profound influence on their adaptation modes. Individuals (e.g., peace corp volunteers) with voluntary motivations to leave a familiar culture and enter a new cultural experience have fewer adaptive problems than do individuals with involuntary motivations (e.g., refugees). Furthermore, sojourners (e.g., international businesspersons) encounter less conformity pressure than do immigrants because of their different role. For sojourners, their temporary residence status is self-contained and their instrumental goal is clear and specific (e.g., training local managers). For immigrants, the permanent residence status evokes a mixture of affective and instrumental stressors. Immigrants often also have more family worries and identity dislocation problems than do sojourners. Lastly, the sense of "no return" (i.e., for immigrants) versus "transitory stay" (i.e., for sojourners) produces different motivational drives for newcomers to acquire the new core rituals, symbols, and scripts suited to their new setting.

Research on sojourners, for example, indicates that over a thousand managers from the United States, Canada, and Europe offered the following reasons why they might accept international assignments from their companies (Adler, 1997). The top reason is opportunity for cross-cultural or personal growth experiences. Over half of the respondents want to see other cultures, travel, learn new languages, and gain a greater understanding of other ways of life. A second reason is the job itself: many of the respondents see global assignments as providing more challenging rewards such as allowing for more autonomy, power, status, and responsibility. A third reason is money: many of the young managers believe that such global positions will enable them to earn a higher salary and benefits than they would receive in a domestic position.

Interestingly, the importance of location is ranked as the number one reason why the young managers would reject an overseas assignment. More than half of the respondents cited "bad location" as the top reason for rejecting a global assignment, especially because of the host country's political instability or high potential for war and public violence. The other two reasons respondents gave for rejecting an overseas assignment are its potential negative impact on their career and concern about their spouse and family.

In the case of long-term stay immigrants, acculturation research indicates that many immigrants have uprooted themselves due to a mixture of "push" factors (e.g., political and economic reasons) and "pull" factors (e.g., the host culture's economic opportunities) (Furnham, 1986). Many immigrants were forced to depart from their home countries because of cultural, religious, or political persecution, as well as economic strains there. By immigrating, they strive to create better opportunities for themselves and their families. Additionally, the new culture's attractions ("pull" factors) include better chances for personal advancement and better job opportunities, greater educational opportunities for the children, an improved quality of life for the family, a better standard of living, and democratic cultural values (Furnham, 1986). In sum, the motivational orientations of people leaving their homelands can greatly affect their expectations and behaviors in the new culture.

Individual expectations have long been viewed as a crucial factor in the intercultural adaptation process. Expectations refer to the anticipatory process and predictive outcome of the upcoming situation. Two observations have often been associated with such expectations: the first is that realistic expectations facilitate intercultural adaptation; the second is that accuracy-based positive expectations ease adaptation stress (Ward, 1996; Ward & Kennedy, 1994). Individuals with realistic expectations are better prepared psychologically to deal with actual adaptation problems than are individuals with unrealistic expectations. Furthermore, individuals with positive expectations tend to create a self-fulfilling prophecy in their successful adaptation (e.g., you think this is a great move and your thinking affects your positive actions); negative expectations tend to produce the opposite effect.

Past research (McGuire & McDermott, 1988) indicates that while international students tend to carry positive expectation images concerning their anticipated sojourn in the new culture, immigrants often carry negative apprehensive images regarding their major relocation move. Overall, realistic and positively oriented expectancy images of the new culture can help to facilitate intercultural adaptation for both sojourners and immigrants. Expectations influence newcomers' mindset, attitudes, sentiments, and behaviors. Research indicates that a positively resilient mindset helps to balance the negative stressors that a newcomer may encounter in her or his adaptive efforts.

Newcomers' *cultural knowledge* and *interaction-based knowledge* about the host culture serves as another critical factor in their adaptation process. Cultural knowledge can include information on the following: cultural and ethnic diversity history, geography, political and economic systems, religious and spiritual beliefs, multiple value systems, and situational norms. Interaction-based knowledge can include language, verbal and nonverbal styles, diversity-related communication issues (e.g., regional, ethnic, and gender differences within a culture), and various problem-solving and decision-making styles. Fluency in the host culture's language, for example, has been found to have a direct positive impact on sociocultural adaptation, such as developing relationships with members of the host culture (Ward & Kennedy, 1993). In contrast, language incompetence has been associated with increased psychological and psychosomatic symptoms (e.g., sleeplessness, severe headaches) in immigrants to the United States from India (Krishman & Berry, 1992). Beyond language fluency, interaction-based pragmatic competence such as knowing "when to say what appropriately, under what situations" is critical in adapting to a new environment.

In regard to *personality attributes*, such personality profiles as high tolerance for ambiguity (i.e., high acceptance of ambiguous situations; Cort & King, 1979), internal locus of control (i.e., inner-directed drives and motivations; Ward & Kennedy, 1993), and personal flexibility and openness (Ruben & Kealey, 1979; Kim, 1988, 1995) have been consistently related to positive psychological functioning in a new culture. Ward (1996) suggests a "cultural fit" proposition, which emphasizes the importance of a good match between personality types (such as extraversion and introversion) of the acculturators and the host cultural norms. For example, we can speculate that independent self sojourners may be more compatible with individualistic cultural norms, whereas interdependent self sojourners may be more compatible with collectivistic cultural norms. The synchronized match between a particular personality type and the larger cultural norms produces a "goodness of fit" and possibly cultivates a positive adaptive experience for strangers.

Additionally, demographic variables such as age and educational level have also been found to affect adaptational effectiveness, with the younger children having an easier time adapting to the new culture than adults. However, younger children typically experience more stress and confusion in reentry culture shock stage than do adults. Individuals with higher educational levels tend to adapt more effectively than do individuals with lower educational levels (Berry et al., 1987; Yum, 1982). We should note here that most of the cited studies are based on sojourners' and immigrants' experiences in the settings of Australia, Canada, and the United States. Thus, the research conclusions summarized in this chapter are reflective of adaptation norms in individualistic cultures more than in collectivistic cultures. Obviously, more intercultural adaptation research needs to be conducted in other world regions and with other types of sojourners and immigrants.

We now turn to a discussion of some of the interpersonal-related factors that affect newcomers' adaptive change process.

Interpersonal-Level Factors

Interpersonal-level factors can include relational face-to-face network factors (e.g., social network), mediated contact factors (e.g., use of mass media) (Y. Y. Kim, 1995), and interpersonal skills' factors. Both relational contact networks and the mass media can enhance newcomers' interpersonal coping skills in their culture-learning journey.

By *contact network* we refer to a combination of personal and social ties in the new culture in which affective, instrumental, and informational resources are exchanged (Adelman, 1988). Affective resources include the exchange of identity support and relational empathic messages (e.g., "It must be difficult for you, especially without your parents and friends here"). Instrumental resources include task-related goal support, practical assistance (e.g., offering rides), and tangible resource exchange (e.g., finding jobs, providing assistance such as helping someone to move). Informational resources include sharing knowledge and keeping the other person informed of important news (Furnham & Bochner, 1986). Most personal or social networks serve all three functions.

Through supportive personal and social networks and supportive systems-level treatment, strangers' vulnerable identities are incrementally protected. A supportive social network serves as a buffer zone between a newcomer's threatened identity on the one hand, and the unfamiliar environment, on the other. Overall, studies on immigrants' and sojourners' network patterns have yielded some interesting findings. Ethnic-based social and friendship networks provide critical identity support during the initial stages of immigrants' adaptation process (Mortland & Ledgerwood, 1988). This observation is based on the idea that the density (i.e., ethnic clusters or niches) of the ethnic community is strong and is available as a supportive network. For the newcomers, established individuals from the same or a similar ethnic background can serve as successful role models. They can also provide identity and affective support because they have gone through a similar set of culture shock experiences. These "established locals" can engage in appropriate and effective identity-validation messages (e.g., "I experienced the same confused feelings and loneliness when I first came here") that instill hope and confidence in the newly arrived immigrants or sojourners.

Moreover, immigrants' and sojourners' network ties with members from the dominant cultural group facilitate learning of the mainstream cultural norms (Adelman, 1988; Y. Y. Kim, 1988). Research studies (Y. Y. Kim, 1988; Searle & Ward, 1990) indicate a positive association between newcomers' participation in dominant cultural group activities and favorable attitudes toward the host culture. This line of research probably holds more true for societies with a strong assimilationist stance than for those with a pluralist stance. Additionally, international students reported greater satisfaction with their host culture when they were befriended by host nationals.

It has been found that international students' friendship networks typically consist of the following patterns: (1) a primary, monocultural friendship network that consists of close friendships with other comparriots from similar cultural backgrounds (e.g., German international students develop-ing friendship ties with other European students); (2) a bicultural network that consists of social bonds between sojourners and host nationals whereby professional aspirations and goals are pursued; and (3) a multicultural network that consists of acquaintances from diverse cultural groups for recreational activities (Furnham & Bochner, 1982).

In sum, studies have revealed that in initial adaptation stages an ethnic-based social/friendship network is critical to newcomers in terms of identity-support and emotional-support functions. Similar ethnic friendship networks (especially those with linguistic ties) in initial adaptation stages ease strangers' adaptive stress and loneliness (Furnham & Bochner, 1986). Researchers further encourage such bonds to include eventually bicultural and multicultural networks in order to enrich the mutual learning processes between host nationals and new arrivals. Studies (e.g., Ward & Kennedy, 1993) have also consistently found that the frequency and quality of personal contacts between host nationals and newcomers increase adaptive satisfaction and perceived competence. The higher the quality of personal contact between the locals and the newcomers, the more the new arrivals experience adaptive satisfaction.

These contact networks are often viewed as the "healing webs" that nurture the adaptive growth and inquiry process of newcomers. Both close ties (e.g., relatives, close friends) and weak ties (e.g., acquaintanceships with neighbors, schoolteachers, grocers) provide important identity and informational support functions (Adelman, 1988). In fact, it has been speculated that oftentimes it is the latter connections that may help newcomers to locate their first jobs or solve their everyday problems (Granovetter, 1973).

Ethnic media (such as ethnic publications and broadcasts) also play a critical role in the initial stages of immigrants' adaptation. Due to language barriers, immigrants tend to reach out for ethnic newspapers, magazines, radio, and TV programs when such media resources are available in the local community. Ethnic media tend to ease the loneliness and adaptive stress of the new arrivals. The familiar language and images are identity affirming and offer newcomers a sense of comfort and identity connection in the unfamiliar environment.

On the other hand, research indicates that the host media (such as radio and television) do play a critical educational role in providing a safe environment for newcomers to learn the host language and socialization skills (Chaffee, Ness, & Yang, 1990; Y. Y. Kim, 1979). Overall, the mass media's influence on newcomers' adaptation process is broad but not deep. The influence of personal relationship networks, in comparison, is deep, but not broad. Through the mass media (especially television), immigrants receive a smorgasbord of information concerning a broad range of host national topics but without much informational depth. In contrast, through personal network contacts, newcomers learn about the host culture from a smaller sample of individuals, revolving around a narrower range of topics, but with more depth and specific personal perspectives.

According to research, of all the variables, language competence plays a significant role in host media consumption (Chaffee et al., 1990; J. K. Kim, 1980). The more sophisticated newcomers are in their host culture's language, the more likely they will select host-based media (i.e., host-based newspapers or TV news). While new immigrants tend to use more entertainment-oriented TV shows during their early stages of adaptation, they tend to use more information-oriented shows (e.g., TV news and documentaries) during their later stages of adaptation (perhaps, due to increased host language competence and incremental in-group membership commitment) (Y. Y. Kim, 1988).

International management researchers identify the following *adaptive interpersonal skills* as critical for businesspeople working abroad: maintenance of psychological well-being, appropriate awareness of host values and attitudes, and interpersonal interactions with the host nationals (Black & Mendenhall, 1990). In comparison, intercultural communication researchers define the following abilities as important intercultural skills: (1) ability to manage psychological stress; (2) ability to communicate effectively; and (3) ability to establish meaningful interpersonal relationships (Hammer, Gudykunst, & Wiseman, 1978).

Lastly, the following five steps are equally applicable for sojourners and immigrants in honing their culture-specific interpersonal skills in the new culture (Brislin & Yoshida, 1994):

1. Identify a skill (or a set of skills) that should facilitate better communication with people from a specific culture.
2. Understand why this skill is important—pair specific cultural values with this skill.
3. Find out when, where, and under what situations this skill is appropriately used.
4. Be conscious of the uniqueness of the individual with whom you are interacting—she or he may not fit the "norm."
5. Practice this skill in day-to-day interaction with people from the new culture.

In any successful intercultural learning process, members of the host culture need to act as the gracious hosts while newcomers need to act as the willing-to-learn guests. Without collaborative effort, the hosts and the new arrivals may end up with great frustrations, miscommunications, and identity misalignments. Intercultural adaptation is a collaborative learning journey in which host members should play the helpful host role and new residents should play the mindful discoverer role. In learning from people who are culturally different, both hosts and new arrivals can stretch their identity boundaries to integrate new ideas, expand affective horizons, and respect alternative lifestyles and practices.

INTERCULTURAL ADAPTATION: THE IDENTITY CHANGE PROCESS

The intercultural adaptation process involves identity change and challenges for the newcomers. The challenges include (1) differences in core beliefs, values, and situational norms between the home and host cultures; (2) loss of the valued images of the home culture—all those familiar images and symbols that define a newcomer's once familiar identities have vanished; and (3) the newcomer's sense of social incompetence in responding to the new setting appropriately and effectively.

This section is developed in three parts: the first reviews the meaning and implications of culture shock; the second presents the various developmental models of the sojourners' adjustment process; the third examines immigrants' identity change experience (see Figure 9.1).

Managing the Culture Shock Process

Culture shock refers to transitional process in which an individual perceives threats to her or his well-being in a culturally new environment. In this unfamiliar environment, the individual's identity appears to be stripped of all protection. The previously familiar cultural scenes and scripts are not operable in the new setting, and the previously familiar, cultural safety net has disappeared.

Culture shock produces expectancy violations, which in turn bring about emotional vulnerability. Culture shock is, first and foremost, an emotional phenomenon; then comes cognitive disorientation and identity dissonance. Both short-term sojourners and long-term immigrants can experience culture shock at different stages of their adaptation.

Oberg (1960), an anthropologist, coined the term "culture shock" nearly four decades ago. According to him, culture shock produces an identity disequilibrium state, which can bring about adaptive transformations in a newcomer on moral, affective, cognitive, and behavioral levels. Culture shock involves (1) a sense of *identity loss and identity deprivation* with regard to values, status, profession, friends, and possessions; (2) *identity strain* as a result of the effort required to make necessary psychological adaptation; (3) *identity rejection* by members of the new culture; (4) *identity confusion,* especially as regards role ambiguity and unpredictability; (5) *identity impotence* as a result of not being able to cope with the new environment (Furnham, 1988).

All sojourners and immigrants experience some degree of identity loss and grief in an unfamiliar environment. Culture shock is an inevitably stressful and disorienting experience (Ting-Toomey, 1997b). People encounter culture shock whenever they uproot themselves from a familiar setting to an unfamiliar one (e.g., relocate from Hong Kong to Los Angeles; move from one job to another); since it is unavoidable, just how we manage culture shock will determine the adaptive process and outcome. As Furnham and Bochner (1986) observe insightfully,

Culture shock is precipitated by the anxiety that results from losing all our familiar signs and symbols of social discourse. These signs or cues include a thousand and one ways in which we orient ourselves to the situations of daily life: when to shake hands and what to say when we meet people, when and how to give tips . . . [and] how to make purchases, when to accept and when to refuse invitations, when to take statements seriously and when not. Now these cues which may be words, gestures, facial expressions, customs, or norms are acquired by all of us in the course of growing up and are as much a part of our culture as the language we speak or the beliefs we accept. All of us depend for our peace of mind and our efficiency on hundreds of these cues, most of which we are not consciously aware. (p. 48)

Culture shock can serve both negative and positive implications. Its negative implications include the following: psychosomatic problems (e.g., headaches, stomachaches) due to prolonged stress; cognitive disorientation due to difficulties in making accurate attributions; affective upheavals consisting of feelings of loneliness, depression, and drastic mood swings; and awkwardness in social interaction due to the inability to perform optimally in the new language and setting.

On the other hand, culture shock, if managed mindfully, can have the following positive effects on the newcomer: a sense of well-being and heightened positive self-esteem; cognitive openness and flexibility; emotional richness and enhanced tolerance for ambiguity; competence in social interaction; and enhanced self-confidence and confidence in others. Many sojourners, however, are either paralyzed by their culture shock experience and return to their home culture prematurely or play the "prisoner role" in serving their time abroad, all the while longing to return home. In a study of international managers' experience, two researchers note that "The number of expatriate failures has been variously estimated between 16% to 40% of those assigned. . . . The total cost to the organization for an expatriate employee may be as high as three to five times that employee's annual salary . . . , with the cost of a failure estimated between $250,000 and $1,000,000 per employee" (Bhagat & Prien, 1996, pp. 217–218).

Many of these sojourners can either become very aggressive in the new culture or become totally withdrawn. Anderson (1994), for example, identifies four types of "culture shockers" as follows: (1) the *early returnees*—those who exit at an early stage and use occasional fight-and-flight strategies to deal with the "hostile" environment; (2) the *time servers*—those who are doing a minimally passable job with minimal host contact and who are emotionally and cognitively "serving their time" while eagerly looking forward to returning home; (3) the *adjusters*—those who are doing a moderately effective job and are mixing with host culture members behaviorally but not affectively; and (4) the *participators*—those who are performing optimally in their jobs and are affectively and behaviorally full-fledged participants in the local culture.

Sojourners' Adjustment Models

Crossing boundaries entails changes on many levels. Each cultural boundary parameter has its own traditions and beliefs, value assumptions and communication premises, norms and rules, and rituals and interaction scripts. Individuals who travel across cultural boundaries and stay in other cultures for a lengthy period are inevitably transformed on the cognitive, affective, behavioral, and identity levels. The following subsections explore various developmental models regarding the newcomers' adjustment process in a new environment. Next, we explore the developmental models of the short- to medium-term adjustment process of sojourners. By understanding the developmental processes of adaptive change, we can approach the issue of identity change with some degree of predictability.

Sojourners' Identity Change Models

A number of researchers have conceptualized the sojourners' adjustment process from various developmental perspectives. An interesting consequence of these stage-oriented descriptive models centers around whether sojourners' adaptation is a U-curve or a W-curve process. In interviewing over 200 Norwegian Fulbright grantees in the United States, Lysgaard (1955) developed a three-phase intercultural adjustment model that includes initial adjustment, crisis, and regained adjustment: the first is the optimistic or elation phase of the sojourners' adjustment process; the second is the stressful phase when reality sets in and the sojourners are overwhelmed by their own incompetence; the third is the settling-in phase when sojourners learn to cope effectively with the new environment.

Drawing from the above ideas, Lysgaard (1955) proposed the U-curve model of the sojourners' adjustment process, suggesting that sojourners pass through an initial honeymoon phase, then experience a "slump" or stressful phase, and finally pull themselves back up to an effective phase in managing their assignments abroad. In extending the U-curve model, Gullahorn and Gullahorn (1963) proposed a six-stage W-shaped model, with successive honeymoon, hostility, humorous, at-home, reentry culture shock, and resocialization stages. Expanding the ideas of Gullahorn and Gullahorn, we have developed the following seven-stage revised W-shaped adjustment model to explain sojourners' short-term to medium-term adjustment process (see Figure 9.2).

The *revised W-shaped adjustment model* consists of seven stages: the

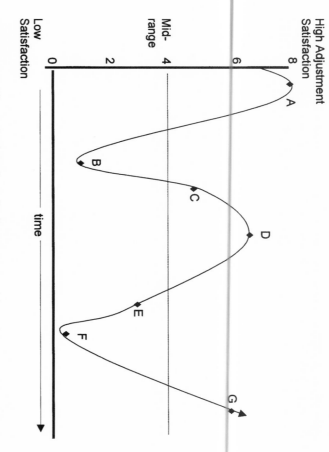

FIGURE 9.2. The revised W-shaped adjustment model: A, honeymoon stage; B, hostility stage; C, humorous stage; D, in-sync stage; E, ambivalence stage; F, reentry culture shock stage; and G, resocialization stage.

honeymoon, hostility, humorous, in-sync, ambivalence, reentry culture shock, and resocialization stages. The model applies especially to international students' experience abroad.

In the *honeymoon stage*, individuals are excited about their new cultural environment. They perceive people and events through pleasantly tinted (or "rose-colored") lenses. Nonetheless, they experience mild identity dislocation and disorientation; they also experience bursts of loneliness and homesickness. However, overall, they are cognitively curious about the new culture and emotionally charged up at meeting new people. They may not completely understand the verbal and nonverbal behaviors that surround them, but they are enjoying their initial "friendly" contacts with the locals.

In the *hostility stage*, sojourners experience severe identity confusion and disorientation. At this stage, nothing is working out. Individuals experience a major loss of self-esteem and confidence. They feel incompetent (e.g., because of task incompetence, language and communication incompetence, or barriers to achieving specific goals) and discouraged. They now often employ one of the following three strategies: flight, fight, or commitment. In using the "flight" strategy, sojourners can either physically or psychologically avoid being in contact with the local people or culture. They may go to school or work in the new culture, but for the most part they hide away in their apartment and count the days until they can go home (i.e., the time servers). They may even exit from the new culture if the stressors become too unmanageable (i.e., the early returnees). In contrast, sojourners who use the "fight" strategy tend to make frequent critical and hostile statements concerning the host culture's customs or practices. Emotionally, they are angry and frustrated. They react with moderately high ethnocentrism: they do not understand why people are acting in such an "uncivilized" or "hypocritical" way. They are at a very emotionally vulnerable stage of either "punching out" someone or quitting altogether. However, with the help of supportive networks, incremental goal progression, and willpower, some sojourners (i.e., the committed participators) are able to pull out from the hostility stage and learn to reclaim their lost sense of self-esteem. Those sojourners who use the "commitment" strategy to manage their ethnocentrism, and instead, employ some ethnorelative thinking, have a good chance of passing on to the next stage and beginning to enjoy themselves in the new culture.

At the *humorous stage*, sojourners learn to laugh at their cultural faux pas and start to realize that there are pros and cons in each culture—just as there are both good and evil people in every society. They experience a mixture of stress–adaptation–growth emotions (Kim, 1988) such as small frustrations and small triumphs. They are able to compare both their home and host cultures in realistic terms, and they no longer take things as seriously as in the hostility stage. They can now take a step backward and look at their own behavior and reactions objectively. Taskwise, they are making progress in attaining their instrumental goals (e.g., achieving their MBA degree, or acquiring new business skills). They are beginning to form new friendships and social networks. These sojourners eventually arrive at the next stage.

At the *in-sync stage*, sojourners feel "at home" and experience identity security and inclusion. The boundaries between outsiders and insiders become fuzzier, and the sojourners experience social acceptance and support. They are now easily able to "make sense" of the "bizarre" local customs and behaviors. They may well be able to converse in the local language with flair, even catching some verbal jokes and puns, and perhaps responding with a one-up joke. They may now even act as role models or mentors to incoming sojourners from their home cultures. During the in-sync stage, sojourners develop a sense of trust and empathy and a wide spectrum of other positive emotions. They become much more creative and adaptive in the new environment. They are capable of making appropriate choices in connection with any new situations that may arise.

Just as they are at a "comfort level" of their sojourn, however, they have to get ready to pack their bags and go home. In the *ambivalence stage*, sojourners experience grief, nostalgia, and pride, with a mixed sense of relief and sorrow that they are going home. They recall their early awkward days in the new culture, and they all count the new friends they have made since then. They also look forward eagerly to sharing all their intercultural stories with their family members and old friends back home. They finally say goodbye to their newfound friends and their temporarily adopted culture.

At the *reentry culture shock stage*, sojourners face an unexpected jolt (see the "Reentry Culture Shock" section below). Because of the unanticipated nature of reentry shock, its impact is usually much more severe, with returnees usually feeling more depressed and stressed than they did with entry culture shock. There is a sharp sense of letdown (e.g., their friends or family members have no interest in hearing all their wonderful intercultural stories) and identity disjunction: the greater the distance (i.e., on the cultural values and communication dimensions) between the two cultures, the more intense the reentry shock. By now, though, most sojourners have become resourceful and resilient individuals. They can recycle some of the commitment strategies they used abroad to pull themselves through to the next stage.

In the *resocialization stage*, some individuals (i.e., the resocializers) may quietly assimilate themselves back to their old roles and behaviors without making much of a "wave" or appearing different from the rest of their peers or colleagues. They bury their newly acquired ideas and skills together with the snapshots in their photo albums and try not to look at them again. Looking at these pictures can only cause identity dissonance and disequilibrium. Other individuals (i.e., the alienators) can never "fit back" in their home cultures again. They are always the first to accept an overseas assignment. They feel more alive abroad than at home. These alienators may eventually become global nomads who claim the world as their home rather than any single place as their base culture. Finally, yet other individuals (i.e., the transformers) are the ones who act as agents of change in their home organizations or cultures. They mindfully integrate their new learning experience abroad with what is positive in their own culture. They apply multidimensional thinking, enriched emotional intelligence, and diverse angles to solve problems or to instigate change for a truly inclusive learning organization.

Transformers are the change agents who bring home with them a wealth of personal and cultural treasures to share, actively and responsibly, with colleagues, friends, and families. They do so with interpersonally sensitive skills—something they have learned in the foreign environment. They have no fears of acting or being perceived as "different"; they now have a "taste" of what it means to be "different" (however, this "taste" of difference is qualitatively different from the "difference" that many minority members experience in their everyday lives). They are comfortable in experiencing the identity double-swing process, for example, individualist *and* collectivist, low context *and* high context. They are more compassionate and committed than before about social injustice issues and human rights' issues on a global scale. Transformers are the individuals who have acquired (and are always in the process of acquiring) mindfulness, compassion, and wisdom.

In sum, the revised W-shaped adjustment model basically emphasizes the following characteristics during the sojourners' identity change process: (1) They need to understand the peaks and valleys, and positive and negative shifts, that constitute identity change in an unfamiliar environment, realizing that the frustration-and-triumph roller-coaster ride is part of the change-and-growth process. (2) They need to be aware and keep track of their instrumental, relational, and identity goals in the new culture; success in one set of goals (e.g., making new friends) can affect triumph in another set of goals (e.g., newfound friends can help to solve a school-related problem). (3) They need to give themselves some time and space to adjust; they should keep a journal to express their daily feelings and random thoughts, and they should also keep in touch with people in their home culture via letters, faxes, and E-mail. (4) They need to develop both strong ties (meaningful friendships) and weak ties (functional social connections, e.g., with supportive teachers, caring counselors or friendly grocers) to cushion themselves and seek help in times of crisis. (5) They need to reach out to participate in the host culture's major cultural events—art and music festivals, parades, local museums, or national sports—and immerse themselves in this once-in-a-lifetime experience and learn to enjoy the local culture as much as possible. The patterns of the revised W-shaped adjustment model consist of back-and-forth looping movements within and between stages. (The factors that influence these movements have been explained above in the "Intercultural Adaptation: Antecedent Factors" section, i.e., systems-level, individual-level, and interpersonal-level factors; see Figure 9.1). Length of sojourn, alone or with families, degree of adaptation commitment, degrees and types of communication competence (e.g., linguistic competence), first-time visit versus repeated visit, and realistic versus unrealistic goals are some other factors that will propel either progressive or regressive loops along the W-shaped model.

Church (1982), in reviewing the literature on these developmental models, comment that both U-curve and W-shape models appear to be too general and do not capture the dynamic interplay between sojourners' and host nationals' factors in the adjustment process (see the above section on "Intercultural Adaptation: Antecedent Factors"—systems, individual, and interpersonal factors). In addition, sojourners adapt and learn at different rates. The data to support either model are based on one-time cross-sectional data (i.e., one-shot data collection) rather than longitudinal data (i.e., collection of data at different points during the 2-year adjustment stages). More controversial is the debate as to the initial phase (i.e., the "honeymoon stage" of adjustment. Recent research (Kealey, 1989; Osland, 1995; Rohrlich &

Martin, 1991) indicates that international students and managers both tend to experience severe identity shock (i.e., the "hostility" stage comes very early, side by side with the fleeting "honeymoon" stage) in the early phase of their sojourn abroad. However, the overseas stressors also motivate them to become more resourceful and resilient in their search for new knowledge and skills in managing the "alien" environment.

Despite some of the limitations of the developmental models, their positive implications are that they offer us a developmental portrait of the culture shock experience, illustrate that culture shock process is filled with peaks and valleys, and contribute to a holistic understanding of the psychological, affective, and identity changes in the new arrivals. Additionally, in the W-shaped model, we are made aware of the importance of understanding the role of "reentry culture shock."

Reentry Culture Shock

The phenomenon of reentry culture shock has received increased attention from intercultural researchers (Martin, 1986; Martin & Harrell, 1996; Sussman, 1986). Reentry shock involves the realignment of one's new identity with a once familiar home environment. After living abroad for an extensive period of time, reentry culture shock is inevitable.

This identity realignment process can sometimes be more stressful and jolting than entry culture shock because of the unanticipated nature of one's own identity change and the accompanying change of one's friends and family in different directions. According to research (e.g., Adler, 1997; Osland, 1995), factors that affect reentry culture shock include the following: (1) sojourners' identity change—the newly acquired values, affects, cognitions, role statuses, managerial methods, and behaviors (on both verbal and nonverbal levels) are not a "good fit" with the once familiar home culture; (2) sojourners' nostalgic and idealized images of their home culture—remembering its positive aspects and forgetting about its negative aspects during their experience abroad; (3) sojourners' difficulty in reintegrating themselves into their old career pathway or career roles because of their new cultural lenses; (4) sojourners' letdown in their expectations as to close ties with family members and friends who have become more distant because of the long separation; (5) family and friends have little interest in listening to the sojourning stories of the returnees and soon become impatient with them; (6) the home culture's demand for conformity and expectations for old role performance; (7) the absence of change in the home culture (the old system or workplace looks "stale" and "boring" in comparison to the overseas adventure) or too much change (such as political or corporate upheavals) can also create immense identity disjunction for the recent returnees.

Thus, reentry culture shock can be understood from three domains: the returnees' readiness to resocialize themselves in the home environment, the degree of change in the returnees' friendship and family networks, and the home receptivity conditions. Sussman (1986) recommends that on the individual level, "awareness of change" should be a major component of reentry training as individuals face a wide range of psychological and environmental challenges. Pusch and Loewenthall (1988) further recommend that preparation for a successful return should include (1) the recognition of what sojourners are leaving behind and what they have gained in their assignments abroad; (2) the emotional costs of transition; (3) the value of "worrying"—anticipating and preparing for difficulties that may occur; (4) the need for support systems and ways to develop them; and (5) the necessity of developing one's own strategies for going home.

Adler (1997) identifies three types of returnee managers in relationship to the specific transition strategies they employ: resocialized returnees, alienated returnees, and proactive returnees. *Resocialized returnees* are the ones who do not recognize having learned new skills in the new culture. They are also psychologically distant from their international experience. They try to use the fit-back-in strategy and resocialize themselves quietly into the domestic corporate structure. They typically rate their reentry experience as quite satisfactory. The *alienated returnees*, on the other hand, are aware of their new skills and ideas in their experience abroad. However, they have difficulty in applying their new knowledge in the home organizations. Rather, they try to use the "distance-rejective" strategy of being onlookers in their home culture. Of all the three types, they are the most dissatisfied group. The *proactive returnees* are highly aware of changes in themselves and the new values and skills they have learned overseas. They try to integrate the new values and practices learned from the sojourning culture into the home culture and develop a synergistic outlook in their reentry phase. While abroad, the proactive managers tend to use proactive communication to maintain close ties with the home organization via formal to informal memo. They also have a home-based mentor to look after their interests and pass on salient corporate information. Their mentor keeps the home-based headquarters informed of their achievements while abroad. Proactive managers might report the acquisition of the following skills in their assignments abroad: alternative managerial skills, tolerance of ambiguity, multiple reasoning perspectives, and ability to work with and manage others. They further report that the new skills improve their self-image and self-confidence level. Not surprisingly, returnees who receive validation (e.g., promotions) from their bosses and recognition from their colleagues report higher reentry satisfaction than do returnees who receive no such validation or recognition (Adler, 1997).

We turn now to examine models of the long-term acculturation of immigrants.

Minority and Immigrants' Identity Change Models

Acculturation is a multidimensional, multifaceted process that involves both systems-level and individual-level change processes. Anthropologists define the term "acculturation" as continuous first-hand contact between groups of individuals that produces subsequent changes in the cultural patterns of either one group or both (Redfield et al., 1936, p. 149). From the intercultural communication discipline, as noted earlier, the term "acculturation" commonly refers to the individual-level change process due to prolonged first-hand contact with a new culture. The term is reserved here to describe immigrants' or subsequent generations' relationships with the dominant culture.

This individual transformation process can occur in a monocultural or a pluralistic society. In a monocultural society with a high demand for conformity (e.g., Japan), acculturation for long-term inhabitants (e.g., Korean Japanese) is typically unidirectional (e.g., minority members attempting to assimilate into the dominant culture). In a pluralistic society (e.g., Canada), acculturation can take many forms and directions. The concept of acculturation involves issues such as in-group/out-group boundaries, conformity pressure, majority–minority group attitudes and relationship, and ethnic heritage maintenance and larger culture assimilation. Many majority–minority group identity models (e.g., Cross, 1991; Helms, 1993; Parham, 1989; Phinney, 1989; Ruiz, 1990; Sue & Sue, 1990; Waters, 1990) have been developed to account for the developmental stages of identity unconsciousness to consciousness in majority and minority group members. The one perspective that seems to capture the essence of immigrants' acculturation process is that of Berry and associates' fourfold typological model (Berry, Kim, & Boski, 1987; Berry, Kim, Power, Young, & Bujaki, 1989) (see Figure 9.3).

From this *typological perspective*, ethnic/cultural identity salience (i.e., the importance of ethnic and cultural identification) can be viewed as a fourfold model that emphasizes an individual's orientation toward issues of ethnic identity maintenance *and* larger cultural identity maintenance. According to Berry et al. (1987; Berry, 1994), immigrants who tend to favor ethnic tradition maintenance while attaching low significance to the values and norms of the new culture practice the *traditional-oriented* or "separation" option. Individuals who favor ethnic tradition maintenance and at the same time display movements (i.e., on the cognitive, affective, and/or behavioral level) to become an integral part of the larger society practice the *bicultural-oriented* or "integrative" option. Individuals who attach low significance to their ethnic values and norms and tend to view themselves as members of the larger culture practice the *assimilation* option. Finally, individuals who lose ethnic/psychological contact with both their ethnic group and the larger society and experience feelings of alienation and loss of identity are undergoing *marginalization*.

Cultural Identity

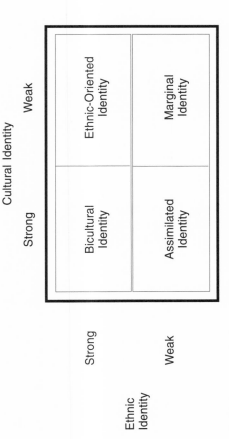

	Strong	Weak
Ethnic Identity Strong	Bicultural Identity	Ethnic-Oriented Identity
Weak	Assimilated Identity	Marginal Identity

FIGURE 9.3. A cultural–ethnic identity typological model. Data from Berry et al. (1987).

For example, a second-generation Asian American or Latino/a American can commit to one of the following four ethnic/cultural identity salience categories: Asian or Latino(a) primarily, American primarily, both, or neither (Chung & Ting-Toomey, 1994; Davis, 1990; Espiritu, 1992). Systems-level antecedent factors, individual and interpersonal factors, and identity-based process-related factors—add together integratively as a net influence on immigrants' adaptive experience and identity change process.

Alternatively, from the *racial/ethnic identity development perspective*, various models have been proposed to account for racial or ethnic identity formation of African Americans (e.g., Cross, 1978, 1995; Helms, 1993; Parham, 1989), Asian Americans (Sodowsky, Kwan, & Pannu, 1995; Sue & Sue, 1990), Latino/a Americans (e.g., Ruiz, 1990), and European Americans (e.g., Helms & Carter, 1993; Rowe, Bennett, & Atkinson, 1994). Racial/ethnic identity development models tend to emphasize the oppressive—adaptive nature of intergroup relations in a pluralistic society. From their perspective, racial/ethnic identity salience concerns the development of racial or ethnic consciousness along a linear, progressive pathway of identity change. For example, Cross (1971, 1991) has developed a five-stage model of African American racial identity development that includes preencounter (stage 1), encounter (stage 2), immersion–emersion (stage 3), internalization (stage 4), and internalization-commitment (stage 5). Helms and her associates (e.g., Helms, 1986, 1993; Parham & Helms, 1985) have amended and refined this five-stage model (i.e., integrating the concept of "worldview" in each stage) into four stages: preencounter, encounter, immersion–emersion, and internalization-commitment. The *preencounter stage* is the high cultural identity salience phase wherein ethnic minority group members' self-concepts are influenced by the values and norms of the larger culture. The *encounter stage* is the marginal identity phase when new racial/ethnic real-ization is awakened in the individuals because of a "racial shattering" event (e.g., encountering racism) and minority group members realize that they cannot be fully accepted as part of the "White world." The *immersion–emersion stage* is the strong racial/ethnic identity salience phase when individuals withdraw to the safe confines of their own racial/ethnic groups and become ethnically conscious. Lastly, the *internalization–commitment stage* is the phase in which individuals develop a secure racial/ethnic identity that is internally defined and at the same time are able to establish genuine inter-personal contacts with members of the dominant group. Racial/ethnic iden-tity, from the above perspective, refers to the "quality or manner of identi-fication with the respective racial groups" (Helms, 1993, p. 5). Phinney (1992; see also Keefe, 1992) has identified four common themes of ethnic identity that are relevant to different group members at any stage of racial/ethnic identity development: ethnic belonging (i.e., positive affiliation with one's own ethnic group), ethnic identity achievement (i.e., active search for ethnic identity knowledge), ethnic practices (i.e., participation in ethnic ac-tivities), and other-group orientation (i.e., attitudes and feelings toward members of other ethnic groups).

Integratively, the foregoing typological and stage perspectives provide a good framework from which we can begin to understand the role of eth-nic/cultural identity salience in a pluralistic society. Neither model, how-ever, fully explains the ethnic/cultural identity salience issue or the ethnic/cultural identity content issue (see Chapter 2).

To summarize, it appears that the study of ethnic identity salience has both ethnic-specific and ethnic-general elements (Phinney, 1990, 1991). As a specific phenomenon, ethnic identity encompasses the unique history, tra-ditions, values, rituals, and symbols of a particular ethnic group. As a gen-eral phenomenon, ethnic identity in a pluralistic society is a composite construct that involves ethnic group belonging and the larger cultural iden-tity issues. Thus, in order to understand the role of ethnic identity salience in a pluralistic society, both ethnic identity maintenance and the larger cul-tural identity maintenance should be taken into consideration. In order to gain a more complete understanding of the influence of ethnic/cultural iden-tity on behavior, the content (e.g., individualistic and collectivistic values, individual power ideology, intergroup expectations and perceived distance) and salience (e.g., degrees of importance and commitment) of ethnic iden-tity should be integrated more closely into these models. Nevertheless, these models portray the broader trends of minority group members' experience in a multicultural environment and depict the ebbs and flows of their struggle for identity. Some of the antecedent factors discussed earlier in this chapter can also account for the wavelike or oscillating movements between stages.

INTERCULTURAL ADAPTATION: EFFECTIVE OUTCOMES

Both systems-level and interpersonal antecedent factors, plus identity-based process factors, influence effective or ineffective intercultural adaptation outcomes. This section is developed in two parts. First we will discuss the costs and rewards of system- and interpersonal-level change, and then we will deal with the costs and rewards of immigrants' adaptive outcomes (refer to Figure 9.1).

Systems-Level and Interpersonal-Level Outcomes

According to a Workforce 2020 report (Judy & Amico, 1997), whereas in the 1980s new immigrants accounted for about one-fourth of the increase in the U.S. workforce, in the 1990s they account for fully half of the increase in the workforce. Each year approximately 500,000 legal immigrants are added to the U.S. workforce (together with an estimated 250,000 illegal entrants). Moreover, skilled and highly educated immigrants (in the areas of computer and engineering service industries) play a vital role in the U.S. advanced-technology industries. As Judy and Amico (1997) comment, "The payroll of leading IT [information technology] companies such as Intel and Microsoft include many highly skilled, foreign-born employees. In their absence it would be difficult for America to regain its global lead in IT" (p. 21). Many U.S. immigrants have contributed positively to the social and economic development of the nation.

As part of a nation in search of a coherent, multicultural policy, U.S. immigrants are here to stay—regardless of whether they are well-educated, skilled, or unskilled individuals. Job training and basic education skills are a must in order to prepare all U.S. immigrants for tomorrow's economy. Additionally, intercultural and diversity training is necessary for both host nationals and immigrants—in achieving pluralistic management goals.

Inattention to diversity issues in the workplace can lead to the following costs: (1) low morale due to culture clash; (2) high absenteeism due to psychic stress; (3) substantial dollars that must be spent due to high employee turnover; (4) much time wasted due to miscommunication between diverse employees; and (5) the enormous waste of personal energy and creativity expended in active resistance to inevitable change (Loden & Rosener, 1991, p. 12).

The long-term advantages of managing diversity effectively at the system or organizational level (Loden & Rosener, 1991) are: (1) full utilization of the organization's human capital; (2) increased knowledge and enhanced mutual respect among diverse employees; (3) therefore, increased commitment among diverse employees at all organizational levels and across all functions; (4) greater innovation and flexibility as *others* participate more fully in problem-solving groups; and (5) improved productivity as more employee effort is directed at achieving the system's missions and goals and less energy is wasted with culture clash issues (p. 220). As two expert management researchers on the U.S. workplace argue, "As humankind confronts the complex economic and social problems of the next millennium . . . a single, homogenized approach to . . . problem solving will be far less likely to succeed. Instead, creative solutions will be far more likely to come from a deep pool of diverse talents, perspectives, and life experiences. As such, it is the richness of [cultural and individual] diversity that will ultimately lead to innovation and productive change in the future" (Loden & Rosener, 1991, p. 222).

Personal Identity Change Outcomes

Intercultural adaptation outcome is an oscillating, dialectical process. Both the outcome and the process are overlapping phenomena; that is, they are interdependent constructs. Newcomers at each adaptation stage have to learn to experiment and reinvent new ways of coping, thinking, feeling, and behaving on a daily basis. The costs of such internal and external struggle and constant reinvention can include everything from identity rejection to identity loss.

When systems-level and interpersonal-level factors are consistently hostile to the newcomers, the newcomers lose their motivations to pursue their adaptive task or socioemotional goals. Additionally, their mental and physical health is affected by all these stressors. Identity confusion and identity loss can occur. In such situations, friends and networks of the newcomers ought to provide them with timely identity support so that they know they are not alone. Institutions (e.g., school teachers and counselors) might well convey more attention and empathy to the newcomers to buffer the psychological stressors that individuals are experiencing. Moreover, the new arrivals should put themselves into situations in which they can maintain some degree of success and self-esteem. They should learn to ask for help when things become too overwhelming and exhausting in the new culture.

Furthermore, immigrants have to realize that their sense of "identity in-betweenness" may stay with them for a long while. The affective struggle of identity rootlessness versus rootedness, especially in immigrants and subsequent generations, is part of this oscillating, dialectical process (Yoshikawa, 1988). Their sense of rootlessness may provide them with the advantage of seeing ideas and practices in their adopted homeland with great clarity. Their sense of developmental rootedness may propel many immigrants and immigrant children to be more committed to social change and correcting social injustice in their adopted society.

Some sojourners and immigrants may arrive at a stage of utilizing a "third culture perspective" (Gudykunst, Wiseman, & Hammer, 1977) in viewing the pros and cons of their culture of origin and the new culture.

Such a perspective enables an individual to integrate the best practices and approaches of the two cultures and work out the task and relational issues synergistically and creatively. Alternatively, J. Bennett (1993) terms some of these individuals "constructive marginals," meaning that they are inclined to interpret and evaluate behavior from a variety of cultural frames of reference and engage in "contextual evaluation" of people's dissimilar actions. They tend to take responsibilities for generating synergistic solutions and help to evaluate alternative outcomes.

In sum, to be a resourceful communicator in a new culture, one has to constantly walk a narrow path while balancing different identity acts. One has to forgo stability in order to regain stability. One has to experience differentiation in order to regain inclusion. One has to risk losing trust in order to regain trust. Finally, a newcomer has to be willing to "become" an anonymity in the unknown territory in order to "be" a full-fledged, recognized member of the new culture. While some travelers view the journey as difficult and hazardous, others take advantage of traversing the hills and valleys along the way as part of a long-term learning process.

RECOMMENDATIONS

Overall, based on existing research findings (e.g., Anderson, 1994; Ward, 1996), here are some recommendations for managing newcomers' culture shock effectively:

1. Newcomers should realize that culture shock is an inevitable experience that most people encounter when relocating from a familiar environment to an unfamiliar one. Culture shock is induced because of identity fear or threat in the unpredictable environment.

2. New arrivals should understand that culture shock arises because of the unfamiliar environment which is saturated with unfamiliar cues. Developing a supportive ethnic-based friendship network and easing themselves into the new setting slowly can help to restore the identity equilibrium state.

3. Sojourners and immigrants should realize that part of the culture stress is due to their sense of acute disorientation with respect to unfamiliar norms and scripts in the new culture. Thus, making an effort to establish contacts with members of the host culture and learning to communicate with them can increase local knowledge and reduce such feelings of vulnerability. Likewise, the more members of the host culture extend a helping hand and the more they attempt to increase their familiarity with the new arrivals, the more they can increase the newcomers' sense of security and inclusion.

4. Culture shock is induced partly by an intense feeling of incompetence. By seeking out positive role models or mentors, newcomers may be

able to find reliable and competent cultural translators in easing the initial and developmental phases of their adaptation.

6. Newcomers should realize that culture shock is a transitional affective phase of stress that ebbs and flows from high to low intensity. New arrivals need to hang onto a resilient sense of humor and emphasize the positive aspects of the environment rather than engaging in prolonged concentration on its negative aspects, realizing that these "growing pains" may lead to long-term personal and professional growth and development.

7. From the identity negotiation theory, the fundamental need for newcomers in an unfamiliar culture is addressing the sense of insecurity and vulnerability. The more competent newcomers are at managing their identity threat level, the more they are able to induce effective adaptation outcomes. New arrivals can defuse their identity threats by (a) increasing their motivations to learn about the new culture; (b) keeping their expectations realistic and increasing their familiarity concerning the diverse facets of the new culture (e.g., conducting culture-specific research through readings and diverse accurate sources, including talking with people who have spent some time in that culture); (c) increasing their linguistic fluency and learning why, how, and under what situations certain phrases or gestures are appropriate, plus understanding the core cultural values linked to specific behaviors; (d) working on their tolerance for ambiguity and other flexible personal attributes; (e) developing strong ties (close friends) and weak ties (acquaintanceships) to manage identity stress and loneliness; (f) using a wide range of mass media to understand the symbolic complexity of the host culture; and (g) being mindful of their interpersonal behaviors and suspend snap evaluations of the host or newly adopted culture.

10

Transcultural Communication Competence

Criteria of Transcultural Communication Competence.............. 262
   The Appropriateness Criterion.. 262
   The Effectiveness Criterion.. 263
   The Satisfaction Criterion.. 265
Components of Transcultural Communication Competence 265
   The Knowledge Blocks Component 266
   The Mindfulness Component 267
   The Communication Skills Component 269
From Intercultural to Transcultural Ethics 271
   Ethical Absolutism versus Ethical Relativism...................... 272
   Moral Exclusion versus Moral Inclusion 275
Final Recommendations.. 276

Transcultural communication competence (TCC) refers to an integrative theory–practice approach enabling us to mindfully apply the intercultural knowledge we have learned in a sensitive manner. Specifically, it refers to a transformation process connecting intercultural knowledge with competent practice. To be a competent transcultural communicator, we need to transform our knowledge of intercultural theories into appropriate and effective performance.

The word "transcultural" conveys the idea that there is an existing body of knowledge and skills in the intercultural communication literature that is designed to help people communicate appropriately and effectively in a wide range of intercultural situations. Culture-specific and ethnic-specific knowledge, in conjunction with a TCC approach, will yield a wealth of interaction skills that permit individuals to cross cultural boundaries flexibly and adaptively.

This chapter serves as a summation of core themes that we have discussed in the previous chapters. It is divided into four main sections: first, criteria of TCC; second, components of TCC; third, a discussion of intercultural ethics; and fourth, some final recommendations.

CRITERIA OF TRANSCULTURAL
COMMUNICATION COMPETENCE

Drawing from the identity negotiation perspective of this book, we reemphasize here that the underlying goal in any intercultural or interethnic situation is to manage content, process, relational and group membership identity issues appropriately, effectively, and satisfactorily. In addition to content-related issues, this view emphasizes the importance of understanding the various identity types and needs (e.g., inclusion vs. differentiation) of individuals from different cultures. It also highlights the different operational skills that are needed in managing diversity in a wide range of intercultural episodes.

The criteria of perceived appropriateness, effectiveness, and satisfaction are inferred through the competent exchange of verbal and nonverbal messages between persons of different cultures. Competent exchange of messages means that both intercultural communicators perceive that they and their messages are being understood in the proper context and with the desirable effects.

The criteria of TCC act as yardstick measures of a competent transcultural communicator. When both communicators and interested parties experience communication appropriateness and effectiveness plus satisfaction, the process and the outcome of communication can be deemed successful. This section is developed in three parts: (1) the criterion of appropriateness; (2) the criterion of effectiveness; and (3) the criterion of satisfaction.

The Appropriateness Criterion

Appropriateness refers to the degree to which the exchanged behaviors are regarded as proper and match the expectations generated by the insiders of the culture. For example, if you are in China, when you offer your guest some food, you should use self-effacing mode of expression such as "The food is not too delicious, but try some. . . ." And if you are an interculturally sensitive guest, you might say something like "All the dishes look so good, you must have been working really hard all day in the kitchen. You're being too humble. . . ." In another example, a Taiwanese top-notch computer programmer might say, "I'm not very familiar with this software program. Please don't expect too much. . . ." You, as a client, might reply with a compliment: "Please don't be so humble. I know your firm's great reputation. If you can't fix this problem, no one can!"

Individuals typically use their own cultural expectations and scripts to approach an intercultural interaction scene. They also formulate their impressions of a competent communicator based on their perceptions of the other's verbal and nonverbal behaviors in relation to the particulars of a situation. While insiders have worked out a smooth script for their everyday interactions, outsiders may be completely baffled by what seem like a "phony" or "hypocritical" way of expression. The first lesson in TCC is to tune in to our own ethnocentric evaluations concerning "improper" dissimilar behaviors. Our evaluations of "proper" and "improper" behavior stem, in part, from our ingrained cultural socialization experiences.

Thus, to understand TCC, we need to understand the impressions people have of each other in conjunction with the specific sets of behaviors that are performed in a particular situation. It is also critical that we gather short-term and long-term data concerning an individual's TCC quotient. TCC is not a one-time episodic phenomenon. Rather, it is a long-term learning and practicing process.

TCC is an incremental learning journey whereby intercultural communicators learn to mutually adapt to each other's behaviors appropriately and flexibly. To understand whether appropriate communication has been perceived, it is vital to obtain competence evaluations from the standpoint of both the communicators and interested observers. It is also critical to obtain both self-perception and other-perception data. We may think that we are acting appropriately, but others may not concur with our self-assessments.

Appropriate communication can be assessed through understanding the underlying values, norms, social roles, expectations, rules, and scripts of the cultural scene. The criterion of communication appropriateness works concurrently with the criterion of communication effectiveness. When we act appropriately in a cultural scene, our culturally proper behaviors can facilitate communication effectiveness. By signaling to the other party that we are willing to adapt our behaviors in a culture-sensitive manner, we convey our respect for the other's cultural frame of reference.

The Effectiveness Criterion

Effectiveness refers to the degree to which communicators achieve mutual shared meaning and desired goal-related outcomes. An effective encoding and decoding process leads to mutually shared meanings. Mutually shared meanings lead to perceived intercultural understanding. Ineffective encoding and decoding by one of the two communicators can lead to intercultural miscommunications and misunderstandings. In addition to the accurate encoding and decoding of messages on the content level, communicators need to cultivate mindful awareness and sensitivity along multiple levels of effective intercultural understanding.

The three layers of meanings that are critical to increase intercultural understanding are content meaning, identity meaning, and relational meaning (see Chapter 1). "Content meaning" refers to the substantive information that is being conveyed to the listener in a particular interaction scene.

Content meaning is tied to factual or digital aspects of the message exchange process (e.g., "Did you like the food?") and is verifiable. However, what you decide to say on the content level can be contingent on the culture in which you are located. You might really not like the food; however, if you are in a high-context culture, you may not want to say "no" as a direct answer. You may have to say something like "It's all delicious, but I'm so full . . . I cannot have another bite. . . ." In many high-context cultures, saving the other's face through an indirect expression is much more important than honest, up-front speech.

"Identity meaning" refers to the following questions: "Who am I and who are you in this intercultural interaction scene?" "How should we act as effective hosts or guests in this relationship?" "How can I find out more about your sense of self, your self-image, your cultural identity?" "How should I convey my sensitivity to or respect for your self-image?" Alternatively, other identity meaning questions include the following: "How do I perceive your attitude toward my cultural identity?" "Is my cultural identity being understood and respected in a sensitive manner?" "How can I learn to save face or give face to you in this situation?" Identity meaning is closely intertwined with content and relationship meanings. When identity meaning is effectively managed, individuals are also more open to renegotiate content and relationship meaning issues.

"Relational meaning" refers to the process of how both communicators define the intimacy distance and power distance of their relationship. Drawing from individualism–collectivism and power distance cultural values, for example, we should realize that individuals in different cultures have different privacy and relational needs, and different status expectations concerning the interaction process itself.

In sum, the effectiveness criterion emphasizes the importance of promoting intercultural understanding on content, identity, and relational levels. It is not enough to just understand the content messages that are being exchanged in the communication process. We also have to pay close attention to the identity-based meanings that underlie the exchanged message. By listening mindfully to the exchanged message and its nonverbal nuances, we can gauge whether the speaker is signaling her or his needs for recognition on the cultural or personal identity level and/or gender or ethnic identity level. We can also match proper cultural values with the meaning level to arrive at a culture-sensitive interpretation of how different cultural strangers are viewing the relationship.

Intercultural interaction effectiveness has been achieved when content, identity, and relational meanings are attended to with accuracy and when desired interaction goals have been reached. Intercultural interaction ineffectiveness occurs when content, identity, and relational meanings have been mismatched and when intercultural noises and clashes have jammed the communication channels.

The Satisfaction Criterion

Identity negotiation theory, in this book, assumes that human beings in all cultures desire positive affirmation from others of group membership identity and personal identity. Individuals tend to be more satisfied in interaction scenes in which their desired identity images are elicited or validated. They tend to experience dissatisfaction when their desired identity images are denied or disconfirmed. Thus, to the extent that the important identities (e.g., cultural or gender) of the intercultural communicators have been positively addressed and sensitively dealt with, they will experience interaction satisfaction. To the extent that important identities of the intercultural communicators have been bypassed or patronized, they will experience interaction dissatisfaction.

In order to achieve interaction satisfaction, we have to understand the cultural premises and assumptions that surround the use of verbal and nonverbal messages in the communication process itself. We have to realize that cultural values such as individualism–collectivism and power distance frame the culture-specific functions of verbal and nonverbal communication. For large power distance cultures, for example, formal verbal and nonverbal interaction is expected. For small power distance cultures, informal verbal and nonverbal interaction is preferred. Additionally, verbal styles of direct or indirect communication and self-enhancing or self-effacing communication can arouse different levels of satisfaction in different cultural communities. For individualists, interaction satisfaction is related to person-based emotions and personal self-worth issues. For collectivists, on the other hand, interaction satisfaction is closely tied to in-group emotional reactions and group-based self-worth issues.

In sum, the criteria of communication appropriateness, effectiveness, and satisfaction can serve as evaluative yardsticks of an intercultural interaction episode. A dynamic transcultural communicator is one who creates and manages meanings appropriately, effectively, and satisfactorily in a diverse range of cultural situations. All three criteria can also be applied holistically to the long-term process of mastery of knowledge, mindfulness, and communication skills in practicing competent transcultural communication.

COMPONENTS OF TRANSCULTURAL COMMUNICATION COMPETENCE

TCC refers to an operationalization process of integrating knowledge, mindfulness, and communication skills in managing group membership differences on a transcultural level. To engage in optimal TCC, we have to acquire in-depth knowledge, heightened mindfulness, and competent communication skills—and, most critically, applying them ethically in a diverse range of intercultural situations. This section is developed in three parts: (1) knowledge blocks; (2) mindfulness; and (3) communication skills. Of the three components of managing intercultural differences, knowledge is the most critical in that it underscores the other two aspects of TCC. We will consider intercultural ethics later.

The Knowledge Blocks Component

Without culture-sensitive knowledge, communicators cannot become aware of the implicit "ethnocentric lenses" they use to evaluate behaviors in an intercultural situation. Without accurate knowledge, communicators cannot accurately reframe their interpretation from the other's cultural standpoint. Knowledge here refers to the process of in-depth understanding of important intercultural communication concepts that "really make a difference."

The knowledge blocks in this book offer you the following information: a set of guiding assumptions about intercultural communication in Chapter 1; a mindful intercultural communication model in Chapter 2; cultural value orientation differences in Chapter 3; language functions and cross-cultural verbal interaction styles in Chapter 4; intercultural nonverbal communication differences in Chapter 5; in-group/out-group boundary regulation and stereotype formation processes in Chapter 6; identity and relational themes in managing the development of intercultural relationships in Chapter 7; factors that affect intercultural conflict management in Chapter 8; identity change and intercultural adaptation in Chapter 9; and TCC and ethical issues in this chapter.

Overall, the knowledge blocks in this book focus on how individualists and collectivists negotiate communication, conflict, and relationship differences via distinctive verbal and nonverbal communication styles. Additionally, individualists and collectivists use distinctive ethnocentric lenses to evaluate dissimilar others' behavior. Our symbolic identities define who we are on group membership and personal identity levels, and our group-based and person-based identities also propel us to choose specific speech codes and nonverbal cues to express our self-images. Our symbolic identity and culture-based identity influence one another. By understanding how intercultural verbal and nonverbal communication works, we can understand the cultural or ethnic identity behind these verbal and nonverbal cues.

By understanding the larger cultural grounding or values that influence the use of specific verbal styles and nonverbal gestures, we can understand the logic that motivates the dissimilar other's behavior. We should emphasize here that not even an insider of a culture can fully explain or interpret every detail of that culture. Obviously, then, the best chance an outsider has is to always underestimate her or his knowledge and always be willing to learn more about the new culture.

In this book, we argue for the importance of understanding cultural values as a starting point for understanding the behavior of ourselves and others. By understanding cultural value orientations, we can understand the "ideal model person" in a culture. If a culture is individualistic, the "ideal model person" will emphasize autonomous values, personal initiatives, and personal distinctions. However, if a culture is group based, the "ideal model person" will emphasize relational values, in-group connections, and in-group reputations. Through understanding cultural values such as individualism–collectivism and power distance, we can also understand the low-context and high-context communication styles that reflect such values. We will understand that individualists express themselves in low-context, direct ways because of their priorities of interpersonal efficiency and self-identity assertion, whereas collectivists convey themselves in high-context, indirect ways because of their preferences for relational harmony and mutual face-saving values. Cultural and personal values frame the identity of the individual with whom we are communicating. The identity of an individual, in turn, is expressed through her or his use of habitual verbal and nonverbal messages and interaction styles.

Transcultural communicators need to develop greater sensitivity concerning the values, identities, behaviors, and situations that constitute intercultural communication. Additionally, these concepts are mediated by the linguistic symbols of that culture. In understanding the language of a culture, we hold the key to the heart of a culture. By understanding the nonverbal nuances, expressions, styles, and boundaries of a culture, we enter the heart of that culture. Acquiring knowledge is a good first step when we are preparing ourselves to enter into any new culture. Knowledge together with mindfulness can help us to be more in tune with ourselves and dissimilar others in a vulnerable identity-contact episode.

The Mindfulness Component

Mindfulness (Thich, 1991) means attending to one's internal assumptions, cognitions, and emotions, and simultaneously attuning to the other's assumptions, cognitions, and emotions. Mindful reflexivity requires us to tune in to our own cultural and personal habitual assumptions in viewing an interaction scene. By being mindful of the "I"-identity or "we"-identity cultural value assumptions, we may be able to monitor our snapshot ethnocentric evaluations reflexively. By being mindful of the "I"-identity or "we"-identity personal variation standpoints, we may be able to monitor our own individual motivations and actions more consciously.

Beyond mindful reflexivity, we also need to be open to novelty or unfamiliar behavior. To be mindful of intercultural differences, we have to learn to see the unfamiliar behavior from a fresh context. In the context of inter-group interaction, we have to simultaneously deal with our own vulnerable emotions regarding unfamiliar behaviors and be open to new interaction scripts. We also need to develop multiple visions in understanding the stylis-tic and substantive levels of the communication process. Integrating new ideas or perspectives into one's value system requires mental flexibility. Mental flexibility requires one to rethink assumptions about oneself and the world. Such rethinking may cause identity dissonance, but inevitably it can also lead to personal growth and resourcefulness (Ting-Toomey, 1993).

According to Langer (1989, 1997), to act mindfully we should learn to (1) see behavior or information presented in the situation as novel or fresh; (2) view a situation from several vantage points or perspectives; (3) attend to the context and the person in which we are perceiving the behavior; and (4) create new categories through which this new behavior may be under-stood (Langer, 1997, p. 111). Additionally, we need to learn to shift our perspective and ground our understanding from the other's cultural frame of reference. This practice of analytical empathy enables communicators to see both differences and similarities between each other's cultural and per-sonal perspectives (Rothman, 1997). Analytical empathy leads to new in-sights and an alternative set of cultural and personal experiences.

On a general level, mindfulness demands creative thinking and living. From a mindful perspective, one's response to a "particular situation is not an attempt to make the best choice from among available options but to create options" (Langer, 1997, p. 114). In an intercultural misunderstand-ing episode, when two individuals either push against or pull away from each other, the problem is never satisfactorily resolved. Intercultural com-municators have to learn to help each other in framing the communication problem from a mutual-interest perspective and collaboratively learn to develop a creative, synergistic solution. Researchers (e.g., Csikszentmihalyi, 1996; Gardner, 1995; Langer, 1997) have found that creative individuals tend to:

1. Cultivate curiosity and interest in their immediate surroundings.
2. Look at problems from as many viewpoints as possible (i.e., open-ness to novelty).
3. Be alert to complexity and distinction within groups or cultures.
4. Be sensitive to different types of situational uniqueness that may occur.
5. Orient themselves to the present with all five senses focused.
6. Cultivate "flow" or enjoyment in their everyday interaction with others.
7. Practice divergent thinking or sideways learning.

Sideways learning, according to Langer (1997), involves attending to "multiple ways of carving up the same domain. It not only makes it possible to create unlimited categories and distinctions . . . but it is essential to mobilizing mindfulness" (pp. 23–24). While a routine thinker practices mindlessness in managing cultural differences, a creative thinker practices mindfulness.

Mindfulness can help us to arrive at the cognitive and affective "readiness" stage to interact with people who are different from ourselves. It can help us to put our own ethnocentric motivations in check. It can prompt us to examine the motivational needs and bases from the other person's frame of reference or standpoint. Mindfulness is the mediating step in linking knowledge with skillful practice.

The Communication Skills Component

"Communication skills" refers to our operational abilities to interact appropriately, effectively, and satisfactorily in a given situation. Many communication skills are useful in enhancing transcultural communication competence. The four core communication skills that are worth resummarizing here and can be used in a diverse range of intercultural situations are mindful observation (Chapter 3), mindful listening (Chapters 4 and 5), identity confirmation (Chapter 6), and collaborative dialogue (Chapter 8).

Mindful observation involves an O–D–I–S (observe–describe–interpret–suspend evaluation) *analysis*. Rather than engaging in snapshot, evaluative attributions, we should first learn to *observe* attentively the verbal and nonverbal signals that are being exchanged in the communication process. We should then try to *describe* mentally and in behaviorally specific terms what is going on in the interaction (e.g., "She is not maintaining eye contact with me when speaking to me"). Next, we should generate multiple *interpretations* (e.g., "Maybe from her cultural framework, eye contact avoidance is a respectful behavior; from my cultural perspective, this is considered a disrespectful sign") to "make sense" of the behavior we are observing and describing. We may decide to respect the differences and suspend our ethnocentric evaluation. We may also decide to engage in open-ended evaluation by acknowledging our discomfort with unfamiliar behaviors (e.g., "I understand that eye contact avoidance may be a cultural habit of this person, but I still don't like it because I feel uncomfortable in such interaction). By engaging in a reflexive dialogue with ourselves, we can monitor our ethnocentric emotions introspectively. We may want to cross-sample a wide variety of people (and in a wide range of contexts) from this cultural group to check if the "eye contact avoidance" response is a cultural or individual trait. We may even decide to approach the person (with the low-/high-context styles in mind) directly or indirectly to meta-communicate about such differences.

In an intercultural exchange episode, communicators have to work hard to *listen mindfully* to the cultural and personal viewpoints that are being expressed in the problematic interaction. To understand identity-salient issues, they have to learn to listen responsively to the tones, rhythms, gestures, movements, nonverbal nuances, pauses, and silence in the interaction episode. They have to learn to listen to the symphony and the individual melodies that are being played out in the interaction scene.

In order to listen mindfully, transcultural communicators have to learn to use paraphrase and perception checking skills in a culture-sensitive manner. Paraphrase is using verbal restatement to summarize the speaker's message. Perception checking skill is to use eyewitness accounts on a descriptive level to check whether the hearer genuinely understands the message or whether she or he has certain unmet needs or wants.

Identity confirmation skills include addressing people by their preferred titles, labels, names, and identities. Addressing people by their desired titles or identities conveys to others our recognitions of their existence and the validity of their experiences. For example, individuals sometimes may identify strongly with their ethnic-based memberships and sometimes their person-based identities. By being sensitive to people' self-images in particular situations and according due respect to their desired identities, we confirm their self-worth. Calling others what they want to be called and recognizing group memberships that are important to them are part of supporting their self-images.

Additionally, using inclusive language rather than exclusive language (i.e., "you people"), and using situational language rather than polarized language are part of identity confirmation skills. Inclusive language means we are mindful at all times of our use of verbal messages when we converse with both in-group and out-group members in a small group setting. We should cross-check our own verbal habits and make sure that we are directing our comments evenly to both in-group and out-group members on an equitable basis. Inclusive language usage also includes the use of inclusive nonverbal behavior (e.g., eye contact is evenly spread out to both in-group and out-group members and not just to in-group members). Situational language means when we observe out-group members' behavior, we are willing to take situational contingencies into account in understanding out-group members' behavior and accord them the same courtesy as we accord in-group members. In sum, we honor the identities of out-group members as if they are members of our in-group rather than overemphasize in-group/out-group circles.

Thus, we confirm and disconfirm dissimilar others by the words we choose to address them and by the attitude behind the words with which we "name" them. Sometimes we may want to downplay group-based identities because members who belong to dissimilar groups do not identify strongly with their groups. However, we may also be interacting with dissimilar individuals who value their group memberships enormously. To communicate sensitively with others, we must pay close attention to their preferences of identity affiliation in particular situations.

Transcultural communicators can practice *collaborative dialogue skills* in their meaning management process. A monologue approach pushes for ethnocentric needs exclusively. A collaborative dialogue approach, on the other hand, emphasizes ethnorelative sensitivity. Collaborative dialogue attempts to discover common ground and share power productively, and it assumes that each cultural team has a piece of the bigger picture (see Chapter 8).

Collaborative dialogue means that people suspend their assumptions and refrain from imposing their views on others. They practice mindful listening and display a respectful attitude regarding the other's viewpoints, needs, and interests. Concurrently, they are also mindful of their own needs, interests, and goals. In collaborative dialogue exchange, individuals orient themselves fully in the present. They are inwardly reflexive and outwardly reflective of identity, relational, and content-based issues.

Many other interaction skills are useful in facilitating transcultural communication competence. To recap, the discussions of these TCC skills appear in the previous chapters: mindful observation skills in Chapter 3; mindful listening skills in Chapter 4; verbal empathy skills in Chapter 4; nonverbal perception checking skills in Chapter 5; mindful stereotyping skills in Chapter 6; culture-sensitive relationship management skills in Chapter 7; constructive conflict management skills in Chapter 8; trust-building and collaborative dialogue skills in Chapter 8; and intercultural adaptation skills in Chapter 9. These skills have been discussed in the "Recommendations" section of each of these chapters. Combining this skills list and the skills that other researchers (e.g., Gudykunst & Kim, 1997; Gudykunst, Ting-Toomey, Sudweeks, & Stewart, 1995; Lustig & Koester, 1996; Wiseman & Koester, 1993) have identified, we can identify seven clear attributes associated with an effective transcultural communicator: tolerance for ambiguity, open-mindedness, cognitive flexibility, respectfulness, situational adaptability, verbal and nonverbal sensitivity, and creative thinking (see Table 10.1).

To act competently across a wide range of cultures, individuals have to increase their knowledge and heighten their mindfulness in practicing adaptive interaction skills in a variety of intercultural situations. Moreover, to engage in optimal TCC, the role of ethics undergirds the other three TCC components.

FROM INTERCULTURAL TO TRANSCULTURAL ETHICS

Ethics are principles of conduct that govern the behavior of individuals and groups. Ethical approaches represent "a community's perspective on what

TABLE 10.1. Transcultural Competence: Attributes and Abilities

Attributes	Abilities
Tolerance for ambiguity	Ability to meet new situations with mindfulness
Open-mindedness	Ability to respond to cultural others in nonevaluative ways
Flexibility	Ability to shift frame of reference
Respectfulness	Ability to show respect and positive regard for another person
Adaptability	Ability to adapt appropriately to particular situations
Sensitivity	Ability to convey empathy verbally and nonverbally
Creativity	Ability to engage in divergent as well as systems-level thinking

is good and bad in human conduct and lead to norms (prescriptive and concrete rules) that regulate actions. Ethics regulate what ought to be and help set standards for human behavior" (Paige & Martin, 1996, p. 36). We will now discuss some of the existing approaches concerning intercultural ethics. While the term *intercultural ethics* is used here to include approaches and issues of ethical absolutism versus ethical relativism, the term *transcultural ethics* probes deeper into the morality stance, characters, and attitudes of the transcultural communicator. Under transcultural ethics, the issues of moral exclusion versus moral inclusion will be considered.

Ethical Absolutism versus Ethical Relativism

Ethical absolutism emphasizes the principles of right and wrong in accordance with a set of "universally" fixed standards regardless of cultural differences. In comparison, ethical relativism emphasizes the principles of right and wrong in terms of the values and goals of a particular cultural group. Each approach has positive and negative implications.

Under the *ethical-absolutism approach*, the importance of cultural context is minimized. Ethical absolutists believe that the same fixed evaluative standards should be applied to all cultures in evaluating "good" and "bad" behavior. Unfortunately, the dominant or mainstream culture typically "defines and dominates the criteria by which ethical behavior is evaluated. Cultural [or ethnic] differences between groups are disregarded" (Pedersen, 1997, p. 154). For example, a dominant culture may view Western medicine as the best "civilized" way of treating a sick person and thus impose its view on all groups. Meanwhile, many nondominant cultural groups may view holistic or spiritual healing as an integral part of curing a sick person. However, their cultural practice is suppressed or denied.

The positive aspect of this approach is that one set of standards is being applied to evaluate a range of practices, thus preserving cross-situational consistency. The negative aspect is that it is an "imposed, universalistic" perspective that is reflective of the criteria set forth by people in the dominant cultures or groups (e.g., "First World" nations vs. "Third World" nations). The ethical-absolutistic approach often results in marginalizing or muting the voices of nondominant groups in domestic and international arenas. It does not take into account the problems of colonial ethnocentrism.

Under the *ethical-relativism approach*, right and wrong are determined predominantly by the culture of the individual. Ethical relativists try to understand each cultural group "in its own terms, with a minimum of 'contamination' by outside influence. Actions are not evaluated or even explained by outside criteria. Psychological [or behavioral] differences are explained by cultural differences" (Pedersen, 1997, p. 155; see also Barnlund, 1980). The positive implication of this approach is that it takes the role of culture seriously in its ethical decision-making process. It takes into account the importance of ethnorelativism rather than ethnocentrism. However, the danger is that it discourages "moral discourse and disregards ethical guidelines outside of each cultural context. Standards of moral behavior are tied to conventional behavior in each cultural context, which might change from time to time, place to place, and person to person" (Pedersen, 1997, p. 155). Intolerable cultural practices (e.g., Chinese footbinding practices of middle- and upper-class women under the Ching dynasty), however, are often preserved by dominant group members to reinforce the status quo or to keep nondominant groups in their subordinate "proper roles."

A third approach, a synthesizing *derived ethical-universalism approach*, emphasizes the importance of deriving universal ethical guidelines while placing ethical evaluations within the proper context, culture, and time. Thus, judgments about ethical behavior require understanding both the "underlying, fundamental similarities across cultures and the idiosyncratic . . . identity features of a culture" (Pedersen, 1997, p. 155). A derived universalistic approach highlights a combined culture-universal and culture-specific evaluative framework. However, this is easier said than done.

While a "derived" universalistic stance is an ideal goal to strive toward, it demands collaborative dialogue, attitudinal openness, and hard work from members of all gender, ethnic, and cultural groups. It demands that all voices be heard and affirmed. It also demands equal power distributions and that representations of members of diverse groups be able to speak up with no fear of sanctions. Most of the current "universal ethics" approaches, unfortunately, are "imposed ethics" that rely heavily on Eurocentric moral philosophies and principles to the exclusion of other cultural groups' voices and standpoints.

A more realistic alternative for guiding our actions in contemporary society may be that of *contextual relativism*, that emphasizes the importance of understanding the problematic practice from a contextual perspective. A contextual perspective means that the application of ethics can only be understood on a case-by-case basis and context-by-context basis. Each ethical case is a unique case, and each context is a unique ethical context that stands alone. With clarity of understanding of the context that frames the behavior in question (on sociocultural, historical, and situational levels), intercultural learners can make a mindful choice concerning their own degree of engagement or disengagement in approaching the context.

Understanding the role of context in making a meta-ethical decision connotes an in-depth understanding of the many factors (e.g., sociohistorical, economic-political, religious or cultural, power dynamics) that frame the questioning behavior (e.g., bribery in Indonesia, child labor in Pakistan, female genital mutilation in Somalia and Sudan). A meta-ethical decision is to move beyond the objectionable practice and go deeper to gather information in an effort to understand the reasons giving rise to such a practice. After understanding the reasons behind that practice, we can then decide to accept, or condemn such problematic "customs." While some questionable behaviors across cultures can be deemed to exist on a mildly offensive continuum (and we may be using our ethnocentric lenses to evaluate such behaviors), other practices are completely intolerable on a humanistic scale.

The contextual reasons have to be placed against the cultural background in which the questionable behavior occurs. We have to also place the ethical dilemma against our own personal, gender, and cultural judgments. We may not personally condone business bribery, but at the minimum we have to understand the conditions that contribute to such a practice. We can then reason that "Bribery, within this cultural context is a common practice because of the following reasons . . . ." or "Unfair child labor practice originated in this cultural context because. . . ."

Once we understand the specific sociohistorical and immediate reasons for a particular practice, we can then evaluate the reasons from an humanistic standpoint with the following questions: Who or which group perpetuates this practice within this culture? Who or which group resists this practice and with what reasons? Who is benefiting? Who is suffering—voluntarily or involuntarily? Does it cause unjustifiable suffering to an individual or a selected group of individuals at the pleasure of another group? What is my role and what is my "voice" in this ethical dilemma? Should I condemn this practice publicly? Should I go along and find a compromising solution (e.g., in the bribery practice case) and reconcile cultural differences (e.g., accept the "appreciation money" and donate it to a local charity, informing your international business partner that it is not customary in your company to accept "appreciation money" and that you have forwarded the money to a charity, thus saving "mutual face"). Should I reject the practice, withdraw from the cultural scene, or act as a change agent in the local scene? Many problematic cultural practices perpetuate themselves because of routinized cultural habits or ignorance of alternative ways of behaving or solving a fundamental problem. Education or a desire for change from within the people in a local culture is usually how questionable practice is ended.

From a contextual–relativistic framework, making a mindful ethical judgment demands both breadth and depth of context-sensitive knowledge, culture-specific knowledge, and genuine humanistic concern. A contextual relativism stance can, perhaps, ultimately lead us to develop a set of derived ethical-universalistic principles. It demands individuals from diverse communities who, with cognitive and emotional integrity, agree upon an ethical-universalistic framework. Struggling with problematic cultural practices is a complex issue—we can commit the error of being either too ethnocentric in our judgment or too ethnorelative in our attention. A mindful inquiring attitude to gather pertinent information may help us in neither hasting to condemn nor lagging in our passivity or naive ignorance.

Moral Exclusion versus Moral Inclusion

Morality involves the cognitive and emotional conditioning of individuals or groups within a particular community or society. It refers to a conception of "wrongness" or "rightness," or "a way of being" (i.e., character, honor, or integrity) concerning ethical dilemmas and choices. Morality forms the deep-seated values and attitudes that drive ethical choices. *Moral exclusion* occurs when "Individuals or groups are perceived as outside the boundary in which moral values, rules, and considerations of fairness apply. Those who are excluded are perceived as nonentities, expendable, or undeserving; consequently, harming them appears acceptable, appropriate, or just" (Opotow, 1990a, p. 1). Moral exclusion can be mild or severe. Severe instances include violations of "human rights, political repression, religious inquisitions, slavery, and genocide. . . . Milder instances of moral exclusion occur when we fail to recognize and deal with undeserved suffering and deprivation" (Opotow, 1990a, p. 2). While moral exclusion applies the scope of justice to a handful of concerned, self-interested communities (e.g., own gender communities), moral inclusion expands the scope of justice (or fairness) to include all individuals across all diverse communities.

The underlying characteristics that constitute moral inclusion (Opotow, 1990a, 1990b) are:

1. The belief that considerations of fairness apply to all other identity groups.
2. The willingness to redistribute economic and social resources to the underprivileged.
3. The willingness to make sacrifices to foster another's well-being.

4. The view that conflicts are opportunities for learning and that individuals are willing to integrate diverse perspectives—so that solutions will include mutually agreed-upon procedures to divide resources fairly.
5. The genuine belief of the "we" group in incorporating individuals from all walks of life—on a truly global level.

The underlying philosophy behind this book echoes the moral inclusion idea: human respect is a fundamental starting point for collaborative, transcultural dialogue. Human respect is a prerequisite for any type or form of intercultural or interethnic communication. Without basic human respect, a community can easily fall apart. In considering a committed, morally inclusive community, Peck (1987) observes that "the spirit of a true community is the spirit of peace. When a group enters [an inclusive] community there is a dramatic change in spirit. And the new spirit is palpable. . . . An utterly new quietness descends on the group. People seem to speak more quietly; yet, strangely, their voices seem to carry better through the room. . . . The people listen and can hear" (p. 76). An inclusive community is a vibrant community that engages in active identity support work. This does not mean that conflicts do not exist. It means, however, that voices of diversity are being listened to and are being understood. As Kale (1991) concludes, "The concept of peace applies not only to relations between cultures and countries but also to the right of all people to live at peace with themselves and their surroundings. As such, it is unethical to communicate with people in a way that does violence to their concept of themselves or to the dignity and worth of their human spirit" (p. 424).

FINAL RECOMMENDATIONS

An ethical transcultural communicator honors the sacredness of her or his sense of self, and the sacredness of others' sense of self. To conclude, an ethical transcultural communicator:

1. Respects people of diverse cultures and groups on the basis of equality.
2. Is willing to engage in a lifelong learning process of culture-universal and culture-specific communication knowledge.
3. Is willing to make mindful choices in response to the various situational contingencies of problematic cultural practices.
4. Is willing to assume a social commitment to work for mindful change so as to create a morally inclusive society.
5. Is willing to uphold the human dignity of others via a respectful mindset, an open heart, inclusive visions through ethnorelative lenses, and practicing mindful transcultural communication competencies.

References

Abrams, D., & Hogg, M. (Eds.). (1990). *Social identity theory: Constructive and critical advances.* New York: Springer-Verlag.

Adelman, M. (1988). Cross-cultural adjustment. *International Journal of Intercultural Relations, 12,* 183–204.

Adler, N. (1995). Competitive frontiers: Cross-cultural management and the 21st century. *International Journal of Intercultural Relations, 19,* 523–537.

Adler, N. (1997). *International dimensions of organizational behavior* (3rd ed.). Cincinnati: South-Western College Publishing.

Agar, M. (1994). *Language shock: Understanding the culture of conversation.* New York: Morrow.

Alba, R. (1990). *Ethnic identity: Transformation of White America.* New Haven, CT: Yale University Press.

Allport, G. (1954). *The nature of prejudice.* Cambridge, MA: Addison-Wesley.

Almaney, A., & Alwan, A. (1982). *Communicating with the Arabs.* Prospect Heights, IL: Waveland.

Altman, I. (1975). *The environment and social behavior.* Monterey, CA: Brooks/Cole.

Altman, I., & Chemers, M. (1980). *Culture and environment.* Monterey, CA: Brooks/Cole.

Altman, I., & Gauvain, M. (1981). A cross-cultural dialectical analysis of homes. In L. Luben, A. Patterson, & N. Newcombe (Eds.), *Spatial representation and behavior across the life span.* New York: Academic Press.

Altman, I., & Taylor, D. (1973). *Social penetration.* New York: Holt, Rinehart & Winston.

Anderson, L. (1994). A new look at an old construct: Cross-cultural adaptation. *International Journal of Intercultural Relations, 18,* 293–328.

Asante, M., & Asante, K. (Eds.). (1990). *African culture: The rhythms of unity.* Trenton, NJ: African World Press.

Auletta, G., & Jones, T. (1994). Unmasking the myths of racism. In D.

Halpern & Associates (Eds.), *Changing the college classroom: New teaching and learning strategies for an increasingly complex world.* San Francisco: Jossey-Bass.

Banks, S. (1995). *Multicultural public relations: A social-interpretive approach.* Thousand Oaks, CA: Sage.

Barkan, E. (1994). Strategies for teaching in a multicultural environment. In D. Halpern & Associates (Eds.), *Changing the college classroom: New teaching and learning strategies for an increasingly complex world.* San Francisco: Jossey-Bass.

Barnlund, D. (1962). Toward a meaning-centered philosophy of communication. *Journal of Communication, 2,* 197–211.

Barnlund, D. (1975). *Public and private self in Japan and the United States.* Tokyo: Simul Press.

Barnlund, D. (1980). The cross-cultural arena: An ethical void. In N. Asuncion-Lande (Ed.), *Ethical perspectives and critical issues in intercultural communication.* Falls Church, CA: Speech Communication Association.

Barnlund, D. (1989). *Communicative styles of Japanese and Americans: Images and realities.* Belmont, CA: Wadsworth.

Basso, K. (1970). To give up on words: Silence in Western Apache culture. *Southern Journal of Anthropology, 26,* 213–230.

Basso, K. (1990). To give up on words: Silence in Western Apache culture. In D. Carbaugh (Ed.), *Cultural communication and intercultural contact.* Hillsdale, NJ: Erlbaum.

Baxter, L. (1990). Dialectical contradictions in relationship development. *Journal of Social and Personal Relationships, 7,* 69–88.

Baxter, L. A., & Montgomery, B. M. (1996). *Relating: Dialogues and dialectics.* New York: Guilford Press.

Belenky, M., Clinchy, B., Goldberger, N., & Tarule, J. (1986). *Women's ways of knowing: The development of self, voice, and mind.* New York: Basic Books.

Bellah, R., Madsen, R., Sullivan, W., Swidler, A., & Tipton, S. (1985), *Habits of the heart: Individualism and commitment in American life.* Berkeley: University of California Press.

Bem, S. (1993). *The lenses of gender: Transforming the debate on sexual inequality.* New Haven, CT: Yale University Press.

Bennett, J. (1993). Cultural marginality: Identity issues in intercultural training. In R. M. Paige (Ed.), *Education for the intercultural experience.* Yarmouth, ME: Intercultural Press.

Bennett, M. (1993). Toward ethnorelativism: A developmental model of intercultural sensitivity. In R. M. Paige (Ed.), *Education for the intercultural experience.* Yarmouth, ME: Intercultural Press.

Berger, C. (1979). Beyond initial interaction. In H. Giles & R. St. Clair (Eds.), *Language and social psychology.* Oxford, UK: Blackwell.

Berger, C., & Kellermann, K. (1983). To ask or not to ask. In R. Bostrom (Ed.), *Communication yearbook 7*. Beverly Hills, CA: Sage.

Berry, J. (1994). Acculturation and psychological adaptation. In A. Bouvy, F. van de Vijver, P. Boski, & P. Schmitz (Eds.), *Journeys into cross-cultural psychology*. Lisse, The Netherlands: Swets & Zeitlinger.

Berry, J., Kim, U., & Boski, P. (1987). Psychological acculturation of immigrants. In Y. Y. Kim & W. Gudykunst (Eds.), *Cross-cultural adaptation: Current approaches*. Newbury Park, CA: Sage.

Berry, J., Kim, U., Power, S., Young, M., & Bujaki, M. (1989). Acculturation attitudes in plural societies. *Applied Psychology, 38*, 185–206.

Berscheid, E., & Reis, H. (1998). Attraction and close relationships. In D. Gilbert, S. Fiske, & G. Lindzey (Eds.), *The handbook of social psychology* (4th ed.). Boston: McGraw-Hill.

Berscheid, E., & Walster, E. (1969). *Interpersonal attraction*. Reading, MA: Addison-Wesley.

Bhagat, R., & Prien, K. (1996). Cross-cultural training in organizational contexts. In D. Landis & R. Bhagat (Eds.), *Handbook of intercultural training* (2nd ed.). Thousand Oaks, CA: Sage.

Bharati, A. (1985). The self in Hindu thought and action. In A. Marsella, G. DeVos, & F. Hsu (Eds.), *Culture and self: Asian and Western perspectives*. New York: Tavistock.

Billig, M. (1987). *Arguing and thinking*. Cambridge, UK: Cambridge University Press.

Birdwhistell, R. (1955). Background in kinesics. *ETC, 13*, 10–18.

Birdwhistell, R. (1970). *Kinesics in context*. Philadelphia: University of Pennsylvania Press.

Black, J., & Mendenhall, M. (1990). Cross-cultural training effectiveness: A review and a theoretical framework for future research. *Academy of Management Review, 15*, 113–136.

Blumer, H. (1969). *Symbolic interactionism: Perspective and method*. Englewood Cliffs, NJ: Prentice-Hall.

Blumstein, P. (1991). The production of selves in personal relationships. In J. Howard & P. Callero (Eds.), *The self-society dynamic: Cognition, emotions and action*. Cambridge, UK: Cambridge University Press.

Boldt, E. (1978). Structural tightness and cross-cultural research. *Journal of Cross-Cultural Psychology, 10*, 221–230.

Bond, M. (1991). *Beyond the Chinese face*. Hong Kong: Oxford University Press.

Bond, M. (Ed.). (1996). *The handbook of Chinese psychology*. Hong Kong: Oxford University Press.

Brake, T., Walker, D., & Walker, T. (1995). *Doing business internationally: The guide to cross-cultural success*. Burr Ridge, IL: Irwin.

Brewer, M. (1988). A dual process model of impression formation. In R.

Wyer & T. Srull (Eds.), *Advances in social cognition* (Vol. 1). New York: Erlbaum.

Brewer, M. (1991). The social self: On being same and different at the same time. *Personality and Social Psychology Bulletin, 17,* 475–482.

Brewer, M. (1996). When contact is not enough: Social identity and intergroup cooperation. *International Journal of Intercultural Relations, 20,* 291–303.

Brewer, M., & Campbell, D. (1976). *Ethnocentrism and intergroup attitudes.* New York: Wiley.

Brewer, M., & Kramer, R. (1985). The psychology of intergroup attitudes and behavior. *Annual Review of Psychology, 36,* 219–243.

Brewer, M., & Miller, N. (1996). *Intergroup relations.* Pacific Grove, CA: Brooks/Cole.

Brislin, R. (1993). *Understanding culture's influence on behavior.* Fort Worth, TX: Harcourt Brace Jovanovich.

Brislin, R., & Yoshida, T. (1994). *Intercultural communication training: An introduction.* Thousand Oaks, CA: Sage.

Broome, B. (1983). The attraction paradigm revisited: Responses to dissimilar others. *Human Communication Research, 10,* 137–152.

Brown, R., & Gilman, A. (1960). The pronouns of power and solidarity. In T. Sebeok (Ed.), *Styles in language.* Cambridge, MA: Technology Press of MIT.

Brown, P., & Levinson, S. (1987). *Politeness: Some universals in language usage.* Cambridge, UK: Cambridge University Press.

Burgoon, J. (1992). Applying a comparative approach to nonverbal expectancy violations theory. In J. Blumer, K. Rosengren, & J. McLeod (Eds.), *Comparatively speaking.* Newbury Park, CA: Sage.

Burgoon, J. (1994). Nonverbal signals. In G. Miller & M. Knapp (Eds.), *Handbook of interpersonal communication* (2nd ed.). Newbury Park, CA: Sage.

Burgoon, J. (1995). Cross-cultural and intercultural applications of expectancy violations theory. In R. Wiseman (Ed.), *Intercultural communication theory.* Thousand Oaks, CA: Sage.

Burgoon, J., Buller, D., & Woodall, W. G. (1996). *Nonverbal communication: The unspoken dialogue* (2nd ed.). New York: McGraw-Hill.

Burke, K. (1945). *A grammar of motives.* Los Angeles: University of California Press.

Buss, D. et al. (1990). International preferences in selecting mates: A study of 37 cultures. *Journal of Cross-Cultural Psychology, 21,* 5–47.

Byrne, D. (1971). *The attraction paradigm.* New York: Academic Press.

Cahn, D. (1987). *Letting go: A practical theory of relationship disengagement and reengagement.* Albany: State University of New York Press.

Cahn, D. (Ed.). (1990). *Intimates in conflict: A communication perspective.* Hillsdale, NJ: Erlbaum.

Cahn, D. (1992). *Conflict in intimate relationships*. New York: Guilford Press.

Carbaugh, D. (Ed.). (1990). *Cultural communication and intercultural contact*. Hillsdale, NJ: Erlbaum.

Carbaugh, D. (1996). *Situating selves: The communication of social identities in American scenes*. Albany: State University of New York Press.

Carroll, R. (1987). *Cultural misunderstandings: The French–American experience*. Chicago: University of Chicago Press.

Casas, J. M., & Pytluk, S. (1995). Hispanic identity development: Implications for research and practice. In J. Ponterotto, J. Casas, L. Suzuki, & C. Alexander (Eds.), *Handbook of multicultural counseling*. Thousand Oaks, CA: Sage.

Cegala, D., & Waldron, V. (1992). A study of the relationship between communicative performance and conversational participants' thoughts. *Communication Studies, 43*, 105–123.

Chaffee, S., Ness, C., & Yang, S. M. (1990). The bridging role of television in immigrant political socialization. *Human Communication Research, 17*, 266–288.

Chaika, E. (1989). *Language: The social mirror* (2nd ed.). New York: Newbury House.

Chen, G. (1995). Differences in self-disclosure patterns among Americans versus Chinese. *Journal of Cross-Cultural Psychology, 26*, 84–91.

Chinese Culture Connection (1987). Chinese values and search for culture-free dimensions of culture. *Journal of Cross-Cultural Psychology, 18*, 143–164.

Chua, E., & Gudykunst, W. (1987). Conflict resolution style in low- and high-context cultures. *Communication Research Reports, 4*, 32–37.

Chung, L. C., & Ting-Toomey, S. (1994, July). *Ethnic identity and relational expectations among Asian Americans*. Paper presented at the annual conference of the International Communication Association, Sydney, NSW, Australia.

Church, A. (1982). Sojourner adjustment. *Psychological Bulletin, 91*, 540–572.

Cissna, K., & Sieburg, E. (1981). Patterns of interactional confirmation and disconfirmation. In C. Wilder-Mott & J. Weakland (Eds.), *Rigor and imagination*. New York: Praeger.

Cissna, K., & Sieburg, E. (1986). Patterns of interactional confirmation and disconfirmation. In J. Stewart (Ed.), *Bridges not walls: A book about interpersonal communication* (4th ed.). New York: Random House.

Cocroft, B.-A., & Ting-Toomey, S. (1994). Facework in Japan and the United States. *International Journal of Intercultural Relations, 18*, 469–506.

Cohen, R. (1987). Problems of intercultural communication in Egyptian–American diplomatic relations. *International Journal of Intercultural Relations, 11*, 29–47.

Cohen, R. (1991). *Negotiating across cultures: Communication obstacles in international diplomacy.* Washington, DC: U.S. Institute of Peace.

Collier, M. J. (1991). Conflict competence within African, Mexican, and Anglo American friendships. In S. Ting-Toomey & F. Korzenny (Eds.), *Cross-cultural interpersonal communication.* Newbury Park, CA: Sage.

Collier, M. J. (1996). Communication competence problematics in ethnic friendships. *Communication Monographs, 63,* 314–336.

Collier, M. J., & Thomas, M. (1988). Identity in intercultural communication: An interpretive perspective. In Y. Y. Kim & W. Gudykunst (Eds.), *Theories of intercultural communication.* Newbury Park, CA: Sage.

Collins, N., & Miller, L. (1994). Self-disclosure and liking: A meta-analytic review. *Psychological Review, 116,* 457–475.

Condon, J. (1984). *With respect to the Japanese.* Yarmouth, ME: Intercultural Press.

Cook, S. W. (1985). Experimenting on social issues: The case of school of desegregation. *American Psychologist, 40,* 452–460.

Cort, D., & King, M. (1979). Some correlates of culture shock among American tourists in Africa. *International Journal of Intercultural Relations, 3,* 211–225.

Costanzo, F., Markel, N., & Costanzo, R. (1969). Voice quality profile and perceived emotion. *Journal of Counseling Psychology, 16,* 267–270.

Cox, T. (1994). *Cultural diversity in organizations: Theory, research, and practice.* San Francisco: Berrett-Koehler.

Cross, W., Jr. (1971). The Negro-to-Black conversion experience: Toward a psychology of Black liberation. *Black World, 20,* 13–27.

Cross, W., Jr. (1978). The Thomas and Cross models on psychological nigrescence: A literature review. *Journal of Black Psychology, 4,* 13–31.

Cross, W., Jr. (1991). *Shades of Black: Diversity in African-American identity.* Philadelphia: Temple University Press.

Cross, W., Jr. (1995). The psychology of Nigrescence: Revising the Cross model. In J. Ponterotto, J. Casas, L. Suzuki, & C. Alexander (Eds.), *Handbook of multicultural counseling.* Thousand Oaks, CA: Sage.

Csikszentmihalyi, M. (1996). *Creativity: Flow and the psychology of discovery and invention.* New York: HarperCollins.

Cunningham, M., Roberts, A., Barbee, A., Duren, P., & Wu, C. (1995). "Their ideas of beauty are, on the whole, the same as ours": Consistency and variability on the cross-cultural perception of female physical attractiveness. *Journal of Personality and Social Psychology, 68,* 261–274.

Cupach, W., & Canary, D. (Eds.). (1997). *Competence in interpersonal conflict.* New York: McGraw-Hill.

Cupach, W., & Imahori, T. (1994). Identity management theory: Communication competence in intercultural episodes and relationships. In R.

Wiseman & J. Koester (Eds.), *Intercultural communication competence*. Newbury Park, CA: Sage.

Cupach, W., & Metts, S. (1994). *Facework*. Thousand Oaks, CA: Sage.

Cushman. D., & Cahn, D. (1985). *Communication in interpersonal relationships*. Albany: State University of New York Press.

Cushner, K., & Brislin, R. (1996). *Intercultural interactions: A practical guide* (2nd ed.). Thousand Oaks, CA: Sage.

D'Andrade, R. (1984). Cultural meaning systems. In R. Shweder & R. LeVine (Eds.), *Culture theory: Essays on mind, self, and emotion*. Cambridge, UK: Cambridge University Press.

Darwin, C. (1965). The expression of the emotions in man and animals. Chicago: University of Chicago Press. (Original work published 1872)

Davis, M. (1990). *Mexican voices/American dream*. New York: Holt.

Davitz, J., & Davitz, L. (1959). The communication of feelings by content-free speech. *Journal of Communication, 9*, 6–13.

Devine, P., Hamilton, D., & Ostrom, T. (1994). *Social cognition: Impact on social psychology*. New York: Academic Press.

Dion, K. K. (1986). Stereotyping based on physical attractiveness: Issues and conceptual perspectives. In C. Herman, M. Zanna, & E. Higgins (Eds.), *Ontario symposium on personality and social psychology* (Vol. 3). Hillsdale, NJ: Erlbaum.

Dion, K. L., & Dion, K. K. (1988). Romantic love: Individual and cultural perspectives. In R. Sternberg & M. Barnes (Eds.), *The psychology of love*. New Haven, CT: Yale University Press.

Dion, K. K., & Dion, K. L. (1996). Cultural perspectives on romantic love. *Personal Relationships, 3*, 5–17.

Duran, R. (1985). Communicative adaptability: A measure of social communicative competence. *Communication Quarterly, 31*, 320–326.

Duran, R. (1992). Communicative adaptability: A review of conceptualization and measurement. *Communication Quarterly, 31*, 320–326.

Edwards, J. (1985). *Language, society, and identity*. Oxford, UK: Blackwell.

Edwards, J. (1994). *Multilingualism*. London: Routledge.

Ekman, P. (1975, September). The universal smile: Face muscles talk every language. *Psychology Today, 9*, 35–39.

Ekman, P., & Friesen, W. (1969). The repertoire of nonverbal behavior: Categories, origins, usage, and coding. *Semiotica, 1*, 49–98.

Ekman, P., & Friesen, W. (1975). *Unmasking the face*. Englewood Cliffs, NJ: Prentice-Hall.

Ekman, P., & Oster, H. (1979). Facial expression of emotion. *Annual Review of Psychology, 30*, 527–554.

Ekman, P. et al. (1987). Universals and cultural differences in the judgment of facial expressions of emotions. *Journal of Personality and Social Psychology, 53*, 712–717.

Engebretson, D., & Fullman, D. (1972). Cross-cultural differences in territoriality: Interaction distances of Native Japanese, Hawaii Japanese, and American Caucasians. In L. Samovar & R. Porter (Eds.), *Intercultural communication: A reader.* Belmont, CA: Wadsworth.

Engholm, C. (1994). *Doing business in Asian's booming "China triangle."* Englewood Cliffs, NJ: Prentice-Hall.

Espiritu, Y. (1992). *Asian American panethnicity.* Philadelphia: Temple University Press.

Farb, P. (1973). *Word play: What happens when people talk?* New York: Bantam Books.

Feagin, J. (1989). *Racial and ethnic relations* (3rd ed.). Englewood Cliffs, NJ: Prentice-Hall.

Ferraro, G. (1990). *The cultural dimension of international business.* Englewood Cliffs, NJ: Prentice Hall.

Fisher, G. (1998). *The mindsets factors in ethnic conflict: A cross-cultural agenda.* Yarmouth, ME: Intercultural Press.

Fisher, R., & Brown, S. (1988). *Getting together: Building relationships as we negotiate.* New York: Penguin Books.

Fisher, R., & Ury, W. (1981). *Getting to yes.* Boston: Houghton Mifflin.

Fiske, A. (1991). *Structures of social life: The four elementary forms of human relations.* New York: Free Press.

Fitch, K. (1994). A cross-cultural study of directive sequences and some implications for compliance-gaining research. *Communication Monographs, 61,* 185–209.

Fitch, K. (1998). *Speaking relationally: Culture, communication, and interpersonal communication.* New York: Guilford Press.

Folger, J., Poole, M., & Stutman, S. (1997). *Working through conflict: Strategies for relationships, groups, and organizations* (3rd ed.). New York: Longman.

Frielich, M. (1989). Introduction: Is culture still relevant? In M. Frielich (Ed.), *The relevance of culture.* New York: Morgan & Garvey.

Furnham, A. (1986). Situational determinants of intergroup communication. In W. Gudykunst (Ed.), *Intergroup communication.* London: Arnold.

Furnham, A. (1988). The adjustment of sojourners. In Y. Y. Kim & W. Gudykunst (Eds.), *Cross-cultural adaptation.* Newbury Park, CA: Sage.

Furnham, A., & Bochner, S. (1982). Social difficulty in a foreign culture. In S. Bochner (Ed.), *Cultures in contact.* Elmsford, NY: Pergamon Press.

Furnham, A., & Bochner, S. (1986). *Culture shock.* New York: Routledge.

Gallois, C., Giles, H., Jones, E., Cargile, A., & Ota, H. (1995). Accommodating intercultural encounters: Elaborations and extensions. In R. Wiseman (Ed.), *Intercultural communication theory.* Thousand Oaks, CA: Sage.

Gao, G. (1991). Stability in romantic relationships in China and the United

States. In S. Ting-Toomey & F. Korzenny (Eds.), *Cross-cultural inter-personal communication*. Newbury Park, CA: Sage.

Gao, G., & Ting-Toomey, S. (1998). *Communicating effectively with the Chinese*. Thousand Oaks, CA: Sage.

Garcia, W. R. (1996). *Respeto*: A Mexican base for interpersonal relation-ships. In W. Gudykunst, S. Ting-Toomey, & T. Nishida (Eds.), *Com-munication in personal relationships across cultures*. Thousand Oaks, CA: Sage.

Gardner, H. (1995). *Leading minds: Anatomy of leadership*. New York: Basic Books.

Gilligan, C. (1988). Remapping the moral domain: New images of self in relationship. In C. Gilligan, J. Ward, & J. Taylor (Eds.), *Mapping the moral domain*. Cambridge, MA: Harvard University Press.

Gochenour, T. (1990). *Considering Filipinos*. Yarmouth, ME: Intercultural Press.

Goffman, E. (1959). *The presentation of self in everyday life*. Garden City, NY: Anchor/Doubleday.

Goleman, D., Kaufman, P., & Ray, M. (1992). *The creative spirit*. New York: Dutton.

Graf, J. (1994). Views on Chinese. In Y. Bao (Ed.), *Zhong guo ren, ni shou le shen me zhu zhou?* [*Chinese people, what have you been cursed with?*] Taipei, Taiwan: Xing Guang Chu Ban She.

Graham, J. (1985). The influence of culture on the process of business nego-tiations. *Journal of International Business Studies, 16,* 81–96.

Granovetter, M. (1973). The strength of weak ties. *American Journal of Sociology, 78,* 1360–1380.

Grinde, D. (1996). Place and kinship: A Native American's identity before and after words. In B. Thompson & S. Tyagi (Eds.), *Names we call home: Autobiography on racial identity*. New York: Routledge.

Gudykunst, W. (1988). Uncertainty and anxiety. In Y. Y. Kim & W. Gudykunst (Eds.), *Theories in intercultural communication*. Newbury Park, CA: Sage.

Gudykunst, W. (1993). Toward a theory of effective interpersonal and in-tergroup communication: An anxiety/uncertainty management (AUM) perspective. In R. Wiseman & J. Koester (Eds.), *Intercultural commu-nication competence*. Newbury Park, CA: Sage.

Gudykunst, W. (1995). Anxiety/uncertainty management (AUM) theory: Current status. In R. Wiseman (Ed.), *Intercultural communication theory*. Thousand Oaks, CA: Sage.

Gudykunst, W. (1998). *Bridging differences: Effective intergroup commu-nication* (3rd ed.). Thousand Oaks, CA: Sage.

Gudykunst, W., & Hammer, M. (1987). The effect of ethnicity, gender, and dyadic composition on uncertainty reduction in initial interactions. *Journal of Black Studies, 18,* 191–214.

Gudykunst, W., & Kim, Y. Y. (1997). *Communicating with strangers: An approach to intercultural communication* (3rd ed.). New York: McGraw-Hill.

Gudykunst, W., Matsumoto, Y., Ting-Toomey, S., Nishida, T., Kim, K. S., & Heyman, S. (1996). The influence of cultural individualism-collectivism, self construals, and individual values on communication styles across cultures. *Human Communication Research, 22,* 510–543.

Gudykunst, W., & Nishida, T. (1984). Individual and cultural influences on uncertainty reduction. *Communication Monographs, 51,* 23–36.

Gudykunst, W., & Shapiro, R. (1996). Communication in everyday interpersonal and intergroup encounters. *International Journal of Intercultural Relations, 20,* 19–45.

Gudykunst, W., & Ting-Toomey, S., with Chua, E. (1988). *Culture and interpersonal communication.* Newbury Park, CA: Sage.

Gudykunst, W., Ting-Toomey, S., Sudweeks, S., & Stewart, L. (1995). *Building bridges.* Boston: Houghton-Mifflin.

Gudykunst, W., Wiseman, R., & Hammer, M. (1977). Determinants of a sojourner's attitudinal satisfaction. In B. Ruben (Ed.), *Communication yearbook 1.* New Brunswick, NJ: Transaction.

Gullahorn, J. T., & Gullahorn, J. E. (1963). An extension of the U-curve hypothesis. *Journal of Social Issues, 19,* 33–47.

Halberstadt, A. (1991). Toward an ecology of expressiveness: Family expressiveness in particular and a model in general. In R. Feldman & B. Rime (Eds.), *Fundamentals of nonverbal communication.* Cambridge, UK: Cambridge University Press.

Hall, E. T. (1959). *The silent language.* New York: Doubleday.

Hall, E. T. (1966). *The hidden dimension* (2nd ed.). Garden City, NY: Anchor/Doubleday.

Hall, E. T. (1976). *Beyond culture.* New York: Doubleday.

Hall, E. T. (1981). *Beyond culture* (2nd ed.). Garden City, NY: Anchor/Doubleday.

Hall, E. T. (1983). *The dance of life.* New York: Doubleday.

Hall, E. T., & Hall, M. (1987). *Hidden differences: Doing business with the Japanese.* Garden City, NY: Anchor Press/Doubleday.

Hammer, M., & Gudykunst, W. (1987). The influence of ethnicity, sex, and dyadic composition on communication in friendships. *Journal of Black Studies, 17,* 418–437.

Hammer, M., Gudykunst, W., & Wiseman, R. (1978). Dimensions of intercultural effectiveness. *International Journal of Intercultural Relations, 2,* 382–393.

Harre, R. (1984). *Personal being: A theory for individual psychology.* Cambridge, MA: Harvard University Press.

Hecht, M., Collier, M. J., & Ribeau, S. (1993). *African American commu-*

nication: Ethnic identity and cultural interpretation. Newbury Park, CA: Sage.

Hecht, M., & Ribeau, S. (1984). Sociocultural roots of ethnic identity. Journal of Black Studies, 21, 501–513.

Hecht, M., Sedano, M., & Ribeau, S. (1993). Understanding culture, communication, and research: Applications to Chicanos and Mexican Americans. International Journal of Intercultural Relations, 17, 157–165.

Heider, F. (1944). Social perception and phenomenal causality. Psychological Review, 51, 258–374.

Heider, F. (1958). The psychology of interpersonal relations. New York: Wiley.

Helms, J. (1986). Expanding racial identity theory to cover counseling process. Journal of Counseling Psychology, 33, 62–64.

Helms, J. (Ed.). (1993). Black and White racial identity: Theory, research, and practice. Westport, CT: Praeger.

Helms, J., & Carter, R. (1993). Development of White racial identity development model. In J. Helms (Ed.), Black and White racial identity: Theory, Research, and practice. Westport, CT: Praeger.

Helms, J., & Parham, T. (1993). Black racial identity attitude scale (Form WRIAS). In J. Helms (Ed.), Black and white racial identity: Theory, research, and practice. Westport, CT: Praeger.

Hewstone, M. (1989). Changing stereotypes with disconfirming information. In D. Bar-Tal, C. Graumann, A. Kruglanski, & W. Stroebe (Eds.), Stereotyping and prejudice: Changing conceptions. New York: Springer-Verlag.

Hewstone, M., & Brown, R. (Eds.). (1986). Contact and conflict in intergroup encounters. Oxford, UK: Blackwell.

Hewstone, M., & Jaspars, J. (1984). Social dimensions of attribution. In H. Tajfel (Ed.), The social dimension (Vol. 2). Cambridge, UK: Cambridge University Press.

Ho, M. K. (1987). Family therapy with ethnic minorities. Newbury Park, CA: Sage.

Hofstede, G. (1980). Culture's consequences: International differences in work-related values. Beverly Hills, CA: Sage.

Hofstede, G. (1991). Cultures and organizations: Software of the mind. London: McGraw-Hill.

Hofstede, G. (1998). Masculinity and femininity: The taboo dimension of national culture. Thousand Oaks, CA: Sage.

Hofstede, G., & Bond, M. (1984). Hofstede's culture dimensions. Journal of Cross-Cultural Psychology, 15, 417–433.

Hogg, M., & Abrams, D. (1988). Social identifications. London: Routledge.

Howell, W. (1982). The empathic communicator. Belmont, CA: Wadsworth.

Hubbert, K., Guerrero, S., & Gudykunst, W. (1995, May). Intergroup com-

munication over time. Paper presented at the annual conference of the International Communication Association, Albuquerque, NM.

Hymes, D. (1972). Models of the interaction of language and social life. In J. Gumperz & D. Hymes (Eds.), *Directions in sociolinguistics: The ethnography of communication.* New York: Holt, Rinehart & Winston.

Imahori, T., & Cupach, W. (1994). Cross-cultural comparison of the interpretation and management of face: U. S. American and Japanese responses to embarrassing predicaments. *International Journal of Intercultural Relations, 18,* 193–220.

Ishii, S., & Bruneau, T. (1991). Silence and silences in cross-cultural perspective: Japan and the United States. In L. Samovar & R. Porter (Eds.), *Intercultural communication: A reader* (6th ed.). Belmont, CA: Wadsworth.

Islam, M., & Hewstone, M. (1993). Dimensions of contact as predictors of intergroup anxiety, perceived outgroup variability, and outgroup attitude: An integrative model. *Personality and Social Psychology Bulletin, 19,* 700–710.

Izard, C. (1980). Cross-cultural perspectives on emotion and emotion communication. In H. Triandis & W. Lonner (Eds.), *Handbook of cross-cultural psychology* (Vol. 3). Boston: Allyn & Bacon.

Jankowiak, W. (Ed.). (1995). *Romantic passion: A universal experience?* New York: Columbia University Press.

Johnson, M. (1991). Commitment to personal relationships. In W. Jones & D. Perlman (Eds.), *Advances in personal relationship* (Vol. 3). London: Kingsley.

Jones, E. (1990). *Interpersonal perception.* New York: Freemen.

Jones, S., & Yarborough, A. (1985). A naturalistic study of the meanings of touch. *Communication Monographs, 52,* 19–56.

Judy, R., & D'Amico, C. (1997). *Work force 2020: Work and workers in the 21st century.* Indianapolis, IN: Hudson Institute.

Kale, D. (1991). Ethics in intercultural communication. In L. Samovar & R. Porter (Eds.), *Intercultural communication: A reader* (6th ed.). Belmont, CA: Wadsworth.

Kanouse, D., & Hanson, L. (1972). Negativity in evaluations. In E. Jones & R. Nisbett (Eds.), *Attribution.* Morristown, NJ: General Learning Press.

Kashima, Y., & Triandis, T. (1986). The self-serving bias in attributions as a coping strategy: A cross-cultural study. *Journal of Cross-Cultural Psychology, 17,* 83–97.

Kashima, Y., Yamaguchi, S., Kim, U., Choi, S.-C., Gelfand, M., & Yuki, M. (1995). Culture, gender and self: Perspective from individualism–collectivism research. *Journal of Personality and Social Psychology, 5,* 925–937.

Katriel, T. (1986). *Talking straight: "Dugri" speech in Israeli Sabra culture.* Cambridge, UK: Cambridge University Press.

Katriel, T. (1991). *Communal webs: Communication and culture in contemporary Israel.* Albany: State University of New York Press.

Kealey, D. (1989). A study of cross-cultural effectiveness: Theoretical issues and practical applications. *International Journal of Intercultural Relations, 13,* 1313–1319.

Kealey, D. (1996). The challenge of international personnel selection. In D. Landis & R. Bhagat (Eds.), *Handbook of intercultural training* (2nd ed.). Thousand Oaks, CA: Sage.

Keefe, S. E. (1992). Ethnic identity: The domain of perceptions and attachment to ethnic groups and cultures. *Human Organization, 51,* 35–41.

Kim, H. K. (1991). Influence of language and similarity on initial intercultural attraction. In S. Ting-Toomey & F. Korzenny (Eds.), *Cross-cultural interpersonal communication.* Newbury Park, CA: Sage.

Kim, J. K. (1980). Explaining acculturation in a communication framework. *Communication Monographs, 47,* 155–179.

Kim, M. S., Hunter, J. E., Miyahara, A., Horvath, A., Bresnahan, M., & Yoon, H. (1996). Individual- vs. cultural-level dimensions of individualism and collectivism: Effects on preferred conversational styles. *Communication Monographs, 63,* 28–49.

Kim, U., Triandis, T., Kagitcibasi, C., Choi, S.-C., & Yoon, G. (Eds.). (1994). *Individualism and collectivism: Theory, method, and applications.* Thousand Oaks, CA: Sage.

Kim, Y. Y. (1979). Toward an interactive theory of communication-acculturation. In D. Nimmo (Ed.), *Communication yearbook 3.* New Brunswick, NJ: Transaction.

Kim, Y. Y. (1988). *Communication and cross-cultural adaptation: An integrative theory.* Clevedon, UK: Multilingual Matters.

Kim, Y. Y. (1991). Intercultural communication competence. In S. Ting-Toomey & F. Korzenny (Eds.), *Cross-cultural interpersonal communication.* Newbury Park, CA: Sage.

Kim, Y. Y. (1995). Cross-cultural adaptation. In R. Wiseman (Ed.), *Intercultural communication theory.* Thousand Oaks, CA: Sage.

Kitayama, S., & Markus, H. (1994). The cultural construction of emotion: Implications for social behavior. In S. Kitayama & H. Markus (Eds.), *Emotion and culture: Empirical studies of mutual influence.* Washington, DC: American Psychological Association.

Kluckhohn, F., & Strodtbeck, F. (1961). *Variations in value orientations.* New York: Row, Peterson.

Knapp, M., & Hall, J. (1992). *Nonverbal communication in human interaction* (3rd ed.). New York: Harcourt Brace.

Kochman, T. (1981). *Black and white styles in conflict.* Chicago: University of Chicago Press.

Kochman, T. (1990). Force fields in Black and White communication. In D.

Carbaugh (Ed.), *Cultural communication and intercultural contact.* Hillsdale, NJ: Erlbaum.

Kohls, L. R. (1996). *Survival kits for overseas living* (3rd ed.). Yarmouth, ME: Intercultural Press.

Kraus, E. (1991). *The contradictory immigrant problem: A socio-psychological analysis.* New York: Lang.

Krishnan, A., & Berry, J. (1992). Acculturative stress and acculturative attitudes among Indian immigrants to the United States. *Psychology and Developing Societies, 4,* 187–212.

Kroeber, A., & Kluckhohn, C. (1952). *Culture: A critical review of concepts and definitions* (Papers of the Peabody Museum, Vol. 47). Cambridge, MA: Peabody Museum.

Labov, W. (1972). Transformation of experience in narrative syntax. In W. Labov (Ed.), *Language in the inner city.* Philadelphia: University of Pennsylvania Press.

LaFrance, M., & Mayo, C. (1978). Cultural aspects of nonverbal behavior. *International Journal of Intercultural Relations, 2,* 71–89.

Laing, D. (1961). *The self and others.* New York: Pantheon Books.

Landis, D., & Bhagat, R. (Eds.). (1996). *Handbook of intercultural training* (2nd ed.). Thousand Oaks, CA: Sage.

Langer, E. (1989). *Mindfulness.* Reading, MA: Addison-Wesley.

Langer, E. (1997). *The power of mindful learning.* Reading, MA: Addison-Wesley.

Lazarus, R. S. (1991). *Emotion and adaptation.* New York: Oxford University Press.

Lederach, J. P. (1997). *Building peace: Sustainable reconciliation in divided societies.* Washington, DC: U.S. Institute of Peace.

Lee, H., & Boster, F. (1991). Social information for uncertainty reduction during initial interactions. In S. Ting-Toomey & F. Korzenny (Eds.), *Cross-cultural interpersonal communication.* Newbury Park, CA: Sage.

Leung, K. (1987). Some determinants of reactions to procedural models for conflict resolution: A cross-national study. *Journal of Personality and Social Psychology, 53,* 898–908.

Leung, K. (1988). Some determinants of conflict avoidance. *Journal of Cross-Cultural Psychology, 19,* 125–136.

Leung, K., Au, Y.-F., Fernandez-Dols, J. M., & Iwawaki, S. (1992). Preference for methods of conflict processing in two collectivistic cultures. *International Journal of Psychology, 27,* 195–209.

Leung, K., & Bond, M. (1984). The impact of cultural collectivism on reward allocation. *Journal of Personality and Social Psychology, 47,* 793–804.

Leung, K., & Iwawaki, S. (1988). Cultural collectivism and distributive behavior. *Journal of Cross-Cultural Psychology, 19,* 35–49.

Lewin, K. (1936). *Principles of typological psychology.* New York: McGraw-Hill.

Leyens, J.-P., Yzerbyt, V., & Schadron, G. (1994). *Stereotypes and social cognition.* London: Sage.

Lim, T.-S., & Choi, S. (1996). Interpersonal relationships in Korea. In W. Gudykunst, S. Ting-Toomey, & T. Nishida (Eds.), *Communication in interpersonal relationships across cultures.* Thousand Oaks, CA: Sage.

Lippman, W. (1936). *Public opinion.* New York: Macmillan

Locke, D. (1992). *Increasing multicultural understanding: A comprehensive model.* Newbury Park, CA: Sage.

Loden, M., & Rosener, J. (1991). *Workforce America! Managing employee diversity as a vital resource.* Homewood, IL: Business One-Irwin.

Lukens, J. (1978). Ethnocentric speech. *Ethnic Groups, 2,* 35–53.

Lustig, M., & Koester, J. (1996). *Intercultural competence: Interpersonal communication across cultures* (2nd ed.). New York: HarperCollins.

Lysgaard, S. (1955). Adjustment in a foreign society. *International Social Science Bulletin, 7,* 45–51.

Maltz, D., & Borker, R. (1982). A cultural approach to male–female communication. In J. Gumperz (Ed.), *Language and social identity.* Cambridge, UK: Cambridge University Press.

Markus, H., & Kitayama, S. (1991). Culture and the self: Implications for cognition, emotion, and motivation. *Psychological Review, 2,* 224–253.

Markus, H., & Kitayama, S. (1994). A collective fear of the collective: Implications for selves and theories of selves. *Personality and Social Psychology Bulletin, 20,* 568–579.

Marsella, A., DeVos, G., & Hsu, F. L. K. (Eds.). (1985). *Culture and self: Asian and Western perspectives.* New York: Tavistock.

Martin, J. (1986). Training issues in cross-cultural orientation. *International Journal of Intercultural Relations, 10,* 103–116.

Martin, J., & Harrell, T. (1996). Reentry training for intercultural sojourners. In D. Landis & R. Bhagat (Eds.), *Handbook of intercultural training* (2nd ed.). Thousand Oaks, CA: Sage.

Matsumoto, D. (1989). American-Japanese cultural differences in the recognition of universal facial expressions. *Journal of Cross-Cultural Psychology, 23,* 72–84.

Matsumoto, D. (1992). Cultural influences on the perception of emotion. *Journal of Cross-Cultural Psychology, 20,* 92–104.

Matsumoto, D., & Kudoh, T. (1993). American-Japanese cultural differences in attributions based on smiles. *Journal of Nonverbal Behavior, 17,* 231–243.

Mayo, C., & LaFrance, M. (1977). *Evaluating research in social psychology.* Monterey, CA: Brooks/Cole.

McCall, G., & Simmons, J. (1978). *Identities and interaction.* New York: Free Press.

McGuire, M., & McDermott, S. (1988). Communication in assimilation, deviance, and alienation states. In Y. Y. Kim & W. Gudykunst (Eds.), *Cross-cultural adaptation*. Newbury Park, CA: Sage.

Mead, G. H. (1934). *Mind, self, and society*. Chicago: University of Chicago Press.

Mehrabian, A. (1981). *Silent messages: Implicit communication of emotions* (2nd ed.). Belmont, CA: Wadsworth.

Merton, R. (1957). *Social theory and social structure*. New York: Free Press.

Mesquita, B., & Frijida, N. (1992). Cultural variations in emotions: A review. *Psychological Bulletin, 112*, 179–204.

Miller, J. (1991). A cultural perspective on the morality of beneficence and interpersonal responsibility. In S. Ting-Toomey & F. Korzenny (Eds.), *Cross-cultural interpersonal communication*. Newbury Park, CA: Sage.

Morrison, T., Conaway, W., & Borden, G. (1994). *Kiss, bow, or shake hands: How to do business in sixty countries*. Holbrook, MA: Adams.

Mortland, C., & Ledgerwood, J. (1988). Refugee resource acquisition. In Y. Y. Kim & W. Gudykunst (Eds.), *Cross-cultural adaptation*. Newbury Park, CA: Sage.

Naotsuka, R., Sakamoto, N., Hirose, T., Hagihara, H., Ohta, J., Maeda, S., Hara, T., & Iwasaki, K. (1981). *Mutual understanding of different cultures*. Tokyo: Taishukan.

Nydell, M. K. (1987). *Understanding Arabs*. Yarmouth, ME: Intercultural Press.

Nydell, M. K. (1996). *Understanding Arabs* (2nd ed.). Yarmouth, ME: Intercultural Press.

Oberg, K. (1960). Culture shock and the problems of adjustment to new cultural environments. *Practical Anthropology, 7*, 170–179.

Ochs, E. (1988). *Culture and language development: Current perspectives*. Beverly Hills, CA: Sage.

Oetzel, J., & Bolton-Oetzel, K. (1997). Exploring the relationship between self-construal and dimensions of group effectiveness. *Management Communication Quarterly, 10*, 289–315.

Okabe, R. (1983). Cultural assumptions of East and West: Japan and the United States. In W. Gudykunst (Ed.), *Intercultural communication theory: Current perspectives*. Beverly Hills, CA: Sage.

Olsen, M. (1978). *The process of social organization* (2nd ed.). New York: Holt, Rinehart & Winston.

Opotow, S. (1990a). Moral exclusion and injustice. *Journal of Social Issues, 46*, 1–20.

Opotow, S. (1990b). Deterring moral exclusion. *Journal of Social Issues, 46*, 173–182.

Orbe, M. (1998). *Constructing co-culture-theory: An explication of cultures, power, and communication*. Thousand Oaks, CA: Sage.

Osgood, C., May, W., & Miron, M. (1975). *Cross-cultural universals of meaning.* Urbana: University of Illinois Press.

Osland, J. (1995). *The adventure of working abroad: Hero tales from the global frontier.* San Francisco: Jossey-Bass.

Padilla, A. (1981). Pluralistic counseling and psychotherapy for Hispanic Americans. In A. Marsella & P. Pedersen (Eds.), *Cross-cultural counseling and psychotherapy.* Westport, CT: Greenwood Press.

Paige, M., & Martin, J. (1996). Ethics in intercultural training. In D. Landis & R. Bhagat (Eds.), *Handbook of intercultural training* (2nd ed.). Thousand Oaks, CA: Sage.

Paniagua, F. (1994). *Assessing and treating culturally diverse clients.* Thousand Oaks, CA: Sage.

Papa, M., & Papa, W. (1997). Competence in organizational conflicts. In W. Cupach & D. Canary (Eds.), *Competence in interpersonal conflict.* New York: McGraw-Hill.

Parham, T. (1989). Cycles of psychological Nigrescence. *The Counseling Psychologist, 17,* 187–226.

Parham, T., & Helms, J. (1985). The relationship of racial identity attitudes to self-actualization of Black students and affective states. *Journal of Counseling Psychology, 32,* 431–440.

Park, M. (1979). *Communication styles in two cultures: Korean and American.* Seoul: Han Shin.

Parson, T. (1951). *The social system.* Glencoe, IL: Free Press.

Patzer, G. (1985). *The physical attractiveness phenomenon.* New York: Plenum.

Peck, M. S. (1987). *The different drum: Community making and peace.* New York: Simon & Schuster.

Pedersen, P. (1997). Do the right thing: A question of ethics. In K. Cushner & R. Brislin (Eds.), *Improving intercultural interactions: Modules for cross-cultural training programs* (Vol. 2). Thousand Oaks, CA: Sage.

Pennington, D. (1990). Time in African culture. In A. Asante & K. Asante (Eds.), *African culture: The rhythms of unity.* Trenton, NJ: Africa World Press.

Pettigrew, T. (1979). The ultimate attribution error. *Personality and Social Psychology Bulletin, 5,* 461–476.

Philipsen, G. (1987). The prospect of cultural communication. In L. Kincaid (Ed.), *Communication theory: Eastern and Western perspectives.* New York: Academic Press.

Philipsen, G. (1992). *Speaking culturally.* Albany: State University of New York Press.

Phinney, J. (1989). Stages of ethnic identity development in minority group adolescents. *Journal of Adolescence, 9,* 34–49.

Phinney, J. (1990). Ethnic identity in adolescence and adulthood: A review. *Psychological Bulletin, 108*, 499–514.

Phinney, J. (1991). Ethnic identity and self-esteem: A review and integration. *Hispanic Journal of Behavioral Sciences, 13*, 193–208.

Phinney, J. (1992). The multigroup ethnic identity measure: A new scale for use with diverse groups. *Journal of Adolescent Research, 7*, 156–176.

Phinney, J., & Chavira, V. (1995). Parental ethnic socialization and adolescent outcomes in ethnic minority families. *Journal of Research on Adolescence, 5*, 31–54.

Puentha, D., Giles, H., & Young, L. (1987). Interethnic perceptions and relative deprivation: British data. In Y. Y. Kim & W. Gudykunst (Eds.), *Cross-cultural adaptation: current approaches*. Newbury Park, CA: Sage.

Pusch, M., & Loewenthall, N. (1988). *Helping them home: A guide for leaders of professional integrity and reentry workshops*. Washington, DC: National Association for Foreign Student Affairs.

Redfield, R., Linton, R., & Herskovits, M. (1936). Memorandum for the study of acculturation. *American Anthropologist, 38*, 149–152.

Richmond, Y. (1996). *From nyet to da: Understanding the Russians* (2nd ed.). Yarmouth, ME: Intercultural Press.

Rohrlich, B., & Martin, J. (1991). Host country and reentry adjustment of student sojourners. *International Journal of Intercultural Relations, 15*, 163–182.

Rosaldo, M. (1984). Toward an anthropology of self and feeling. In R. Shweder & R. LeVine (Eds.), *Culture theory: Essays on mind, self, and society*. Cambridge, UK: Cambridge University Press.

Rosenthal, R., & Jacobson, L. (1968). *Pygmalion in the classroom: Teacher expectation and pupils' intellectual development*. New York: Holt, Rinehart & Winston.

Ross, J., & Ferris, K. (1981). Interpersonal attraction and organizational outcome: A field experiment. *Administrative Science Quarterly, 26*, 617–632.

Rothman, J. (1997). *Resolving identity-based conflict in nations, organizations, and communities*. San Francisco: Jossey-Bass.

Rowe, W., Bennett, S., & Atkinson, D. (1994). White racial identity development models: A critique and alternative proposal. *The Counseling Psychologist, 22*, 129–146.

Ruben, B., & Kealey, D. (1979). Behavioral assessment of communication competency and the prediction of cross-cultural adaptation. *International Journal of Intercultural Relations, 3*, 15–48.

Ruiz, A. (1990). Ethnic identity: Crisis and resolution. *Journal of Multicultural Counseling, 18*, 29–40.

Russell, J. (1991). Culture and the categorization of emotions. *Psychological Bulletin, 110*, 426–450.

Sapir, E. (Ed.). (1921). *Language: An introduction to the study of speech*. New York: Harcourt, Brace & World.

Schaefer, R. (1990). *Racial and ethnic groups* (4th ed.). New York: HarperCollins.

Scherer, K. (1994). Affect bursts. In S. van Goozen, N. Van de Poll, & J. Sergeant (Eds.), *Emotions: Essays on emotion theory*. Hillsdale, NJ: Erlbaum.

Schwartz, S., & Bilsky, W. (1990). Toward a theory of the universal content and structure of values. *Journal of Personality and Social Psychology, 58*, 878–891.

Searle, W., & Ward, C. (1990). The prediction of psychological and socio-cultural adjustment during cross-cultural transitions. *International Journal of Intercultural Relations, 14*, 449–464.

Shuter, R. (1976). Proxemics and tactility in Latin America. *Journal of Communication, 26*, 46–52.

Simmons, C., Vom Kolke, A., & Shimizu, H. (1986). Attitudes toward romantic love among American, German, and Japanese students. *Journal of Social Psychology, 126*, 327–336.

Simmons, C., & Wehner, E., & Kay, K. (1989). Differences in attitudes toward romantic love of French and American college students. *International Journal of Social Psychology, 129*, 793–799.

Singelis, T. (1994). The measurement of independent and interdependent self-construals. *Personality and Social Psychology Bulletin, 20*, 580–591.

Singelis, T., & Brown, W. (1995). Culture, self, and collectivist communication: Linking culture to individual behavior. *Human Communication Research, 21*, 354–389.

Smith, P., & Bond, M. (1993). *Social psychology across cultures*. New York: Harvester.

Snyder, M., & Cantor, N. (1998). Understanding personality and social behavior: A functionalist strategy. In D. Gilbert, S. Fiske, & G. Lindzey (Eds.), *The handbook of social psychology* (4th ed.). Boston: McGraw-Hill.

Sodowsky, G., Kwan, K.-L., & Pannu, R. (1995). Ethnic identity of Asians in the United States. In J. Ponterotto, J. Casas, L. Suzuki, & C. Alexander (Eds.), *Handbook of multicultural counseling*. Thousand Oaks, CA: Sage.

Sorrells, B. (1983). *The nonsexist communicator*. Englewood Cliffs, NJ: Prentice-Hall.

Spitzberg, B., & Cupach, W. (1984). *Interpersonal communication competence*. Beverly Hills, CA: Sage.

Steinfatt, T. (1989). Linguistic relativity: A broader view. In S. Ting-Toomey & F. Korzenny (Eds.), *Language, communication, and culture: Current directions*. Newbury Park, CA: Sage.

Stephan, C., & Stephan, W. (1992). Reducing intercultural anxiety through intercultural contact. *International Journal of Intercultural Relations, 16*, 89–106.

Stephan, W., & Stephan, C. (1996). *Intergroup relations.* Boulder, CO: Westview.

Stewart, E., & Bennett, M. (1991). *American cultural patterns: A cross-cultural perspective* (2nd ed.). Yarmouth, ME: Intercultural Press.

Stimpson, D., Jensen, L., & Neff, W. (1992). Cross-cultural gender differences in preference for a caring morality. *Journal of Social Psychology, 132,* 317–322.

Stryker, S. (1981). Symbolic interactionism: Themes and variations. In M. Rosenberg & R. H. Turner (Eds.), *Social psychology: Sociological perspectives.* New York: Basic Books.

Stryker, S. (1987). Identity theory: Developments and extensions. In K. Yardley & T. Honess (Eds.), *Self and society: Psychosocial perspectives.* Chichester, UK: Wiley.

Stryker, S. (1991). Exploring the relevance of social cognition for the relationship of self and society: Linking the cognitive perspective and identity theory. In J. Howard & P. Callero (Eds.), *Self-society dynamic: Emotion, cognition and action.* Cambridge, UK: Cambridge University Press.

Sue, D., & Sue, D. (1990). *Counseling the culturally different: Theory and practice* (2nd ed.). New York: Wiley.

Summer, W. (1940). *Folkways.* Boston: Ginn.

Sussman, N. (1986). Reentry research and training: Methods and implications. *International Journal of Intercultural Relations, 10,* 235–254.

Sussman, N., & Rosenfeld, H. (1982). Influence of culture, language, and sex on conversational distance. *Journal of Personality and Social Psychology, 42,* 66–74.

Tajfel, H. (1981). *Human groups and social categories.* Cambridge, UK: Cambridge University Press.

Tajfel, H., & Turner, J. (1986). The social identity theory of intergroup relations. In S. Worchel & W. Austin (Eds.), *Psychology of intergroup relations.* Monterey, CA: Brooks/Cole.

Tannen, D. (1990). *You just don't understand: Women and men in conversation.* New York: William Morrow.

Tannen, D. (1994). *Talking 9 to 5.* New York: William Morrow.

Thich, N. H. (1991). *Peace is every step: The path of mindfulness in everyday life.* New York: Bantam Books.

Thornton, M. (1992). The quiet immigration: Foreign spouses of U. S. citizens, 1945–1985. In M. Root (Ed.), *Racially mixed people in America.* Newbury Park, CA: Sage.

Ting-Toomey, S. (1980). Talk as a cultural resource in the Chinese American speech community. *Communication, 9,* 193–203.

Ting-Toomey, S. (1981). Ethnic identity and close friendship in Chinese American college students. *International Journal of Intercultural Relations, 5,* 383–406.

Ting-Toomey, S. (1985). Toward a theory of conflict and culture. In W. Gudykunst, L. Stewart, & S. Ting-Toomey (Eds.). *Communication, culture, and organizational processes.* Beverly Hills, CA: Sage.

Ting-Toomey, S. (1986). Conflict communication styles in Black and White subjective cultures. In Y. Y. Kim (Ed.), *Interethnic communication: Current research.* Newbury Park, CA: Sage.

Ting-Toomey, S. (1988). Intercultural conflict styles: A face-negotiation theory. In Y. Y. Kim & W. Gudykunst (Eds.), *Theories in intercultural communication.* Newbury Park, CA: Sage.

Ting-Toomey, S. (1989a). Identity and interpersonal bonding. In M. Asante & W. Gudykunst (Eds.), *Handbook of international and intercultural communication.* Newbury Park, CA: Sage.

Ting-Toomey, S. (1989b). Culture and interpersonal relationship development: Some conceptual issues. In J. Anderson (Ed.), *Communication yearbook 12.* Newbury Park, CA: Sage.

Ting-Toomey, S. (1991). Intimacy expressions in three cultures: France, Japan, and the United States. *International Journal of Intercultural Relations, 15,* 29–46.

Ting-Toomey, S. (1993). Communicative resourcefulness: An identity negotiation perspective. In R. Wiseman & J. Koester (Eds.), *Intercultural communication competence.* Newbury Park, CA: Sage.

Ting-Toomey, S. (1994a). Managing intercultural conflicts effectively. In L. Samovar & R. Porter (Eds.), *Intercultural communication: A reader* (7th ed.). Belmont, CA: Wadsworth.

Ting-Toomey, S. (1994b). Managing conflict in intimate intercultural relationships. In D. Cahn (Ed.), *Intimate conflict in personal relationships.* Hillsdale, NJ: Erlbaum.

Ting-Toomey, S. (Ed.). (1994c). *The challenge of facework: Cross-cultural and interpersonal issues.* Albany: State University of New York Press.

Ting-Toomey, S. (1997a). Intercultural conflict competence. In W. Cupach & D. Canary (Eds.), *Competence in interpersonal conflict.* New York: McGraw-Hill.

Ting-Toomey, S. (1997b). An intercultural journey: The four seasons. In M. Bond (Ed.), *Working at the interface of cultures: Eighteen lives in social science.* London: Routledge.

Ting-Toomey, S., Gao, G., Trubisky, P., Yang, Z., Kim, H. S., Lin, S.-L., & Nishida, T. (1991). Culture, face maintenance, and styles of handling interpersonal conflict: A study in five cultures. *International Journal of Conflict Management, 2,* 275–296.

Ting-Toomey, S., & Korzenny, F. (Eds.). (1989). *Language, communication, and culture: Current directions.* Newbury Park, CA: Sage.

Ting-Toomey, S., & Kurogi, A. (1998). Facework competence in intercultural conflict: An updated face-negotiation theory. *International Journal of Intercultural Relations, 22,* 187–225.

Ting-Toomey, S., Yee, K., Shapiro, R., Garcia, W., Wright, Y., & Oetzel, J. (in press). Ethnic/cultural identity salience and conflict styles in four U.S. ethnic groups. *International Journal of Intercultural Relations*.

Trager, G. (1958). Paralanguage: A first approximation. *Studies in Linguistics, 13*, 1–12.

Triandis, H. (1972). *The analysis of subjective culture*. New York: Wiley.

Triandis, H. (1988). Collectivism vs. individualism: A reconceptualization of a basic concept in cross-cultural psychology. In G. Verma & C. Bagley (Eds.), *Cross-cultural studies of personality, attitudes and cognition*. London: Macmillan.

Triandis, H. (1989). Self and social behavior in differing cultural contexts. *Psychological Review, 96*, 269–289.

Triandis, H. (1990). Theoretical concepts that are applicable to the analysis of ethnocentrism. In R. Brislin (Ed.), *Applied cross-cultural psychology*. Newbury Park, CA: Sage.

Triandis, H. (1994a). *Culture and social behavior*. New York: McGraw-Hill.

Triandis, H. (1994b). Major cultural syndromes and emotion. In S. Kitayama & H. Markus (Eds.), *Emotion and culture: Empirical studies of mutual influence*. Washington, DC: American Psychological Association.

Triandis, H. (1995). *Individualism and collectivism*. Boulder, CO: Westview Press.

Triandis, H., Brislin, R., & Hui, H. (1988). Cross-cultural training across the individualism-collectivism divide. *International Journal of Intercultural Relations, 12*, 269–289.

Triandis, H., McCusker, C., Betancourt, H., Iwao, S., Leung, K., Salazar, J. M., Setiadi, B., Sinha, J., Touzard, H., & Zaleski, Z. (1993). An etic-emic analysis of individualism-collectivism. *Journal of Cross-Cultural Psychology, 24*, 366–383.

Trompenaars, F. (1994). *Riding the waves of culture: Understanding diversity in global business*. Burr Ridge, IL: Irwin.

Trubisky, P., Ting-Toomey, S., & Lin, S.-L. (1991). The influence of individualism-collectivism and self-monitoring on conflict styles. *International Journal of Intercultural Relations, 15*, 65–84.

Tung, R. (1994). Strategic management thought in East Asia. *Organizational Dynamics, 22*, 55–65.

Turner, J. C. (1985). Social categorization and the self-concept: A social cognitive theory of group behavior. In E. Lawler (Ed.), *Advances in group processes* (Vol. 2). Greenwich, CT: JAI Press.

Turner, J. C. (1987). *Rediscovering the social group: A self-categorization theory*. Oxford, UK: Blackwell.

Turner, J. H. (1987). Toward a sociological theory of motivation. *American Sociological Review, 52*, 15–27.

Turner, J. H. (1988). *A theory of social interaction*. Stanford, CA: Stanford University Press.

van Knippenberg, A. (1989). Strategies of identity management. In J. Van Oudenhoven & T. Willemsen (Eds.), *Ethnic minorities: Social psychological perspectives*. Amsterdam: Swets & Zeitlinger.

Ward, C. (1996). Acculturation. In D. Landis & R. Bhagat (Eds.), (1996). *Handbook of intercultural training* (2nd ed.). Thousand Oaks, CA: Sage.

Ward, C., & Kennedy, A. (1993). Where's the culture in cross-cultural transition? Comparative studies of sojourner adjustment. *Journal of Cross-Cultural Psychology, 24,* 221–249.

Ward, C., & Kennedy, A. (1994). Acculturation strategies, psychological adjustment, and socio-cultural competence during cross-cultural transitions. *International Journal of Intercultural Relations, 18,* 329–343.

Ward, C., & Searle, W. (1991). The impact of value discrepancies and cultural identity on psychological and socio-cultural adjustment of sojourners. *International Journal of Intercultural Relations, 15,* 209–225.

Waters, M. (1990). *Ethnic options: Choosing identities in America*. Berkeley: University of California Press.

Watson, O. (1970). *Proxemic behavior: A cross-cultural study*. The Hague: Mouton.

Watzlawick, P., Beavin, J., & Jackson, D. (1967). *The pragmatics of human communication*. New York: Norton.

Wheeler, L., & Kim, Y. (1997). What is beautiful is culturally good: The physical attractiveness stereotype has different content in collectivistic cultures. *Personality and Social Psychology Bulletin, 23,* 795–800.

Whorf, B. (1952). *Collected papers on metalinguistics*. Washington, DC: U.S. Department of State, Foreign Service Institute.

Whorf, B. (1956). *Language, thought and reality*. New York: Wiley.

Wiemann, J., Chen, V., & Giles, H. (1986, November). *Beliefs about talk and silence in a cultural context*. Paper presented at the annual meeting of the Speech Communication Association, Chicago.

Wills, T. (1991). Similarity and self-esteem in downward comparison. In J. Suls & T. Wills (Eds.), *Social comparison: Contemporary theory and research*. Hillsdale, NJ: Erlbaum.

Wilmot, W., & Hocker, J. (1998). *Interpersonal conflict* (5th ed.). Boston: McGraw-Hill.

Wiseman, R. (Ed.). (1995). *Intercultural communication theory*. Thousand Oaks, CA: Sage.

Wiseman, R., & Koester, J. (Eds.). (1993). *Intercultural communication competence*. Newbury Park, CA: Sage.

Wood, J. (1995). The part is not the whole: Weaving diversity into the study of relationships. *Journal of Social and Personal Relationships, 12,* 563–567.

Wood, J. (1996). Gender, relationships, and communication. In J. Wood (Ed.), *Gendered relationships*. Mountain View, CA: Mayfield.

Wood, J. (1997). *Gendered lives: Communication, gender, and culture* (2nd ed.). Belmont, CA: Wadsworth.

Wyatt, T. (1995). Language development in African American English child speech. *Linguistics and Education, 7*, 7–22.

Yinger, M. (1994). *Ethnicity*. Albany: State University of New York Press.

Yoshikawa, M. (1988). Cross-cultural adaptation and perceptual development. In Y. Y. Kim & W. Gudykunst (Eds.), *Cross-cultural adaptation*. Newbury Park, CA: Sage.

Young, L. (1994). *Crosstalk and culture in Sino–American communication*. Cambridge, UK: Cambridge University Press.

Yum, J. O. (1982). Communication diversity and information acquisition among Korean immigrants in Hawaii. *Human Communication Research, 8*, 154–169.

Yum, J. O. (1988a). The impact of Confucianism in interpersonal relationships and communication in East Asia. *Communication Monographs, 55*, 374–388.

Yum, J. O. (1988b). Locus of control and communication patterns of immigrants. In Y. Y. Kim & W. Gudykunst (Eds.), *Cross-cultural adaptation*. Newbury Park, CA: Sage.

Zanna, M., & Olson, J. (Eds.). (1994). *The Ontario symposium: Vol. 7. The psychology of prejudice*. Hillsdale, NJ: Erlbaum.

Zuckerman, M., Lipets, M., Koivumaki, J., & Rosenthal, R. (1975). Encoding and decoding nonverbal cues of emotion. *Journal of Personality and Social Psychology, 32*, 1068–1076.

Index

Accented speech patterns, 86, 87
Acculturation
  definition, 235, 254
  identity change models, 254–256
  motivational factors, 239, 240
Activity orientation, and values, 64, 65
Adaptation, intercultural, 233–260
  antecedent factors, 234–244
  and culture shock, 245–247
  effective outcomes, 257–259
  identity changes, 245–260
    outcomes, 258, 259
  individual-level factors, 239–241
  interpersonal factors, 241–245
    outcomes, 257, 258
  model of, 236
  systems-level factors, 235–237
    outcomes, 257, 258
Adaptors, in conversational management, 126
Adjustment, intercultural, 235
Adoptive family metaphor, 238
Adornments, as identity marker, 117, 118
Affective dimension
  intergroup communication, 159, 160
  language group identity function, 93
  in semantics, 89
African Americans
  activity values, 64
  Black English use, 92, 93
  conflict style, 217, 218
  versus European Americans, verbal style, 109, 110
  eye contact patterns, 126
  human nature orientation, 63
  identity development, 255, 256
  interpersonal synchrony, 138
  proxemic behaviors, 130

temporal orientation, 62, 135
self-disclosure, 190, 191
workforce trends, 5–7
Africans
  interpersonal synchrony, 138
  time orientation, 62, 135
Age factors, and adaptation, 241
Ambivalence stage, sojourners, 249, 250
American English, and power, 93
Ancestry, and ethnic identity, 31
Anger
  facial expression, 121
  vocalics, 122
Anxiety, and intergroup cooperation, 180
Anxiety/uncertainty management theory, 25, 182, 183
Apache culture, concept of silence, 111
Arab cultures
  greeting rituals, 139
  home environment, 133
  personal space, 128
  privacy concept, 134
  self-enhancement style, 108, 109
  time orientation, 136
  vocal expression, 122, 123
Arm's-length prejudice, 168
Asian Americans
  activity orientation, 64, 65
  conflict style, 217
  eye contact, 126
  facework, 217
Asian culture, self-effacement style, 107–109
Assimilationist societies
  identity change models, 254–256
  and immigrant adaptation, 235–237, 254–256
Attentiveness, 191, 192

Attitudes
and interpersonal attraction, 187
nonverbal expression, 119–123
Attributions
inherent biases, 153, 154
principle of negativity, 153
Authoritarian personality, 164, 165
Autonomy-connection theme
in close relationships, 184–186
in identity negotiation, 43, 44
individualist versus collectivist cultures,
184–186
Autostereotype, 161, 162
"Average person" myth, 140

B

Bicultural orientation, 254, 255
Bigotry, 167, 168
Black English, 92, 93
Body posture
in conversational management, 126
and credibility, 127
"Brainstorming," 226

C

Caring perspective, and gender, 178
Causal referents, language structure, 96
Che-myon, 98
Chinese culture
causal referents, language, 96
indirect verbal interaction style, 104, 105
privacy negative connotation, 134
role of silence, 110
self-construal, 78
Chinese Culture Connection group,
74
Chronemics, 134–137
"Circus of Peace," 226
Climate, and personal contact, 129
Close relationships (*see* Personal relationships)
Code-switching, and Black English, 92, 93
Collaborative dialogue
in conflict management, 224–226
in meaning management, 271
paradigm shift in, 225
problem-solving sequence, 226
Collateral relationships, 65, 66
Collective self, 79
Collectivist cultures
autonomy-connection issue, 184–186
companionate love emphasis, 176, 177,
184–186

conflict management, 196–198, 202–204,
210–212, 215–230
cultural identity dimension, 30, 31
emotional expression, 120–122, 215
gender differences, 69
indirect verbal interactive style, 103–106
individualist cultural differences, 66–69
particularistic-based interactions, 81, 82
self-effacement style, 109, 154
self-esteem influence, 80, 81
time orientation, 136, 137
values of, 67, 68
and interdependent self-construal, 76–79
intergroup attributions, 155
interpersonal synchrony, 138, 139
openness–closedness theme, 191
self-construal, 78
and conflict norms, 214–216
home setting, 133
Communication accommodation theory,
118, 119
Companionate love, 176
Competitive tasks, 180
Confianza, 78, 223
Confirming communication, 47
Conflict goals, 195–198
Conflict management, 194–230
adaptive communication, 226, 227
collaborative dialogue in, 224–226
ethnocentrism problem, 198–201, 218
face-saving issues, 196–198
facework strategies, 210–212, 216–218,
222
and individualistic-collectivistic values,
202–204
low-context versus high-context styles,
208, 209
mindful listening/reframing, 220
norms for, 214–216
outcome-oriented model, 210–212
power distance values in, 204, 205
process goals, 197, 198, 210–212
relational issues, 196
self-construal effect on, 205–208
styles of, 216–218
and temporal orientation, 212, 213
trust-building skills, 222–224
Confucianism, 74, 75
conflict style, 217
core values, 75

facework relationship, 75, 217
self-construal influence, 78
Connotative meaning, 88, 89
Content meaning, 19, 263, 264
Contextual factors, 23 (see also High-
    context communication; Low-context
    communication)
Conversational management, 123–126
    interpersonal synchrony in, 138, 139
    interruptions in, 125
    kinesics and oculesics in, 123–126
Cooperative tasks, 180
Coyuntura, 223
Creativity
    characteristics, 268, 269
    human diversity role, 8
    language function, 98–100
Cuello, 223
Cultural community, 18, 19
Cultural display rules, 215
Cultural distance, 238
"Cultural fit" proposition, 241
Cultural norms
    in conflict management, 214, 215
    definition, 11
    and role identity, 36, 37
    and stereotypes, 161, 162
Cultural pluralism (see Pluralistic societies)
Cultural relativists, 119
Cultural universalists, 119
Culture shock
    management of, 245–247
    negative and positive implications, 246
    principle aspects, 245
    sojourners, 245–247, 250
    types of, 246, 247

D

Deception, in close relationships, 189, 190
Denotative meaning, 88, 89
Digital communication, 17
Direct verbal interaction
    versus indirect style, 103–106
    individualistic cultures, 103
Disconfirming communication, 47
Discrimination, 166–169
    basic forms of, 166
    and fear, 169
    mindset analysis, 169–171
    prejudice relationship, 166–168
    reduction of, 169–171
    typology, 167, 168
Dispositional attributions, 155

Diversity, 6
Downward social comparison, 151

E

Ebonics, 92, 93
Ecological adaptation, 14
Educational level, and adaptation, 241
Emblems
    in conversational management, 123, 124
    cultural differences, 124
Embracing, 130
Emic meanings, 89, 90
Emotional expression, 119–123 (see also
    Facial expression)
    in conflict negotiation, 214, 215
    cultural influence theories, 119, 120
    individualist–collectivist cultures, 120–
        122
Empathy, intergroup communication, 160
Enculturation, 235
English language, person orientation of,
    106, 107
Environmental factors, and boundary
    regulation, 131–133
Equity norm
    in conflict negotiation, 214, 215
    individualistic cultures emphasis, 214
Ethics, 271–276
    absolutism versus relativism, 272–275
    contextual relativism approach, 274, 275
    derived-universalism approach, 273
Ethnic identity (see also Identity negotiation
        theory)
    and ancestry, 31
    salience of, 32, 33, 146, 147
    subjective experience of, 32, 33
    typology, 254, 255
Ethnic media, 243, 244
Ethnocentrism, 157–161
    and communication, 157–161
    definition, 14, 157
    differential degrees of, 158, 159
    intercultural conflict cause, 198–201, 218
Ethnorelativism
    communication aid, 158–161
    and mindfulness, 161
    relative degrees of, 158, 159
Etic meanings, 89, 90
European Americans
    activity values, 64
    versus African Americans, verbal style,
        109, 110
    eye contact pattern, 126

European Americans (*continued*)
human nature orientation, 63, 64
labor force percentage, 5
personal space, 128, 130
self-disclosure, 190, 191
temporal orientation, 62, 63, 136, 137
Exclusive language, 270
Expectancies
and intercultural adaptation, 240
social categorization consequence, 149, 150
Expectancy violations theory, 25
Exploitation, prejudice theory, 164
Eye contact, 126

F

Face painting techniques, 117, 118
Face-saving issues, 196–198
Facework
in conflict negotiation, 210–212, 216–218
Confucian influence, 75
definition, 38
in identity negotiation, 37, 38
linguistic codes, Koreans, 98
Facial expression, 119–123
and credibility, 127
cultural relativist approach, 119
cultural universalist approach, 119
decoding of, 121
individualist–collectivist cultures, 120–122
neuroculture theory, 120
Familismo, 94
Family relationships
gender role socialization, 73
and relational identity, 37
uncertainty avoidance dimension, 71, 72
Fear, prejudice role, 169
"Feminine" cultures, 72–74
family socialization, 73
"masculine" culture differences, 72–74
Filipino culture
power distance values, 204, 205
vocal expression, 122, 123
French culture
conversational interruption pattern, 125
role of silence in communication, 111
temporal orientation, 63
Friendship networks, and adaptation, 242, 243
"Fundamental attribution error," 153
Future-oriented time sense, 61–63, 135, 136

G

Games, gender identity development, 177
Gan qing, 94
Gender differences
individualist–collectivist values, 69
self-disclosure, 190
Gender roles
cultural differences, 72–74, 177, 178
family socialization, 73
and language, 99
learning of, 34, 69
and personal relationships, 177, 178
Giving face, 222, 228
Globalization, and workplace diversity, 4, 5
Grammar
and morphemes, 87, 88
thought process influence, 95, 96
Greeting rituals, 139
Group identity, language function, 91–93
Group inclusion
communication effects of, 22
cultural function, 13
Group relations (*see* Intergroup communication/contact; Transcultural communication competence)

H

"Hai, hai," 125, 126
Han xu, 94
"Healing webs," 243
Haptics, 130, 131
Handholding, 130
Hand gestures, 123–126
Handshakes, 130
Heterostereotype, 161, 162
High-contact cultures, 129
High-context communication
and conflict negotiation, 208, 209
cross–cultural differences, 100–103, 208, 209
definition, 100, 208–209
Hindu culture, 78
Hispanics, diversity trends, 6, 7 (*see also* Latino/a)
"Home," 12
Home environment, 132, 133
Honeymoon stage, sojourners, 248, 251, 252
Hopi language, 95
"Horizontal self" spectrum, 208
Hostility, in sojourners, 248, 249
Human nature orientation, 63, 64

Index

I

"I" identity (*see* Individualistic cultures)
Identity being–identity becoming theme, 234
Identity change, 233–260
   antecedent factors, 234–244
   and intercultural adaptation, 245–260
   minorities and immigrants, 254–256
   sojourners, 247–252
Identity confirmation skills, 270
Identity negotiation theory, 25–54
   background, 27, 28
   conceptual aspects, 39–54
   core assumptions, 40–45
   and ethnic identity consciousness, 32, 33, 146, 147
   and motivation, 52, 53
   primary domains, 28–36
   and self-esteem, 80
   and situational factors, 36–39
   social structure influence, 75, 76
Identity valuation skills, 53, 54
Illustrators, in conversational management, 124, 125
Immigrants
   in assimilationist versus pluralistic societies, 237
   cultural distance factor, 238
   culture shock, 245–247
   expectancies, 240
   identity change models, 254–256
   intercultural adaptation, 234–244
   mass media influence, 243, 244
   motivational orientation, 239, 240
   personality factors, 241
   social networks, 241–243
   "third culture perspective," 258, 259
   U.S. diversity trends, 5–7
Impression management, 126, 127
Inclusion–differentiation theme, 43
Inclusive language, 270
Independent self-construal, 76–79
   characteristics, 79
   and close relationships, 178, 179
   and conflict management, 205–208, 211
   identity negotiation, 35, 80
   individualism emphasis, 76–79
   and moral responsibility, 78
   outcome-oriented model, 211
   power distance influence, 205–208
Indirect verbal interaction
   collectivist cultures, 103
   versus direct style, 103–106

Individualistic cultures
   autonomy–connection theme, 184–186
   close relationships in, 176, 177, 184–186
   collectivism differences, 66–69
   conflict management, 196–198, 202–204, 210–212, 216–230
   cultural identity dimension, 30, 31
   direct verbal interaction style, 103–106
   emotional expression, 120–122
   gender differences, 69
   and independent self-construal, 76–79
   intergroup attributions, 155
   interpersonal synchrony, 138, 139
   openness–closedness theme, 191
   romantic love emphasis, 176, 177, 184–186
   self-enhancement style, 109
   self-esteem influence, 80, 81
   self-serving biases, 154
   universalist-based interaction, 81, 82
   and values, 65–67
Information technology, 257
In-group favoritism principle, 148
Ingroup interactions
   boundary regulation, 146–152
   and conflict negotiation, 214, 215
   cultural influences, 13, 14
   and ethnocentrism, 158–160
   identity negotiation theory, 42, 43
   intergroup attributions, 154, 155
   loyalty and preference in, 147, 148
   mindful versus mindless stereotyping, 163, 164
   mindsets, 156–171
   "particularistic" societies, 81, 82
   social identity theory, 147–152
Institutional policies, 237, 238
Institutional racism, 170
Intercultural adaptation (*see* Adaptation, intercultural)
Intercultural communication (*see* Transcultural communication competence)
Interdependent self-construal, 76–79
   characteristics, 79
   and close relationships, 178, 179
   collectivism emphasis, 76–79
   and conflict management, 205–208, 211, 212
   identity negotiation, 35, 80
   and moral responsibility, 78
   power distance effect, 205–208
   process-oriented model, 211, 212

306

Intergroup attributions, 154, 155
Intergroup communication/contact, 145–173
  attribution biases, 152–155
  boundary regulation, 13, 14, 146–152
  definition, 16
  mindsets, 156–171
  social identity theory, 28, 146–152
  stereotyping, 161–164
International business, trends, 4, 5
International students, 242, 243
Interpersonal perceptions, 28
Interpersonal relationships (*see* Personal relationships)
Interpersonal synchrony, 137–139
Interrogation strategy, 189
Interruption, in conversational regulation, 125
Intimacy
  language function, 97, 98
  and self-disclosure, 188, 189
Intrapersonal space, 133, 134
Isomorphic attribution, 159
Italian culture, hand gestures, 124

J
Japanese culture
  conflict management style, 209
  emotional expression identification, 121
  high-context interaction style, 102, 103, 209
  home environment, 133
  indirect verbal interaction, 105, 106
  private self, 188
  proxemics, 130
  self-effacement style, 107, 108
  status-oriented verbal style, 106, 107
  use of silence in communication, 110
Justice perspective, gender differences, 178

K
Kibun, 105
Kinesics
  in conversational management, 123–126
  and emotional expression, 119
Kissing, 130, 131
Knowledge
  intercultural communication component, 50–52, 266, 267
  "mindfulness" role in, 51
  racism reduction, 170, 171
Korean culture
  facework codes, 98
  indirect verbal behavior, 105
  status orientation, 107

L
"Languaculture," 112
Language, 84–114
  cognitive reasoning function, 94–97
  creativity function, 98–100
  distinctive features of, 85–90
  group identity function, 91–93
  and mindful communication, 84–114
  perceptual filtering function, 94
  Sapir–Whorf hypothesis, 94–97
  sexism in, 99
  status and intimacy function, 97, 98
Language borrowing, 98
Language fluency, 241, 244
Lateral social comparison, 150, 151
Latino/a
  activity orientation, 65
  conflict style, 217
  eye contact pattern, 126
  touch behaviors, 131
  workforce trends, 5
Leakage cues, 189
Lineal relationships, 65, 66
  in individualistic versus collectivist cultures, 176, 177, 184–186
Linguistic relativity hypothesis, 95, 96
Linguistic similarity, 187
Location, and sojourner motivation, 239
Love relationships
  autonomy–connection theme, 184–186
  cross-cultural differences, 100–103, 208, 209
Low-context communication
  and conflict negotiation, 208, 209
  cross-cultural differences, 100–103, 208, 209
  definition, 100, 208–209
Low-context cultures, 129
Loyalty, in-group characteristic, 147, 148
Lying
  cross-cultural differences, 189, 190
  detection of, 189

M
Ma, 110
Machismo, 94
Marginalization, immigrants, 254, 255
Marianismo, 94
"Masculine" cultures, 72–74
  family socialization, 73

Index

feminine culture differences, 72–74
organizational behavior, 72–74
Masculine generics, 99–100
Mass media, 243, 244
Mexican Americans
  conflict style, 217
  temporal orientation, 62
Mian zi, 94
Mindfulness, 25–54, 84–114
  and conflict negotiation, 220–222
  and creativity, 268
  criteria and components, 48–54, 267–268
  definition, 16, 23, 46, 267
  intercultural communication outcomes, 46, 47
  language influence, 84–114
  and listening skills, 112
  model of, 48, 49
  nonverbal messages, 114–141
  role of knowledge in, 50–52
  and self-esteem, 80
  skills in, 53, 54
  and stereotyping, 163, 164
Mindless stereotyping, 163, 164
Mindlessness, 46
Mindsets, intergroup perception, 156
Minimal Group Paradigm project, 148
Minority groups, 254–256 (*see also* Prejudice)
Monochronic time schedule, 135–137
  and conflict negotiation, 212, 213
  cultural values effect, 135–137
Monocultural society
  identity change models, 254–256
  and immigrant adaptation, 235–237, 254–256
Moral exclusion, 275
Moral inclusion, 275, 276
Morphemes, 87, 88
Motivation
  identity negotiation theory context, 52, 53
  and intercultural adaptation, 239, 240

N
Naming process, and group identity, 92
Native Americans
  activity orientation, 65
  ethnic identity, 32
  eye contact, 126
  human nature orientation, 63, 64
Navajo tribe, silent behavior, 111

Negative correlation principle, 153
Negative emotions
  in conflict negotiation, 215
  identification of, 122
Negative stereotypes, power of, 162
Negotiated shared meanings, 19, 40
Neuroculture theory, 120
Nonverbal communication, 114–141
  and conversational management, 123–126
  cross-cultural interpretation, cautions, 139, 140
  distinctive characteristics, 116
  emotional expression, 119–123
  functions and patterns, 115–127
  as identity marker, 117–119
  and interpersonal boundaries, 128–137
  interpersonal synchrony, 137–139
  in symbolic exchange, 17
Norms (*see* Cultural norms)
Nunchi, 105

O
Oculesics, 1232–126
O-D-I-S method, 83, 269
Openness–closedness theme
  ethnic differences, 190, 191
  and intimacy, 188, 189
  in personal relationships, 188–192
Organizational values
  cultural differences, 66–76
  masculinity–femininity dimension, 72–74
  uncertainty avoidance dimension, 71, 72
Other-oriented communication, 77
Outcome-oriented models, 210–212, 219, 220
Out-group interactions
  attributional biases toward, 153–155
  boundary regulation, 146–152
  and conflict negotiation, 214, 215
  cultural influences, 13, 14
  ethnocentrism consequences, 158–160
  identity negotiation perspective, 42, 43
  mindful versus mindless stereotyping, 163, 164
  mindsets, 156–171
  social identity theory, 147–152
  societal influences, 81, 82

P
Palanca, 78
Papago Indian tribe, 111
Paraphrasing skills, 112, 113, 270

Parent–child relationship, 70
Particularistic societies, 81, 82
Past-oriented time sense, 61–63, 135, 136
Perception checking, 141, 159, 270
Perceptiveness, 191, 192
Person-oriented verbal style
   in individualistic cultures, 106
   versus status-oriented style, 106, 107
Personal identities, 34–36
Personal racism, 170
Personal relationships, 174–193
   autonomy-connection theme, 184–186
   contextual conditions, 175–181
   cultural and ethnic values, 176, 177
   development themes, 174–193
   intercultural adaptation factor, 241–245
   outcomes, 257–258
   openness–closedness theme, 188–192
   personality factors, 178, 179
   similarity-attraction hypothesis, 186–188
   situational conditions for, 179, 180
   vulnerability-security theme, 181–183
Personal space, 128–130
Personal stereotypes, 162
Personalismo, 89, 90
Personality factors
   in close relationships, 178, 179
   in identity negotiation process, 35, 36
   and identity security, 45
   and intercultural adaptation, 241
Phonology, 86, 87
Physical appearance
   intergroup attraction factor, 187
   and perceived attractiveness, 127
Physical boundaries, regulation of, 131–133
Play behavior, and gender identity, 177
Pluralistic societies
   minority and immigrants identity change,
      254–256
   newcomer adaptation, 237
Polarized thinking, 149, 150
Polychronic time schedule, 135–137
   and conflict negotiation, 212, 213
   cultural values effect, 135–137
Positive stereotypes, power of, 162
Power distance values, 69–71
   cultural differences, 69–71
   and emotional expression, 120
   intercultural conflict role, 204, 205
   and parent–child relationship, 70
   in work situations, 70, 71

Pragmatic language rules, 90
Preference, in-group characteristic, 147, 148
Prefixes, morphology, 88
Prejudice, 164, 165
   authoritarian personality approach, 164,
      165
   definition, 164
   discrimination relationship, 166–168
   exploitation theory of, 164
   and fear, 169
   functions, 165
   and intergroup attraction, 187
   mindset analysis, 169–171
   reduction of, 169–171
   scapegoating theory of, 164
   structural approach, 165
   typology, 167, 168
Premarital chastity, 177
Privacy
   and home environment, 132, 133
   in intercultural communication, 17, 18
Private self
   cultural and gender loadings, 188
   and individualistic cultures, 79
Probability statements, and language, 95,
   96
Process-oriented model
   in conflict negotiation, 210–212, 220
   psychological level, 133, 134
Proxemics, 128–130
Public self, 79, 188

R

Racism (see also Prejudice)
   continuum of, 170
   and identity development, 255, 256
   and intergroup boundaries, 168, 169
   and interpersonal attraction, 187
   reduction of, 170, 171
Reentry culture shock, 252, 253
Reframing, in conflict negotiation, 221, 222
Refugees (see Immigrants)
Regulators, in conversational management,
   125, 126
Relational culture, 175, 176
Relational dialectics, 27
Relational identity, 37
Relational meaning, 20, 264
Relational orientation, 65, 66
Ren qing, 94
Resocialization, sojourners, 250
Respeto, 94, 97

Responsiveness, 191, 192
Role identity, 36, 37
Romantic love
  autonomy–connection conflict, 184, 185
  individualistic versus collectivist cultures, 176, 177
Russian culture, facial expressions, 121, 122

S

Sapir–Whorf hypothesis, 94–97
Scapegoating, 164
Security–vulnerability theme, 42
Self-conception
  consequences of, 76–82
  layers of, 79
Self-construal (see Independent self-construal; Interdependent self-construal)
Self-disclosure
  in close relationships, 189
  ethnic differences, 190, 191
  individualistic versus collectivist cultures, 190
  and intimacy, 188, 189
  sex differences, 190
  strategies, 189
  uncertainty reduction, 189
Self-effacing verbal style
  Asian cultures, 107–109
  versus self-enhancement style, 107–110
Self-enhancement verbal style
  African Americans, 109, 110
  Arab cultures, 108, 109
  versus self-effacing style, 107–110
Self-esteem, 80, 81
Self-fulfilling prophecy, and stereotyping, 162
Self-image, 26
Self-serving bias, 154
Semantics, 88–90
Sensory exposure needs, 129
Sex differences (see Gender differences)
Sex roles (see Gender roles)
Sexism, 99
Shared meanings, negotiation of, 19
Sideways learning, 269
Silence, 110, 111, 216
Similarity–attraction perspective
  and complementarity, 187, 188
  intergroup–interpersonal context, 186–188
Skills, and mindful communication, 53, 54

Smiles, cultural meanings, 121, 122
Social categorization
  consequences, 149, 150
  and mindfulness, 150
Social comparison
  in groups, 150–152
  and social identity, 150–152
Social identity theory, 27, 28, 146–152
  derivation, 43
  and group boundary regulation, 146–152
  identity negotiation relationship, 146–152
  salience conditions, 146, 147
Social network, 241–243
Social penetration theory, 188, 189
Social structure, 75, 76
Socioeconomic conditions, and adaptation, 235
Sociotypes, 161
Sojourners, 247–253
  adjustment models, 247–253
  culture shock, 245–247, 250
  definition, 235
  identity change models, 247–252
  intercultural adaptation, 234–253
  motivation, 239
  personality factors, 241
  reentry culture shock, 252, 253
  "third culture perspective," 258, 259
Spanish culture
  hand illustrators, 124
  status and intimacy in, 97, 98
  time sense, 95, 96
Spatial boundaries (interpersonal), 128–134
  environmental aspects, 131–134
  haptics, 130, 131
  proxemics, 128–130
Speech community, 90
Speech pattern, as identity marker, 118, 119
Stability–change theme, 44
Status differences
  high-context cultures, 106, 107
  language function, 97, 98
Stereotypes
  attribution biases, groups, 153, 154
  communication effect of, 161–164
  definition, 161
  and expectancies, 149, 150
  mindful versus mindless form of, 163, 164, 169
  power of, 162
  and self-fulfilling prophecies, 162
Stigma, and stereotyping, 162

Subjective culture, 11
Suffixes, morphology, 87, 88
Support networks, 241–243
Symbolic exchange, 17
Symbolic interactionism
  and identity negotiation, 38, 39
  theory, 27, 28
Symbolic racism, 168, 169
Synchrony, interpersonal, 137–139
Syntax, 88
Systems perspective
  communication influence, 23, 24
  emphasis of, 25

T
Television, 243, 244
Temporal orientation
  and conflict negotiation, 212, 213
  and cultural values, 61–63, 134–137
  linguistic influences, 95, 96
  patterns of, 135,136
Territoriality, 131–133
"Third culture perspective," 258, 259
Time orientation (*see* Temporal orientation)
Ting, 220
Ting hua, 94
"Tokenism-type" prejudice, 168
Tolerance for ambiguity
  close relationships factor, 178
  and identity security, 45
Tone of voice, 122, 123
Touch behavior, 130, 131
Transcultural communication competence,
  261–276
  appropriateness criterion, 262, 263
  collaborative dialogue in, 271
  conceptualization, 16, 17
  criteria, 262–265
  definition, 261
  effectiveness criterion, 263, 264
  identity confirmation skills in, 270
  knowledge role in, 266, 267
  mindfulness component, 267–270
  satisfaction criterion, 265
Translation problems, 89
Trust-building skills
  in conflict negotiation, 222–224
  and power distance values, 223
Tu, 97

U
Uncertainty avoidance

  definition, 71
  individualistic versus collectivist cultures,
    190
  in organizations, 71, 72
  and self-disclosure, 189
Uniforms, as identity marker, 118
Unconscious competence, 52
Universalistic societies, 81, 82
Upward social comparison, 151
Usted, 97
Uye-ri, 107

V
Value orientations, 57–83
  organizational dimension, 66–76
  self-conception consequences, 76–82
  universal assumptions, 59–66
Verbal communication, 84–114 (*see also*
  Language)
  cross-cultural styles of, 100–111
  direct and indirect styles, 103–106
  low- versus high-context, 100–103
  and mindfulness, 84–114
  person- versus status-oriented styles, 106,
    107
  self-effacement style, 107–110
  self-enhancement style, 107–110
"Vertical self" spectrum, 208
Vietnamese Americans, time orientation, 62
Vínculos, 78
Vocabulary, and communication, 96
Vocalics, 118, 122, 123
Vocalizations, as identity marker, 118
Voice qualifiers, 118
"Voiceprints," 87
Vulnerability-security theme
  and anxiety, 182, 183
  in close relationships, 181–183
  contextual conditions influence, 181, 182

W
"We"-identity (*see* Collectivist cultures)
"Well-meaning clashes," 22, 23
Work situations (*see* Organizational values)
Workforce 2020 report, 4, 257

X
Xiao, 94
Xin ren, 223

Z
Zuo ren, 78